Backyard Buckaroos
Collecting
Western Toy Guns

By Jim Schleyer

Dedication:

This Book is Dedicated to My Family, Who Like This Effort, are a Proud and Joyous Labor of Love.

Art Director:　　　　　*Jim Schleyer*
Design Consultant:　　　*Matthew Schleyer*

ISBN: 089689-121-6

700 E. State Street • Iola, WI 54990-0001
Telephone: 715/445-2214

JIMMY

JENNY

DAVE

AMANDA

MATT

BRIAN

TRAVIS

KENDALL

Contents

Introduction.. 1
Western Characters:
    Alan Ladd................................... 17
    Annie Oakley.............................. 18
    Bat Masterson........................... 20
    Billy the Kid.............................. 22
    Bobby Benson........................... 23

    Bonanza.................................... 23
    Buffalo Bill................................ 26
    Cheyenne.................................. 30
    Cisco Kid.................................. 32
    Colt .45..................................... 33

    Cowboy in Africa...................... 34
    Davy Crockett........................... 35
    Dale Evans................................142
    Deputy..................................... 39
    Gene Autry................................ 41

    Gray Ghost................................ 60
    Gunsmoke................................. 60
    Have Gun, Will Travel-Paladin..............63
    High Chapparal......................... 65
    Highway Patrol......................... 65

    Hopalong Cassidy...................... 66
    How the West Was Won................ 65
    Jesse James............................... 76
    Johnny Ringo........................... 76
    John Wayne.............................. 77

    Kit Carson................................ 77
    Laramie.................................... 79
    Lawman.................................... 98
    Lone Ranger.............................. 80
    Maverick.................................. 98

    Overland Trail.......................... 103
    Pecos Bill................................. 103
    Pecos Kid................................. 104
    Planet of the Apes..................... 104
    Range Rider............................. 104

    Rebel......................................105
    Red Ryder..............................106
    Restless Gun.............................106
    Rifleman..................................108
    Rin Tin Tin & Rusty...................109
    Roy Rogers............................. 111

Western Characters Continued:
    Sergeant Preston...................... 146
    Tombstone Territory.................. 147
    Tom Mix.................................. 147
    Trackdown................................ 148
    Wagon Train............................ 148

    Wanted Dead or Alive................. 152
    Wells Fargo.............................. 154
    Wild Bill Hickok....................... 156
    Wyatt Earp.............................. 160
    Zorro....................................... 168

Abbreviations Utilized...........................D

Ammunition................................... 412
Badges.. 435
Belt Buckles.................................. 417
Bibliography................................. 16
Boots.. 406

Boxes.. 394
Collectors & Dealers..................... 441
Derringers....................................377
Gloves... 392
Grip Details.................................. 429

Gun Engraving.............................426
Hand Cuffs................................... 407
Hats & Belts................................. 408
Holsters.. 345
Holster Details..............................421

ID & Tidbits.................................. 434
Kerchiefs & Bandannas................. 404
Knives & Tomahawks.................... 402
Lariats & Lassos............................393
Miscellaneous Guns......................382

Pop-Cork & Shot Guns..................332
Rifles.. 311
Spurs.. 384
Steel/Tin Guns............................. 380
Toy Gun Displays......................... 432

Value System................................14
Western & Toy Museums................16
Western Outfits............................. 410
WesternToy Guns.......................... 169
Wrist Cuffs...................................388

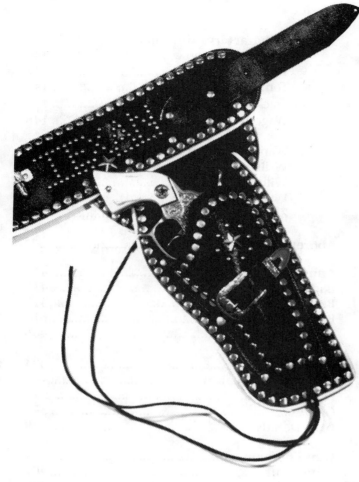

Abbreviations:

Ant Brnz	Antique Bronze Finish
ARCOR	American Rubber Corp.
B&W	Black and White
B&T	Black and Tan
Blk	Black
Blu	Blue
Brnz	Bronze Finish
Buk	Buckle
Bul	Bullets
CI	Cast Iron
Cross Strap	Small Strap Across Holster Front
CW	Civil War
DC	Die Cast
Dk	Dark or Blue/Black Finish
Drngr	Derringer
Eng	Engraved
Engrv	Engraved
Esq	Esquire Novelty Co.
Esq Nov	Esquire Novelty Co.
Frng	Fringe
Gunfighter	Mexican-loop holster and belt
Gunslinger	Drastic low-slung holster
Jwls	Jewels
Key Bros	Keyston Brothers Holsters
Keyston B	Keyston Brothers Holsters
KB	Keyston Brothers Holsters
Kilg	Kilgore Co.
Laced Edge	Edge of Holster or Belt has Lacing
LB	Long Barrel
L-H	Leslie-Henry Co.
Loop Style	Holsters with belt loop on top
L	Lower
Mfg	Manufacturing
Nik	Nickel Finish
O/U	Over and Under Barrels
RC	Revolving Cylinder
Rep	Repeater
R-L	Right to Left
RR	Roy Rogers
Scalloped	Edge of Belt or Holster is Scalloped
Sil	Silver
Sm	Small
S-M	S Bar M (Logo for Service Mfg. Co.)
SS	Single Shot
Stds	Studs
3-D	Three Dimensional-Sculptured
T	Top
Turq	Turquoise Green
WW II	World War II Era
Y&•	Wyandotte Metal Co.
Yel	Yellow Color

Backyard Buckaroos
Jim Schleyer
A Guide Book to Western Toy Guns, Holsters & Related Items

Introduction:

Values listed in this book are a culmination of many years of personal buying experience, toy show prices, auction sales, dealer's lists, periodical price listings and the agreement of numerous experts in this field of western toy collectibles. The prices listed are intended as a guide to current market values and should not be construed as actual costs. Prices vary according to location, condition, rarity, individual purchaser's whims and desires, personal opinions and the degree of collector demand. The author and the publisher can not be held responsible for any losses or gains directly related to these price estimations, as they only represent approximate current values. Many months transpire between writing a guide book and actual publication, so prices may be directly influenced by changeable collecting trends.

The author and publisher apologize for any errors, omissions, or unintentionally missed expressions of appreciation. A book of this magnitude makes it impossible to eliminate all errors, even though every effort was made to do so. Many of the western character's names and logos are copyrighted and protected. They are used in this book only as a visual aid for identifying the items depicted as reference material for collectors and researchers.

This book would not have become a reality if it wasn't for the multitude of dedicated men and women who labored in numerous toy factories around the world to produce these wonderful toys. Their craftsmanship and dedication to quality are the envy of all collectors, as we become the present curators of their efforts. It is difficult to view an engraved cap gun, a finely crafted leather holster, or piece of apparel without marveling at the quality of these rare toys. All toy guns have inherent smiles, memories and a history of less stressful times as children. Relive those memories as you read on!

Acknowledgments:

A reference and price guide of this complexity only becomes reality through the persistence and generosity of many individuals. I am forever grateful to the numerous friends, collectors and dealers who graciously shared their collectibles with me. The items depicted in this book represent the most complete and in-depth accumulation of western toy guns, holsters and related items ever assembled. The following list of curators permitted the use of their toys, reference materials and memories: Bill Adams, Roland Adams, Beth Alphin, Steve Arlin, Paul Batson, Charles Best, J.C. Black, Ray Brandes, Ellis Brown, Bill Campbell, Denny Carper, Dave Case, Howard Caulkins, Doug Candler, Lin Clayberg, Dennis Clements, Wayne Conover, Rudy D'Angelo, Ron Doub, Marvin Fairchild, Ron Fulcher, Dave Frederickson, Jim Geuy, Jimmy Glover, Terry Graham, Ben Graves, Ted Hake, Bill Hamburg, Tony Horne, Paul Hotchkiss, Robert Johnston, Pete Karp, Mark King, Tom Kolomjec, Jim Krantz, Bob Lauver, Tom Lockart, Sam Logan, Bill Longstreet, Dave Luellen, Jim Moore, Tony Musco, George Newcomb, Talley Nichols, Tom Parin, Gerald Preston, Marcel Quintilli, Don Raker, Brian Roeder, Stanley Rojo, Jack Rosenthal, Bob Saylor, Ron Scisciani, Stuart Schneider, Steve and Mike Schoff, Bob Skaggs, Dave Storrs, Eston & Debbie Stowers, Ted Stowers, "Pete" & Herb Taylor, Tom Vandell, Earl Wagner, Penn Waldron, Andy Weber, Bob Williamson, Tom Winge, Ron Witman, and Brian Wolf. I must also acknowledge all the past members of the Toy Gun Purveyor's Club who submitted information and memories.

Special thanks to all who helped with the production and review of this book. Their understanding and patience in working with me was laudatory! I am forever grateful for the encouragement, love and assistance of: Chris, Jenny, Dave, Matt, Tim, Stephanie and Emma.

The American Cowboy

Perhaps the most unlikely hero should have been the American Cowboy. Few occupations were more mundane, dangerous, lonely, meager paying and unrewarding. Yet the cowboy has left an indelible mark not only on the range, but in the hearts and minds of millions of aficionados!

The cowboy was born and nurtured on a daily diet of hostile trails, ornery cattle, choking dust, soaking rain, bone-chilling winds, freezing blizzards, scorching sun, rustler and Indian raids, lack of medical attention, mediocre vittles, saddle sores, aching bones, rope burns, rattlesnakes, wild animals, minimal friendships, and the prairie for a bed. Hardly a glamorous career, and a far cry from the heroic image portrayed by the radio, books, T.V. and silver screen!

The cowboy's meager belongings were reduced to what he wore and carried on his horse. He had a few personal items in his saddlebags, a handgun and holster, perhaps a rifle, a canteen, a pocket watch, his blanket, a saddle, a wide-brimmed hat, a bandanna, maybe an extra shirt, leather chaps, a pair of gloves, a rain slicker, extra ammunition, a small flask of medicinal liquid, his lariat, a pocket or sheath knife, boots, spurs, his good luck piece, perhaps a Bible, and an abundance of raw courage and determination.

The world's image of this range and ranch worker has been greatly enhanced by the media of the past and present. Every boy or girl who was raised during the 1930-to-1965 era wanted to be a cowboy or cowgirl. The cowboy generated imaginary visions of a great hero and thousands couldn't wait to follow in his bootsteps! Dime novels and early radio glamorized him as a daring horseman, sharpshooter, bronco-buster, cattle baron, town Marshal, stagecoach driver, Texas Ranger, train robber, rustler, wagon master, gold miner, bandit, bank thief, sheriff, gun fighter, gambler, Indian fighter, bounty hunter, saloon and bawdy house patron, and a horse lover. The media provided this rogue with a positive marketing plan that was second to none! Head west, young man...become a cowboy! Yahoooo!

The Mexican Vaqueros were the first real western cowboys as they herded cattle in Mexico and what is now, Texas. Their apparel, horsemanship, work habits and courage became the pattern for the American Cowboy. These men spent endless days on long, dangerous and boring cattle drives. The terms Cowpoke and Cowpuncher refer to those who punched or poked cattle with sticks through open slatted railroad cars to keep the cattle standing, thus utilizing less space. A Tenderfoot or Pilgrim, was a newcomer to the range. A Dude referred to someone who wore extra fancy clothes that were far removed from being utilitarian. A Sheriff or Marshal was often a man who wore a tin star. A vigilante was an unauthorized lawman. Pards were partners or cohorts. Mavericks were cattle without a brand. Red-eye was straight whiskey. The cookie, or beanmaster, was the chuckwagon cook. A cowboy's food was referred to as chuck, and usually consisted of bacon, beans, corn bread, pancakes, stews, chili, rice, wild game, sourdough bread and coffee. The list of cowboy-related terms grows to include pony boys, cowgirls, cowhands, bronco-busters, steer-wrestlers, calf-ropers, range boss, foreman, vigilante, gunfighters, regulators, greenhorns, bunkhouse bums, ranch hands, cattlemen, rustler, saddle tramps, posse, top hand, lawman, range riders, etc.

If the pulp novels with their exaggerated exploits were the foundation for radio serials, then the super structure was the Saturday western movie matinees, comic books, and early television. Hollywood created a glamorous figure and we all leaped into the saddle. The real western cowboy era was short-lived, as were the years of western TV stars. From the mid-1950s until the mid-1960s, virtually every network filled their imaginary range with western shows. The list of western characters is almost endless, and spans the careers of the Lone Ranger, Buck Jones, Tom Mix, Hoot Gibson,

Buffalo Bill, Annie Oakley, Hopalong Cassidy, Roy Rogers, and Gene Autry to the baby-boomer era of the Rifleman, Wild Bill Hickok, Wagontrain, Gunsmoke, Paladin, Bonanza, Maverick, Wyatt Earp, and numerous others. The popularity of recent films like *Pale Rider, Silverado, Lonesome Dove, Wyatt Earp, Riders of the Purple Sage* and *Unforgiven* continue to nourish the cowboy mystique!

Every boy and girl wanted a toy gun that resembled a Colt .45 or Winchester rifle. Holsters gleaming with faux jewels, silver studs and dummy bullets were belongings eagerly requested, as were western clothes and various accessories. There were six guns, rifles, der-ringers, cap shooters, water pistols, clickers, dart guns, rubberband shooters, pop guns, wartime composition guns, rubber, plastic and miniatures. Who would have imagined that these toy guns and items of apparel would attain their current value as investment col-lectibles? Backyard buckaroos were almost as harsh on their equipment as the real cowboys were. The mortality rate of these somewhat fragile toys was extremely high, and few have survived the rigors of play and passage of time. It is my belief that of all the toys owned by children, toy guns have survived in alarmingly short supply. Virtually everyone of us had a toy gun, many had more than one. Where are they now? Lost, broken, handed-down, or perhaps still in some dark and dusty attic waiting to be discovered by a modern day curator.

Toy manufacturers were very accurate in pro-ducing quality play items that resembled the real cowboy regalia. Many toy guns and acces-sories are nearly identical copies of the origi-nals. It boggles my mind to see prices of toy guns rivaling, or surpassing, the asking prices for real guns! In some instances, it is easier to find and purchase a real Colt or Winchester rather than some particular toy guns. As the western cowboy era of 1940-65 began to diminish, so did the quality of the toys. The western-styled cast iron toy guns and the early production of die cast maintain their promi-nent place as investment collectibles. I have

attempted to write a book that would pay homage to the real cowboy, the backyard buckaroo, and the quality examples of toy guns that remain as, true and lasting testament to an American era unrivaled by fact and fic-tion! The American Cowboy lives forever in our hearts, imagination and collections.

Investment Collectibles

The current rage of authentic and toy cowboy collectibles has driven the prices of even the most common items into oblivion. In my opinion the demand far outweighs the supply, and prices for quality items will continue to escalate. Until recently, toy guns have received only minimal attention in the antique col-lectible market. This has changed drastically however, as investors, collectors and dealers discover their innate charm, value, quality and rarity! In the very near future I believe that western-styled toy guns, holsters and acces-sories will rival, and possibly surpass, the mar-ket value and investment potential of real western antiques.

Published reports on investing usually promote diversification in anyone's portfolio. In the past few years, many articles have suggested investing in collectibles, and many writers have recently urged purchasing western charac-ter and early TV related items. Perhaps the true respect due toy guns, and their potential, is finally becoming a reality. American's love affair with their childhood memories has pushed the demand for quality toy guns far beyond what is currently available on the col-lector market.

Condition & Demand

Toy guns were seldom pampered and many had to withstand the rigors of rough play. Few mint examples exist of items from the early 1930-50 era. Most toy guns were played with, so condition can vary considerably. As with any antique collectible, condition is the prime factor in determining value. Having the origi-nal box can add generously to the market value. Obviously, familiar western character names such as: Gene Autry, Roy Rogers, Hoppy, Paladin, Maverick, Lone Ranger, etc., push the demand and value even higher. Generic names such as: Pony Boy, Texan, Cowhand, Ranger, Marshal, etc., have lesser appeal. Generally, collectors seek large six-guns that closely resemble the real Colts. Makers such as: Nichols, George Schmidt, Leslie-Henry, Mattel, Hubley, Marx, etc., produced top quality western-styled die cast guns. It is difficult to ignore the inherent quality and workmanship of the early cast iron toy guns produced by Hubley, Kilgore, Kenton, Stevens and Dent. Use caution in purchasing broken or damaged toys as it is often difficult, expensive or impossible to repair them. New selective reproduction parts, springs, grips, etc. are now available.

Dummy Varieties

Many states and cities have banned or restricted fireworks and caps. Among them were: New York City, Washington, D.C., Colorado, Idaho, Delaware, Iowa, New Jersey, New Mexico, West Virginia, Mississippi and Wisconsin. About 1941, the toy gun manufacturers complied with these regulations by producing dummy guns in both cast iron and die cast that were similar to normal guns except they were incapable of firing caps. Since these varieties were manufactured in lesser quantities, they are rarer and more valuable to collectors. A word of caution: dummy-styled hammers are being reproduced and installed in existing toy guns to increase their value. It is obvious that if an original gun was a dummy, no caps could be fired in it. This would leave a gun with no corrosion and in virtually mint condition around the hammer area. If you notice a heavily corroded cap box area on a gun with a dummy hammer, I would be skeptical of its authenticity. It is also difficult to match the cast metal color of an old gun with a new cast hammer. If the color varies, be careful, it may be a replacement.

Toy Gun Legislation

Present day laws and restrictions have been enacted that ban certain replicas, real gun look-alikes and some toy guns. The use of these guns in the commission of crimes and as a scare tactic in many cities and schools has prompted this legal action. Check your local and federal regulations concerning the purchase, transportation and display of your collection.

There are many American cities and foreign countries that have a legal ban on real handguns or guns in general. Collectors in these specific locations have only toy guns to cherish. Toy gun collectors must share their potential holdings with collectors of real western items, the various character collectors, (such as Hoppy, Roy, Gene, and TV character collectors), toy collectors in general, Baby-Boomers, and real gun collectors. There is lots of competition for so few collectibles.

I often ponder the fact that despite the exposure to toy guns as children, very few of us became criminals. Children experts have often tried to link violence and crime to toy guns. I find it interesting that the reduction and almost total absence of toy guns today seems to have little or no impact on diminishing crime. I'm sure you recall that Hoppy, Roy and Gene just had to wing the bad guy, never kill him. Fists were used more often than guns! I believe the ethical framework often established by these highly moral, western heroes, and their youth clubs, impacted our personal values. They stressed rules and strict codes of ethics that greatly influenced our future, much like the 4-H, Boy Scouts and Girl Scouts did. Perhaps the naive innocence we experienced was influential, but the lasting impact was certainly more beneficial than today's cynical violence! The credo set forth in our youth emphasized clean living, good vs. evil, family values, patriotism and religion. Today's movies and TV leave absolutely nothing to your imagination... violence, crime and killing have become common place and acceptable. Apparently, all of our cowboy exposure was to "G" rated material only! They weren't just heroes... they were excellent role models!

Reproductions & Counterfeits

As with all collectibles, once values and demand increase, so do the number of unethical people. I urge you to use caution when making major purchases and buy from reputable dealers or have your item examined by an expert prior to purchasing. If you are buying by mail or through an auction, make sure you have return rights if the toy is questionable. Some early toy guns have been reproduced and others are probably in production as I write this book. If it looks too good, or is priced as a bargain, the buyer must beware. It is possible to restore old guns with acid cleaning, replating, airbrushing black or dark blue finishes, buffing, adding new cast grips, replacing broken parts and springs, welding old cracks, etc. I have no problem with the proper restoration of any antique as long as the buyer is well aware of this at the time of purchase. New finishes and parts intended to deceive or create a rarer version are unethical and criminal. Holsters and related items, such as spurs, cuffs, clothes, badges, etc., are also being reproduced. A number of western-styled items are currently being newly manufactured.

The new color copiers and laser reproducing machines make it relatively easy to copy original boxes and construct nearly identical ones. Carefully inspect all boxes. If the original had a tear or marred finish it will show in the copy, but touching those areas will reveal no texture. It is virtually impossible to detect if the original box was absolutely mint. Check to ensure that any imperfection is on the actual box and not a copy.

A few reproduction holsters and limited editions have been recently introduced. These should be priced and advertised as such. A number of quality craftsmen are making exact copies of western character gun rigs in adult or children sizes. The workmanship on many is

superb and prices are quite high for all the hand labor.

Nothing that is collectible is immune to unethical practices. Take the time to do research, carefully examine original specimens, ask lots of questions from experts, and spend your investment money wisely. It is far better to own one or two authentic, top quality toys than a huge accumulation of lesser examples.

Holsters

The current collector vogue is fancy holster sets with jewels, studs, cutouts, fringe, conchos and fake bullets. The more decoration, the more desirability, the more collector value. Any holster with a western character name is in higher demand than generic ones. Earlier leather holsters tend to be of higher quality than more recent ones. Actually, many of the early toy gun sets were made by real holster manufacturers and are stamped on the back. Keyston Brothers of San Francisco were makers of fine western leather goods for nearly a hundred years, and they were also prolific makers of toy holsters and accessories. Their examples are among the finest examples known. Many of their 1950-era holsters contain studs or rivets with a tiny running buffalo logo stamped on them.

Holsters made of synthetic materials, such as Dura-Hide and Neolite, are less desirable and examples from the 1960s have limited collector appeal. There is a certain charm and allure in the very early holsters that is difficult to explain. Most early sets were for a single gun. Fancy double holster sets were at their ultimate peak in the late 1950 era. Hubley, Halco, Graton & Knight Co., Classy, Keyston Brothers, Tex-Tan, Esquire Novelty, S-Bar-M (Service Manufacturing Co.), Western Boy, Leslie-Henry, State Ranger, and Boyville produce some exceptional, high quality holster sets. Many display higher quality workmanship than real holsters. Holsters intended for cowgirls are difficult to find and in constant demand. Most girl sets are white leather with red hearts, jewels and fringe. They were made in lesser numbers and demand premium prices. Character sets intended for cowgirls such as: Dale Evans, Sally Star and Annie Oakley are very choice items.

It was a common practice for holster manufacturers to produce sets that were oversized for many toy guns. This enabled distributors to utilize a wider latitude of toy guns in them. At times, the holsters appear huge for the smaller guns in them. These larger holsters could accept big and small guns making them more accommodating to catalog companies and stores. Of course, collectors and dealers constantly change guns and holsters today. A review of old toy gun or holiday catalogs will reveal the dates of availability and depict sets with the guns in place. It takes considerable room to display a collection of holsters so plan accordingly. Many of the original toy gun holster sets were made in small, unknown factories that hired mostly women seamstresses to produce them for large companies.

Condition & Care

Inspect holsters for broken stitches, missing studs and jewels, torn leather, etc. Leather can be repaired and most can be enhanced with a mild leather cleaner or softener. Reproduction bullets are available to replace missing ammo. I urge collectors to regularly inspect guns stored in holsters, or leave guns out of them. The salts used in the tanning of leather can mar or corrode the metal finish. Some collectors put plastic sandwich bags over their guns prior to placing them in holsters. It is advisable to check all the guns periodically.

Western Accessories

Initially collectors wanted just toy guns. Then they included the holsters. Now collectibles encompasses anything related to a young buckaroo's imaginary day in the saddle! The escalating prices of many toy guns and holster sets forced many collectors to seek more reasonable western toy items. Now, even their availability and value have made them scarce.

It appears that the major demise of the western toy collector is due to the limited, remaining examples. I have always maintained western collectibles were very rare compared to other toys.

The backyard buckaroo used the identical items a real cowboy utilized. To prevent rope burns, he needed leather gloves and wrist cuffs. To ward off brambles, chaparral and cactus, he wore a vest and chaps. To encourage his horse, he used spurs. To rope a longhorn steer, he needed a lariat. To cut food, or a tobacco plug, he used his knife. For his meager belongings, he carried a saddle bag. A buckaroo needed a scabbard for his Winchester rifle, and kerchiefs to ward-off dust and the cold. He wore a wide-brimmed hat for weather protection, fanning a fire's embers, or watering his horse. Boots were a necessity for his roaming feet. Obviously, he also had to have extra ammunition, a good luck piece and spending money for the saloon!

The young buckaroo had them all... rubber knives, play money, caps, shootin' shells, cowboy hats, character clothes, jeweled wrist cuffs, fringed gloves, trick lariats, bike saddle bags, decorative kerchiefs and slides, boots or fake shoe tops, a Marshal's badge, root beer and sasparilla! Every item is every bit as rare as the cowboy originals! Try to find an early rubber knife, fancy set of spurs or an old box of caps! Playtime on the imaginary range was rough and tumble, so few examples of these children's western accessories exist today. Newly manufactured spurs, plastic knives and lawmen badges exist, so use caution when purchasing these items. The quality is very good, but they should be priced accordingly.

Interesting Tidbits

I find it amazing that virtually everyone I talk with about western toy guns remembers the very distinct smell of a fired cap. It is probably the one thing everyone specifically mentions.

Many of the toy gun manufacturers hired women workers. They reported to work at 9:00

A.M. and left at 3:00 P.M. to be home when the children left and returned from school. They were hard workers, weren't bored on the assembly line, accepted minimal wages and their small hands were most desirable in assembling small springs, internal parts and screws in the toy guns. Men primarily did the marketing, pre-production models, planning, mold preparation, plating, metal casting and heavier machine work.

A number of teachers purchased toy guns to present as awards for the boys who were the highest achievers during the school year. Many teachers became collectors as their hoard of confiscated guns was discovered after retirement. This was especially true of water pistols!

One older gentleman was ecstatic about having his confiscated toy pistol returned to him nearly 45 years later. Upon visiting his mother in a retirement community, he was surprised to learn his old grammar school teacher resided at the same home. After a brief visit and discussion he learned that the teacher still retained a box of guns she took from him and other students decades before. A few days later he was reunited with his original Hubley Cowboy, that still contained a roll of caps! It even worked perfectly as he fired off a cap!

Many people recalled taking their six-gun and holster to the hospital when they had their tonsils or appendix removed as a child. Strapped over the end of the hospital bed it provided the security a sick cowboy or cowgirl needed to mend quickly.

Theater managers and ushers recall stopping Saturday matinees to remove cap guns from young buckaroos who were firing at the screen during a thrilling western episode! Many theaters gave away cap guns and tin clickers as promotional items for their cowboy movies. As with the teachers, many theater workers started their present-day collections after discovering guns they had confiscated years before.

Some of the mail order catalogs of the 1948-1955 era mention that cap guns cannot be sold to minors under 16 in Ohio and Washington. This is of interest as both Kenton and Kilgore were located in Ohio, and if cap guns weren't toys for kids, who were their customers?

Clothing and shoe stores regularly gave away toy guns with new outfits, boots, costumes, or store purchases. Some of these have store advertisements printed on them. Many local and national contests awarded toy guns as prizes. Selling garden seeds provided many a toy gun.

The company stores in many mining regions of the Appalachians used expensive toy gun sets as incentives to keep their workers in debt. At Christmas time and around July 4th, the stores would stock elaborate holster sets to entice the worker's children. The worker, of course, had little choice but to purchase the toys and become further indebted to the company store. The fancier the set, the more in debt, so many fine ones are discovered in these regions of the country.

Between the major rush to fill Christmas orders and the July 4th demand, many of the toy gun companies made other items such as: hinges, bolts, latches, hardware items, tools, and metal castings. It is also of interest that during this lull in the toy manufacturing, many workers recall spending extra time in buffing and polishing the guns. This helps to explain the rather scarce number of polished varieties of cast iron toy guns. Apparently only a few guns were ever polished. It was also noted that the salesmen samples were often given special finishes or polishing to promote sales.

Virtually all the major shipping of early cast iron toy guns was by Railway Express. The cost of shipping this heavy inventory is really what prompted the manufacturers to find alternate materials to reduce their shipping costs. The use of die cast zinc, plastics, aluminum and metal alloys opened the door to a flood of new technologies for toy guns.

Research indicates that many of the toy gun companies located in the mid-West utilized scrap metal and imperfect castings from the automobile industry for their supply of metal. Each week trucks would deliver this metal to be melted down and cast into toy guns. Perhaps your Gene Autry, Hopalong Cassidy or Big Horn originally was an imperfect hood ornament, cigarette lighter or door handle for a Ford, Packard, Desoto, or Edsel!

Interviews with factory workers indicate that when polishing and nickel plating became too expensive, many of the toy guns were simply sprayed or dipped in paint for their final finish. A number of companies did provide a dark or blue-black finish in their regular lines. Kilgore cast iron guns have exceptionally beautiful painted finishes which were intended to resemble the metallic blue finish of a real gun. Nichols' "Steel-Blu" guns are rare and desirable.

A large number of collectors recall receiving a new cap gun every July 4th to celebrate Independence Day. I remember my Aunt Mary visiting every July 4th from Brooklyn, and always bringing me a new cap pistol from Macy's. I recall being terribly disappointed with a particular dummy Texan that wouldn't shoot caps! I often wonder where it is now.

After a toy gun article I wrote appeared in the *Washington Post* newspaper, I received a phone call from a woman who remembered growing up in Oklahoma and playing cap guns with her brothers, sisters and friends. She noted the pungent smell of fired caps and the great times they had as they rode their real horses. She mentioned that she reminisced and started to cry, as all her relatives and friends had passed on. But then she remarked, I started to smile as I recalled all the pleasant memories your article had resurrected, and how those memories would never die. She concluded by saying my article on toy guns had made an 89 year old woman very, very happy!

A fellow collector remembered how many toy guns he had owned as a child. He broke many

as he tried to perfect his fast draw and twirling abilities. Some were simply lost. Others vanished or were traded away. He recalled cutting grass, raking leaves, shoveling snow and delivering newspapers to earn enough funds to buy another gun! He vividly remembered his first sighting of a Texan for one dollar, and then the best... a Long Tom that actually fired six shots! He recalled finally owning the huge Nichols' Stallion .45 that accepted and used bullets! Golly, those were the days! Carefree, imaginative and filled with fun to share with friends.

One letter writer remembered taking apart a tin clicker pistol so that the two halves would provide him with a double set of guns like Hoppy!

A sizable number of correspondents related that they never had a double holster set, just a single. Some noted they didn't have any holsters at all. Most never saw a gold-plated toy gun, fancy holster sets or any related accessories. A large number had a Kenton Gene Autry cast iron or a Roy Rogers pistol by Classy, Leslie-Henry or George Schmidt. Only a few recalled owning a Hoppy, and they were Wyandotte guns. Virtually no one remembered having a Lone Ranger gun. Rifles were pretty scarce until you get to the Mattel Shootin' Shell Winchesters of the early 1960s. Mattel Fanners were extremely popular! The most desired gun was probably a Nichols' Stallion .45. What a great toy... an absolutely all time Classic Western Toy Gun. I tip my hat to Talley Nichols and his co-workers. One man remembered wanting a short-barreled Colt like many of the western stars, so he proceeded to cut off the barrel of his Nichols' Stallion .45 at the ejector rod! Horrors!!!

Catalog pages and advertising research, indicate that cast iron guns were still being manufactured as late as 1951-53. I believe that the Kenton Lawmaker, Bullseye and engraved Gene Autry guns, as well as the Stevens' Billy the Kid, were the last made. It may be the reason that these particular guns are relatively rare.

Many have asked what is my favorite toy gun? What a difficult question to answer. I guess it could be my first gun, my next gun, or any in between! I was most fortunate that my mother kept a few of my toys. I have often asked myself why she did, as anything old was usually discarded. When my mom died, I went through many items in her attic. Here among the Christmas ornaments and old gift boxes were some of my childhood treasures! I was literally shocked to find them. A small box containing years of memories! Here was my Kenton, orange-handled, Gene Autry, my Hubley die cast Cowboy, a Keyston holster, my three-fingered Ballhawk baseball glove, an old match safe, my Barlow pocket knife, a few 1950-era baseball cards, a small hunting sheath knife and two western comic books. These are among my most cherished belongings, and I hope to retain them for future generations.

I had other guns. I remember a Texan, Jr., the Texan dummy, many tin clickers and dart pistols, a few composition and rubber guns during W.W. II, a Hubley Pirate pistol, a pop gun, some wooden guns my dad made and a rather rare, Daisy Model 141 Defender BB gun. I am presently the curator for many others, but I am especially fond of the Kilgore, cast iron Big Horn of the 1940 era. This particular model is beautifully made, has a revolving cylinder, fires six shots, has stag grips, is perfectly balanced, fits your hand comfortably and looks like a Colt Peacemaker. If I could have only one... it would be a Big Horn, but my salvaged Kenton Gene Autry would be a very close second! Note the photograph of me on the back cover, the gun in my hand is my childhood treasure... the Kenton Gene Autry!

A haphazard survey of many toy gun collectors indicates a preference for many of the same models. Those guns on the most liked or most wanted list include: the Kilgore cast iron American, Big Horn, Long Tom and Lone Ranger, the Kenton Gene Autry and Lawman, the Hubley cast iron Texan, Texan, Jr., and the die cast Colt .45 and Cowboy, the George Schmidt Hoppy, Alan Ladd and Roy guns, the Nichols' Stallion .45 Mark II, the Mattel Shootin' Shell, Fanner .45 and Fanner 50, and all the many Leslie-Henry character guns. Many collect just revolving cylinder guns, those that accept bullets, special finishes like gold. Some prefer one company, one character, colorful grips, and most of us, like them all!

Research indicates that between February and August of 1938, Kenton made over one million Gene Autry cap guns. By late 1939, they went over the two million mark! In 1947 Kenton employed about 125 people exclusively manufacturing these guns. It is estimated that by the time Kenton ceased making Gene Autry guns in late 1951, a total exceeding 6 million had been produced. A royalty check of nearly $12,000 was reportedly paid to Gene Autry in 1938.

The Nichols Industries, "Circle N Ranch" of Pasadena and Jacksonville, Texas, produced their first toy guns in 1946. After producing over 30 various models, they sold the company in 1965 to Kusan Manufacturing Company of Nashville, TN, which continued to manufacture toy guns until late 1982. Within these years some of the finest toy guns were produced. During the Kusan era, many guns closely resembling previous Nichols' models were made for Daisy, Halco and others. Some of these guns, made both here and possibly abroad, contain no markings. Kusan sold the cap guns molds and materials in early 1983 to Strombecker of Chicago, IL.

In the late 1950s, Actoy guns were apparently manufactured and distributed by the Esquire Novelty Corp., of Jersey City, NJ. One boxed item from 1960, displays an Esquire address of Amsterdam, NY. They produced a wide variety of western character holster sets and guns. A small horsehead, or pony medallion usually appears on Actoy gun grips. Their Lone Ranger, Restless Gun, Wyatt Earp, Wells Fargo, Rin Tin Tin, Johnny Ringo and antique bronze-finished guns are especially desirable.

Many toy guns were shipped with decorative boxes usually printed in patriotic red, white and blue. A number contain western illustrations. Some distributors preferred to have no boxes as the guns were to be used in holster sets or simply displayed on a counter top. In lieu of boxes, some of the toy makers would provide a reduced price, special finish or perhaps a colorful jewel to the customer. Very few, if any of us, kept the box the gun came in. Like most toys, the original boxes for guns are much rarer than the toy itself. Boxes have not surfaced for many varieties of toy guns, but those that do exist are highly coveted. It is not uncommon to find certain desirable boxes selling for hundreds of dollars. This is especially true of specific western character boxes.

Various toy guns exist that are nearly identical copies of Hubley models. Some are marked Long Island Die Casting Inc., Inwood 95, L.I., N.Y., and others are marked Service Mfg. Co. (S Bar M Brand), Yonkers, N.Y. They are so identical that it appears these variations are from the same molds. They may have been subcontractors to help Hubley meet the toy gun demands of the late 1950s. During the early 1950s, S Bar M also made some exceptional quality leather holster sets. L.I. Die Casting, Inc., produced a few identical Hubley Wyatt Earp guns, with the addition of engraving on the frame and barrel. Many of these Hubley copies have the familiar Star medallion, but a few have a small "V" with "Service" above it on the medallion. Other toy guns made by Lone Star, Crescent and British Cast Metals of England, Modern Toys of Japan and Lincoln Industries Ltd. of New Zealand also have many similar details to various Hubley guns. Imitation is still the best form of flattery!

Hubley Manufacturing of Lancaster, PA, introduced the new Colt .38 pistols in their 1958 catalog. The huge Colt .45 and Remington .36 with short barrel were introduced in 1959. In 1960, Hubley announced the new Panther wrist derringer, Ric-O-Shay, Dagger Derringer, the Model 1860 .44 Cal. and the Wyatt Earp "Buntline Special" with extra-long barrel and Canyon brown grips! The 1961 releases were the rare long-barreled, Remington .36 as a Civil War replica, and the extremely rare Texan .45 variation of the big Colt .45 as a special limited edition for the 125th Anniverary of the Republic of Texas. Apparently, a very limited number were produced for a toy distributor in Texas. Hubley was sold to Gabriel in 1966.

Perhaps the most mysterious of all the toy gun manufacturers, is the famous George Schmidt Manufacturing Company, 716 East 14th Street, Los Angeles 21, California. Extensive research has yielded very minimal information on this company and their fine quality toy guns and spurs. It appears they were in business from just prior to 1950 until they ceased to exist in the 1960s. The following companies apparently had some contact with Schmidt during this timeframe: Tumbleweed Togs of Arcadia, Calif., Duncan Sales Co. of L.A., Rodeo King Western Holsters of L.A., Keyston Bros. of San Francisco who had an office on W. 3 St. in L.A., LATCO of L.A. (Los Angeles Toy Co.), Viril Mfg. of L.A. and Halco of Pittsburg (The J. Halpern Co.). George Schmidt produced some of the finest quality western character toy guns, including: Roy Rogers, Hopalong Cassidy, Alan Ladd, Maverick, Wyatt Earp, Dale Evans, Lasso Em Bill, etc. A few clues indicate they were possibly an import-export company. Any information would be greatly appreciated.

The letters "M.A.H.-1946" found stamped on the bottom of many Gene Autry holsters stands for Milton A. Henry of Mount Vernon, N.Y. His company produced many Gene Autry and western items from the late 1930s until the mid 1940s. There also was a M.A. Henry Limited in Scarborough Junction, Ontario, Canada, and another in Santa Monica, CA. His son's nickname was supposedly "Buzz", and is found on some smaller toy guns. There is a possible connection with the Feinburg-Henry Mfg. Co. of NY during the 1940s.

Apparently he joined with Leslie around 1950 to form the Leslie-Henry Co. They produced some of the finest western character guns. The larger .44 model Leslie-Henry guns with revolving cylinders have either an "H" or "L-H" medallion on the grip. Those with the "H" medallion usually have cylinders that accept small copper or brass bullets. Guns with the "L-H" usually have solid cylinders. In recent years some new L-H .44 models have been reproduced without character name and usually a painted, antique bronze finish. These were probably made by Parris Mfg. Co. I believe that any Leslie-Henry guns with the square hole-type assembly screws were made in Canada, as these appear on guns usually found in Canada or near the border.

During the mid 1960s, several L-H guns appear on display cards marked: Leslie-Henry, Wilkes Barre, PA. In the late 1960s and early 1970s, display cards with L-H guns appear that are marked "Western Man" with the manufacturer listed as: Roth American Inc., Wilkes Barre, PA. There is apparently a connection. The later quality is inferior to earlier toys manufactured in Mt. Vernon, NY.

The big and beautiful Mattel Fanner .45 is an awesome toy! It is nearly identical to a real Colt Peacemaker. It was introduced in the 1959 Mattel catalog and on national TV as a super-size, barrel-smoking, realistic cartridge-shootin' shell .45! It has beautiful stag grips and polished nickel finish. I believe it was only made for two years, and due to its fragile nature only a small number have survived. It fits nicely into many of the larger holsters.

In the 1965-68 era, Mattel produced the Agent Zero series of toy guns which also had the designation of Secret Frontier Defender. All these guns had a paper Agent Zero sticker on the right-hand grip. In the early 1960s Mattel introduced the "Dura-Hide" holsters which were washable, and wouldn't tear, crack or ever lose their shape. Their color was permanent and they had a hand-tooled appearance of a fine western saddle. Unfortunately, most collectors detest these synthetic holsters and place little value on them.

The J. Halpern Company (Halco) was founded about 1909 in Pittsburg, PA. They were a high-volume distributor who concentrated on traditional quality and value throughout the year rather than concentrating on seasonal sales. They provided millions of toy gun sets and were well known for their extensive selection of character and children's costumes. Research indicates that in some years, over 3 million toy gun holster sets were sold by them to Western Auto, Montgomery Wards, Woolworth's, Sears, Macy's, Eaton's, Speigels, Schwartz Toys, J.C. Penney's, Marshal Fields, and other companies. In the 1940-60 era, Halco purchased large numbers of Nichols, Hubley, Schmidt, Leslie-Henry, Kenton and Kilgore toy guns for their extensive line of holster sets. They also purchased large numbers of western character and generic holsters from various manufacturers and then assembled and boxed the sets for distribution. Their southern representative was the River Company of Memphis, TN. Literally, millions of toy gun rigs we cherish today went through Halco's hands.

About 1960, the Barash Co., Inc., of NYC, introduced holster sets made from Neolite, a new synthetic material from Goodyear Co. The holsters were not rubber, or plastic, but this new material that would withstand abuse and ensure durability. It was made to resemble fine tooled leather. Barash Co. produced a number of boxed salesman sample cases containing Lone Ranger holsters made from Neolite. The sets usually included Hubley Texas Jr. guns.

Parris Mfg. Co, of Savannah, TN, made thousands of toy guns. During WW II they made over 2 million dummy training rifles for the Army and Navy due to the shortage of real guns. They were presented the Army-Navy "E" Award for their excellent effort.

In the 1955-60 era, Kilgore produced perhaps, the finest gold-plated guns. They used 24 Karat gold plate on highly polished guns and the results are beautiful! These guns are quite rare and usually have black grips. The Eagle, Grizzly and Kit Carson are great toy guns. In this same time period, Hubley and George Schmidt also produced limited numbers of exceptional gold-plated guns. A few collectors specialize in gold-plated guns only.

During WW II, severe restrictions were placed on the use of metals for toys or items considered non-essential. All metal was reserved for the war effort. During this time many of the toy manufacturers such as Nichols, Hubley, Wyandotte, Parris and others, produced defense items including: bomb fuses, M-1 rifle clips, training rifles, equipment components, screws, bolts, rivets, etc. The toy guns produced during this period utilized rubber, plastic and a composition material similar to a mixture of paper pulp, sawdust and glue. Many of the existing gun molds were used, but casting was done with rubber or this composition material in lieu of metal. Some highly detailed guns were made by Molex. Most were painted black and since there were no moving parts... you provided the bang! All of these guns were extremely fragile and only a mere handful have survived the backyard battles.

Even Daisy made a number of wooden "Victory" model guns with patriotic decals. These wartime toys are an important historical segment of the toy gun legacy, but unfortunately, most collectors ignore them.

It would be impossible to do a book on cowboys without including the Indians. Most of us were nurtured on a diet of cowboy and Indian tales, stories and images. Only a few toy guns and accessories have survived that honor this first American pioneer of the west. A number of cap guns have names like: Chief, Warrior, Big Injun, Big Chief, Apache, Chieftain, Little Beaver, Indian, Cheyenne, Mohawk, Mohican, Brave, and Sioux. Strangely, there is no Tonto, Sitting Bull, Geronimo or Cochise gun. A few holsters exist with Tonto, and there is an Indian Scout Rifle, but the selection is mighty sparse. Some Indian-style accessories exist and a few toy guns that have been owner-modified to depict Indian usage.

Films and early TV usually depicted the good guys wearing white hats and the bad guys wearing black ones. It is interesting to note that Nichols provide both a black and white pair of grips with their Stallion .45 Mark II. Perhaps you could become a good or bad guy simply by changing your gun's grips.

During the golden era of cap guns, Kilgore brought local kids to the factory and had them use, and comment on various models prior to actual production. Many free guns were given away as rewards for this invaluable customer research.

To help identify their toy guns, original owners often scratched their initials in the bottom of the grip, or placed a piece of paper containing their name under the grip if it was removable. I have found a number of guns that were similarly identified. I have one Hubley die cast Cowboy dummy with the owner's name professionally engraved on the frame. Another gun had the owner's original library card under the grip. I was pleasantly surprised to find my own Kenton Gene Autry had my name and address still folded under the grip!

Many who read this book have never experienced the thrill and excitement of listening to the western heroes on the radio. We rushed home to let our imaginations run wild as we rode the range with these cowboys. I will never forget the anticipation I experienced waiting for the mailman to deliver those cherished, but often disappointing, radio premiums. Was it just me... or did it really take months to arrive? Another box of cereal! Ugh!

Numerous small companies produced various hardware items and their toy gun output was limited to certain periods of the year. Dent had an extensive line of hardware items. A pair of toy, cast iron handcuffs dated 1924, were made by the Gardner Screw Co. of Gardner, Mass. Other companies also made toy banks, trucks, vehicles and doll house items. Many smaller foundries made toy gun parts and castings for the larger manufacturers.

During the depression years of the late 1920s and early 1930s, company sales were drastically limited. The Ansley H. Fox Gun Co., of Philadelphia, PA, produced some of the finest double-barrel shotguns ever made in America. Due to reduced gun sales, they decided to offer a toy double-barrel shotgun between 1929 and 1931. This superb toy is of the highest quality and chambered two shot-shells that enabled the user to fire round wooden balls at targets. They shoot with amazing authority! These very rare, reduced scale shotguns are premier additions to a toy, or real double-barrel gun collection. What western lawman didn't grab a double-barrel shotgun when trouble was eminent?

I have attempted to bring respectability to toy gun collecting, reveal their true scarcity and investment potential, and more importantly... expose the imaginative and creative child in all of us! Do you recall radio, Chinese checkers, dominoes, mumbly peg, Monopoly, kick the can, Old Maid, jump rope, pickup sticks, jacks, marbles, stoop ball, rummy, and trading cards? Some people thought we only played with toy guns. I often wonder if today's kids ever have the fun and imaginative playtime we experienced 30 to 50 years ago. Will these present generations recall TV, electronic games, Internet, CD Rom, computers and day care centers with the same intense memories we retain? They certainly will remember dominoes... but probably only as a pizza delivery!

Most people remember their toy gun as being really big! They are generally surprised to realize how small the guns are. It is easy to forget what size we were as children. I do wonder, however, how kids could play with guns as large as the Marx Thundergun or Hubley Ric-O-Shay and Colt .45. I have been often reminded that 45 years ago, toy guns were still popular with teenagers as old as 14-16!

Many holster sets came with a supply of fake cartridges. In most instances, the makers are unknown. Materials vary, but most were made of plastic, wood or metal. Some are two piece with a brass color case and lead color bullets.

Some came apart to insert caps, others had bullets that actually shot from the gun! Caps, the ammo for cap guns, came in a myriad of varieties: sheets of single shot caps, rolls of 50 shot caps, boxes of 250, 500 and even over a 1000! Generic names proliferate, but western character names are noticeably absent. Colors are usually the familiar, patriotic ones... red, white and blue. A few toy guns actually fired blank cartridges made by the normal ammunition companies. The two dummy bullets found in Kenton cast iron Lasso 'Em Bill guns were produced by the Remington Gun Co. They were nickel-plated, included a lead bullet and had a small hole drilled at the bottom of the case. The first bullets used by Nichols in their .45 and .38 Stallion guns were manufactured by the Winchester Repeating Arms Co. Later, after receiving competitive bids, Remington Arms Co. produced them. All the bullets are unmarked so it is impossible to identify the makers. Dummy .38 caliber, nickel-plated shells by Peters can occasionally be found in the ammo loops of early1950 Sears holster sets made by Boyville.

A large portion of correspondence I have received, indicates that "aunts" were among the most prolific providers of toy guns to children. I personally received a number of guns from my Aunts Mary, Nellie and Blanche. Probably my Aunt Blanche had the most impact on my love of cowboys and toy guns. On many a Saturday she took me to the matinee to see the cowboy movies, especially Gene Autry. Then after the show, she took me to the Olympia ice cream parlor for a banana split! She purchased many toy guns for me and was a constant supplier of caps. She treated me to my first cowboy rodeo... staring Gene Autry at Madison Square Garden in New York City. Thanks, Aunt Blanche, for all the super great memories!

Toy Gun Care & Maintenance

As curators of toy guns, it is imperative that we protect and maintain them for future generations. Cleaning and polishing toy guns must be done carefully to protect the finishes. Gold guns have an extremely thin plating so they demand closer scrutiny when cleaning. Machine buffing can quickly ruin a fine collectible and should only be attempted by skilled craftsmen. I recommend using any fine jeweler's cleaner such as, Simichrome, Top-Brite or Metal-Glo that can be applied with a toothbrush and hand wiped with a soft cloth. Even toothpaste can be used as a cleaner. As with any type of cleaning or polishing, be careful and proceed on small portions at a time to reduce any possible damage. The patina garnered by a collectible over the years is part of its legacy. Caution should be taken before you remove this past and possibly reduce the value. If you desire to have anything refinished, seek professional help. A few drops of quality gun oil can be applied to internal moving parts. I suggest a quarterly inspection of your collectibles to check for rust, corrosion, or damage. Plastic grips demand extreme caution as they are especially susceptible to damage from polishing and the chemicals in some cleaners.

Toy Gun Values:

What's it worth? Probably the most asked question about any collectible. In my opinion, prices are totally dependent on availability, rarity, desirability, popularity, emotional attachment, condition, location in the country and the willingness of buyers to part with their money. Most dealers depend on auction prices, value guides, the old supply and demand syndrome or simple greed! Remember that auction prices are only the result of two or more individuals wanting the same item. The prices realized are not a true indication of actual value as the bidders get caught in the frenzy of bidding and skewed by their personal desires. Any value guide is just that... a guide or average suggestion. If a price is close to what you feel is reasonable and you want the item... make an offer, or pay the asking price.

It is virtually impossible to appease everyone when you try to place a value or price estimate on any collectible. There are so many factors

that determine value, and everyone's opinion on condition and scarcity varies considerably. I have gone to great lengths to ensure that the values I've assigned met with the approval of a select review board of toy gun experts and toy dealers. I did not treat this assignment lightly. I have decided to give most items a price value range. The lower figure designates an item in excellent condition with no broken parts, most of the original finish, operating properly and exemplifying a well cared for collectible. The high value designates an item in mint, or near-mint condition, and as close to the way it left the factory.

Many of the related items have only one price, which indicates the value of an average to excellent example. Holster values do not include the guns shown in the photographs. Boxes, holsters and certain items, especially with Character names, are those deemed the most desirable in the market place. They are assigned very high values. Some items, although rare, or seldom seen, might have minimal value directly related to collector demand and interest. Buyer demand determines the higher value, not rarity! Some of the rarest items are seldom offered for sale, so the task of assigning a value was virtually impossible. I have given these a reasonable assessment.

Original Prices:

Some items in this book had the original price tag still attached and I have tried to make special note of this. If you do some simple mathmatical figuring you will be surprised at how expensive many toy guns were. A double holster set for $9.98 in 1951 was a very costly toy when you consider that the minimum hourly wage was only about $.75!

Grid System

Many of the toy guns and accessories in this book were photographed on a one-inch grid to aid in accurately determining their size.

CHIP

LIN

DOUG

JOHN

Western Museums:

Gene Autry Western Heritage Museum................ Los Angeles, CA
Cowboy Hall of Fame..Oklahoma City, OK
Roy Rogers and Dale Evans Museum.................... Victorville, CA
Cowgirl Hall of Fame...Hereford, TX
Tom Mix Museum.. Dewey, OK
Will Rogers Memorial..Claremore, OK
Rex Allen Museum...Willcox, AZ
William S. Hart Museum.. Newhall. CA
Daisy Gun Museum.. Rogers, AR
Winchester-Buffalo Bill Museum...........................Cody, WY
Rockwell Museum- American West .... Corning, NY

Bibliography:
(Recommended reading for additional information on real and toy western collectibles.)

Cast Iron Toy Guns & Cap Shooters.....................Sam Logan & Charles Best
Collecting Toys Volume 7...................................... Richard O'Brien
History of Nichols Industries, Inc. (Toys).............. Talley Nichols
Radio Premiums...Tom Tumbusch
Six-Gun Heros..Hake & Cauler

Guide to Cowboy Character Collectibles...............Ted Hake
Cowboy Collectibles...Heide & Gilman
Cowboy Collectibles & Western Memorabilia...... Ball & Vebell
Steel Canvas..R.L. Wilson
Cowboy Culture..M. Friedman

Packing Iron..Richard Rattenbury
The Peacemakers..R.L. Wilson
The Wild West.. Time-Life Books
Age of the Gunfighter.. J. Rosa
Roy Rogers... Robert Phillips

Hoppy Collectors Guide...Joe Caro
Cowboy & Gunfighter Collectibles ....Bill Mackin
Box Office Buckaroos...Heide & Gilman
I Had One of Those Toys..Robin Sommer
Official TV Western Books......................................Neil Summers

Toy Gun Purveyors - Newsletters...........................Jim Schleyer
The Big Toy Box at Sears.. Fritz & Mautner
Toy Gun Collectors of America - Newsletters.......Jim Buskirk

Correspondence: Jim Schleyer, Box 243, Burke, VA 22015
For all correspondence and inquiries, please include a self-addressed and stamped envelope if you expect a response. Information and detailed photographs on items not included in this book are welcomed. Research on companies who produced toy guns, holsters and accessories is appreciated.

Alan Ladd-Shane

G. Schmidt- 1952-53. Very rare, chromed die cast with copper stag grips. Name on side frame. One of the most difficult character toy guns to find. Original tan and dark brown box.

Value: $150-325 (Gun) - $75-125 (Box)

AL-1

Alan Ladd-Shane

G. Schmidt- 1952-53. Close-up detail of AL-1 showing frame lettering and AL circle medallion on stag grips. Beautifully polished and chrome plated gun.

AL-2

Alan Ladd-Shane Holster

Possibly Canadian- 1952-55. Extremely rare tan leather holster set with silver conchos and studs. Shane on the holster front. Set advertised in Eaton's Catalogs. An Alan Ladd gun fits in this holster.

Value: $250-350 (Holster only)

AL-3

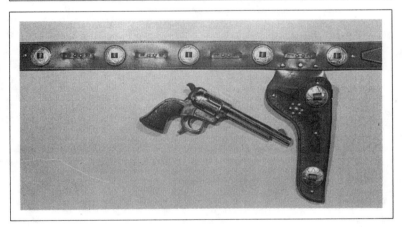

Alan Ladd-Shane Holster

Unknown- 1952-55. Close-up detail of the holster, AL-3 above. Note the dark brown western-style lettering of "Shane" on the holster front. Star, silver conchos and G. Schmidt polished toy gun.

AL-4

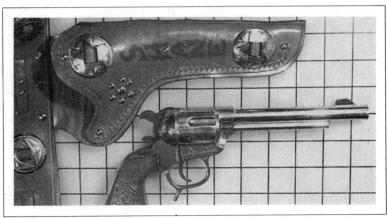

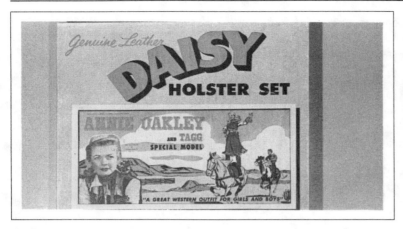

Annie Oakley

Daisy, Plymouth, MI-1955 era. Full color box for a set of very rare Annie Oakley holsters. All sets intended for cowgirls are seldom seen, as very few were made.

Value: $75-125 (Box only)

AO-1

Annie Oakley

Daisy- 1955 era. Very rare, dark blue and buckskin leather holsters. Annie Oakley's brand on top of holster. Sets usually contain generic guns, such as Texan, Jrs.

Value: $125-225 (Box & holster set)

AO-2

Annie Oakley

Daisy- 1955 era. Close-up detail of brand found on AO-2. The "A" has the rifle as the crossbar. The "O" forms part of a target's bullseye. The outer circle completes the brand. Great logo design!

AO-3

Annie Oakley

Leslie-Henry- 1955 era. Rare and unusual variation. This gun has Gene Autry cast on the left side and Annie Oakley on the right. Both TV shows were produced by Gene's, Flying "A" Ranch Productions.

Value: $135-250

AO-4

Annie Oakley

Leslie-Henry- 1955 era. Very rare nickel die cast with white horsehead grips. Very few toy guns were made for cowgirls. It is one of the most difficult character guns to locate.

Value: $135-250

AO-5

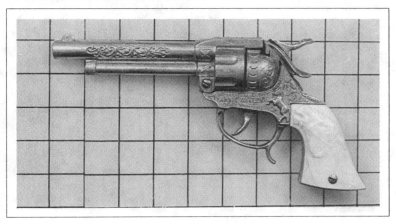

Annie Oakley

Leslie-Henry- 1955 era. Close-up detail of AO-5 showing name and incised engraving. Note flower decoration on hinge screw.

AO-6

Annie Oakley Holster

Unknown- 1955 era. Very rare cross-draw, highly decorated holsters in white and red leather. Name on the belt with silver studs, red jewels, fringe and hearts. Guns are Latco Ruff Rider with scroll grips.

Value: $250-500 (Holsters & guns)

AO-7

Annie Oakley Set

Daisy- 1956 era. Ad for rare set including smoke & pop rifle with gold finish & blue sling. Canteen is white with blue strap. Logo on stock. Catalog page from the Christmas 1956 Western Auto Store.

Value: $85-175 (Rifle and canteen)

AO-8

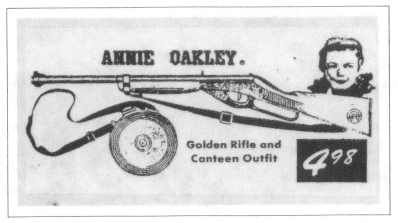

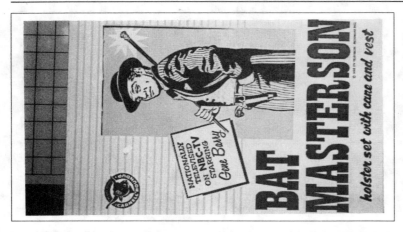

Bat Masterson

Carnell Mfg. Brooklyn- 1959-60 era. Box for a complete set that includes holster, gun, cane and vest. Research indicates that the guns were made by Lone Star in England. Halco distributed similar guns.

Value: $165-350 (Box & complete set)

BM-1

Bat Masterson

Carnell Mfg.- 1959-60. Complete contents of box BM-1 shown above. Note: vest is gold and black. Holster and cane are also black with gold details and lettering. The gun is nickel with stag grips.

Value: $165-350 (Box & complete set)

BM-2

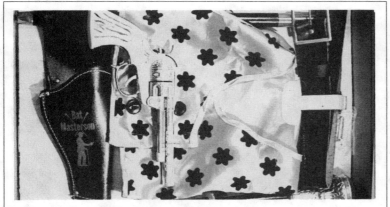

Bat Masterson

Carnell Mfg.- 1959-60. Black leather loop-style holster with artwork in gold on holster front. Gun is Lone Star in nickel.

Value: $125-245 (Holster & gun)

BM-3

Bat Masterson

Carnell Mfg.- 1959-60. Rare display box for the revolving cylinder Carnell gun. This variation also accepts two-piece bullets. Artwork on the acetate box cover. Gun BM-5 came in this box.

Value: $45-100 (Box only)

BM-4

Bat Masterson

Carnell Mfg.- 1959-60. Very rare nickel gun with revolving cylinder which also accepts 6 bullets. Gun has details similar to some Lone Star guns. Grips are stag. Note the "C" circle medallion on grips.

Value: $250-400

BM-5

Bat Masterson

Carnell Mfg.- 1959-60. Similar to the gun BM-5 above, except in the rarer gold finish, black stag grips. Revolving cylinder is copper plated. A nickel variation also exists with the same copper cylinder.

Value: $300-500 (Gold)

BM-6

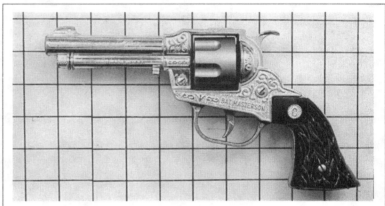

Bat Masterson

Lone Star, Eng.- 1960 era. Nickel plated repeater with stag grips. Cylinder does not revolve. Halco utilized some similar generic guns in their holster sets.

Value: $85-150 (Nickel)

BM-7

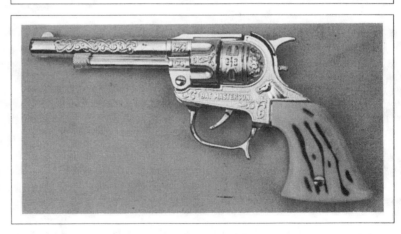

Bat Masterson

Lone Star, Eng.- 1960 era. Similar to gun BM-7 above, except in the very rare antique bronze finish. Stag grips. Some of the Lone Star variations are found with Notch-Bar grips in lieu of stag.

Value: $100-185 (Antique Bronze)

BM-8

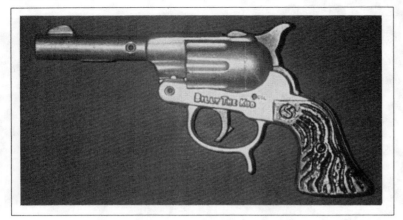

Billy the Kid

Stevens- 1950 era. One of the last cast iron guns made. Rather rare toy gun. The grips are usually painted black. Repeater.

Value: $100-165

BK-1

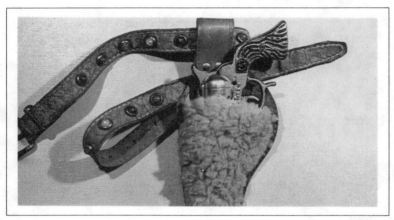

Billy the Kid

Unknown- 1950 era. Unusual leather holster set with sheepskin wooly front. Belt has many multi-colored jewels. This left-handed holster has a C.I. Billy the Kid.

Value: $150-200 (Holster & gun)

BK-2

Billy the Kid

Stevens- 1955-60 era. Die cast in nickel with painted black grips. "S" medallions on grips. Repeater in the original red and white box.

Value: $75-125 (Box & gun)

BK-3

Billy the Kid

Stevens- 1955-60 era. Close-up of the gun BK-3 shown above. Note barrel engraving and painted black grips. Seldom seen character toy.

BK-4

Bobby Benson

Unknown- 1931-35 era. An early black leather holster with studs and metal letters. B-Bar-B Ranch. Gun is a Western by Kenton. Some have the H-Bar-O gun by Kilgore. Radio sponsor was Hecker's Oats.

Value: $125-225 (Holster & either gun)

BB-1

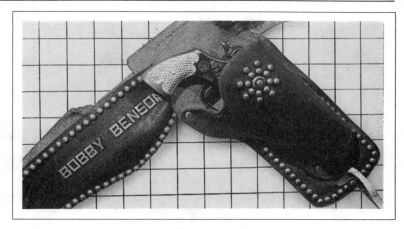

Bonanza

Leslie-Henry- 1959-65. 9" in the dull gray finish with black stag grips. All Bonanza marked guns are fairly rare toys.

Value: $85-165 (Dull finish)

B-1

Bonanza

Leslie-Henry- 1959-65. Nickel finish with white grips and black star inserts. Similar to above gun except for better finish and grip variation.

Value: $95-175 (Nickel)

B-2

Bonanza

Hubley-Halco- 1963-65 era. Late production in nickel finish with nice engraving. One-piece stag grips in red-brown and tan. Bonanza on left side, Halco on the right. Made by Hubley. Star medallion.

Value: $85-145

B-3

Bonanza

Leslie-Henry- 1959-65 era. Very rare long barrel in dull nickel finish. Black stag grips. All L-H guns with longer barrels are very rare. Gun is 10 1/2".

Value: $100-200

B-4

Bonanza

L-H- 1959-65 era. Close-up detail of B-4 above showing the lettering and engraving.

B-5

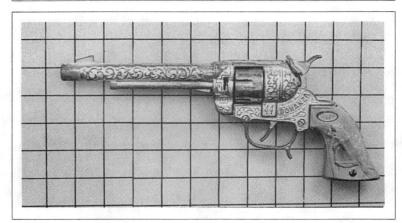

Bonanza

Leslie-Henry- 1965 era. Late production, large .44 model in the dull painted silver finish. One of the rarer L-H .44 models. Has horsehead grips.

Value: $100-200

B-6

Bonanza

L-H- 1965 era. Close-up detail of B-7 gun above. Note lettering, the silver painted finish and "H" oval medallion.

B-7

Bonanza

Pilen, Spain- 1960-65 era. Unusual foreign gun and original box. Nickel with brown checkered grips. Stamped Bonanza. Ben Cartwright is on the full color box.

Value: $85-150 (Gun & box)

B-8

Bonanza

Marx- 1966. Hoss Range Pistol is large six shooter clicker, made of plastic & metal. On original display card.
(Photo courtesy of Hake's Americana, PA)

Value: $85-150 (Gun on Card)

B-9

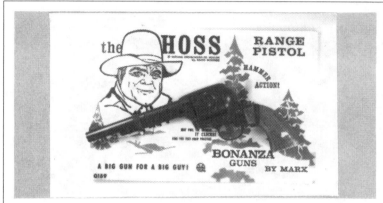

Bonanza Holster

Leslie-Henry- 1965. Double holster set in original box. Dark brown leather with gold horsehead conchos and gold lettering. Guns are L-H .44 Models in nickel finish with dark brown stag grips. Rare.

Value: $350-600 Complete set with guns

B-10

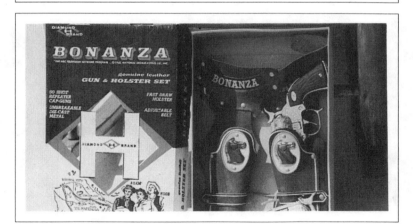

Bonanza Holster

Halco- 1960-65 era. Very rare set with a large Halco .45 Bonanza gun with revolving cylinder and stag grips. Holster is brown & black leather with gold coins embossed on the front. Name on strap.

Value: $350-500 (Holster & Halco gun)

B-11

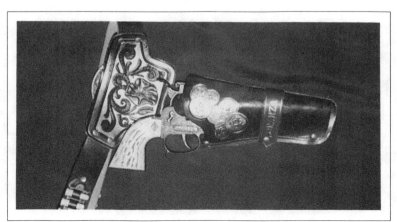

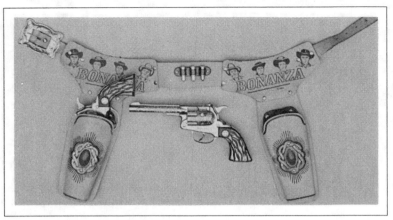

Bonanza Holster

Halco- 1960-65. Light tan leather double set with the four Cartwrights on each side. Large silver conchos with brown-red jewel on holsters. Guns are Hubley-Halco die cast.

Value: $200-300

B-12

Bonanza

Leslie-Henry- 1960-65. Russet tan leather set with tooling and name embossed on holster straps. Holsters have the very rare long barreled L-H guns with black star inserts. Rare character set.

Value: $325-475 (Holsters & guns)

B-13

Bonanza

Marx- 1960-65 era. Ranch set. Has 24" Winchester cap carbine, holster, cartridge belt and 9" plastic & metal Colt clicker. (Photo courtesy Hake's Americana, PA)

Value: $100-165 (complete set)

B-14

Buffalo Bill

Ives- 1880 era. Extremely rare cast iron 7" single shot marked Buffalo Bill No. 71.

Value: $250-450

BF-1

Buffalo Bill

Stevens- 1890 era. Very early cast iron cap gun with long barrel. Single shot. Name on barrel. Spur trigger. Quaint engraving.

Value: $225-350

BF-2

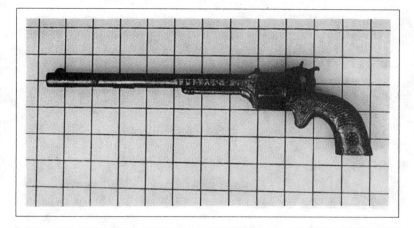

Buffalo Bill

Kenton- 1930 era. Extremely rare, very long barrel cap gun. Single shot. 13 1/2" long. All long barreled cast iron guns are quite rare and desirable as many barrels were cracked or broken-off from play.

Value: $350-600

BF-3

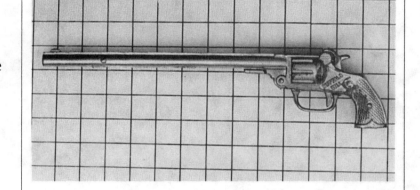

Buffalo Bill

Kenton- 1920 era. Rare long barrel cast iron single shot. Later variety with large, wide hammer.

Value: $225-350

BF-4

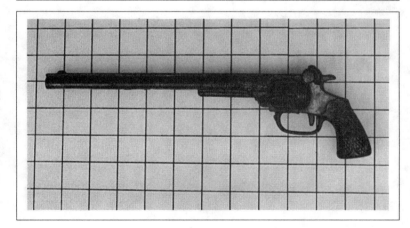

Buffalo Bill

Kenton- 1920 era. Pair of rare long barrel single shots. Early variety with the very narrow hammers. The gun on top is the normal casting. The bottom one is mis-cast with no second "F" in Buf_ alo Bill.

Value: $235-365

BF-5

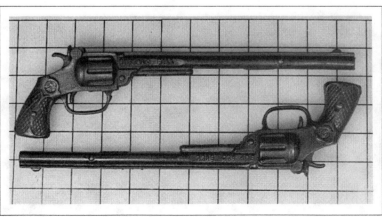

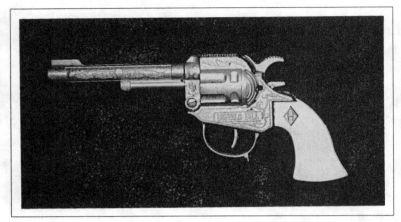

Buffalo Bill

Leslie-Henry-Halco- 1960. Unusual die cast in nickel with engraving. Has white stag grips with diamond "H" medallions. This 9" pistol is rather uncommon.

Value: $35-85

BF-6

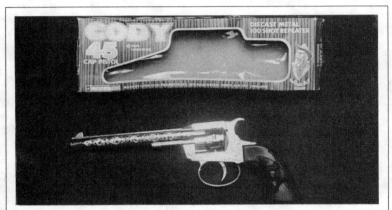

Buffalo Bill- Cody .45

Lone Star, Eng.- 1975. Die cast repeater in polished chrome with black steerhead grips. Engraved with Cody .45 on frame.

Value: $35-75 (Gun & box)

BF-7

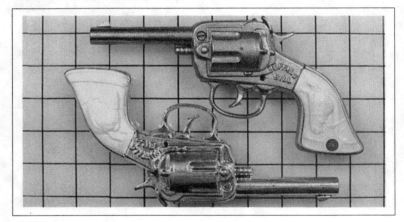

Buffalo Bill

Stevens- 1940-45. Top: Normal cast iron with white horsehead grips with red or green jewels. Lower: Later variety with silver painted finish and no jewels.

Value: $65-135   (Either finish)

BF-8

Buffalo Bill

Stevens- 1940 era. Early flat frame variety with no raised side plate casting behind the cylinder access door. Seldom seen.

Value: $75-150

BF-9

Buffalo Bill

Stevens- 1950-55 era. Rare die cast nickel repeater with ivory white grips with Buffalo Bill busts. Unusual toy gun.

Value: $75-145

BF-10

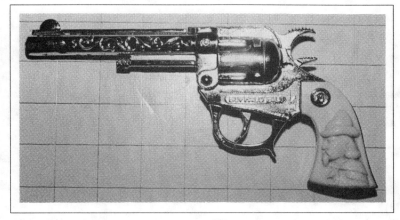

Young Buffalo Bill

Halco/L-H- 1955-60 era. Nickel single shot with Diamond "H" medallion on white stag grips.

Value: $30-65

BF-11

Young Buffalo Bill

L-H/Halco- 1955-60 era. Slightly larger than BF-11, but nearly identical. Has transparent amber horsehead grips.

Value: $35-70

BF-12

Buffalo Bill

Unknown- 1960 era. Possibly a Halco gun with an unusual barrel extension. This 11" gun has the barrel extension permanently attached and in identical finish to the remainder on the gun. Stag grips.

Value: $45-85

BF-13

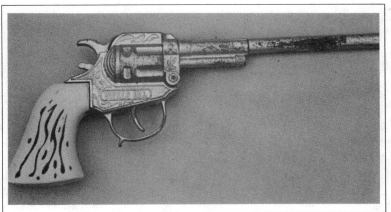

Buffalo Bill Holsters

Keyston Bros.- 1940 era. Nearly identical holsters found in a Keyston box. One is black leather, the other in tan. Both have red jewels and numerous silver studs. The name is made of studs. Beautiful and rare holsters. Gun is a rare Lasso Em Bill.

Value: $125-235 (Either holster only)

BF-14

Buffalo Bill Holster

Unknown- 1940-50 era. Very ornate set in black and white leather with fringe, gold lettering, silver studs, red jewels, bullets and silver conchos. Guns are cast iron.

Value: $125-200 (Holsters only)

BF-15

Cheyenne

Kilgore- 1955-62 era. Extremely rare 9" die cast repeater in nickel finish with stag grips.

Value: $85-150

CY-1

Cheyenne

Hamilton- 1955-60 era. 9 1/2" die cast in nickel finish with smooth white grips that have "CS", Cheyenne Shooter, logo in gold on right grip. Seldom seen. Very rare original box.

Value: $100-175 (Gun with box)

CY-2

Cheyenne

Hamilton- 1955-60 era. Similar to CY-2, except in the dull gray finish and with a left-handed tooled leather holster that has likeness of Cheyenne embossed in top strap.

Value: $100-185 (Gun and holster)

C-3

Cheyenne

Daisy- 1960 era. Fast draw holster set in tan leather with embossed bust on strap. Gun is a Nichols Stallion .45. Seldom seen character set in original box. Can be found in identical double holster set.

Value: $300-500 (Holster, box & gun)

CY-4

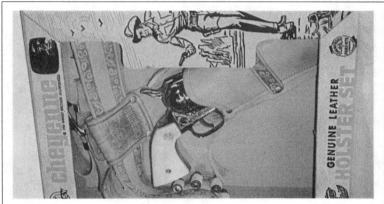

Cheyenne Peacemaker

Empire, Tarboro, NC- 1960. Large 13 1/2" plastic clicker in brass and black colors. Walnut color grips. Large Colt Dragoon style pistol. Unusual toy.

Value: $30-60

CY-5

Cheyenne Hanger

Daisy- 1961. Extremely rare accessory is this wall hanger made like a tan and black leather saddle. It holds the Daisy Ricochet Cheyenne rifle and the above holster set. The original price was $9.95.

Value: $85-150

CY-6

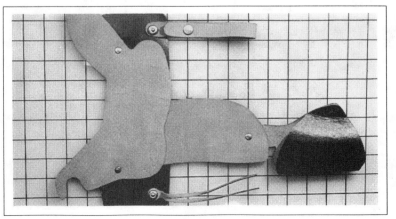

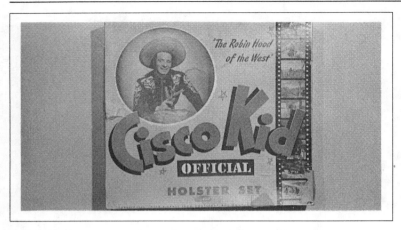

Cisco Kid

Cisco Kid Leather & Metal Products, Inc. CA 1950-55 era. Very rare character set in the original full color box for a double holster and gun set. Company located in the Redwine Bldg., Los Angeles, CA.

Value: $75-150 (Box only)

CK-1

Cisco Kid

Cisco Kid Products, Inc.- 1950-55 era. Rare double holster set in black and white leather with cut-outs, Cisco bust conchos, silver studs, red jewels and gold lettering. Guns are Kilgore Rangers.

Value: $500-750 (Complete boxed set)

CK-2

Cisco Kid

Cisco Kid Products, Inc.- 1950-55. Close-up detail of holster shown in CK-2. Note the highly detailed silver bust of Cisco, the decorative cut-outs, silver studs and red jewels. A very high quality holster set.

CK-3

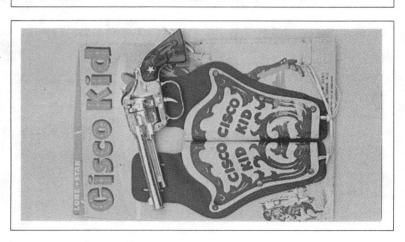

Cisco Kid

Lone Star, Eng.- 1955 era. Rare double set on the original card. Black, white and red leather with printed artwork. Set has two Lone Star die cast guns.

Value: $150-300 (Complete with guns)

CK-4

Cisco Kid

Lone Star- 1955 era. Close-up detail of the gun shown in CK-4. Note the beautiful casting and finish, the red horsehead grips with silver star and the Cisco Kid lettering in the checkered circle. Rare.

Value: $65-130 (Gun only)

CK-5

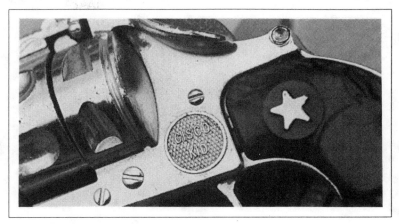

Colt .45

Hubley- 1957-60 era. Black leather set has gold lettering, gold studs and buckles. Large loop-style holster to accommodate the Hubley Colt .45 gun.

Value: $225-335 (Gun & holster)

CF-1

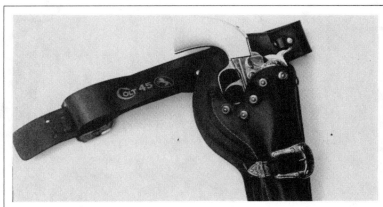

Colt .45

Hubley- 1957-60 era. Gunfighter-style set in black leather with gold lettering and horsehead. Has six bullets and Colt .45 gun by Hubley.

Value: $225-335 (Gun & holster)

CF-2

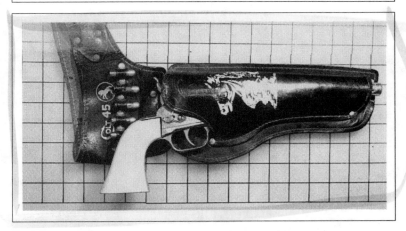

Colt .45

Hubley- 1957-60 era. Gunfighter-style set in russet brown leather with gold lettering on the holster cross strap. Bullets on back of gun belt. Gun is Colt .45.

Value:$ 225-335 (Gun & holster)

CF-3

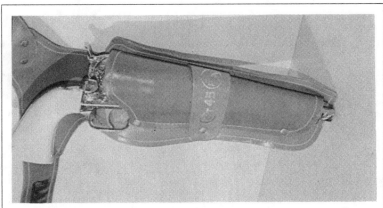

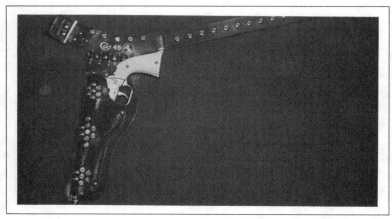

Colt .45

Hubley- 1957-60 era. Gunslinger-style set in black leather with numerous silver studs, pearl jewels and gold lettering. Bullets above holster. Gun is a Colt .45. This is a very decorative holster set.

Value: $225-350 (Gun & holster)

CF-4

Cowboy in Africa

Mattel- 1962 era. Seldom seen display box with the Mattel Fanner-50 in the black finish with the white Impala grips.

Value: $100-225 (Gun & box)

CA-1

Cowboy in Africa

Mattel- 1962 era. Single Dura-Hide in the black finish with two Mattel Fanner-50 variations. Top one in polished chrome, the lower in black. Both have the white Impala grips.

Value: $100-200 (Either gun & holster)

CA-2

Cowboy in Africa

Mattel- 1962 era. Rarer double holster set in Dura-Hide with matching pair of Mattel Fanner-50s in polished chrome. The name is on front of both holsters.

Value: $200-325 (Holsters & guns)

CA-3

Davy Crockett

Leslie-Henry- 1955. Rare boxed set in tan leather with silver studs and the very rare 9" L-H Crockett gun. The box is in antiqued tan and black with frontier artwork.

Value: $250-450 (Boxed set with gun)

DC-1

Davy Crockett

Leslie-Henry- 1955. Extremely rare 9" die cast gun is one of the most difficult character guns to find. Nickel with white or light tan horsehead grips.

Value: $175-350

DC-2

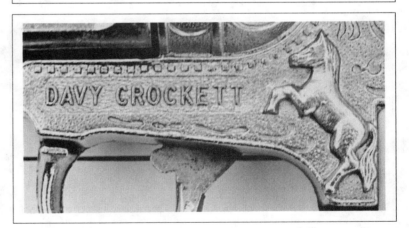

Davy Crockett

Leslie-Henry- 1955. Close-up detail of gun DC-2 shown above. Note the name, rearing horse and fine engraving by L-H.

DC-3

Davy Crockett

Leslie-Henry- 1955. Extremely rare die cast is this smaller nickel repeater with full size white horsehead grips. Most collectors don't realize this variety exists.

Value: $150-325

DC-4

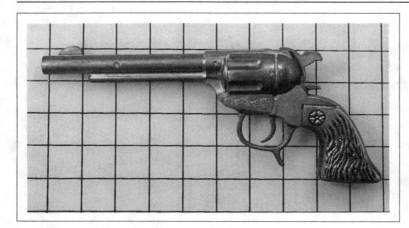

Davy Crockett

G. Schmidt- 1955. Another very rare die cast. Among the rarest of G. Schmidt guns. Dull gray finish with copper stag grips. Also found in the nickel finish.

Value: $200-350

DC-5

Davy Crockett

G. Schmidt- 1955. Close-up detail of gun DC-5 showing the Davy Crockett name on the side frame. It is surprising that so many western-style guns were used for a frontier hero who used a flintlock!

DC-6

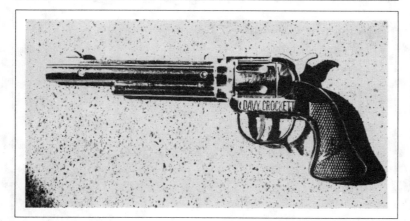

Davy Crockett

G. Schmidt- 1955. Extremely rare, single shot, die cast with polished chrome finish and copper checkered grips. Name is on the side of the frame.

Value: $165-300

DC-7

Davy Crockett

G. Schmidt- 1955. Rare revolving cylinder die cast in polished chrome with checkered stag grips. Has a secret compartment in the grip for caps and a small compass. Similar to the rare Schmidt "Pathfinder."

Value: $265-425

DC-8

Davy Crockett

Leslie-Henry- 1955. Full color box for a double holster set showing a cowboy on rearing horse for Crockett set! Contents shown below in DC-10.

DC-9

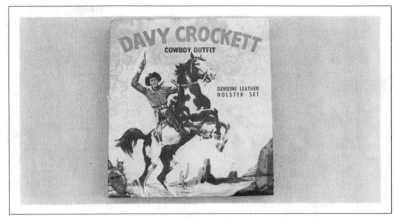

Davy Crockett

Leslie-Henry- 1955. Double holster set from above box. Tan and brown leather with large silver horse and diamond conchos. Artwork on holsters. Very rare 9" L-H die cast guns.

Value: $500-800 (Box, holsters & guns)

DC-10

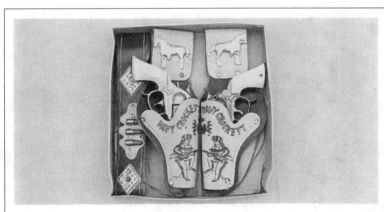

Davy Crockett

Ohio Art Co., OH.- 1955-60 era. Unusual pressed steel clicker in very colorful red, white, yellow, black and brown. Came in tan and black leather holster with fringe.

Value: $45-100 (Gun and holster)

DC-11

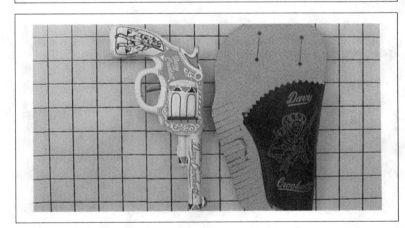

Davy Crockett Holster

Unknown- 1955 era. Rare holster set in tan and fur cowhide with matching knife sheath. Silver steerhead conchos. Bullets, silver buckles and fringe. No gun or play knife. Unusual holster set.

Value: $100-185

DC-12

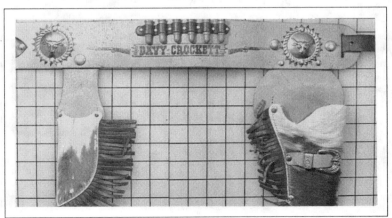

Davy Crockett

Unknown- 1955. Small leather holsters in black and tan fur cowhide. Name on holster straps. Silver studs. Guns are small Hubley die cast single shots.

Value: $30-50 (Holsters & guns)

DC-13

Davy Crockett

Daisy- 1955. Smoke & bang rifle 35" long in blue finish with leather boot & name on the stock. Came with leather fringed plastic powder horn. Shown with the rare L-H 9" DC cap gun. Seldom seen set.

Value: $100-225 (Rifle & powder horn)

DC-14

Davy Crockett

Halco- 1955. Frontier set with buckskin leather holster with fringe and Crockett buckle. Box has red and black artwork. Gun is a Hubley over-under Flintlock.

Value: $85-125 (Box, holster & gun)

DC-15

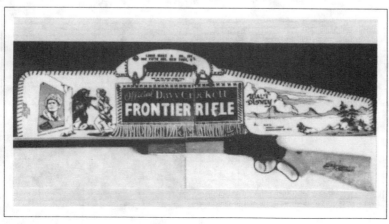

Davy Crockett Rifle

Marx- 1955. Frontier Rifle. 32" cap firing Winchester in original colored cardboard scabbard. Seldom seen rifle. Another of the western guns for a Frontiersman.
(Photo courtesy Hake's Americana, PA)

Value: $150-250 (Rifle & scabbard)

DC-16

Deputy-Simon Fry

Halco- 1960. Rare boxed double holster set in black leather with white artwork. L-H die cast guns with stag grips and Diamond H medallion. Box is green and black.

Value: $150-300 (Box, holsters & guns)

D-1

Deputy-Simon Fry

Hubley- 1960 era. Unusual die cast with ribbed barrel, beautiful engraving and all metal, Tiffany-style grips. Complete with red and silver Deputy badge and box.

Value: $65-120 (Box, badge & gun)

D-2

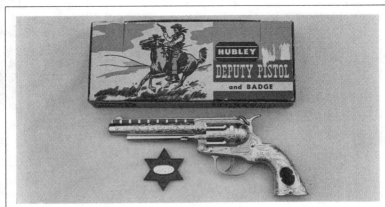

Deputy-Simon Fry

Hubley- 1960 era. Almost identical to D-2 *Top:* rarer dull finish, black painted grips with push-button latch behind cylinder. *Lower:* nickel finish, silver grips with the open latch on bottom of the barrel.

Value: $65-120 (Either variety)

D-3

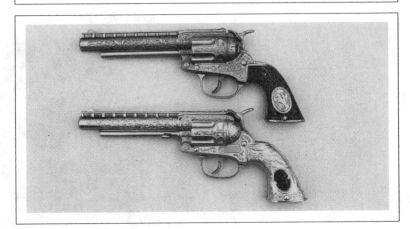

Deputy-Simon Fry

Kilgore- 1960 era. Very rare die cast in all metal. Nickel finish with a raised silver bullet on the grips. Name on frame. This repeater is seldom seen.

Value- $75-135

D-4

Gene Autry at the Kenton factory in Ohio, about 1938, reviewing the cast iron replicas of his six shooter. Note all the women workers assembling the toy guns.

Gene Autry

Kenton- 1938-39 box. During the first year of production the imitation pearl grips were left blank. Note that the gun on the box has no name or horse. Red, white and blue color.

Value: $75-135 (Box only)

GA-1

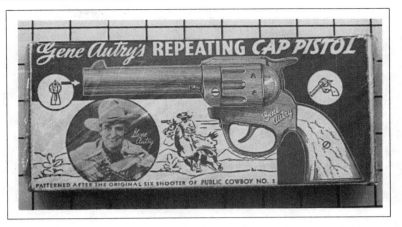

Gene Autry

Kenton- 1938 First model. Long barrel, cast iron with no artwork on the grips. This gun is in the dark finish with imitation pearl grips. Also in nickel finish.

Value: $165-250

GA-2

Gene Autry

Kenton- 1938. Early model. Short barrel, cast iron with name on grips. *Top:* nickel gun has the raised circle on the frame and orange grips. *Bottom:* nickel with raised circle and red jewel.

Value: T-$150-200 B-$175-225 (Jewel)

GA-3

Gene Autry

Kenton- 1939 Second model. Long barrel cast iron with rearing horse and rider artwork on pearl grips. *Top:* dark finish. *Bottom:* nickel finish. These variations are seldom found.

Value: $175-265

GA-4

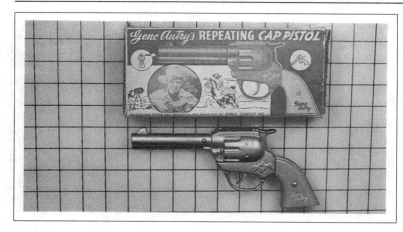

Gene Autry

Kenton- 1940-50 era. 3rd model cast iron with original box. In 1940 all the grips contained Gene's signature.

Value: $150-250 $75-100 (Box)

GA-5

Gene Autry

Kenton- 1940-50 era. Short barrel, cast iron, dark finish with original box. Signature in gold on red grips.

Value: $150-200 $75-100 (Box)

GA-6

Gene Autry

Kenton- 1940-50 era. Short barrels in nickel finish cast iron. *Left:* signature on frame and red grips. *Center:* Raised circle with red grips. *Right:* Raised circle, red jewel and white signature grips.

Value: $150-200 $175-225 (Jewel)

GA-7

Gene Autry

Kenton- 1940-50 era. Short barrel, nickel finish cast iron with the raised circle and signature orange grips. Note that this is a rare dummy variety.

Value: $200-250

GA-8

Gene Autry

Kenton- 1940-50 era. Short barrel, cast iron in the dark finish with circle on the frame. This is the rare dummy variety.

Value: $200-250

GA-9

Gene Autry

Kenton- 1940-50 era. Short barrel, cast iron in the dark finish with circle on frame containing a red jewel. This is the rare dummy variety.

Value: $225-275

GA-10

Gene Autry

Kenton- 1940-50 era. Long barrel, cast iron in polished nickel finish with orange grips. This is the rare dummy variety with early-style hammer.

Value: $250-350

GA-11

Gene Autry

Kenton- 1940-50 era. Long barrel, cast iron in the dark finish with pearl grips. This is the rare dummy variety with early-style hammer.

Value: $250-350

GA-12

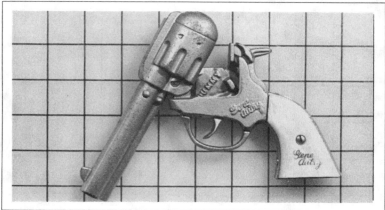

Gene Autry

Kenton- 1950 era. Long barrel, cast iron in the nickel finish with pearl grips. This is a very rare dummy variety with the late-style, scalloped hammer.

Value: $265-375

GA-13

Gene Autry

Kenton- 1950 era. Long barrel, cast iron of lighter alloy in a silver paint-type of finish. This is a very rare dummy variety with the late-style, scalloped hammer.

Value: $265-375

GA-14

Gene Autry

Kenton- Late 1940 era. The upper gun is a long barrel, cast iron in the rare highly polished finish. When this gun was recently discovered, in a linen drawer, it had the hat and spur white grips.

Value: $175-300 (Polished model)

GA-15

Gene Autry

Kenton- 1950 era. Short barrel, cast iron in the extremely rare engraved variety. *Upper:* Nickel finish with orange grips. Lower: Dark finish with white grips. Only produced in the 1950-52 era.

Value: $350-600

GA-16

Gene Autry

Kenton- 1950 era. Long barrel, cast iron in the extremely rare engraved variety. *Upper:* Nickel finish with orange grips. *Lower:* Dark finish with white grips. Only produced in the 1950-52 era.

Value:$400-700 -Box very rare $200-300

GA-17

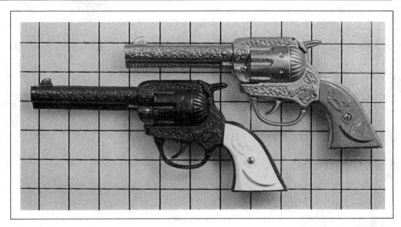

Gene Autry

Kenton- 1950 era. Long barrel, cast iron extremely rare engraved pistol in the even rarer, dummy variety in the nickel finish.

Value: $500-800

GA-18

Gene Autry (Bulls Eye)

Kenton- 1950 era. These three cast iron guns look almost identical. *Left:* a Bulls Eye found with Gene Autry signature grips. *Center: and Right:* are regular Gene Autry engraved varieties.

Value: $100-175 (Bulls Eye)

GA-19

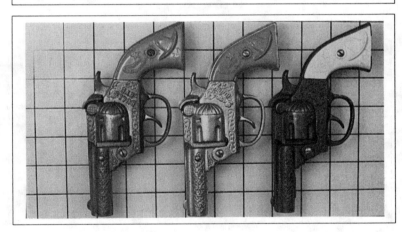

Gene Autry (Boxes)

Kenton- 1938-50 era. Original boxes. *Left:* 1939-50 with pistol showing signature. *Center:* Early 1938 box with blank grips. *Right:* 1940-50 box for the short barrel cast iron variety.
Value: $75-150 each.

GA-20

Gene Autry

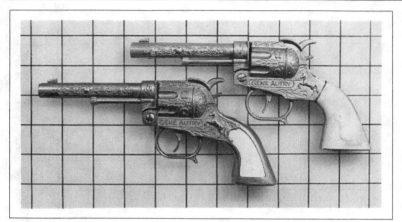

Buzz Henry- 1950-60 era. *Upper:* This die cast, nickel gun has the rarer full size white horsehead grips. *Lower:* The more common nickel gun with insert white grips.

Value: $85-150 (Full) $75-125 (Insert)

GA-21

Gene Autry

Buzz Henry- 1950-60 era. *Upper:* This die cast, rarer gold gun, has unusual full size transparent amber, horsehead grips. *Lower:* Dull gray finished, nickel die cast with white full size grips.

Value: $100-175 (Gold) $75-125 (Dull G.)

GA-22

Gene Autry

Buzz Henry- 1950-60 era. The rarer die cast in gold finish with yellow ivory color inset grips. Can also be found with red or black grips.

Value: $100-175 (Gold)

GA-23

Gene Autry

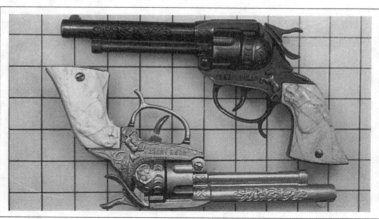

Leslie-Henry- 1950-60 era. *Upper:* This die cast gun is in the extremely rare antique bronze finish with butterscotch grips. *Lower:* This die cast gun is in the nickel finish with white horsehead grips.

Value: $150-325 (AB) $100-175 (Nickel)

GA-24

Gene Autry

Leslie-Henry- 1950-60 era. This very rare, nickel, die cast gun has the extra long barrel. It is believed that these were made in Canada. Light orange grips.

Value: $175-275

GA-25

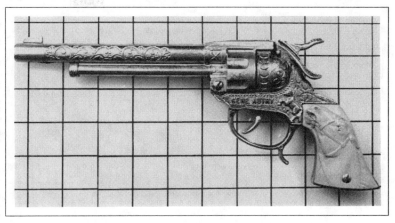

Gene Autry

Leslie-Henry- 1950-60 era. A rare pair of die cast in the gold finish. Both have incised engraving. The upper gun has light tan grips, the lower has white.

Value: $ 175-300 (Gold)

GA-26

Gene Autry

Leslie-Henry- 1950-60 era. Extremely rare die cast gun with the pop-up cap box and in gold finish with black grips. Also found in nickel finish. Can be found in metallic front holster sets.

Value: $225-350 (Gold) $220-325 (Nic)

GA-27

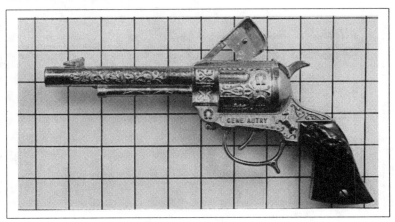

Gene Autry

Leslie-Henry .44- 1950-60 era. Large die cast guns in nickel finish. *Upper:* "H" ovals on transparent amber grips is rarer and takes 6 small, solid metal bullets. *Lower:* is normal with "L-H" ovals.

Value: $175-275 (Bullets) $125-175 (LH)

GA-28

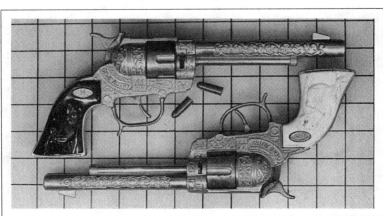

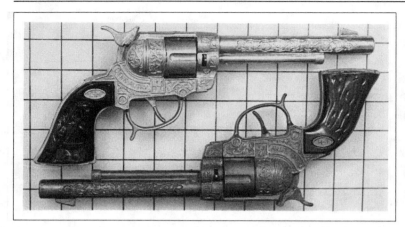

Gene Autry

Leslie-Henry .44- 1950-60 era. *Upper:* Very rare gold finish with black grips. *Lower:* Very rare antique bronze finish with black stag grips. Both die cast with "L-H" ovals on the grips. Seldom found.

Value: $175-350 (Gold) $165-250 (AB)

GA-29

Gene Autry

Leslie-Henry .44- 1950-60 era. A detail close-up of the name and the "L-H" oval medallions on the grips.

GA-30

Gene Autry-Champion

Leslie-Henry- 1950-60 era. "Champion" die cast, early first model nickel with extra heavy frame and having very simple scroll engraving on the barrel.

Value: $125-175

GA-31

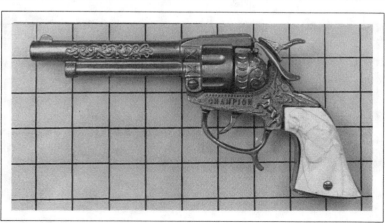

Gene Autry-Champion

Leslie-Henry- 1950-60 era. "Champion" die cast nickel regular frame and engraving. White horsehead grips.

Value: $100-155

GA-32

Gene Autry-Champion

Leslie-Henry- 1950-60 era. Die cast in the low hammer variety with the rarer gold finish and black grips. This is the raised engraving variation.

Value: $150-250 (Gold)

GA-33

Gene Autry

Marx-Britain- 1950-60 era. Extremely rare double barrel souvenir "pop" gun for the Autry Western Show at Empress Hall in London. Shown with poster. Artwork is either back or brown on wood stock.

Value: $225-350

GA-34

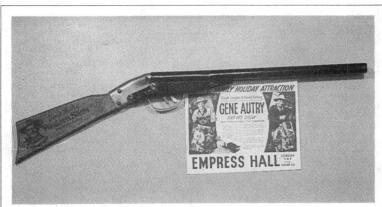

Gene Autry Gun Boxes

Leslie-Henry- 1950-60 era. *Left:* Original box for a gold plated die cast. *Center:* An early box for a nickel die cast. *Right:* An early box for a Buzz Henry with inset grips.

Value: $75-150

GA-35

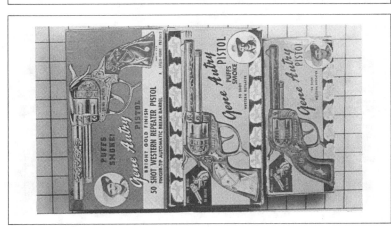

Gene Autry Gun Box

Leslie-Henry .44- 1950-60 era. The rare antique bronze G. Autry, and extremely rare original silver-blue and black box marked "Western Bronze Finish".

Value: $125-300 (Box only)

GA-36

Gene Autry Gun Box

Leslie-Henry .44- 1950-60 era. Original box for a nickel die cast gun. This box is red with dark blue guns. Note, revolving barrel rather than cylinder.

Value: $100-150

GA-37

Gene Autry Gun Box

Leslie-Henry .44- 1950-60 era. Original box for a nickel die cast gun. This box is blue, red and yellow.

Value: $100-150

GA-38

Gene Autry Gun Box

Leslie-Henry .44- 1950-60 era. This box is similar to the one above except for the illustration of the bullets and belt clip. It is a rather elusive box in the same color scheme. Bullets and clip included in box.

Value: $100-165

GA-39

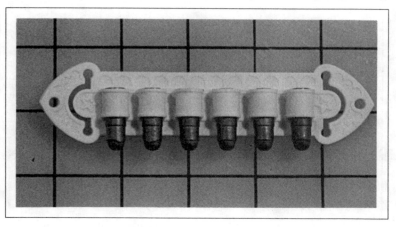

Gene Autry Bullets

Leslie-Henry .44- 1950-60 era. Close-up detail of the white plastic, belt, bullet clip and six bullets included with the box. The bullets are heavy solid copper metal. Some contain brass bullets.

Value: $75 (Clip and 6 bullets)

GA-40

Gene Autry Box

Kenton- 1950 era. Among the rarest of all toy gun boxes is the one for the cast iron engraved Gene Autry. Only a handful are known to exist. Black, red and yellow.

Value: $200-350 (Box only)

GA-41

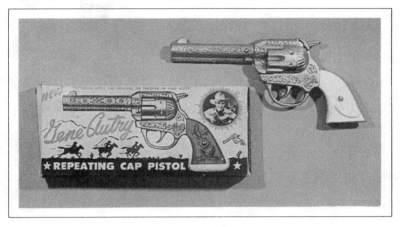

Gene Autry Ranch Set Box

M.A. Henry- 1945-50 era. Box top for the Ranch Set which included a holster, lariat, kerchief and gun. Some sets have cast iron Kenton guns, some composition guns and others copies of Texan, Jrs.

Value: $75-150 (Box only)

GA-42

Gene Autry Ranch Set

M.A. Henry- 1945-50 era. Detail of Ranch Set showing holster, lariat and a die cast, Canadian copy of a Hubley Texan, Jr. The kerchief and slide are not in photo.

Value: $100-225 (Complete set with box)

GA-43

Gene Autry Counter Display

Leslie-Henry- 1950-60 era. Very rare counter top display for a Gene Autry .44. This cardboard display is black, blue and orange and folds to hold one gun.

Value: $150-400 (Display only)

GA-44

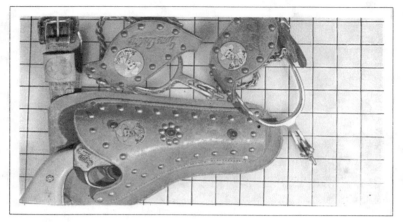

Gene Autry Holster

Keyston Brothers, Calif.- 1940 era. Early tan leather holster with a decal of Gene on the holster, spurs and belt. Spurs are cast iron. Red jewels and silver studs.

Value: $150-200 (Hol.) $200-350 (Spurs)

GA-45

Gene Autry Boxed Set

Keyston Brothers, Calif.- 1940 era. Superb boxed set! Keeper strap over gun. Tan leather with red jewels and silver studs. Box is orange and black. Gene decals.

Value: $300-650 (Without gun)

GA-46

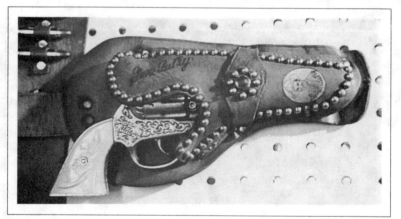

Gene Autry Holster

Keyston Brothers, Calif.- 1940 era. Tan leather with red jewels and silver studs. Gene decal. Nice early set.

Value: $150-250 (Without gun)

GA-47

Gene Autry Holsters

M.A. Henry, NY- 1945-50 era. *Left:* Tan leather with red jewels and silver studs. *Center:* Red and white with cutout, red jewels and studs. *Right:* Black leather and composition board with red jewels.

Value: $75-125 each

GA-48

Gene Autry Holster

M.A. Henry, NY- 1945-50 era. Early black and tan leather with red artwork, yellow, red and blue jewels with silver studs.

Value: $85-145

GA-49

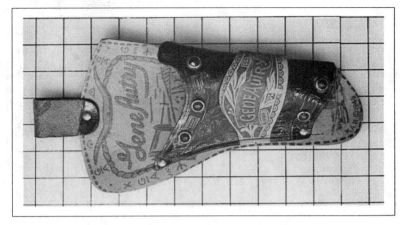

Gene Autry Holster

M.A. Henry, NY- 1945-50 era. Similar to holster above except has Champion art on the top of the back piece. Multi-color jewels. Tan leather.

Value: $85-145 (Holster only)

GA-50

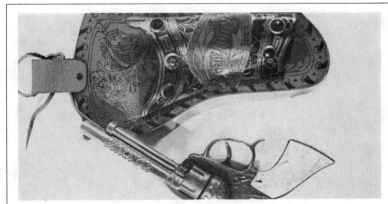

Gene Autry Holster

Unknown- 1950-55 era. Black leather with gold and silver steerhead conchos, red jewels and silver studs. Name in white. Uncommon for a Gene set.

Value: $95-150 (Holster only)

GA-51

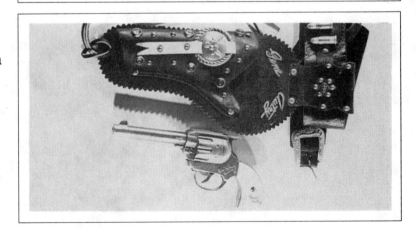

Gene Autry Holster

M.A. Henry, NY- 1945-50 era. Black leather front with composition board back. Green jewels with silver conchos. White art work. Carved front.

Value: $65-100

GA-52

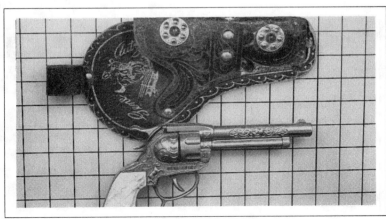

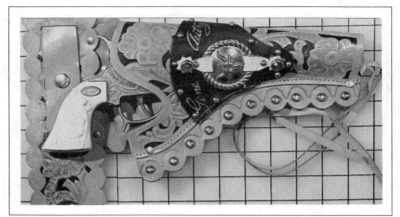

Gene Autry Holster

Halco, Pitts.- 1955 era. Very large tan leather holster with black keeper band, entirely tooled, Gene concho on back of belt, Gold and silver steerhead concho on front. Red jewels and silver studs.

Value: $150-250 (Holster only)

GA-53

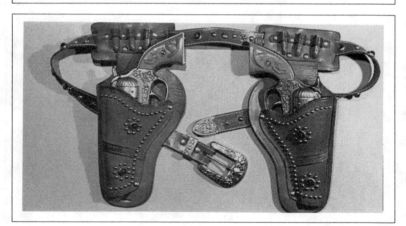

Gene Autry Holster & Belt.

M.A. Henry, NY- 1945-50 era. Two tone tan leather with tooling and multi-color jewels. Superb Gene Autry belt with a bucking bronc rider, scrolls and pearl.

Value: $100-150 (Holster & belt)

GA-54

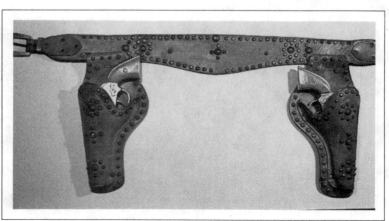

Gene Autry Double Holster

Keyston Brothers, Calif.- 1940 era. Tan leather with red jewels, silver studs and bullets. Early set with a pair of engraved Kenton guns.

Value: $135-175 (Holster & belt only)

GA-55

Gene Autry Double Holster

Keyston Brothers, Calif.- 1940 era. Early tan leather set with red jewels and silver studs.

Value: $135-175

GA-56

Gene Autry Holster

Keyston Brothers, Calif.- 1940 era. Close-up detail of holster GA-56 showing the embossed lettering on the back of gun belt.

GA-57

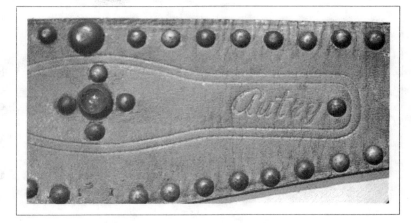

Gene Autry Double Holster

Halco, Pitts.- 1955-60 era. Large set shown in many mail order catalogs. Tan and black tooled leather with silver conchos, silver lettering and bullets.

Value: $150-300

GA-58

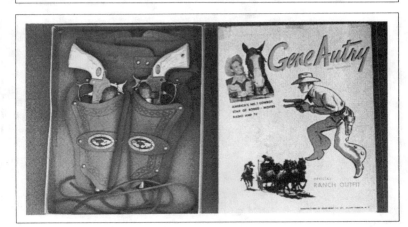

Gene Autry Double Holster

Leslie-Henry, NY- 1950-55 era. Boxed set with tan tooled holsters. Has bullets and gold and silver, oval steerhead, conchos.

Value: $225-450 (Box and holsters)

GA-59

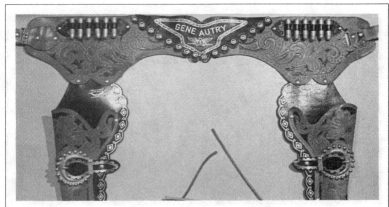

Gene Autry Double Holster

Unknown- 1955-60 era. Superb set with floral and scroll, embossed, gold metallic fronts on the holsters. Black and tan leather with color appliques and silver studs. Gene's name on back of gun belt.

Value: $250-450 (Holsters only)

GA-60

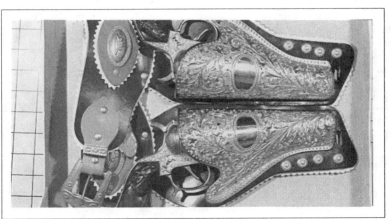

Gene Autry Double Holster

Halco, Pitts.- 1955-60 era. Tan and black leather. Flying A Ranch set, with silver conchos, studs, jewels and bullets. Large cowboy silver buckle.

Value: $150-300

GA-61

Gene Autry Detail

Halco, Pitts.- 1955-60 era. Detail of above holster showing Flying A Ranch brand and Gene's signature embossed on back of gun belt.

GA-62

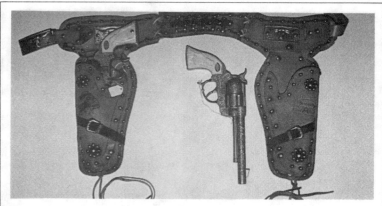

Gene Autry Double Holster

Halco, Pitts.- 1950-60 era. Light tan leather with large silver steerhead conchos and matching buckle. Studs and bullets. Flying A Ranch brand on front of holsters.

Value: $250-450 (Holster set only)

GA-63

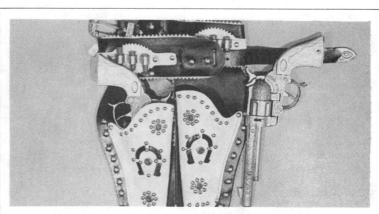

Gene Autry Double Holster

Leslie-Henry- 1955-60 era. Red and white leather set probably intended for a cowgirl. Cutout horseshoes, red jewels and silver studs.

Value: $165-265 (Holster set only)

GA-64

Gene Autry Double Holster

Unknown- 1955-60 era. Tan and black leather set with silver metallic fronts with scrolls and vines. Stamped with Flying A Ranch. Steerhead silver buckle. Smaller size holsters for small guns.

Value: $225-400 (Holsters only)

GA-65

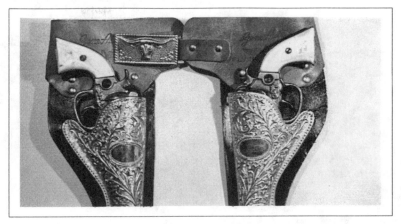

Gene Autry Holster Detail

Unknown- 1955-60 era. Detail of Gene's embossed signature on rear of gun belt for the above set number GA-65.

GA-66

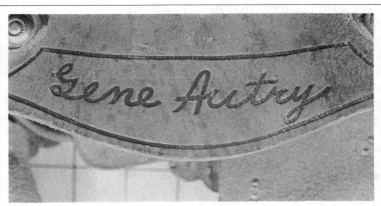

Gene Autry Double Holster

Leslie-Henry- 1955-60 era. White and black leather probably intended for a cow girl. Set has name on holsters and contains cutouts, blue jewels and silver studs.

Value: $100-165

GA-67

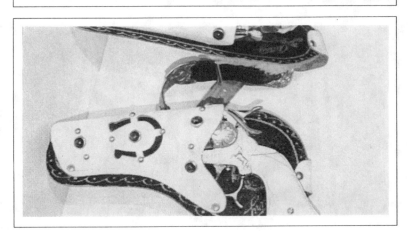

Gene Autry Double Holster

Unknown- 1955-60 era. Black leather set with silver metallic fronts with scrolls and vines. Signature and Flying A Ranch in silver with steerhead buckle. Accepts larger guns.

Value: $250-450 (Holsters only)

GA-68

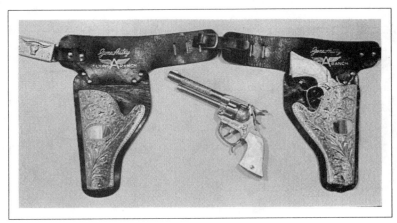

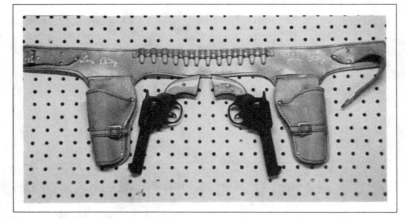

Gene Autry Double Holster

Unknown- 1950 era. Unusual tan loop holster set with Gene's name in silver. Has 12 red, wooden bullets.

Value: $125-165 (Holsters only)

GA-69

Gene Autry Counter Card

Kenton- 1938. During the August, 1938 visit by Gene Autry to Kenton, Ohio, he and many factory workers signed this counter display card that had a cast iron gun attached. Perhaps one-of-a-kind.

Value: $750 (?) (Including gun)

GA-70

Gene Autry Holster

Leslie-Henry- 1950 era. Red & white holster set intended for a cowgirl. Red felt backing. Set came in a G. Autry marked box, but no name on holsters. Guns are Buzz Henry models in nickel finish.

Value: $150-225 (Holster set only)

GA-71

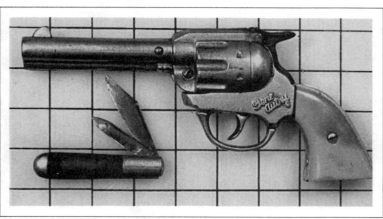

Gene Autry

Kenton- 1945 era. This is the actual Gene Autry cap pistol I played with as a child. This nickel finished gun with orange handles was a constant companion as I rode the imaginary range. For reasons unknown, my mother had saved this toy and barlow pocket knife, among other items from my youth. I'm fortunate to have them back, as they are priceless!

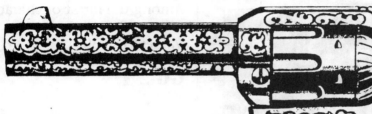
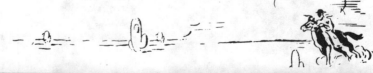

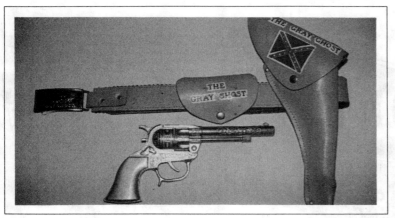

Gray Ghost

Lone Star, Eng.- 1957. An extremely rare character set. Gray leather Civil War rig with silver buckle and ammo pouch. Has C.S.A. flag on flap. Gun is very rare die cast nickel with smooth silver grips.

Value: $300-500 (Gun & holster set)

GG-1

Gray Ghost-Major Mosby CSA

Lone Star, Eng.- 1957 era. Extremely rare die cast in nickel finish with silver grips. Among the rarest of character guns.

Value: $150-300

GG-2

Gray Ghost

Lone Star, Eng.- 1957 era. Close-up detail of the lettering and engraving on the frame. Note horsehead & smooth grips.

GG-3

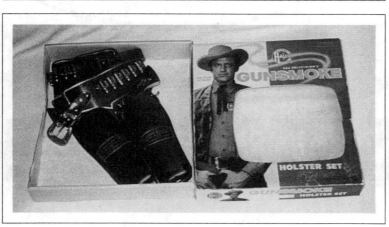

Gunsmoke-Matt Dillon

Halco- 1955-75. Boxed double holster set. Russet leather with gold lettering and bullets above holster. The L-H 9" guns have copper steerhead-Marshal grips.

Value: $300-500 (Box, holster & guns)

GS-1

Gunsmoke-Matt Dillon

Leslie-Henry- 1955-75 era. Similar to GS-1, except lettering above holsters & bullets on the back. All artwork and borders in gold on russet leather. L-H 9" guns with copper Matt Dillon & steerhead grips.

Value: $250-500 (Holster & guns)

GS-2

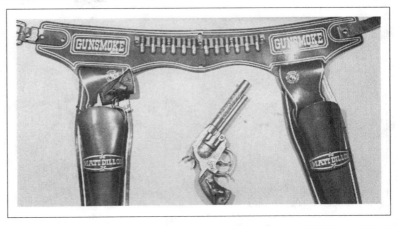

Gunsmoke-Matt Dillon

Hubley- 1955-75. Tan leather double set with red jewels & silver studs. Embossed lettering. Guns are Hubley Marshal die cast with steerhead grips.

Value: $100-225 (Guns & holsters)

GS-3

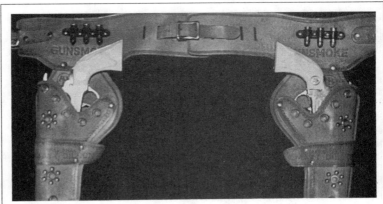

Gunsmoke-Matt Dillon

Hubley- 1955-75. Tan leather double set with embossed lettering, red jewels and double holster straps with name. Guns are late-style Hubley Marshals with one piece stag grips.

Value: $85-200

GS-4

Gunsmoke-Matt Dillon

Leslie-Henry- 1955-75. Black double holster set with silver lettering and borders. Large silver conchos with red and green jewels. L-H 9" nickel guns with white horsehead grips.

Value: $160-325 (Holsters & guns)

GS-5

Gunsmoke-Matt Dillon

Leslie-Henry- 1955-75. Beautiful early style die cast with nice engraving, heavy frame, low hammer and black horsehead grips.

Value: $85-165

GS-6

Gunsmoke-Matt Dillon

Leslie-Henry- 1955-75. Nickel finish die cast with high hammer. Has rarer copper steerhead grips with Marshal Matt Dillon lettering which are more desirable. Also found with rarer longer barrel.

Value: $95-185 - (Long barrel) $125-220

GS-7

Gunsmoke-Matt Dillon

Halco/L-H- 1955-75. Very rare die cast in nickel finish with the pop-up cap box. An unusual variety with copper steer-head and Matt Dillon lettering.

Value: $135-250

GS-8

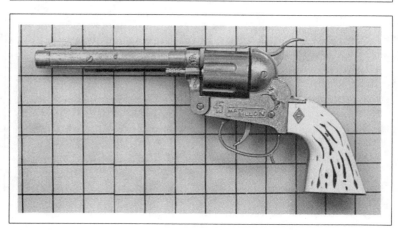

Gunsmoke-Matt Dillon .45

Halco/L-H- 1955-75. Extremely rare D.C. Matt Dillon. Very large revolving cylinder that accepts bullets. Has fanner-type hammer, stag grips with the Diamond H logo. The rarest of the Gunsmoke guns.

Value: $175-350

GS-9

Have Gun, Will Travel

Halco- 1957-63. Full color box for the Paladin double holster set. Black leather with silver 3-D horseheads and lettering. No guns.

Value: $225-350 (Box & holsters)

HG-1

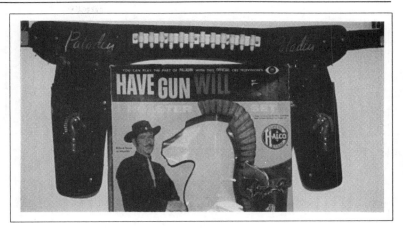

Have Gun, Will Travel

Halco- 1957-63. Black leather double set with silver 3-D horseheads, lettering and bullets. Pair of rare L-H- 9" Paladin, die cast guns with horseshoe black insert grips.
Value: $350-700 (Holsters & guns)

HG-2

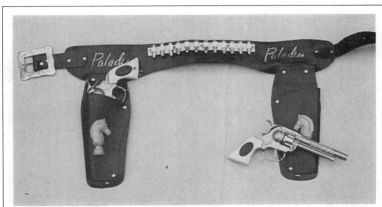

Have Gun, Will Travel

Halco- 1957-63. Large black double holster with silver horsehead conchos, bullets and silver outlined Paladin lettering. No guns.

Value; $200-300 (Holsters only)

HG-3

Have Gun, Will Travel

Unknown- 1957-63. Large double holster in black leather have silver horseheads, bullets, buckle, white Paladin lettering & hat artwork. No guns. Many Paladin sets use L-H & Hubley generic guns-Colt .45s.

Value: $200-300 (Holsters only)

HG-4

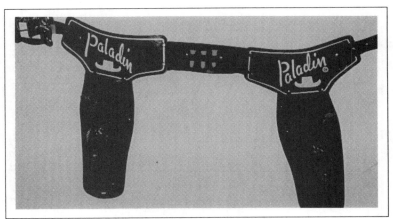

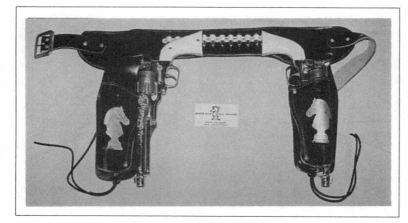

Have Gun, Will Travel

Halco- 1957-63. Large double holster in black leather with embossed horsehead art on front. 12 bullets. Guns are Hubley Colt .45s. Note Paladin calling card.

Value: $350-500 (Holsters & guns)

HG-5

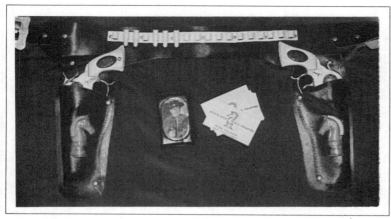

Have Gun, Will Travel

Halco- 1957-63. Black leather double set with 3-D silver horseheads with 18 bullet loops! Has pair of rare L-H Paladin guns with black horseshoe insert grips. Note cards and rare carrying case.

Value: $300-600 (Holsters & L-H guns)

HG-6

Have Gun, Will Travel

Leslie-Henry- 1957-63. Very rare Paladin 9" nickel die cast with black insert white grips. A seldom seen L-H character gun.

Value: $100-245

HG-7

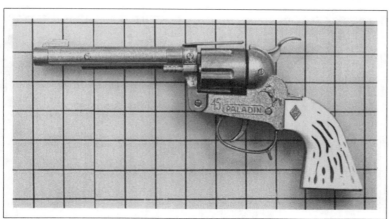

Have Gun, Will Travel

Halco/L-H- 1957-63. Extremely rare DC in nickel finish with revolving cylinder that accepts bullets. Fanner-type hammer and stag grips. Also antique bronze. "Paladin" .45 model. Diamond "H" medallions.

Value: $175-400

HG-8

Have Gun, Will Travel

Hubley-Halco- 1960-63. Perhaps the rarest Paladin toy gun. 10" DC repeater made by Hubley with Halco on the right side. Paladin on left frame under cylinder. Has two piece stag grips. Polished nickel.

Value: $150-275

HG-9

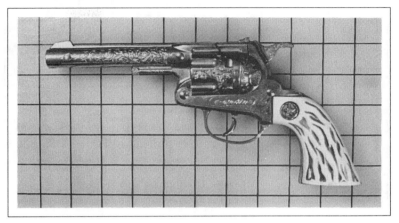

High Chaparral

Daisy- 1960-65 era. Unusual tan & buckskin double holster set with fringe, large silver conchos, studs, turquoise jewels and bullets. Pair of Hubley Western guns with turquoise steerhead grips.

Value: $85-165 (Holsters & guns)

H-1

Highway Patrol

Halco- 1960 era. Dan Mathews was not a western character but the Highway Patrol set is western-style. Black leather with art in silver. Gun is a G. Schmidt "Patrol", which is a rare die cast western-style.

Value: $75-150 (Complete set & gun)

HP-1

How the West Was Won

Nichols (Kusan?)- 1978. Box with tooled vinyl double holster. Guns are late-style unmarked 8" with one-piece stag. Box marked Nichols (?). Single holster sets also exist.

Value: $100-150 (Complete set in box)

HW-1

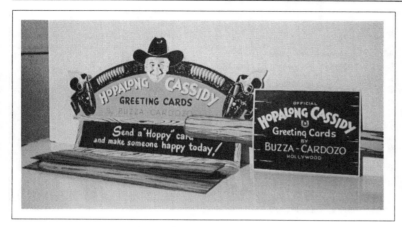

Hopalong Cassidy Display

Buzza-Cardozo, CA- 1955 era. Rare store display rack for Hopalong greeting cards. Graphics closely depict the actual holster set worn by Hoppy. Full color artwork.

Value: $350-650

HC-0

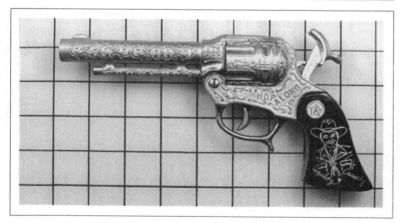

Hopalong Cassidy

Wyandotte- 1950-55 era. Pair of 9" Hoppy guns. *Top:* Nickel finish with ivory white, incised grips. *Lower:* Gold with black incised grips. All Hoppy guns are scarce.

Value: $225-400 (Nic.) - $250-450 (Gold)

HC-1

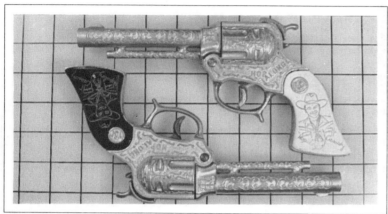

Hopalong Cassidy

Wyandotte- 1950-55 era. Similar to HC-1, but this gold gun is the very rare dummy variety.

Value: $250-500 (Dummy-Gold)

HC-2

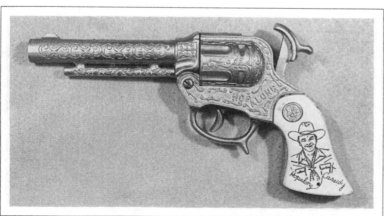

Hopalong Cassidy

Wyandotte- 1950-55 era. Similar to HC-1, but this nickel gun is also the very rare dummy variety. Extremely few Hoppy guns exist in the dummy variety.

Value: $250-500 (Dummy-Nickel)

HC-3

Hopalong Cassidy

Leslie-Henry- 1955 era. Probably made in Canada. Extremely rare Hoppy gun. Only a few known to exist. Nickel with black grips. Note square hole grip screw. Also found in gold finish.

Value: $250-500 (Nik.) $300-550 (Gold)

HC-4

Hopalong Cassidy

Wyandotte- 1955 era. Rare single shot in the nickel finish with blue incised name on ivory-white grip. Nice engraving. The small ejector rod is often missing.

Value: $125-235 (Nickel with ejector rod)

HC-5

Hopalong Cassidy

Wyandotte- 1955 era. Rare single shot in the gold finish with gold incised name on black grip. Note, ejector rod mentioned above in HC-5 is missing on this gun.

Value: $140-250 (Gold with ejector rod)

HC-6

Hopalong Cassidy

G. Schmidt- 1950-55 era. An early Buck'n Bronc with large lettering, full engraving with black grips and white Hoppy busts. Also in white with black bust. Very desirable Hoppy gun.

Value: $200-425

HC-7

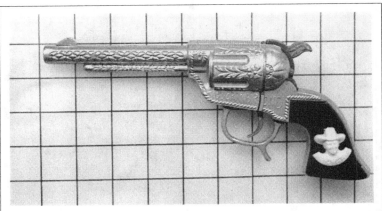

Hopalong Cassidy

G. Schmidt- 1950-55 era. Buck'n Bronc with the small lettering, full engraving, nickel finish with black grips and white Hoppy busts. Also white with black bust.

Value: $200-425

HC-8

Hopalong Cassidy

G. Schmidt- 1950-55 era. One of the very rarest Hoppy guns. Early Buck'n Bronc in full engraving with large lettering in the gold finish with black grips and black Hoppy busts. Schmidt gold is superb!

Value: $275-500 (Gold)

HC-9

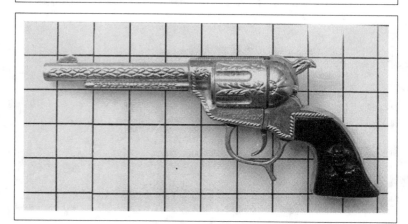

Hopalong Cassidy

G. Schmidt- 1950-55 era. Equally as rare as HC-9 above, is this fully engraved gun marked Hopalong Cassidy with black grips and black Hoppy busts.

Value: $275-500 (Gold)

HC-10

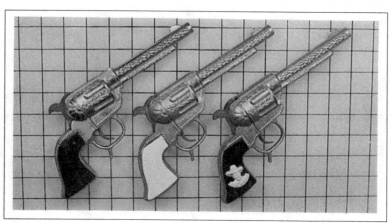

Hopalong Cassidy

G. Schmidt- 1950-55 era. *Left:* Silver paint finish with rare black grips and red jewel. *Center:* Nickel with plain white grips. *Right:* Nickel with normal black grips and white busts. Many grip varieties do exist.

Value: $200-425 (Any grip variety)

HC-11

Hopalong Cassidy

G. Schmidt- 1950-55 era. Pair of rare, long ribbed barrel Buck'n Bronc guns with the Hoppy busts. Schmidt put Hoppy grips on various Buck'n Bronc models to meet the customer demands. Seldom seen.

Value: $200-425

HC-12

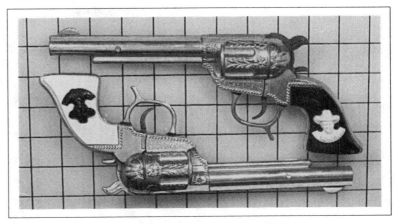

Hopalong Cassidy

G. Schmidt- 1950-55era. Extremely rare nickel finish Hopalong Cassidy with the white grips and the black busts, in the dummy variety. Very few known to exist.

Value: $250-500

HC-13

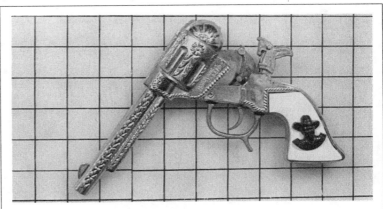

Hopalong Cassidy

G. Schmidt- 1950-55 era. Close-up detail of HC-13 above showing the very rare dummy hammer. *Top:* Note the special dummy hammer that can't strike the cap anvil. *Lower:* Regular hammer casting.

HC-14

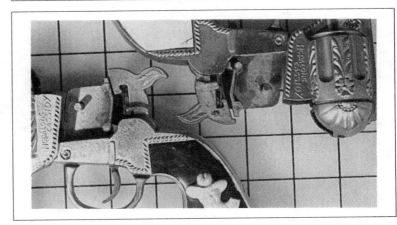

Hopalong Cassidy Holster

Wyandotte- 1950-55 era. Single, black leather with silver studs, silver and gold steerhead concho and name on the belt. Shown with nickel gun.

Value: $100-175 (Holster only)

HC-15

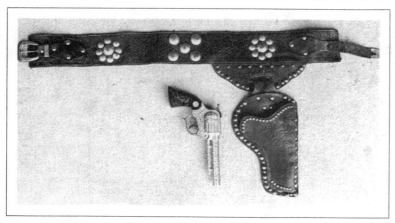

Hopalong Cassidy Holster

Unknown- 1950 era. Early, black leather with large and small silver studs with an embossed horse and rider on the holster front. Very rare Hoppy set. Shown with gold Wyandotte gun.

Value: $150-285 (Holster only)

HC-16

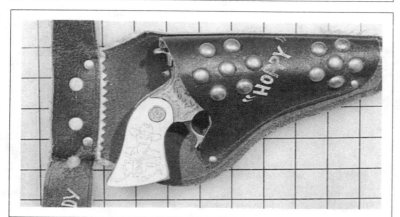

Hopalong Cassidy Holster

Unknown- 1950 era. Rare, early holster in black leather with fur cowhide front and conchos. Red jewels and silver studs. The name is on the belt. Heart-shaped holster strap. Possibly for a cowgirl. Schmidt gun

Value: $200-350 (Holster only)

HC-17

Hopalong Cassidy Holster

Unknown- 1950 era. Early black holster with silver studs and name on both holster and belt. Unusual treatment. Nickel Wyandotte gun.

Value: $125-200 (Holster only)

HC-18

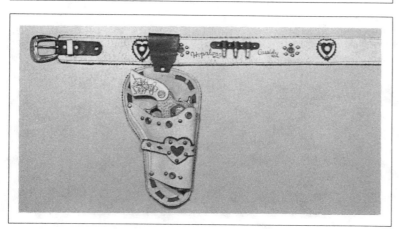

Hopalong Cassidy Holster

Unknown- 1955 era. Rare and unusal girl set in white and red leather with silver studs, red jewels, red heart cut-outs, and red lettering on the belt. Hoppy girl sets are seldom seen. Wyandotte nickel gun.

Value: $165-325 (Holster only)

HC-19

Hopalong Cassidy Holster

Wyandotte- 1950-55 era. Black leather with red jewels, silver studs and a silver and gold steerhead concho. Name is on the belt. Diamond pattern silver studs. The gun is a Wyandotte in nickel.

Value: $150-250

HC-20

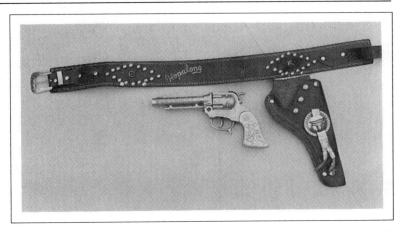

Hopalong Cassidy Holster

Wyandotte- 1950-55 era. Black leather with red jewels, silver and gold steerhead concho and circle pattern of silver studs. Name is on the belt. In original brown and green box including Wyandotte gun.

Value: $550-900 (Complete set in box)

HC-21

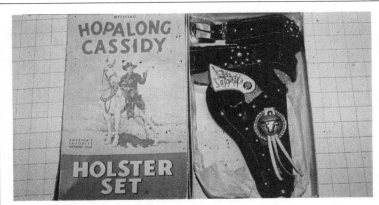

Hopalong Cassidy Holster

Unknown- 1950 era. Very early black leather set with white trim, cut-out letters, white jewels and many silver studs. Rare and unusual double set.

Value: $185-350 (Holster only)

HC-22

Hopalong Cassidy Holster

Unknown- 1950 era. Early black leather with numerous white leather cut-outs, numerous gold and silver stars and studs. Name on gun belt. Uncommon set with a pair of rare, gold G. Schmidt guns.

Value: $185-375 (Holster only)

HC-23

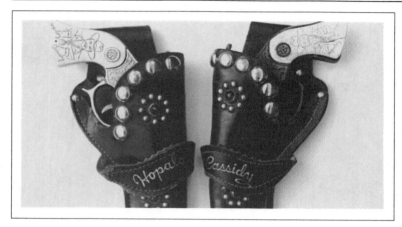

Hopalong Cassidy Holster

Unknown- 1950 era. Early black leather with large silver studs on top, small studs in circular pattern and red jewels. Name on cross-straps with decorative felt. Guns are Wyandotte nickel repeaters.

Value: $155-250 (Holsters only-no belt)

HC-24

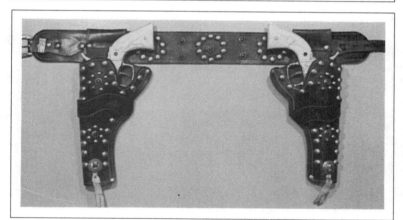

Hopalong Cassidy Holster

Unknown- 1950 era. Similar to HC-24 but has smaller silver studs, studs on cross-straps, red jewels and name on belt. Very desirable early, large set. Black leather.

Value:$ 300-600 (holsters and belt)

HC-25

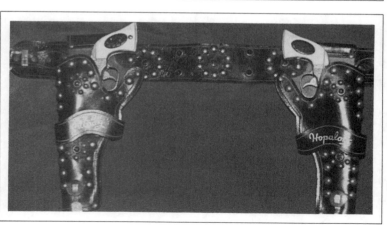

Hopalong Cassidy Holster

Unknown- 1950 era. Like HC-25 in black leather with different stud pattern and name on holster straps. The jewels are red, blue, yellow, and green. Has silver conchos with white straps. Large & rare. (Guns are Nichols Stallion .45.)
Value: $300-600 (Holsters and belt only)

HC-26

Hopalong Cassidy Holster

Unknown- 1950 era. Identical to HC-26 in black leather with similar silver stud patterns. All jewels on this set are red, not multi-colored. Halco Marshal guns. Rare.

Value: $300-600 (Holsters and belt only)

HC-27

Hopalong Cassidy Holster

Wyandotte- 1950-55 era. Black leather set with large silver and gold Hoppy bust conchos, silver studs and red jewels. Note oval concho on belt with name. Loop style holsters.

Value: $185-325 (Holster only)

HC-28

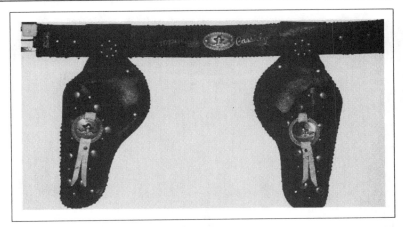

Hopalong Cassidy Holster

Wyandotte- 1950-55 era. Unusual black leather set with white cut-outs and silver studs. Name on top flap of holsters. Guns are Wyandotte. Two piece box is black and orange. Seldom seen set.

Value: $500-1,000 (Box, holsters & guns)

HC-29

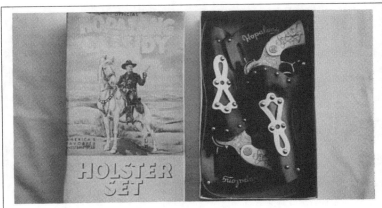

Hopalong Cassidy Holster

Wyandotte- 1950-55 era. Very rare set in black leather with silver stars and studs. Name is on belt. Nickel Wyandotte guns. Two piece box is black and orange. Extra nice.

Value: $800-1,500 (Box, holsters & guns)

HC-30

Hopalong Cassidy Holster

Wyandotte- 1950-55 era. Unusual black leather with "S" pattern silver studs on belt, Hoppy gold and silver busts on holsters with large silver studs as well.

Value: $185-325 (Holsters only)

HC-31

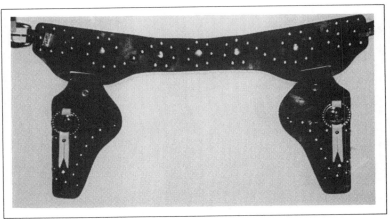

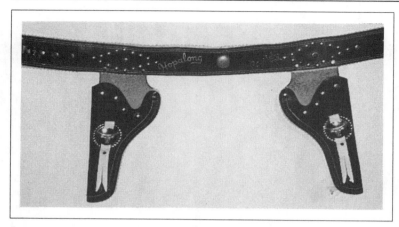

Hopalong Cassidy Holster

Wyandotte- 1950-55 era. Black leather with silver studs in a diamond pattern with red jewels and steerhead gold and silver conchos. Name on belt. Early style.

Value: $185-325 (Holsters only)

HC-32

Hopalong Cassidy Holster

Unknown- 1950-55 era. Early style set in black leather with simple silver studs. Has "Hoppy" on both holsters and belt. G. Schmidt nickel guns.

Value: $185-325 (Holsters only, no guns.)

HC-33

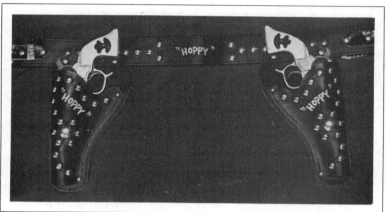

Hopalong Cassidy Holster

Wyandotte- 1950-55 era. Black leather in simple, silver stud triangle pattern with red jewels and name on the belt. Gold and silver steerhead conchos. Has nickel Wyandotte guns. Early-style decoration.

Value: $185-325 (Holsters only, no guns.)

HC-34

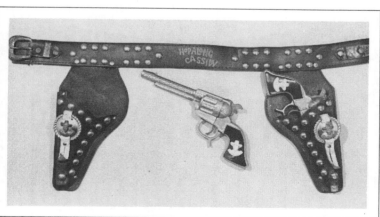

Hopalong Cassidy Holster

Wyandotte- 1950-55 era. Unusual black leather with large silver studs in a line with name on belt and Hoppy silver and gold bust conchos. G. Schmidt guns.

Value: $185-325 (Holsters only, no guns.)

HC-35

Hopalong Cassidy Holster

Wyandotte- 1950-55 era. Extremely rare set in black leather with silver studs, red jewels, silver & gold steerhead conchos. Matching wrist cuffs & spurs. Rare gold Wyandotte guns. Unbelievable set!

Value: $650-1,300 (Complete set & guns.)

HC-36

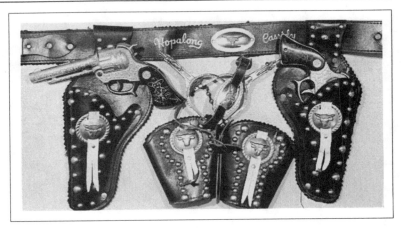

Hopalong Cassidy Holster

J. Schleyer-1985 Creation. Custom quality set in black leather with red jewels, silver studs, has black Hoppy busts and name on loop holsters & Bar 20 Ranch on belt. G. Schmidt nickel guns with black busts.

Value: $500 (Holsters only-one-of-a-kind)

HC-37

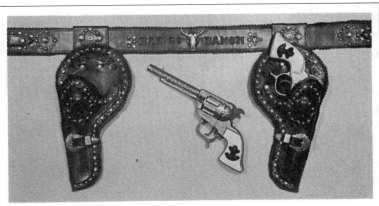

Hopalong Cassidy Holster

Western Creations, PA- 1993. New, limited edition set produced for the 1993 Hoppy Festival in Cambridge, OH. Black leather, silver studs and white lettering. Silver boxes are serial numbered, not holsters.

Value: $150-225 (Boxed set- no guns)

HC-38

Hopalong Cassidy

George Schmidt- 1950. Illustration from an early Schmidt ad shows "Hopalong" in one word on gun's frame. I have never seen an actual gun with this casting. All models found have "Hopalong Cassidy" on both sides.

HC-39

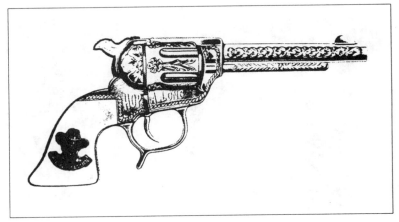

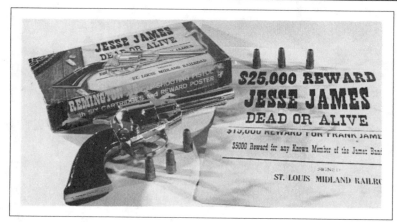

Jesse James

Hubley- 1960 era. Unusual boxed set and rarely seen. Set includes a wanted poster and a Hubley Remington .36 short barrel with black grips. Revolving cylinder that accepts bullets. Gun not marked Jesse J.

Value: $100-250 (box, poster & gun)

JJ-1

Johnny Ringo

Marx- 1960 era. Rare dragoon-style with unusual firing mechanism activated by the lanyard ring tong. Huge, 10 1/2" has beautiful engraving and ivory grips with a steer and horsehead on them. On card.

Value: $125-250 Card, gun & vinyl hols.

JR-1

Johnny Ringo

Esquire-Actoy- 1960. Very rare 9" die cast character gun. Engraved, polished nickel finish with white stag grips and pony medallions. Only a few exist.

Value: $100-175

JR-2

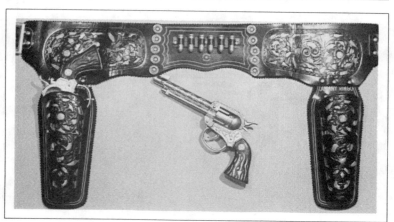

Johnny Ringo

Esquire Novelty-Actoy- 1960 era. Beautiful double holster in black leather with red & gold embossed cut-outs. Silver studs. Name above holster. Guns are Actoy 250 Shot with black & gold stag to match set.

Value: $200-400 (holster & guns)

JR-3

John Wayne

Chancy Novelty Co., Inc. Bklyn, NY- 1950 Very rare character set. Multi-color box, black & tan leather with name on straps & embossed Wayne busts. Set originally came with red pressed steel clicker guns.

Value: $800-1,200 (Box & holsters)

JW-1

John Wayne

Chancy Co., Inc.- 1950 era. Rare single set with tan and black leather holster with signature and embossed bust on holster front. Gun is a Kilgore die cast Ranger.
Value: $500-750 (Holster & gun)

JW-2

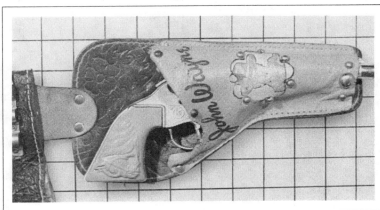

Kit Carson

Kenton- 1930 era. *Top:* Normal cast iron with grips painted white. *Lower:* the rare blue finish with nickel trigger and hammer. Long barrel cast iron.

Value: $125-225 (Either variety)

KC-1

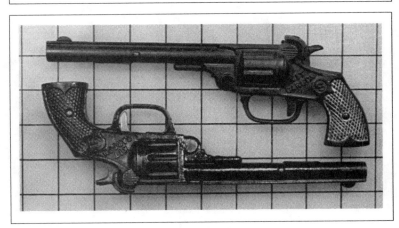

Kit Carson

Unknown- 1955-60 era. Double holster in black leather with gold embossed metalic fronts. Gold lettering. Kilgore die cast Kit Carson guns in gold finish with white grips.

Value: $135-265 (Holsters & guns)

KC-2

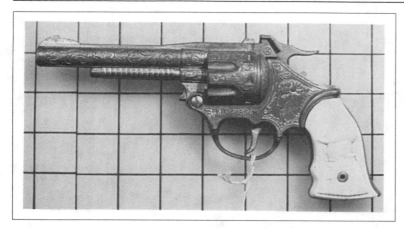

Kit Carson

Kilgore- 1955-60 era. Short barrel 8" gun in dull finish with white grips. Very nice engraving. Uncommon variety to find.

Value: $45-100

KC-3

Kit Carson

Kilgore- 1955-60 era. Long barrel 9 1/2" guns. *Top:* Nickel with black grips. *Lower:* The rarer and highly polished in 24 karat gold finish. Kilgore produced some of the most fantastic gold finished guns.

Value: $75-125 (Nic) - $100-200 (Gold)

KC-4

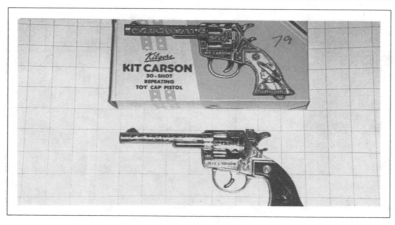

Kit Carson

Kilgore- 1955-60 era. 8" die cast in nickel finish with black grips and lanyard ring. Original box marked $.79!

Value: $45-115 (Gun & box)

KC-5

Kit Carson

Kilgore- 1955-60 era. Similar to KC-5 gun shown above, except in the rarer gold finish with white grips. Nice engraving. Note the bust of Kit Carson on the grips.

Value: $60-125

KC-6

Laramie

R & S Toy Mfg. Co. Inc.- 1959-63. Rare double holster set in black and white leather with silver conchos, lettering and red jewels. Full color box. Note BBC-TV on box. Set possibly made by Lone Star.

Value: $150-250 (Box & holsters)

L-1

Laramie

*R & S Toy Mfg. Co. Inc.-*1959-63. Boxed double holster set in tooled tan, black and orange leather. Hubley die cast Marshal guns with stag handles.

Value: $200-325 (Box, holsters & guns)

L-2

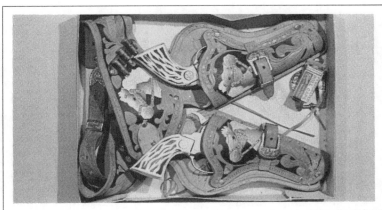

Laramie

Leslie-Henry- 1960 era. An extremely rare character gun. Nickel finish, low hammer with white horsehead grips. This is among the rarest of western toy guns.

Value: $150-250

L-3

Laramie

Leslie-Henry- 1960 era. Close-up detail of L-3 shown above. Note that the lettering is identical in style to that used on the actual show. Very rare toy gun.

L-4

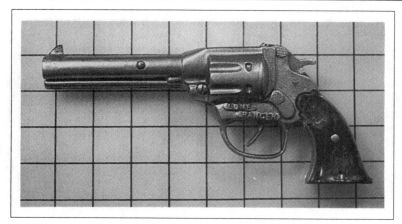

Lone Ranger

Kilgore- Mid 1930s. Extremely rare, cast iron, that may be a factory prototype. It is polished nickel with black grips. Note, lettering and unusual safety on the side.

Value: $300-500

LR-1

Lone Ranger

Kilgore- Mid 1930s. Close-up detail of the LR-1 shown above. Lettering is crudely cast in a raised configuration with large safety lever. Charming, and very rare, early western character toy gun.

LR-2

Lone Ranger

Kilgore- 1940 era. 1st model with narrow hammer in the rare polished nickel with fantastic pearl-blue swirl grips. Gun was found in original box marked "Special". Very rare variation. Cast iron.

Value: $200-375

LR-3

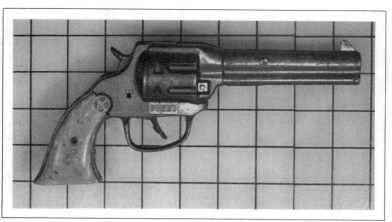

Lone Ranger

Kilgore- 1940 era. Extremely rare, C.I., 1st model, dark finish, dummy variation. It can't fire caps. Note "Dummy" sticker adhered to left frame that is orange and yellow. Butterscotch tan swirl grips.

Value: $185-350

LR-4

Lone Ranger

Kilgore- 1940 era. *Top:* 1st model, narrow hammer in nickel finish, friction close with butterscotch-tan swirl grips. *Lower:* 2nd model, wide hammer, friction close in nickel with black grips. Cast iron.

Value: $165-325 (1st) $150-300 (2nd)

LR-5

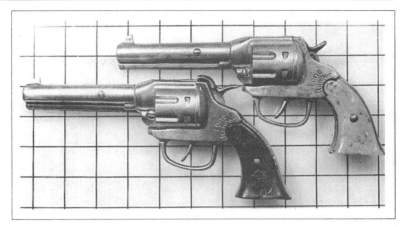

Lone Ranger

Kilgore- 1940 era. Close-up detail of 1st Model cast iron with the very narrow hammer. Note the brown and white swirls in the butterscotch color grips.

LR-6

Lone Ranger

Kilgore- 1940 era. Close-up detail of 2nd Model cast iron with wide hammer. Gun has black "HI-YO SILVER" grips with the rearing horse and rider.

LR-7

Lone Ranger

Kilgore- 1940 era. Rare 2nd Model C.I., in the polished nickel finish with the original box, which is very rare. The grips are black and gun is friction open. Note the price of $.50 on the box!

Value: $185-300 (Gun) $85-150 (Box)

LR-8

Lone Ranger

Kilgore- 1940 era. *Left:* Ist Model black finish. *Center:* 2nd Model in black finish with white grips. *Right:* 2nd Model in nickel finish with red grips. All cast iron, with friction open.

Value: $150-325

LR-9

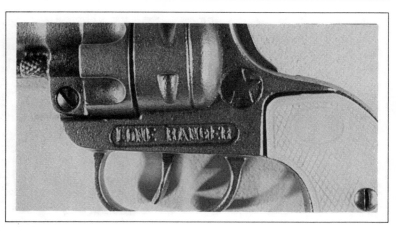

Lone Ranger

Kilgore- 1940 era. Cast iron 3rd Model in nickel finish, wide hammer and push button opener. Note the tag on this gun indicating the push button release. Black grips. With rare original, red & blue box.

Value: $150-285 (Gun) $85-150 (Box)

LR-10

Lone Ranger

Hubley- 1940 era. Extremely rare cast iron that may be a factory prototype. Similar to Hubley C.I Cowboy. Nickel finish has checkered white grips with plain ovals.

Value: $750-1,000

LR-11

Lone Ranger

Hubley- 1940 era. Close-up detail of cast iron LR-11 shown above. Note the Lone Ranger casting. A similar prototype gun has a Roy Rogers casting. Apparently, Hubley never acquired the license.

LR-12

Lone Ranger Holster

Unknown- 1945 era. Early holster in tan leather with fur cowhide front. Silver studs and embossed strap. Gun is a cast iron, 2nd model Kilgore wide hammer.

Value: $ 65-100 (Holster only)

LR-13

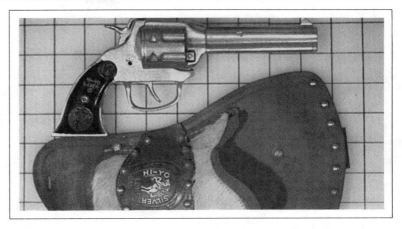

Lone Ranger Holster

Unknown- 1945 era. Detail of the holster strap of LR-13 above. Artwork is red and white and embossed in the leather.

LR-14

Lone Ranger Holster

T.L.R. Inc.- 1962. Tan and dark green set with orange jewel, silver studs and embossed art. 1st Model Kilgore cast iron gun with narrow hammer.

Value: $65-100 (Holster only)

LR-15

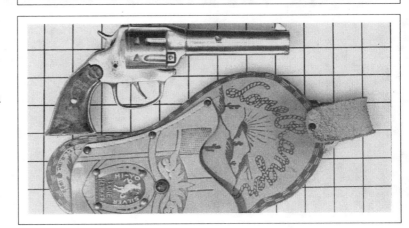

Lone Ranger

Mattel- 1960 era. Seldom seen, die cast in high polished chrome has non-revolving cylinder and slick white grips. This was used in the Mattel Lone Ranger holster sets. No Lone Ranger markings.

Value: $75-165

LR-16

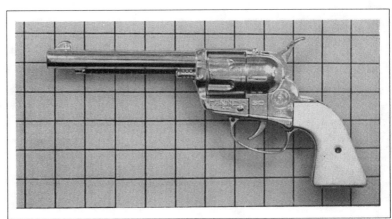

Lone Ranger

Actoy- 1960 era. Engraved die cast in the antique bronze finish with white stag grips. Found with, or without, lanyard ring. All Lone Ranger guns are difficult to find, especially in die cast.

Value: $135-225

LR-17

Lone Ranger

Actoy- 1960 era. Rare nickel finished die cast with white stag grips and no lanyard ring. Most Actoy Lone Ranger guns are in antique bronze.

Value: $145-250

LR-18

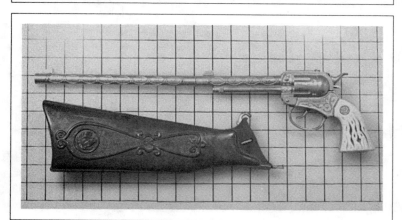

Lone Ranger

Actoy- 1960 era. Extremely rare nickel die cast with frame made to accept an extension barrel and shoulder stock to create a carbine. Only a handful exist! Similar to Restless Gun variation by Actoy-Esquire.

Value: $450-800

LR-19

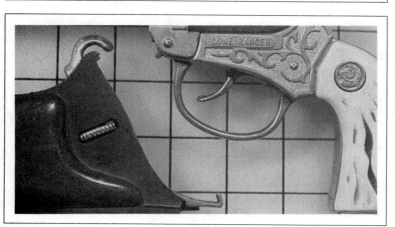

Lone Ranger

Actoy- 1960 era. Close-up detail of LR-19 showing the Lone Ranger stamping and attachment hooks on the detachable stock which fit special castings on frame.

LR-20

Lone Ranger .32

Actoy- 1960 era. Rare die cast engraved gun in the nickel finish with red-brown scroll grips. Also found in antique bronze.

Value: $125-200

LR-21

Lone Ranger

Lone Star, Eng.- 1960-65 era. Rare chrome finished die cast engraved with red-black swirl grips. 9 1/2" repeater. Possibly more recent manufacture.

Value: $100-175

LR-22

Lone Ranger

Marx- 1935-40 era.Very rare pressed steel clicker with ivory celluloid inset grips. It has red jewels and L.R. artwork on the grips. Research indicates these were given away at movie theaters.

Value: $85-150

LR-23

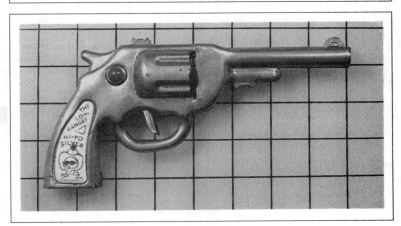

Lone Ranger

Marx- 1935-40 era. Pressed steel clicker in black paint with chrome cylinder. Red jewel on right and L.R. decal of the left. A rather common toy gun.

Value: $35-85

LR-24

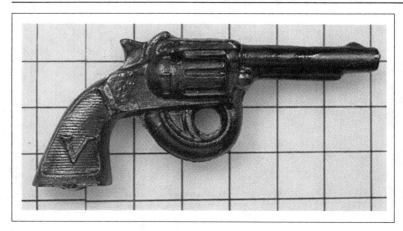

Lone Ranger

Unknown- 1940-45 era. A wood-pulp type composition gun from WW II. A cereal premium (Cheerios). Note Victory "V" on the grip. L.R. cast into frame on both sides. Black painted finish. Very rare.

Value: $85-150

LR-25

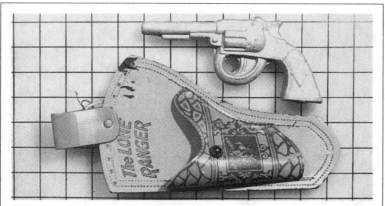

Lone Ranger

Esquire Novelty- 1945 era. A wood-pulp composition gun similar to LR-25, but slightly smaller and in the silver paint finish. With rare cardboard fiber holster, which is tan with black art & blue jewel.

Value: $100-165 (Gun and holster set)

LR-26

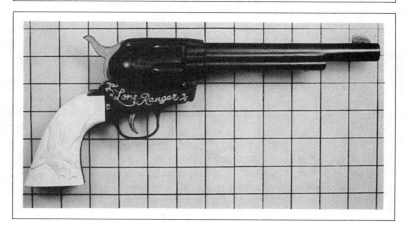

Lone Ranger

Marx- 1955 era. Prototype gun from the Erie, PA plant. Large plastic, clicker gun with fantastic flying eagle, ivory grips and L.R. lettering on side frame. Rare.

Value: $125-185

LR-27

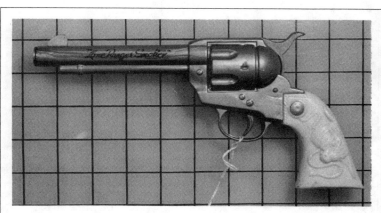

Lone Ranger

Marx- 1955 era. Unusual, smoking-clicker gun. Plastic and metal. Lettering in blue on the barrel with white steerhead grips on silver finish gun. Also came in black.

Value: $85-150

LR-28

Lone Ranger Set

Smallman & Sons Co., Paterson, NJ- 1945 era. Cardboard-fiber holster, belt and wrist cuff set. Tan with black artwork. Unusual set in box.

Value: $85-150

LR-29

Lone Ranger Holster

Esquire Novelty- 1945 Era. Marx all black clicker in a tan and dark brown fiber and cardboard holster with brown artwork and orange jewel.

Value: $45-85

LR-30

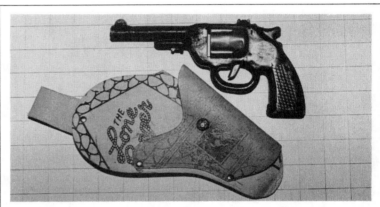

Lone Ranger Holster

Unknown- 1940-45 era. Tan leather with silver studs, red jewels and embossed L.R. artwork. Early holster with Tonto on the top. Gun is a Marx steel clicker.

Value: $65-100

LR-31

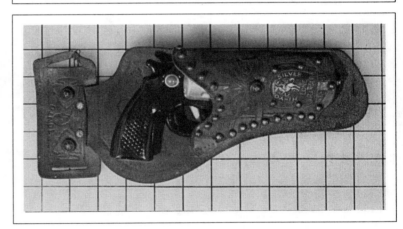

Lone Ranger Holster

Unknown- 1940-45 era. Close-up detail of LR-31. Note the Tonto artwork, flowered studs and red jewels on the top belt loop part of the holster.

LR-32

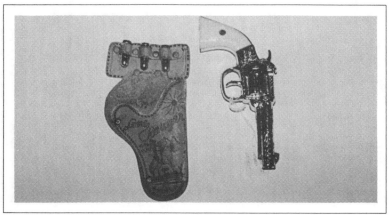

Lone Ranger Holster

Unknown- 1940-45 era. Early tan leather holster with 3 silver bullets and L.R. artwork embossed on the front. Gun is a cast iron engraved Big Scout by Stevens. This gun found in many early L.R. sets.

Value: $65-100 (Holster only)

LR-33

Lone Ranger Holster

Unknown- 1945 era. Unusual pebble-grain black leather with silver artwork and orange jewel.

Value: $50-85

LR-34

Lone Ranger Holster

Feinburg-Henry Mfg. Co. NY- 1940 era. An early L.R. and Tonto holster and belt in beautiful full color box. All L.R. boxes are quite rare and seldom seen.

Value: $135-250 (Box and holster set)

LR-35

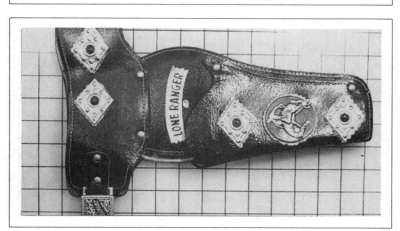

Lone Ranger Holster

Esquire Novelty- 1950 era. Black leather, left handed holster with silver horse & diamond conchos with red jewels. Note unusual & rare L.R. silver, black and red belt buckle.

Value: $100-165

LR-36

Lone Ranger Holster

Esquire Novelty- 1960 era. Black leather in the basketweave pattern with silver conchos and red stars. White lettering. Gun is the rare Actoy Lone Ranger .32.

Value: $65-125 (Holster only)

LR-37

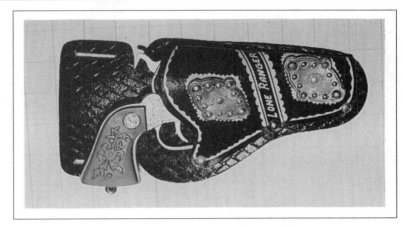

Lone Ranger Holster

Unknown- 1945-50 era. Highly decorated black leather loop holster with numerous silver studs and pearl jewels. Name on holster is embossed and painted silver. Gun is a Kilgore C.I. with maroon grips.

Value: $125-200 (Holster only)

LR-38

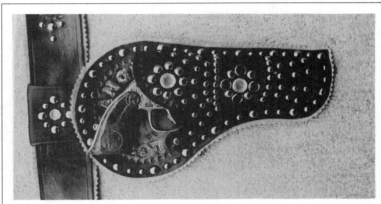

Lone Ranger Holster

Esquire Novelty- 1940 era. An early leather double set with embossed art on holsters and loops. Silver bullets with a pair of dark finished Stevens C.I. Scouts with white grips.

Value: $85-165 (Holsters only)

LR-39

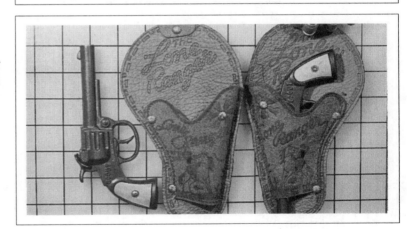

Lone Ranger Holster

Esquire Novelty- 1940 era. Unusual early cross-draw set in tan leather with black embossed art and red jewels. Note the extra wide belt has the Lone Ranger, Tonto and Silver in the middle. Rare set.

Value: $100-185

LR-40

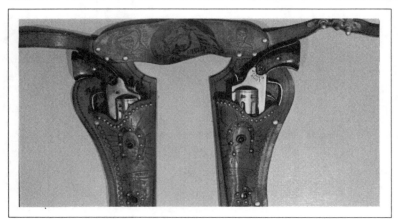

Lone Ranger Holster

Esquire Novelty- 1940-45 era. Similar to LR-40 except for much larger guns. Red jewels and silver studs. Embossed art and similar belt treatment. Rare set with the Kilgore C.I. nickel guns with black grips.

Value: $125-250 (Holsters only)

LR-41

Lone Ranger Holster

Esquire Novelty- 1940-45 era. Close-up detail of the wide belt showing the embossed black artwork of the Lone Ranger, Tonto and Silver. Rare set.

LR-42

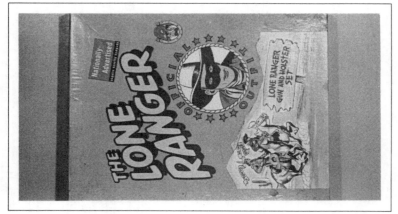

Lone Ranger Holster

Esquire Novelty- 1940 era. Rare, full color box for a double holster set. Outstanding artwork. WW II era set. Contents below.

Value: $125-200 (Box only)

LR-43

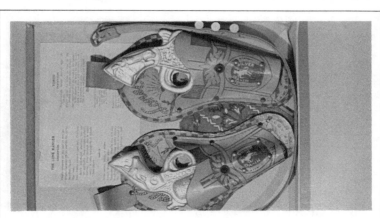

Lone Ranger Holster

Esquire Novelty- 1940 era. Cardboard-fiber double set in tan with dark brown artwork. Orange jewels and silver studs. The composition, silver painted guns, do not match! Set found as shown.

Value: $100-185 (Holster set and guns)

LR-44

Lone Ranger Holster

Feinberg-Henry Mfg. Co.- 1950 era. A full color box for a double holster set. The artwork is exceptional. Contents below.

Value: $125-235

LR-45

Lone Ranger Holster

Feinberg-Henry Mfg. Co.- 1950 era. Double holster set in tan leather with embossed black and brown artwork. Silver studs red jewels and silver bullets. Set includes a kerchief.

Value: $100-225 (Holsters and kerchief)

LR-46

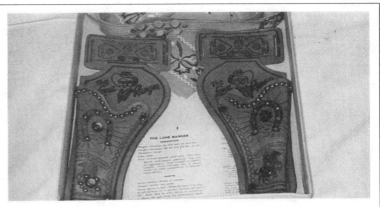

Lone Ranger Holster

Esquire Novelty- 1960 era. Large black leather set white artwork, silver conchos and bullets. Red jewel. Antique bronze die cast Actoy guns with lanyard rings.

Value: $135-225 (Holsters only)

LR-47

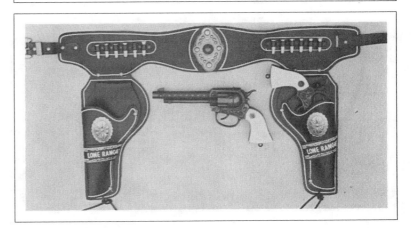

Lone Ranger Holster

Unknown- 1960 era. Double tan and black tooled leather set with tan fringe, silver conchos and adjustable belt. Silver L.R. buckle. Red Ranger Wyandotte guns.

Value: $125-200 (Holsters only)

LR-48

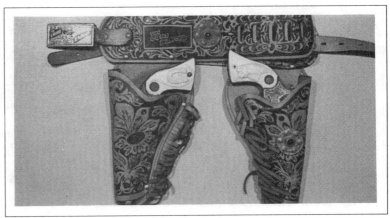

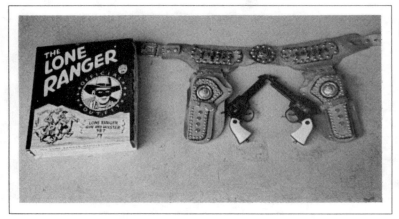

Lone Ranger Holster

Esquire Novelty- 1955-60 era. Large tan leather set with numerous silver studs, horsehead conchos, bullets and red jewels. L.R. silver buckel. Antique bronze Actoy guns. Original full color box.

Value: $350-650 (Holsters, guns and box)

LR-49

Lone Ranger Holster

Esquire Novelty- 1955-60 era. Nearly the same as LR-49 except adjustable belt, no center concho on belt, less silver studs and jewels on holsters. Variation of belt buckle. Name on back of belt.

Value: $145-265 (Holsters only)

LR-50

Lone Ranger Holster

Esquire Novelty- 1955-60 era. Close-up detail of LR-50 showing adjustable belt buckle and silver lettering on belt.

LR-51

Lone Ranger Holster

Esquire Novelty- 1950 era. Black leather with silver horses, conchos and studs. It has an adjustable belt and red jewels. The original full color box included. This set is similar to LR-36.

Value: $225-450 (Holsters and box)

LR-52

Lone Ranger Holster

Esquire Novelty- 1955-60 era. Unusual and highly decorated black leather set with large silver conchos and numerous red jewels. Adjustable belt with rare bullet holder. Schmidt Buck'n Bronc guns.

Value: $145-245 (Holsters only)

LR-53

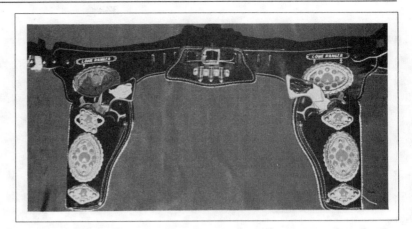

Lone Ranger Holster

Barash Co. Inc. NY- 1955-60 era. Salesman sample case for the new Neolite holsters. Brown cardboard with Lone Ranger on the cover. Very rare boxed set.

Value: $225-350 (Box & holsters-no gun)

LR-54

Lone Ranger Holster

Barash Co. Inc. NY- 1955-60 era. Holsters found in the above salesman's case. Very decorative set with deep floral tooling, silver studs and L.R. bust. Texan, Jr. guns. Made of tan color synthetic Neolite.

Value: $125-225 (Holsters only-no guns)

LR-55

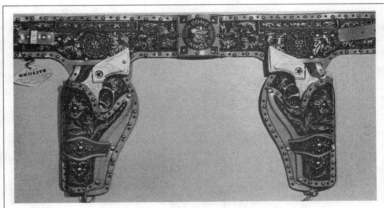

Lone Ranger Holster

Barash Co. Inc. NY- 1955-60 era. Holster tag from the above set. Neolite material made by Goodyear Tire & Rubber Co., Akron, OH. Holsters by Barash of NYC. Limited collector appeal for Neolite or Dura-hide synthetic material holsters.

LR-56

Lone Ranger Holster

Barash Co. Inc. NY- 1955-60 era. Holster similar to LR-55 except in the black Neolite rather than tan. Silver studs and large horsehead conchos above holsters. Guns are Texan, Jr. die cast by Hubley.

Value: $135-235

LR-57

Lone Ranger Holster

J. Schleyer- 1994. Child-size, double black leather set nearly identical to the holster actually worn by Clayton Moore. Tooled with silver studs, conchos, buckles and 20 silver bullets. C.I. Kilgore nickel guns.

Value: $500 (Holsters only one-of-a-kind)

LR-58

Lone Ranger Target Set

Marx- 1945 era. Sheet metal target set with pressed steel dart pistol. Beautiful full color artwork in the original box. A seldom seen target set.

Value: $150-275 (Complete with box)

LR-59

Lone Ranger Miniatures

Super Toys, Peoria, IL.- 1955 era. A rare complete set of six western miniature guns. Solid castings on original card. Note the price of $.49.

Value: $65-100 (Complete set)

LR-60

Lone Ranger

Unknown- 1940 era. Unusual and rare L.R. belt accessory with a tooled leather strap, silver bullet, miniature Colt gun and metal holster with floral treatment and red jewel.

Value: $30-55

LR-61

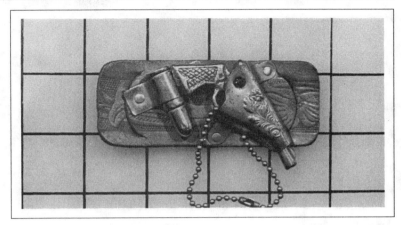

Lone Ranger Ring

General Mills- 1947. Store poster for the 6 Shooter ring from Kix cereal for only one box top and $.15! The ring is currently valued at near $100.

Value: $100-225 (Poster only)

LR-62

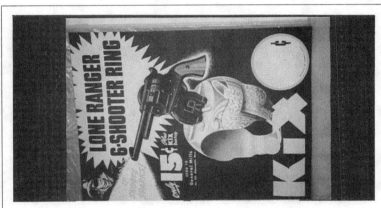

Lone Ranger Rifle

Marx- 1955-60 era. Extremely rare rifle similar to a deluxe Winchester '94 with engraving, checkered stock and is a lever action cap gun. With very rare, full color cardboard rifle scabbard. Name in gold.

Value: $165-300 (Gun and scabbard)
(Other L.R. rifles in Rifle Section)

LR-63

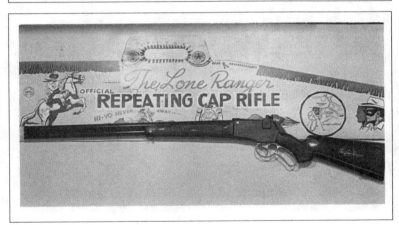

Lone Ranger Carbine

Actoy- 1960 era. Full size view of the rare carbine with detachable stock and barrel extension. Note that the grips are larger and slightly different from normal Actoy guns. The grips also have ivory-tan color with a different stag pattern. See LR-19.

LR-64

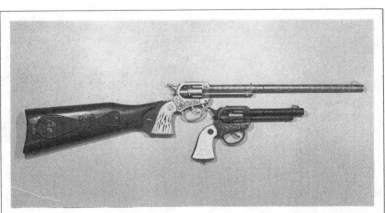

Lone Ranger-Tonto

Esquire Novelty- 1960 era. Rare, complete Tonto outfit includes: box, drum, beaded head-dress with feathers, fringed holster, knife and sheath, and tomahawk. Name on holster. Multi- colored. Generic gun.

Value: $200-450 (Box & complete set)

LR-65

Lone Ranger-Tonto

Esquire Novelty- 1960 era. Holster similar to set LR-65. Beaded art with name on belt rather than holster. Fringe and silver concho. Beaded silver buckle. Gun is a generic Halco. No Tonto guns exist.

Value: $75-150 (Holster only)

LR-66

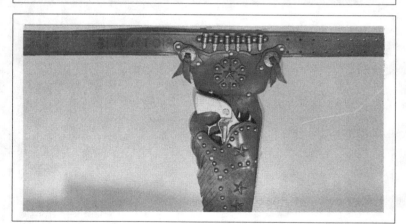

Lone Ranger-Tonto

Unknown- 1955 era. Tan & buckskin set with gold stars, studs and conchos. Tonto on gun belt. Fringe & 6 bullets. The gun is a Stevens Big Chief with grips that have a superb Indian Chief. Rare.

Value: $125-250 (Holster and gun)

LR-67

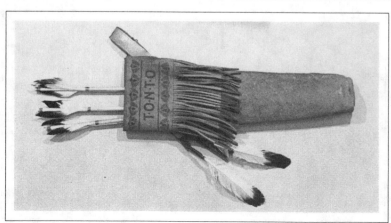

Lone Ranger-Tonto

Unknown- 1955 era. Arrow quiver in tan buckskin with fringe that has similar details to LR-67. Note Tonto and art are identical & both printed in dark brown. The quiver has 3 rubber tipped arrows.

Value: $85-165

LR-68

MIKE

GLEN

BOB

BILL

BEATRICE

STEVE

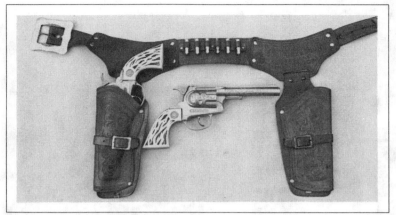

Lawman - Marshal Dan Troop

Halco- 1960 era. Very nice tooled tan leather double holster. Unusual and seldom seen gun rig. Late model Hubley Marshal die cast guns with stag grips.

Value: $115-235 (Holsters & guns)

LM-1

Lawman - Marshal Dan Troop

Halco- 1960 era. Close-up detail of the tooling and lettering on the holster. Note engraving on Hubley Marshal.

LM-2

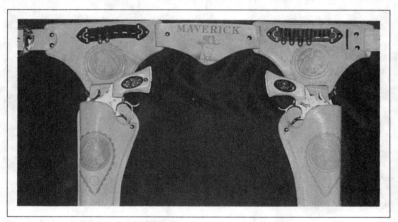

Maverick

Esquire Novelty Co.- 1960 era. Light tan double set with embossed horseheads, name and bust. Pair of L-H long barreled die cast with insert grips.

Value: $250-450 Holsters & Long Barrels

MK-1

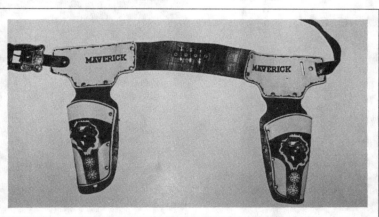

Maverick

Unknown- 1960 era. Large black & white leather set with silver & gold saddle conchos and buckle. Name on belt. No guns.

Value: $75-150 (Holsters only)

MK-2

Maverick

Halco- 1960 era. Black leather double set with gold lettering, silver cochos and turquoise jewels. Guns are L-H short barrels with rare transparent amber grips with white inserts.

Value: $165-325 (Holsters & guns)

MK-3

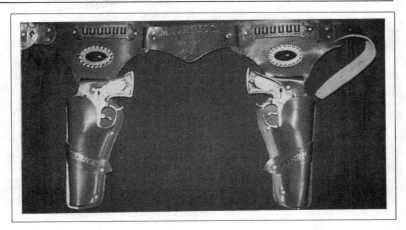

Maverick

R & S Toy Co.- 1960 era. Black & white leather with silver cochos and red jewels. Name on the holsters. Guns are Halco or Leslie-Henry die cast in nickel with white stag and Diamond "H" medallions.

Value: $125-225 (Holsters & guns)

MK-4

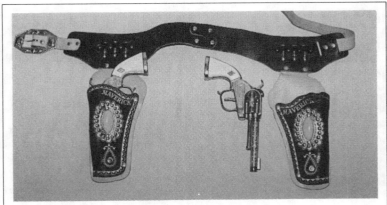

Maverick

Unknown- 1960 era. Black leather single gunslinger-style with gold lettering and red bullets. Very plain set with no gun.

Value: $75-135 (Holster only)

MK-5

Maverick

Unknown- 1960 era. Very ornate black leather set with white artwork, large silver conchos, buckle and studs. Lone Star die cast guns in nickel finish with stag notch-bar grips.

Value: $125-235 (Holsters & guns)

MK-6

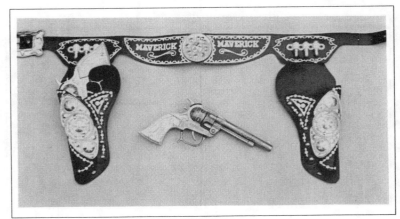

Maverick

Carnell, Bklyn.- 1960 era. Rare & unusual boxed set with strange rifle, tan & white double leather holsters, wrist cuffs and spurs with silver conchos, studs, buckles & red jewels. Guns are Hubley Westerns.

Value: $225-450 (Complete box with all)

MK-7

Maverick

Leslie-Henry- 1960 era. 9" die cast nickel finish with rare transparent amber grips and white star inserts. Short barrel variation.

Value: $75-165

MK-8

Maverick

Leslie-Henry- 1960 era. *Top:* Very rare long barrel variety in nickel. *Lower:* This is a normal 9" variety in nickel. Both guns have the white grips with black horseshoe inserts.

Value: $100-250 (Long barrel)

MK-9

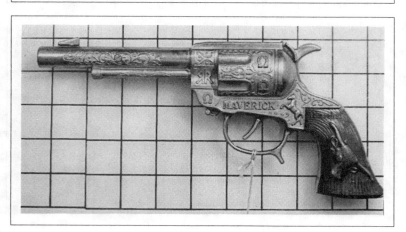

Maverick

Leslie-Henry- 1960 era. Rare die cast with the pop-up cap box in nickel. Has rarer steerhead and Marshal copper grips.

Value: $125-265

MK-10

Maverick

Leslie-Henry- 1960 era. Rare die cast with pop-up cap box in dull finish. Has white grips with black star inserts.

Value: $125-265

MK-11

Maverick

Leslie-Henry- 1960 era. Very rare die cast with pop-up cap box in gold finish. Has butterscotch horsehead grips. Very few pop-up cap box varieties exist in gold.

Value: $145-285

MK-12

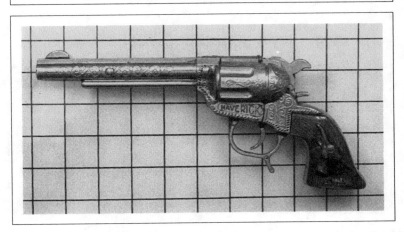

Maverick

G. Schmidt- 1960 era. Extremely rare character gun. Long, ribbed barrel totally engraved with Marshal & steerhead copper grips similar, but smaller than those by Leslie-Henry. Name is on the side.

Value: $250-350

MK-13

Maverick

G. Schmidt- 1960 era. Close-up detail of MK-13. Note the raised scroll engraving, copper steerhead grips and the name on the side plate. The few examples were found in Canada or near the border. This exact gun is featured in the 1959 Nerlich & Company Holiday catalog.

MK-14

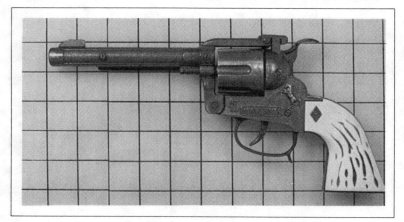

Maverick

Halco/L-H- 1960 era. Rare, large die cast with revolving cylinder that accepts bullets. Antique bronze finish with stag grips and Diamond "H" medallion.

Value: $175-325

MK-15

Maverick

Leslie-Henry- 1960 era. Unusual die cast in nickel finish with inset stag grips with Diamond "H" medallions. Seldom seen variety.

Value: $85-165

MK-16

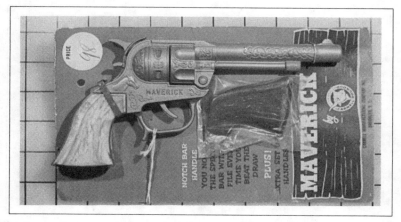

Maverick

Lone Star, Eng.- 1960 era. Dull nickel finish gun with notch-bar grips. On a card by Carnell, Bklyn, NY. Note price of $.98. Also found in a longer barrel model.

Value: $85-165 (Either length barrel)

MK-17

Maverick

Lone Star, Eng.- 1960 era. Same as MK-17 except in polished nickel finish. Has stag notch-bar grips. Also found in a longer barrel model.

Value: $85-165 (Either length barrel)

MK-18

Overland Trail - Kelly & Flip

Hubley- 1960 era. Box for a seldom seen set for the Overland Trail. Show starred William Bendix as Kelly & Doug MClure as Flip.

Value: $150-200 (Box only)

OT-1

Overland Trail

Hubley- 1960 era. Black leather double set with white lettering & artwork. The guns are quite rare, Hubley "Flip" models with black stag grips.

Value: $350-600 (Box, holsters & guns)

OT-2

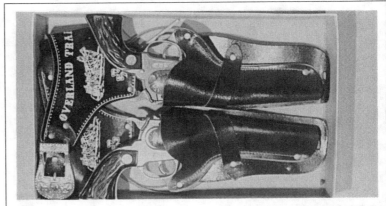

Overland Trail

Halco- 1960 era. Similar to OT-2, except gun belt has 6 silver bullets and holster straps have silver conchos. Guns are Halco Marshals with revolving cylinders.

Value: $300-500 Holsters & Marshal guns

OT-3

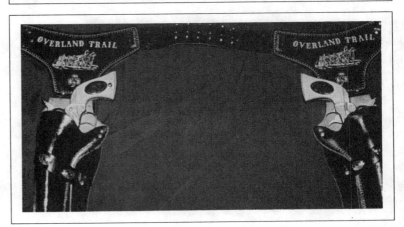

Pecos Bill

Mondial, Italy- 1955-65 era. Unusual die cast in blue finish with ivory grips with a cowboy in full color! Beautiful artwork. A high quality, 8 shot revolving cylinder.

Value: $65-125 (Box & gun)

PB-1

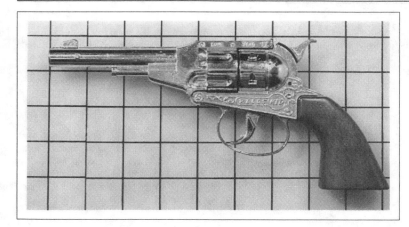

Pecos Kid

Lone Star, Eng.- 1965 era. Unusual die cast repeater with one-piece simulated walnut grips. Could be more recent manufacture.

Value: $35-75

PK-1

Planet of the Apes

Mattel- 1960 era. Secondary western set. Unusual boxed holster in dura-hide with an antique bronze Fanner 50 with black Impala grips. Seldom seen Mattel model.

Value: $85-165 (Box, holster & gun)

PA-1

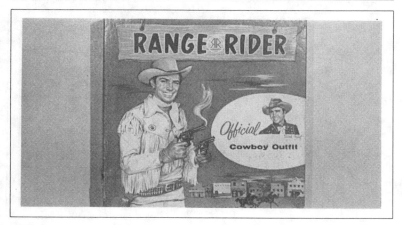

Range Rider

Leslie-Henry- 1950-55era. Very rare boxed set with double holsters and Buzz Henry guns. Show was a Gene Autry Flying A Ranch Production with Jock Mahoney.

Value: $85-150 (Box only)

RN-1

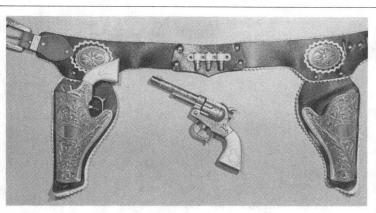

Range Rider

Leslie-Henry- 1950-55 era. Generic double holster set in box RN-1 above. Has black leather with metalic silver floral fronts & silver conchos. Guns are Buzz Henry die cast Ranger repeaters with white grips.

Value: $300-450 (Box, holsters & guns)

RN-2

Range Rider

G. Schmidt- 1950-55 era. Rare die cast in ribbed long barrel with checkered copper grips. A seldom seen, rather plain, western character gun.

Value: $85-175

RN-3

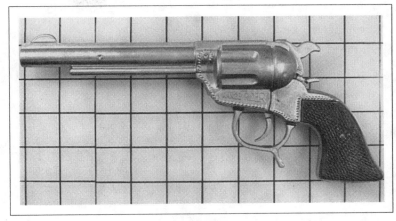

Range Rider MK II

Lone Star, Eng.- 1955-60. A large 12 1/4" die cast with revolving cylinder, bullets & engraving. Chrome finish with black grips with stars & small jewels. Similar to the Nichols MK II Stallion. Rare toy.

Value: $165-325

RN-4

Rebel - Johnny Yuma

Classy Prod.- 1960 era. Extremely rare set with original box. The Scattergun used 2 rolls of caps and came in either a brown wood-grain or black stock. The black holster has C.W. style buckle. Rebel pistol.

Value: $250-500 (Box & shotgun only)

R-1

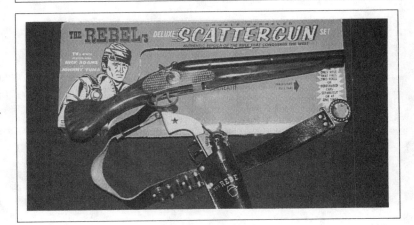

Rebel - Johnny Yuma

Classy Prod..- 1960 era. Detail of lettering on black pistol with white grips & star. It was made by Lone Star. The gun and the holster shown in R-1 came as a set. Rare.

Value: $135-225 (Holster & pistol)

R-2

Red Ryder

Unknown- 1940 era. Primarily associated with Daisy BB guns. This double holster set is tan, basketweave leather. A rather unusual set. I guess 1940, because those found had composition molded guns.

Value: $75-165 (Holsters only)

RD-1

Red Ryder

Unknown- 1940 era. Detail, close-up of the holster strap shown in RD-1. Note the embossed Red Ryder name and silver studs. Gun belt has rope and horsehead silver conchos.

RD-2

Restless Gun - Vint Bonner

Actoy-Esquire- 1957-59. *Top:* Polished & chrome plated die cast with transparent amber grips. *Lower:* Similar, but in the dull nickel. Both guns have a secret compartment for caps in the grip.

Value: $65-145 (Either variety)

RG-1

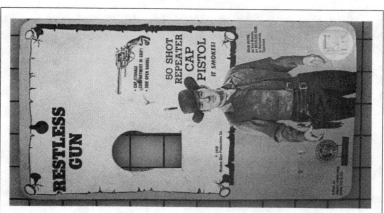

Restless Gun

Esquire Novelty Co.- 1957-59. Original card for RG-1 gun shown above. Price tag of $1.19 is from McCrory's.

Value: $25-50 (Card only)

RG-2

Restless Gun

Actoy- 1957-59. Large die cast repeater in nickel finish with stag grips and pony medallions. No provision for detachable stock.

Value: $85-165

RG-3

Restless Gun

Esquire-Actoy- 1957-59. Large holster in black leather with silver studs and silver embossed artwork. Gun is an Actoy in nickel finish. Silver bullets on belt.

Value: $125-225 (Holster & gun)

RG-4

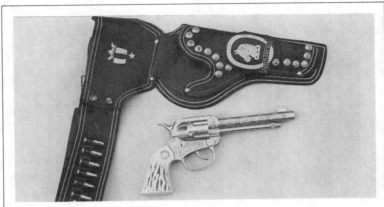

Restless Gun

Esquire-Actoy- 1957-59. Rare set to find complete. Nickel pistol with a detachable carbine stock and barrel extension. Black leather rig holds pistol, stock and extra barrel. Silver star triangle conchos.

Value: $225-450 (Complete set & holster)

RG-5

Restless Gun

Esquire-Actoy- 1957-59. Rare assembled carbine complete with pistol, detachable brown stock and screw-in barrel extension. Usually some piece is missing.

Value: $200-400 (Complete gun & pieces)

RG-6

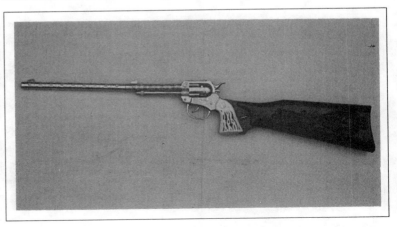

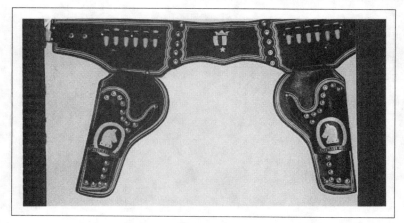

Restless Gun

Esquire Novelty Co.- 1957-59. Rare double holster set in black leather, silver studs, red bullets, white and gold artwork. The double sets are seldom seen.

Value: $65-125

RG-7

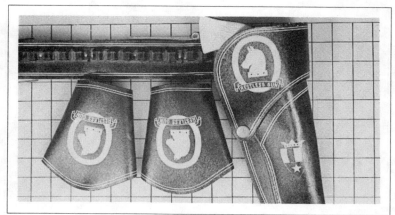

Restless Gun

Esquire Novelty Co.- 1957-59. An unusual holster set in black leather with white artwork. Has a hooded top & matching wrist cuffs. Gun is a large Actoy Restless Gun with lanyard ring.

Value: $135-235 (Holster, cuffs & gun)

RG-8

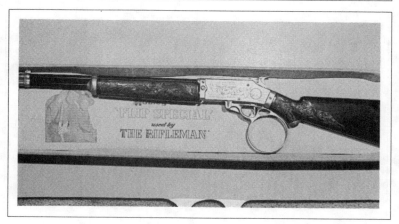

Rifleman - Lucas McCain

Hubley- 1958-63. "Flip Special" ring rifle in nickel die cast with a brown plastic stock. In original box. Popular model.

Value: $250-450 (Box & rifle)

RM-1

Rifleman - Lucas McCain

Hubley- 1958-63. Close-up detail of the beautiful receiver engraving on the Rifleman rifle shown in RM-1. Note the Hubley logo in rope circle.

RM-2

Rin Tin Tin

Actoy- 1955 era. 9" die cast in the rather rare nickel finish. Has white stag grips and lanyard ring (usually missing).

Value: $75-150

RT-1

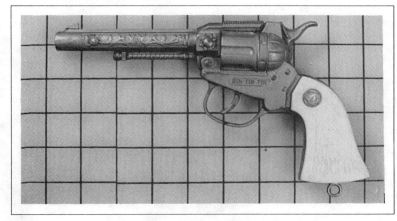

Rin Tin Tin

Actoy- 1955 era. Normal antique bronze finish with white stag and lanyard ring. Note in this photo the gun belt buckel showing Rin Tin Tin & Cpl. Rusty.

Value: $65-135 (Gun only - Ant. Bronze)

RT-2

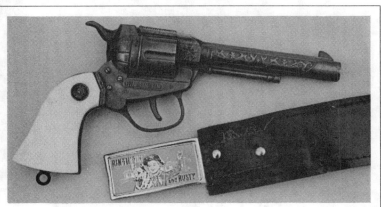

Rin Tin Tin

Esquire Novelty Co.- 1955 era. Rare holster set complete with trooper-style flap holster, bullet pouch, telescope, silver buckel & bronze Actoy pistol. Seldom complete. Black leather with yellow & blue artwork.

Value: $135-250 (Complete set & gun)

RT-3

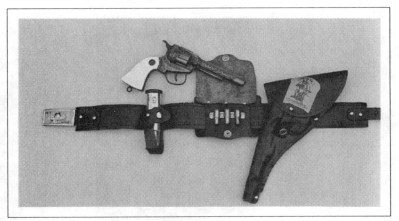

Rin Tin Tin - Cpl. Rusty

Esquire Novelty Co.- 1955 era. Very rare double holster set in black leather with silver conchos, red jewels, silver borders., buckles and bullets. Cpl. Rusty-Top Gun on holsters. Probably had Actoy pistols.

Value: $100-175 (Holsters only)

RT-4

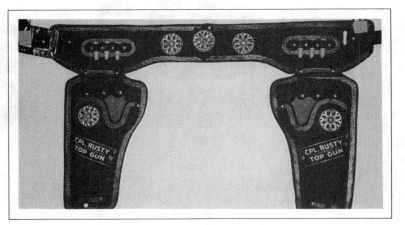

GLEN

ESTON

MIKE

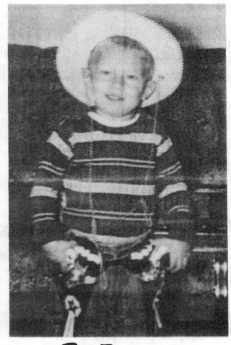

BOB

Roy Rogers

Hubley- 1940-45 era. Extremely rare cast iron, that may well be a one-of-a-kind factory prototype. Similar to the Hubley cast iron Cowboy model. White grips with Colt logo.

Value: $850-1,000

RR-1

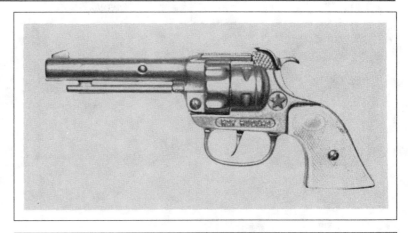

Roy Rogers

Kilgore- 1938-45 era. Pair of very rare cast iron Roy's, in the polished finish with long top strap and riveted stag grips. The name is on top of the grips. One of the most desirable character guns.

Value: $850-1,300 (Each)

RR-2

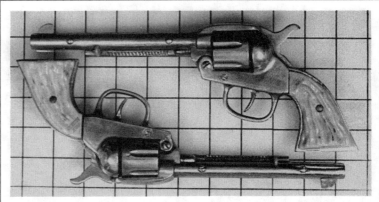

Roy Rogers

Kilgore- Detail photo of the extended top strap, polished finish, cast iron cylinder, and rivited Roy Rogers grip.

RR-3

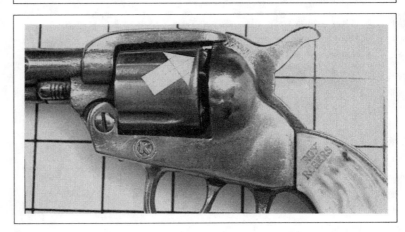

Roy Rogers

Kilgore- 1938-45 era. *Top:* Roy variation with short top strap, cast iron cylinder and Roy grips. *Lower:* Long Tom variety with two piece steel cylinder and rarer etched side plate.

Value: $850-1,300

RR-4

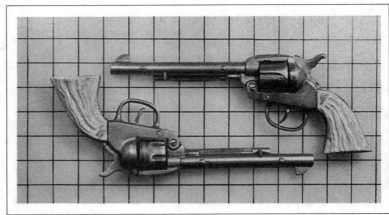

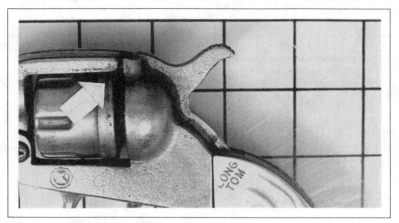

Roy Rogers

Kilgore- Detail of the Long Tom variety showing short top strap, two piece steel cylinder, Long Tom grips and etched side plate. Etching is barely visible.

RR-5

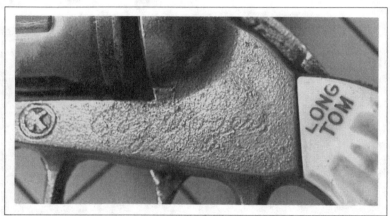

Roy Rogers

Kilgore- Detail of the etched side plate, under the cylinder of the Long Tom. The early Kilgore catalogs depict the name and location. It can be found on either side of the gun.

RR-6

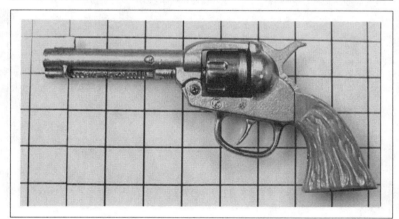

Roy Rogers - Big Horn

Kilgore- 1938-45 era. Very rare Big Horn models by Kilgore can also be found with Roy Rogers lightly etched on either side of the gun' s frame. This example has unusual, cherry red stag grips.

Value: $850-1,300

RR-7

Roy Rogers

Kilgore- Detail of the etched side plate on the Big Horn shown above in RR-7. The etched varieties are very light and almost invisible. Look very closely with a good magnifying glass.

RR-8

Roy Rogers

Leslie-Henry- 1950 era. First model with extra heavy frame and very simple scroll engraving on the barrel. Low hammer in nickel with white horsehead grips.

Value: $150-285

RR-9

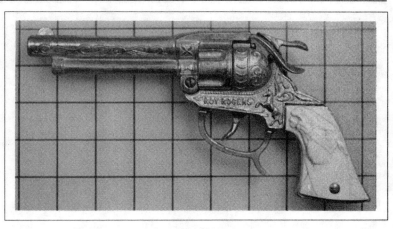

Roy Rogers

Leslie-Henry- 1950-60 era. *Top:* 1st model with high hammer in polished nickel. *Lower:* 2nd Model in rarer, gold finish and black grips. This is also the smoker model with tiny holes in the cap anvil.

Value: $150-250 $175-375 (Gold)

RR-10

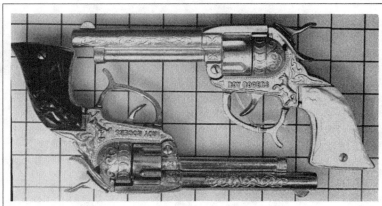

Roy Rogers

Leslie-Henry- 1950-60 era. *Left:* 2nd model in dull nickel. *Middle:* 1st model in nickel with low hammer. *Right:* Very rare, nickel 2nd model, with the dummy hammer.

Value: $150-275 $200-350 (Dummy)

RR-11

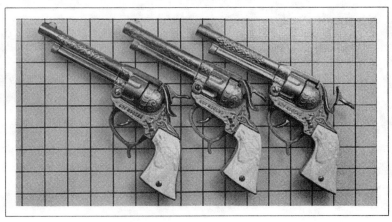

Roy Rogers

Buzz Henry- 1950-60 era. In dull finish nickel with white inset grips.

Value: $85-150

RR-12

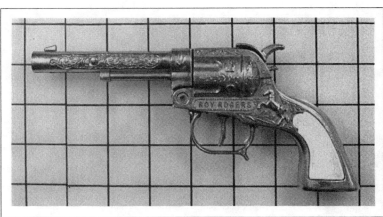

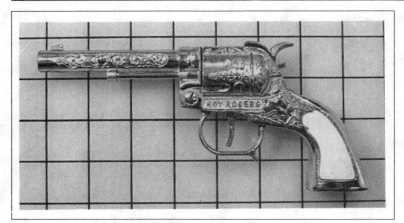

Roy Rogers

Buzz Henry- 1950-60 era. Polished and chrome plated with light blue inset grips.

Value: $85-150

RR-13

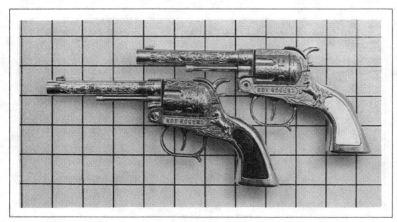

Roy Rogers

Buzz Henry- 1950-60 era. *Top:* Regular nickel finish with white inset grips. *Lower:* Rare gold finish with black inset grips.

Value: $85-150 $100-175 (Gold)

RR-14

Roy Rogers

Buzz Henry- 1950-60 era. Very unusual, and perhaps, one-of-a-kind with nickel finish and red inset grips. The right side is stamped Roy Rogers and the left side Dale Evans! See left side below.

Value: $100-175

RR-15

Roy Rogers

Buzz Henry- 1950-60 era. Left side of above gun showing the Dale Evans stamping.

(* A few 9 inch Leslie-Henry guns exist with a combination of Gene Autry/ Champion or Annie Oakley/Gene Autry.)

RR-16

Roy Rogers

Kilgore- 1955 era. 8" nickel die cast with short ejector rod and white-purple swirl horsehead grips.

Value: $100-175

RR-17

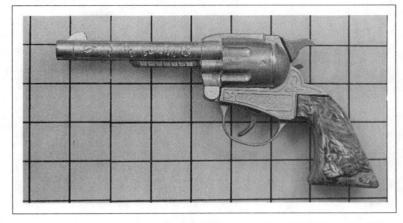

Roy Rogers

Kilgore- 1955 era. 9" nickel die cast with long ejector rod and tan-chocolate swirl horsehead grips.

Value: $100-175

RR-18

Roy Rogers

Kilgore- 1955-60 era. Rare, large nickel finish, with six shot revolving cylinder, white grips and engraving. Seldom seen gun. I have never seen a gold plated one.

Value: $175-350

RR-19

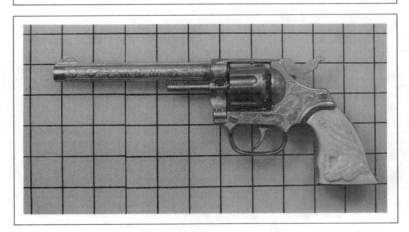

Roy Rogers

Classy- 1955-60 era. Model R-90, die cast in nickel finish, rearing horse metal grips and no engraving. 9 inch length.

Value: $100-175

RR-20

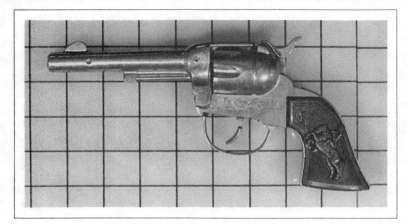

Roy Rogers

Classy- 1955-60 era. Model R-90 die cast in gold finish with dark bronze grips. 9"

Value: $175-300 (Gold)

RR-21

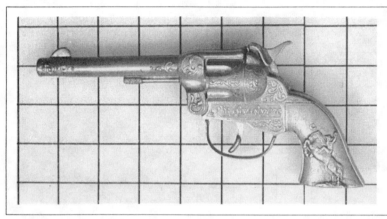

Roy Rogers

Classy- 1955-60 era. Model R-60 die cast nickel with engraving. Metal rearing horse grips. 8" length.

Value: $150-275

RR-22

Roy Rogers

Classy- 1955-60 era. Model R-60 die cast in rarer gold finish with engraving and rearing horse gold grips.

Value:$200-300

RR-23

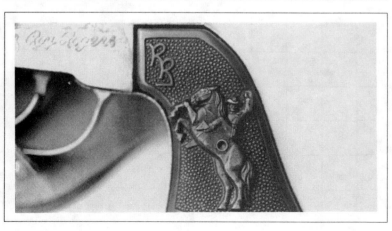

Roy Rogers

Classy- 1955-60 era. Detail - Model R-90 gold die cast with bronze grips - RR-21. Some grips have horse and rider hand-painted in color which adds $10 value.

RR-24

Roy Rogers

Classy- 1955-60 era. Detail of Model R-60 nickel die cast with engraving. RR-22.

RR-25

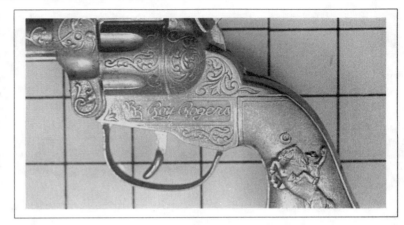

Roy Rogers

Classy- 1955-60 era. Large die cast in nickel finish. *Top:* Has gold finished scroll grips. *Lower:* Has pewter gray finished scroll grips.

Value: $150-325

RR-26

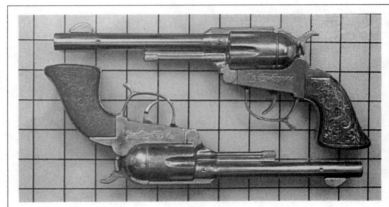

Roy Rogers

Classy- 1955-60 era. Rare variation has nickel frame, gold barrel and cylinder and gold scroll grips. Research indicates this gun was a prize for a cereal contest.

Value: $200-375

RR-27

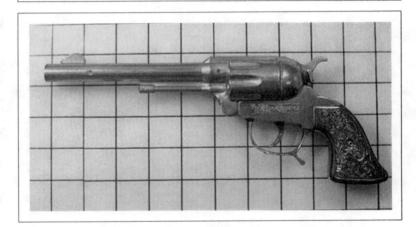

Roy Rogers

Classy- 1955-60 era. Very rare matching pair of completely gold plated guns with gold stag grips. They were prizes awarded by Quaker Oats in the mid 1950s.

Value: $400-700 (Each)

RR-28

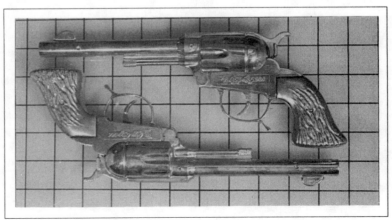

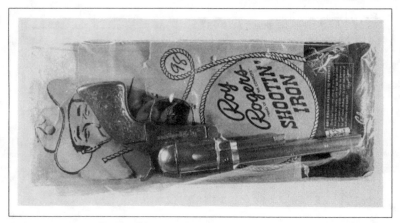

Roy Rogers

Classy- 1955-60 era. Nickel die cast with gold scroll grips still mounted on the original card for only $.98!

Value: $450 (Mint on card)

RR-29

Roy Rogers

Classy- 1955-60 era. Detail of gold scroll grips on RR-27.

RR-30

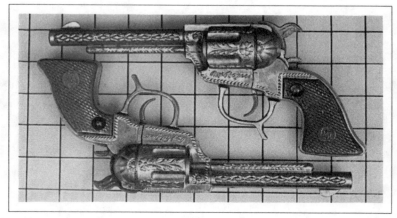

Roy Rogers

G. Schmidt- 1950 era. Pair of early and very rare guns. Nickel finish, with short barrels, engraving and checkered copper RR grips with jewels. Jewels came in red, yellow, blue and green.

Value: $250-425 (Each)

RR-31

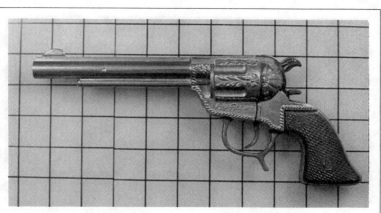

Roy Rogers

G. Schmidt- 1950-60 era. Rare die cast in nickel with long ribbed barrel and fully engraved frame. Checkered copper grips with RR & Trigger. Also with red jewels.

Value: $150-300   - $165-325 (Jewels)

RR-32

Roy Rogers

G. Schmidt- 1950-60 era. Pair of highly polished and chrome plated guns. *Top:* Gun has checkered copper grips with RR & Trigger. *Lower:* Gun has copper stag grips with RR.

Value: $150-245

RR-33

Roy Rogers

G. Schmidt- 1950-60 era. Nearly identical pair of chrome guns. *Top:* Very rare gun with Roy Rogers name incised on the frame. *Lower:* Normal raised name on frame. Guns have copper RR stag grips.

Value: $165-250 (Incised name)

RR-34

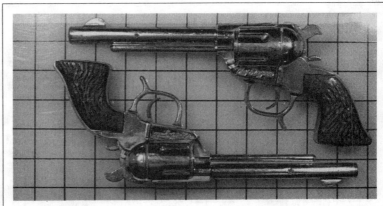

Roy Rogers

G. Schmidt- 1950-60 era. Detail of RR-34 above showing the rare incised name on the frame and RR on the copper stag.

RR-35

Roy Rogers

G. Schmidt- 1950-60 era. Original green and brown box for a Roy Rogers Shoot'n Iron. Gun is the rarer long ribbed barrel with engraved frame in nickel finish.

Value: $85-150 (Box only)

RR-36

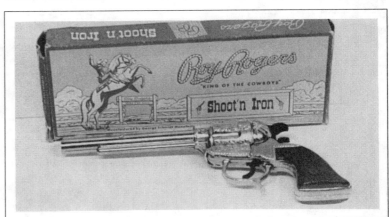

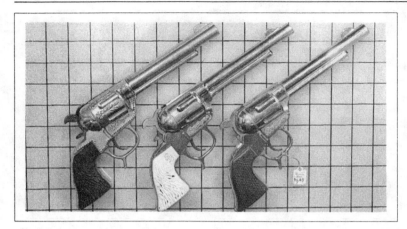

Roy Rogers

G. Schmidt- 1950-60. *Left:* Long ribbed barrel, with engraving and RR stag grips. *Center:* Chrome long barrel, no engraving white RR stag grips. *Right:* Chrome long barrel, no engraving with checkered RR & Trigger grips. Note- $1.49 price tag!

Value: $135-250 (Each)

RR-37

Roy Rogers

G. Schmidt- 1950-60 era. Small frame 9", very rare, nickel die cast. *Top:* Dale Evans with copper DE Butterfly grip. *Lower:* Roy Rogers with RR stag copper grips. Seldom seen.

Value: $175-250

RR-38

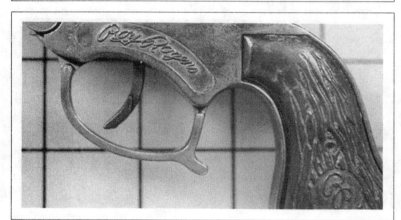

Roy Rogers

G. Schmidt- 1950-60 era. Detail of the small frame lettering and grip shown in the RR-38, Roy photo above.

RR-39

Roy Rogers

Lone Star, Eng.- 1955 era. Very rare, 10", nickel, die cast, fully engraved gun with superb Indian Chief grips. Came in some Classy holsters sold by catalogs in the mid 1950s. (Similar to Hubley Cowboys.)

Value: $200-450

RR-40

Roy Rogers

Lone Star, Eng.- 1955 era. Pair of extremely rare gold plated die cast guns. Came in many mid 1950s holster sets. Fully engraved with ivory white Indian Chief grips.
Value: $265-500 (Each)

RR-41

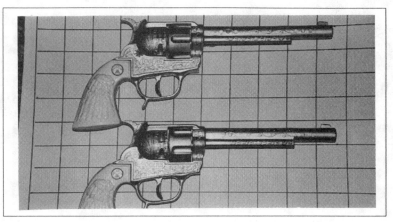

Roy Rogers

Lone Star, Eng.- 1955 era. Detail of RR-41 above, showing the revolving cylinder that accepts small brass and lead bullets.

Value: $15 (Each bullet - Rare)

RR-42

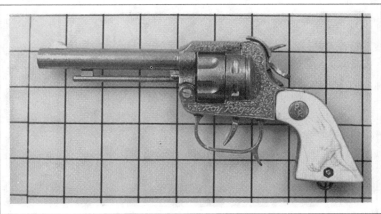

Roy Rogers

Balantyne Mfg. Co. Chicago- 1950. Rare pressed steel .45 with revolving cylinder. This polished gun has white grips with Roy & Trigger. plus name. Unusual toy.

Value: $200-400

RR-43

Roy Rogers

Lone Star, Eng.- 1950-55 era. Nickel 9", Roy Rogers Round-Up. Engraved with RR medallion and steerhead white grips with lanyard ring. Extremely rare gun.

Value: $250-450

RR-44

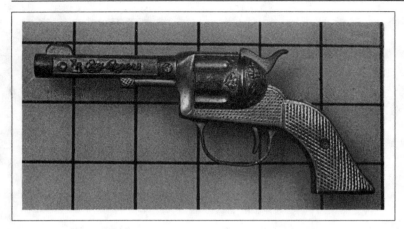

Roy Rogers

Classy- 1959-60. Model R-30 all metal die cast, 5 1/2" Pee Wee, single shot in the iridite finish. Seldom seen little gun. Roy on barrel. Engraved.

Value:$ 45 -125

RR-45

Roy Rogers

Classy- 1955-60 era. Model R-50 all metal die cast, 8" single shot, fully engraved in the iridite finish with RR stag grips. Very rare lttle gun.

Value: $75-150

RR-46

Roy Rogers

Classy- 1955-60 era. Model R-20 all metal die cast is fully engraved with RR on the checkered grips. This tiny single shot has a spur trigger and is quite rare. Also can be found in the rarer, bronze or gold.

Value: $45-100 - $55-125 (Bronze-Gold)

RR-47

Roy Rogers

Classy- 1959-60 era. Very small die cast, Tuck-A-Way on the original card. Single shot in nickel finish with engraving. A rare little gun. Note the price of $.29.

Value: $45-100 (Gun & card)

RR-48

Roy Rogers

Classy- 1959-60 era *.Left:* Model C-31 on a Tuck-A-Way card. Small die cast with engraving. Rare gun. Note price $.39. *Right:* Model R-20 spur trigger in a mini tan leather holster with embossed RR.

Value: $45-100 (Either set)

RR-49

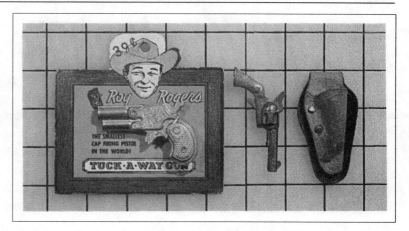

Roy Rogers

Classy- 1959-60. Model R-30 Pee Wee in a very rare mini fringed holster with Roy embossed on the front. Tan and red.

Value: $ 65-100 (Gun & holster)

RR-50

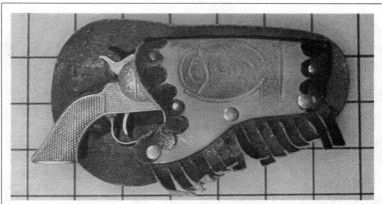

Roy Rogers-Trigger

Stevens- 1950-60 era. Unusual die cast in a dull finish with engraving. The white grips have checkering and a horse. The only known gun with "Trigger" on it. A variety with a nickel finish does exist.

Value: $65-100

RR-51

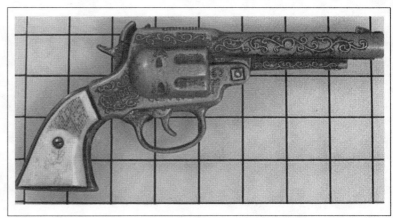

Roy Rogers - Box

Buzz Henry- 1950-55 era. Very rare gold foil presentation box for a gold Roy with white inset grips. Interior dark blue. Two piece box.

Value: $75-150 (Box only)

RR-52

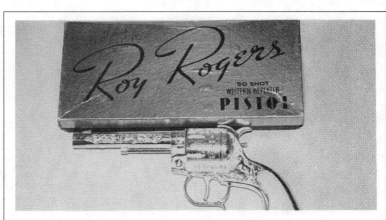

Roy Rogers - Box

Kilgore- 1938-40 era. Very rare box for the cast iron Roy. Red, white and blue box with dark blue interior. Two piece box.

Value: $300-500 (Box only)

RR-53

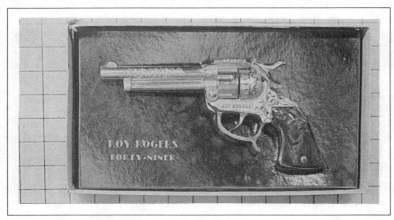

Roy Rogers - Box

Leslie-Henry- 1950-55 era. Rare box for a gold Forty Niner 9". Two piece box in dark blue and yellow with red interior.

Value: $100-175

RR-54

Roy Rogers - Box

Leslie-Henry- 1950-55 era. Detail of box interior of RR-54 above showing gold gun.

RR-55

Roy Rogers - 49er Set

Leslie-Henry- 1950-55 era. Two piece box in dark blue and gold with red interior. It includes 9" gold gun and set of spurs with white straps, red jewels and studs.

Value: $700-1,000 (Complete set)

RR-56

Roy Rogers - 49er Set

Leslie-Henry- 1950-55 era. This boxed set is nearly identical to RR-56. The leather spur straps contain silver and gold steerhead conchos and the box lid says "puffs smoke". Gold gun is a smoker variety. Value: $700-1,000 (Complete set)

RR-57

Roy Rogers - Box

Classy- 1955-60 era. Full color, two piece box for a single holster set. Beautiful artwork. Rarely seen in this size.

Value: $100-225

RR-58

Roy Rogers - Box

Daisy Mfg. Co. Ltd. of Canada- 1960 era. Very unusual one piece display-type box in brown and yellow. Includes a Kilgore D.C. gun and holster with turquoise jewels and studs. From Preston, Ontario.

Value: $200-400 (Complete set)

RR-59

Roy Rogers - Boxed Set

Classy- 1955-60 era. Full color two piece box. Russet & Tan leather holsters. Silver conchos and unusual Roy buckle. Pair of Classy guns in nickel with gold grips.

Value: $850-1,500 (Complete Set)

RR-60

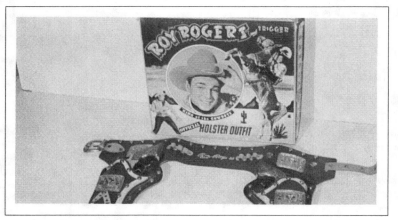

Roy Rogers - Boxed Set

Classy- 1955-60 era. Full color, two piece box with a superb holster set. Brown, tan and white leather with cut outs and four large silver conchos with Roy's bust. Pair of Classy guns with gold scroll grips are in the holsters.

Value: $850-1,500 (Complete set)
RR-61

Roy Rogers - Boxed Set

Classy- 1955-69 era. Nearly identical to RR-61 above except holsters are brown and black tooled leather with numerous RR studs and large Roy buckle. Guns are chromed G. Schmidt's, with copper stag.

Value: $850-1,500 (Complete set)

RR-62

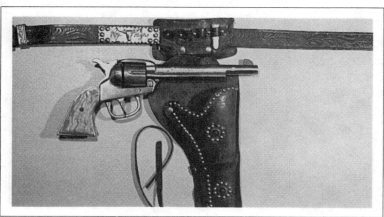

Roy Rogers - Boxed Set

Classy- 1955-60 era. Full color box with smaller two-tone leather holsters with 9" smaller gold Classy guns. Limited decorations on the simple holster set.

Value: $750-1,200 (Complete set)

RR-63

Roy Rogers Holster

Keyston Bros.- 1940 era. Rare, extra long holster for the cast iron Kilgore Roy gun. Roy's name is on the gun belt. Red jewels and silver studs on brown leather.

Value: $200-300 (Holster only)

RR-64

Roy Rogers

Frontiers, Inc.- 1959-60 era. Small folder included with each Classy, Roy Rogers "Flash-Draw" holster sets as shown below in RR-66. Explains how to use the Flash-Draw holsters.

RR-65

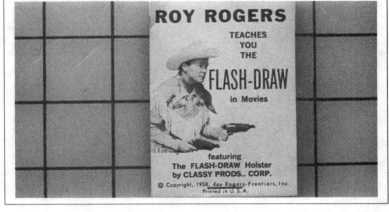

Roy Rogers Holsters

Classy- 1959-60 era. Very rare double set of Flash-Draw holsters with a pair of Classy gold guns with gold stag grips. Black leather with gold decoration and lettering. Classy model-2998 Retail $7.98.

Value:$1,200-2,000 (Complete set)

RR-66

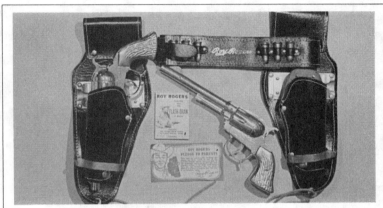

Roy Rogers Holster

Unknown- 1940-50 era. High quality tan leather holster for the long barrel cast iron. Holster and belt have numerous silver studs, red jewels, cut outs and four piece belt.

Value: $100-175 (Holster only)

RR-67

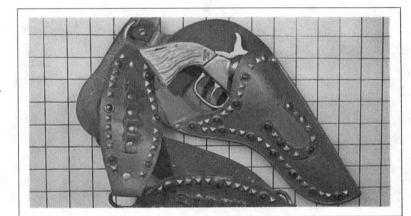

Roy Rogers Holster

Unknown- 1940 era. Very rare, early tan leather holster for the Roy long barrel cast iron. Gun was found in this holster. Belt has 12 bullets and Roy's name.

Value: $175-300 (Holster only)

RR-68

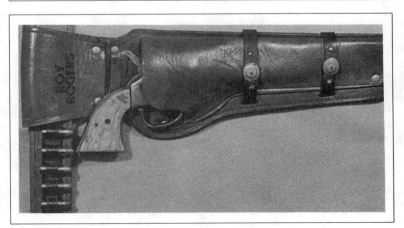

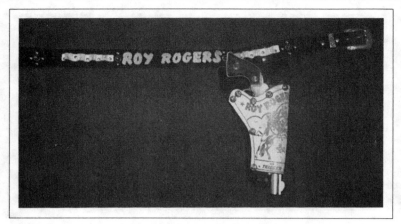

Roy Rogers Holster

Perhaps, Leslie-Henry- Early 1950s. This early holster is black and white with Roy and Trigger on the front. Red jewels and containing a G. Schmidt with checkered copper, RR and Trigger grips.

Value: $125-200 (Holster set only)

RR-69

Roy Rogers Holster

Classy- Early 1950s. Early black leather holster with white cut-outs, gold studs and gold embossed RR. Matching belt has Classy stamping. Small, rare set. Had very rare small Schmidt with jewels in it.

Value: $125-200 (Holster set only)

RR-70

Roy Rogers Holster

Unknown- 1950 era. Large, dark brown tooled leather holster with silver studs and metal letters on the belt. Laced edge. Unusual, early set.

Value: $135-225

RR-71

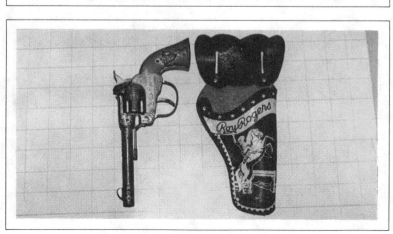

Roy Rogers Holster

Unknown- 1950-55 era. Very simple, blue and white leather holster possibly intended for a cowgirl. Artwork printed on front of holster. Classy R-60 gun.

Value: $65-100 (Holster only)

RR-72

Roy Rogers Holster

Classy- 1959-60. Rare, black leather set with simple RR logo on top. Seldom seen holster that came with Lone Star Apache guns. Classy Model-906 Retail $4.98. Was also available as a double- Model-2906.

Value: $100-165 (Holster only)

RR-73

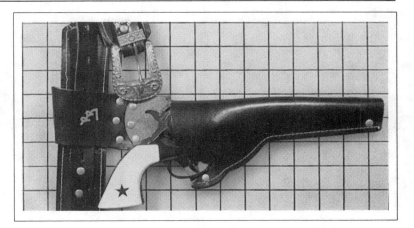

Roy Rogers Holster

Unknown- 1955-60 era. Small white and tan leather, left-handed set. Large RR conchos and silver studs. Roy & Trigger embossed on holster front. L-H gold gun.

Value: $150-225 (Holster only)

RR-74

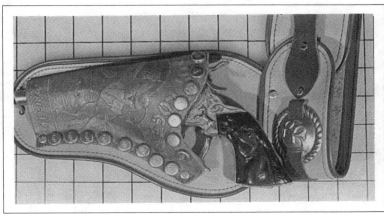

Roy Rogers

Unknown- Detail of the holster shown above, RR-74. Note the RR on each silver stud and the high quality embossed art on the holster.

RR-75

Roy Rogers Holster

Keyston Brothers- 1950 era. Very rare, tan leather holster for the rare small frame George Schmidt guns. Roy's name is embossed on the keeper strap. RR also on the small metal snap. Unusual holster.

Value: $85-150 (Holster only)

RR-76

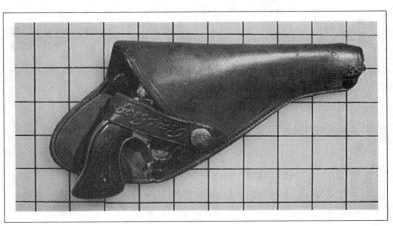

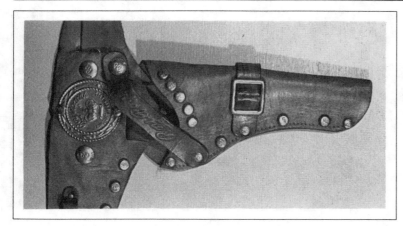

Roy Rogers Holster

Unknown- 1950 era. Rare tan leather holster for a long Schmidt gun. Has many RR silver studs, keeper strap and large "King of the Cowboys" concho!

Value: $150-300 (Holster and belt)

RR-77

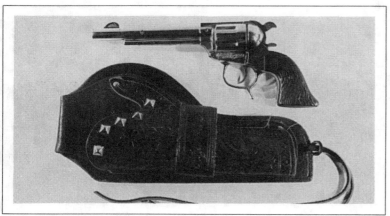

Roy Rogers Holster

Unknown- 1950 era. Unusual dark brown leather holster with silver studs and Roy's name embossed on the cross strap. Left-handed, loop style has Schmidt gun.

Value: $85-150 (Holster only)

RR-78

Roy Rogers Holster

Unknown- 1955-60 era. Tan leather, left-handed holster with silver studs, red jewels and Roy artwork embossed on front. Set originally had Kilgore DC guns not a cast iron variety.

Value: $135-200

RR-79

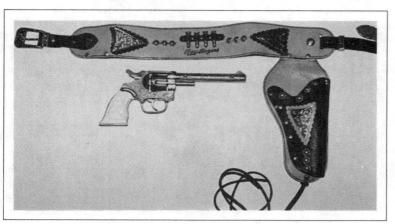

Roy Rogers Holster

Possibly, Halco- 1950-55 era. Large, black and tan set with RR triangle conchos and silver studs. Gun is the rare revolving cylinder Kilgore die cast.

Value: $150-250

RR-80

Roy Rogers Holster

Classy- 1959-60 era. Unusual buckskin leather gun-slinger set with silver steer-head conchos, studs and bullets. Schmidt gun. Classy Model-928 Retail $3.98. Rare. Also came as a double set, Model-2928.

Value: $150-235 (Holster only)

RR-81

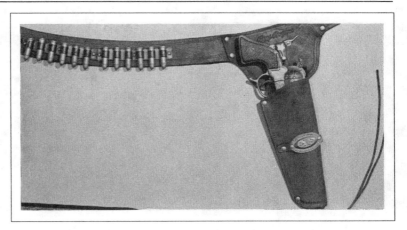

Roy Rogers Holster

Unknown- 1950 era. Early, simple holster in red leather with white artwork of Roy & Trigger.

Value: $85-150

RR-82

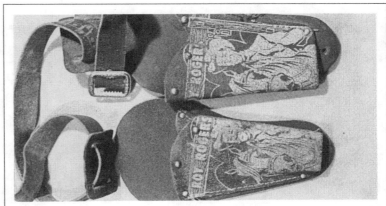

Roy Rogers Holster

Unknown- 1950 era. Early, simple holster in blue and white leather with white art-work of Roy on a rearing Trigger. Guns are Kilgore Bucks.

Value: $85-150 (Holster only)

RR-83

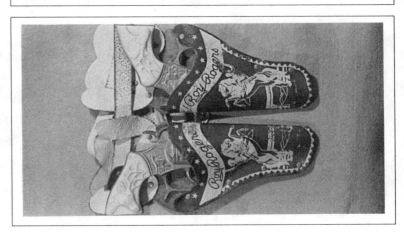

Roy Rogers Holster

Classy- 1959-60. Tan and black tooled leather with white fringe. RR on holster, studs and red jewels. Model-2925-$4.98. Kilgore die cast guns.

Value: $200-300 (Holster only)

RR-84

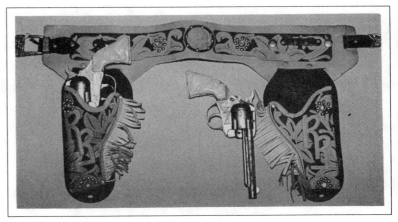

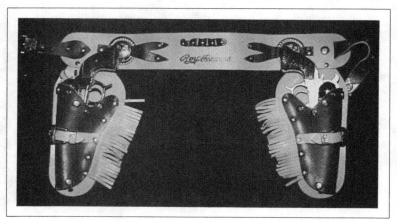

Roy Rogers Holster

Unknown- 1955-60 era. Burgundy & tan leather holster with fringe, RR studs and large RR silver conchos. Schmidt guns.

Value: $150-250 (Holsters only)

RR-85

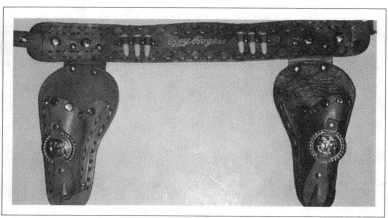

Roy Rogers Holster

Unknown- 1950-55 era. Dark brown tooled leather with large silver and gold RR conchos. Laced edges of holster and belt. RR studs.

Vale: $200-325

RR-86

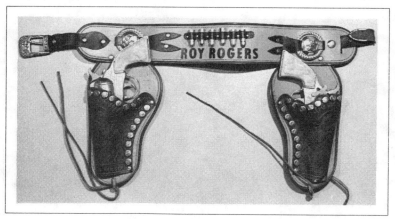

Roy Rogers Holster

Unknown- 1955-60 era. Brown and tan leather with Roy & Trigger embossed on the front. Large RR silver conchos and studs. Kilgore die cast guns.

Value: $150-250 (Holsters only)

RR-87

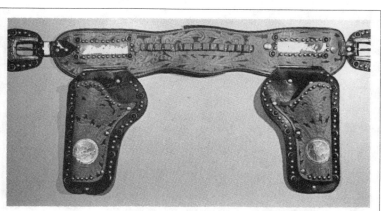

Roy Rogers Holster

*Classy Prod.-*1960 era. Superb, large set in tan and russet, tooled leather with rare metallic silver foil decoration. Has silver studs and two large buckles.

Value: $275-500

RR-88

Roy Rogers Holster

Halco- 1950-55 era. Large tan leather set with numerous RR silver studs and Roy's bust embossed on holsters and belt. Large silver buckel. Guns are cast iron by Kilgore.

Value: $200-375 (Holsters only)

RR-89

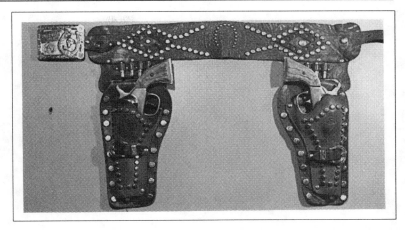

Roy Rogers Holster

Unknown- 1955-60 era. Tan and white tooled leather with tan fringe, orange jewels and silver studs. Probably a cowgirl set. Pair of rare Schmidt short barrels with green jewels.

Value: $165-275 (Holsters only)

RR-90

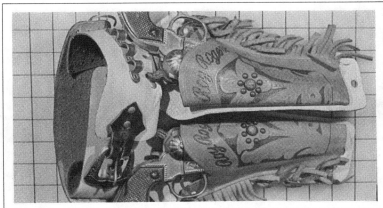

Roy Rogers Holster

Unknown- 1960 era. Black and tan tooled leather with the rare, flower-type silver studs. RR silver buckles. Unusual set.

Value: $175-300

RR-91

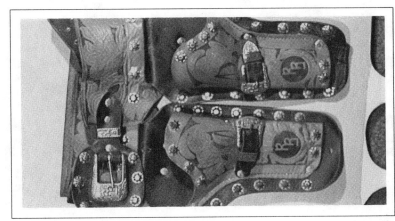

Roy Rogers Holster

Unknown- 1955-60 era. Similar to RR-87, but has light tan tooled leather with minimal silver RR studs and conchos.

Value: $135-225

RR-92

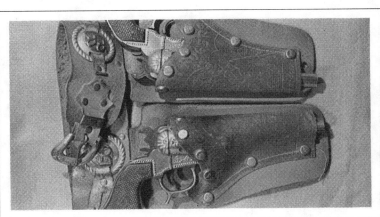

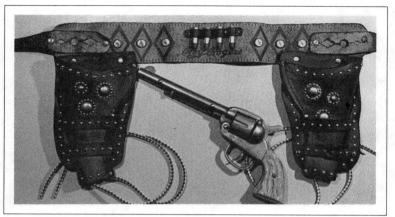

Roy Rogers Holster

Unknown- 1960 era. Very large, tan and red brown set with numerous small and large silver studs. Some RR studs. Shown with a cast iron Kilgore.

Value: $175-300 (Holsters only)

RR-93

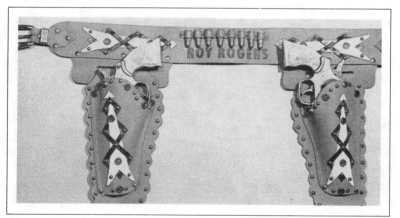

Roy Rogers Holster

Unknown- 1945-50 era. Large, early set in black leather with gold studs & metallic 3-D lettering. Unusual and rare set. Guns are Hubley die cast Cowboys.

Value: $200-350 (Holsters only)

RR-94

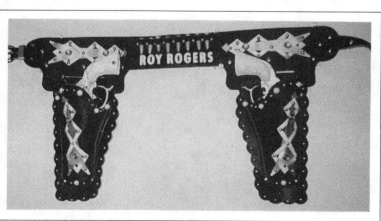

Roy Rogers Holster

Leslie-Henry- 1955 era. Unusual set in tan leather with black and white arrow cut-outs. Silver studs with red and yellow jewels. Seldom seen decorations. Kilgore die cast guns.

Value: $175-300 (Holsters only)

RR-95

Roy Rogers Holster

Leslie-Henry- 1955 era. Similar to RR-95, but in black leather with white & metallic silver arrow cut-outs. Red jewels and silver studs. Unusual set. L-H 9" guns.

Value: $200-350 (Holsters only)

RR-96

Roy Rogers Holster

Halco- 1950-55 era. Similar to RR-89, but in tan and black leather with additional RR silver studs and conchos. Guns are George Schmidt. Large rare set.

Value: $200-375 (Holsters only)

RR-97

Roy Rogers Holster

Unknown- 1950-55 era. Unusual russet and tan leather set with horsehead and border edging cut-outs. Red jewels with silver RR studs. Triangle silver conchos. Guns are 9" Leslie-Henry.

Value: $175-300 (Holster only)

RR-98

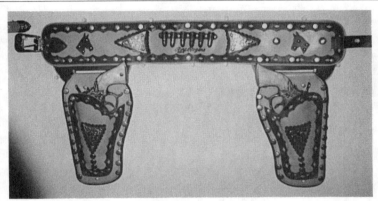

Roy Rogers Holster

Unknown- 1955 era. Tan and brown tooled leather set with RR silver studs. RR embossed on holsters. Kilgore die cast guns.

Value: $ 175-300 (Holsters only)

RR-99

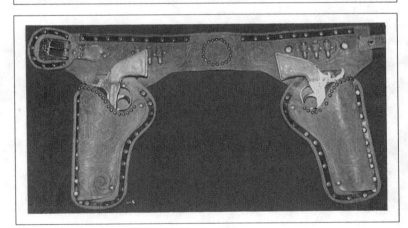

Roy Rogers Holster

Unknown- 1960 era. Very rare, white and metallic silver leather set with gold RR triangle conchos, studs and buckles. Red jewels. Intended for a cowgirl. Kilgore die cast guns. Beautiful holsters.

Value: $250-400 (Holsters only)

RR-100

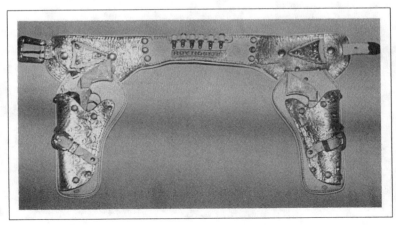

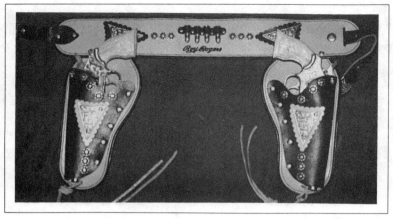

Roy Rogers Holster

Unknown- 1960 era. Tan and black leather with flower-type studs and silver triangle RR conchos. Rare Kilgore die cast guns with revolving cylinders.

Value: $ 175-300 (Holsters only)

RR-101

Roy Rogers Holster

Unknown- 1955-60 era. Very large, light tan leather set with rare, Roy bust silver conchos with turquoise jewels. Fancy silver buckle with red jewels. Silver studs. A seldom seen variety. Schmidt guns.

Value: $ 265-500 (Holsters only)

RR-102

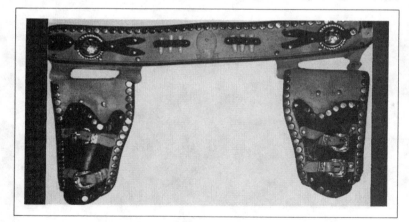

Roy Rogers Holster

Unknown- 1955-60 era. Black and tan leather with large silver RR conchos and RR studs. Double RR holster buckles. Roy embossed on gun belt.

Value: $150-265

RR-103

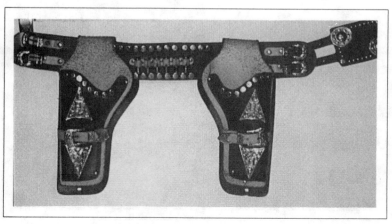

Roy Rogers Holster

Unknown- 1955-60 era. Unusual, large set in black and light gray leather. Loop-style with silver RR triangle conchos, RR studs and buckles. Unusual large buckle.

Value: $250-375

RR-104

Roy Rogers Holster

Classy P.- 1960 era. Large, and extremely fancy, tan and dark brown leather set, completely tooled with numerous silver studs, RR buckles and red jewels. Rare set with Classy guns having gold grips.

Value: $300-450

RR-105

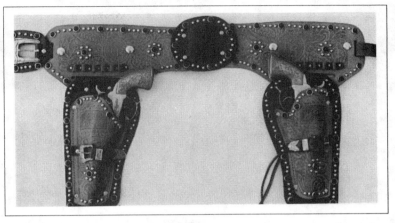

Roy Rogers Holster

Unknown- 1955 era. Very desirable tooled tan leather set similar to real set actually worn by Roy. Silver studs and RR buckles. Unusual, large gun belt buckle. Guns are chromed G. Schmidts with stag grips.

Value: $185-325 (Holsters only)

RR-106

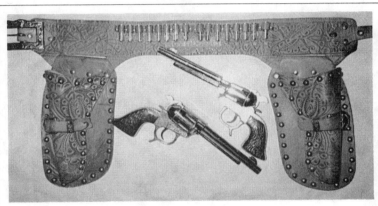

Roy Rogers Holster

Unknown- 1955 era. Similar to RR-106, but has tooled black and tan leather with numerous RR silver studs and buckles. Has the large Roy buckle with horseshoe. Guns are Classy with gold scroll grips.

Value: $200-375 (Holsters only)

RR-107

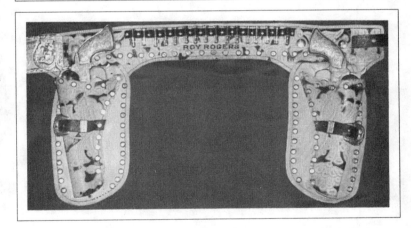

Roy Rogers Holster

Classy- 1959-60. Small and very simple tan leather set. Classy Model-2923-$2.98. Guns are die cast Hubley Rodeos. Almost no decoration. RR and name embossed. Bullets loops on the front of holster.

Value: $75-135 (Holsters only)

RR-108

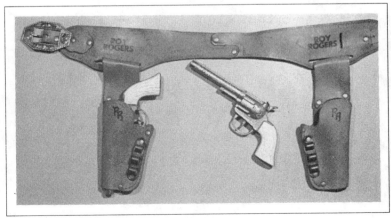

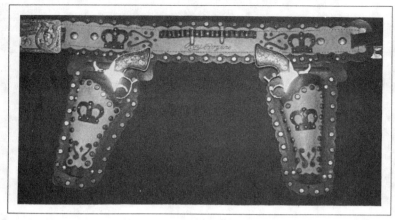

Roy Rogers Holster

Unknown- 1950-55 era. Similar detailing to RR-98. Dark brown and tan leather with border, scroll and King crown cut-outs. Numerous RR silver studs. Rare Roy in horseshoe silver buckle. Classy guns.

Value: $200-375 (Holsters only)

RR-109

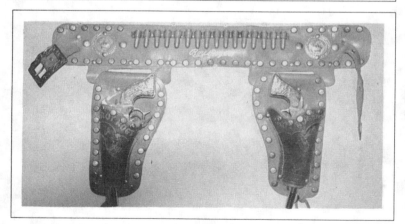

Roy Rogers Holster

Classy P.- 1955 era. Extra fancy tan and black leather with silver conchos, triangles, RR studs, cut-outs and RR buckle. Guns are G. Schmidts.

Value: $200-375 (Holsters only)

RR-110

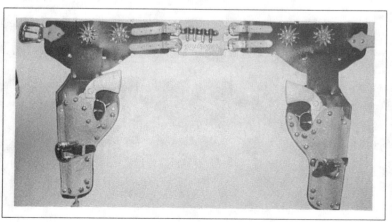

Roy Rogers Holster

Classy P.- 1955 era. Russet tan leather with numerous RR studs, large RR King conchos and Roy embossed on front. G. Schmidt guns.

Value: $175-300 (Holsters only)

RR-111

Roy Rogers Holster

Unknown- 1960 era. Similar detailing to RR-91 with tan and russet tooled leather. Unusual starburst silver conchos, flower studs and 3 piece gun belt with 5 buckles. Very rare Lone Star gold guns.

Value: $175-300 (Holsters only)

RR-112

Roy Rogers Holster

Unknown- 1955 era. Large tan and brown tooled leather loop holsters. Silver studs. Roy embossed on belt and cross straps. Rare Lone Star nickel guns.

Value: $165-275 (Holsters only)

RR-113

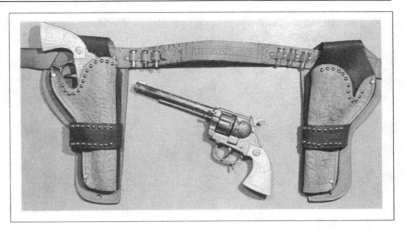

Roy Rogers Holster

Classy P.- 1955 era. Similar detailing to RR-110 Tan set with black holsters. Silver RR triangle & round conchos. RR studs. Embossed bust on center of belt. Horse & Roy buckle. Kilgore die cast guns.

Value: $200-375 (Holsters only)

RR-114

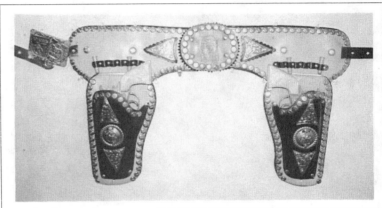

Roy Rogers Holster

Unknown- 1955-60 era. Black and white tooled leather with similar details to RR-103. Gold studs, RR buckles and RR conchos. G. Schmidt guns.

Value: $150-265 (Holsters only)

RR-115

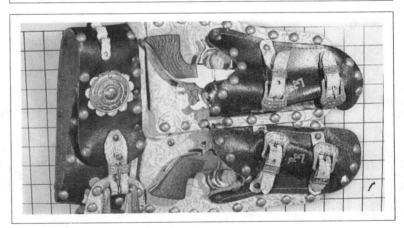

Roy Rogers Holster

Unknown- 1955-60 era. Similar to RR-115. Light tan and russet with silver RR studs and triangle conchos. RR buckles. Guns are G, Schmidts.

Value: $150-265 (Holsters only)

RR-116

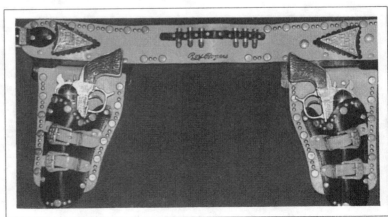

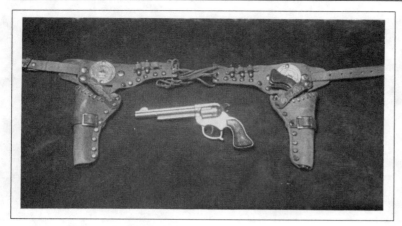

Roy Rogers Holsters

Keyston Bros.- 1950-55 era. Rare, small, tan leather set with silver RR studs and King of the Cowboy conchos. Roy on the keeper straps. 2 piece belt. Made for the rare, small frame G. Schmidts. See RR-76.

Value: $150-235 (Holsters only)

RR-117

Roy Rogers Holster

Keyston Bros.- 1950-55 era. Detail of the small holster above, RR-117, showing the silver concho, RR studs and name on the gun keeper strap.

RR-118

Roy Rogers Holster

Unknown- 1955 era. Tan and black tooled leather with silver flower studs. RR buckles. RR embossed on belt. 16 bullet loops! Large holsters. Note large belt buckle.

Value: $175-275

RR-119

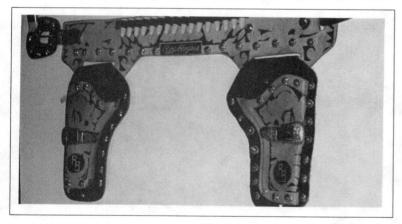

Roy Rogers Holster

Unknown- 1955 era. Large tan and black, tooled holster with red and orange jewels, silver studs and buckles. Name on belt. Note the unusual diagonal holster straps. Kilgore die cast guns.

Value: $175-300 (Holsters only)

RR-120

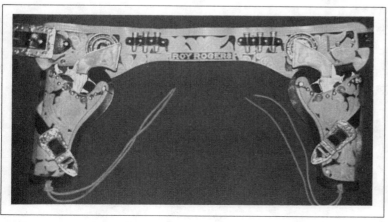

Roy Rogers Holster

Unknown- 1955-60 era. Large set in tan and russet tooled leather with flower studs and RR conchos. Embossed Roy bust on belt. Chrome Schmidt guns.

Value: $200-325 (Holsters only)

RR-121

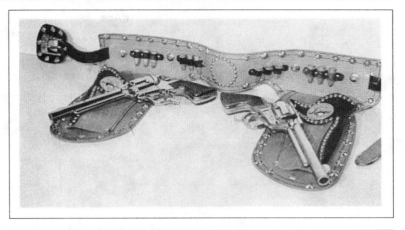

Roy Rogers Holster

Classy P.- 1960 era. Extremely fancy set similar in details to RR-105. Black leather with tooling and silver metallic foil covering. Red jewels and silver studs. Silver buckles. Classy guns with pewter grips.

Value: $325-500 (Holsters only)

RR-122

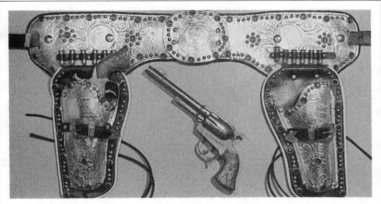

Roy Rogers Holster

Classy P.- 1960 era. Extremely fancy set similar to RR-122 above. Black leather with tooling and gold metallic foil covering. Red jewels and gold studs. Gold buckles. Classy guns with gold grips.

Value: $325-500 (Holsters only)

RR-123

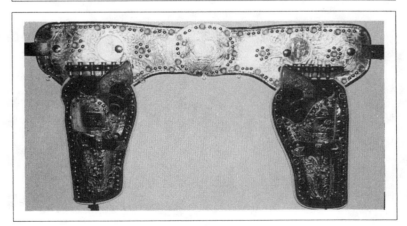

Roy Rogers Holster

Unknown- 1955-60 era. Similar to RR-116 in tan and dark brown. Numerous silver studs, red jewels and large conchos. RR buckles, name on belt, with diamond cut-outs. G. Schmidt nickel guns.

Value: $150-265 (Holsters only)

RR-124

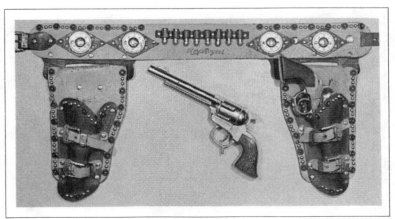

Dale Evans

G. Schmidt: 1950-55 era. Very rare, long, ribbed barrel with engraved frame and checkered copper grips with red jewel and DE butterfly. Very rare original box. All cowgirl toy guns are seldom seen.

Value: $250-450 Gun   Box- $200-400

DE-1

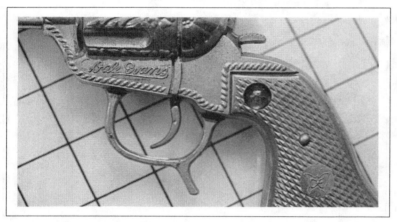

Dale Evans

G. Schmidt- 1950-55 era. Close-up detail of gun shown above - DE-1. Note the name, jewel, engraving and DE within the butterfly on the grips. Gun is in the polished nickel finish with copper grips.

DE-2

Dale Evans

G. Schmidt- 1950-55 era. Same gun as DE-1 except in the unusual dark gray finish rather than polished nickel. Seldom seen variety.

Value: $250-450

DE-3

Dale Evans

Buzz Henry- 1950-55 era. Engraved in the dull finish nickel with pale green inset grips. A rare cowgirl toy gun.

Value: $200-350

DE-4

Dale Evans

Buzz Henry- 1950-55 era. Same as DE-4 except in the polished nickel finish. Rare cowgirl toy gun. This gun has pale red inset grips.

Value: $200-350

DE-5

Dale Evans

Buzz Henry- 1950-55 era. Same as DE-4 except in the very rare gold finish with black grips. Seldom seen variety.

Value: $250-400

DE-6

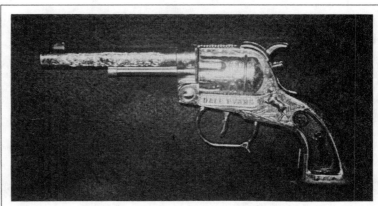

Dale Evans

G. Schmidt- 1950-55 era.The very rare small frame Schmidt with Dale Evans name and copper grips with DE butterfly. One of the rarest cowgirl guns. Nickel.

Value: $250-425

DE-7

Dale Evans

G. Schmidt- 1950-55 era. Close-up detail of gun above - DE-7. Note the name and copper stag grips with DE within the butterfly.

DE-8

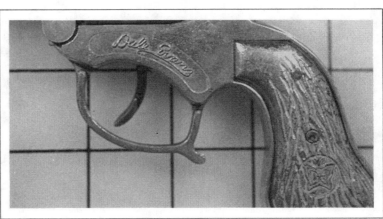

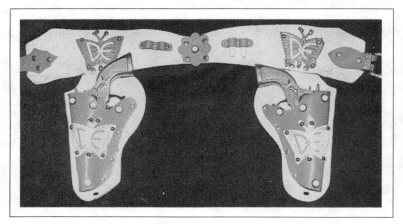

Dale Evans

Classy- 1960 era. Extremely rare double holster set in white and red leather with butterfly cut-outs and white jewels. Include pair of nickel Buzz Henry guns with red handles. Classy Model 2977.

Value: $700-1300 (Set including guns.)

DE-9

Dale Evans

Buzz Henry- 1950-55 era. Extremely rare double holster set in white and purple leather with matching wrist cuff and spurs.Red jewels and silver studs. Made for Buzz Henry pistols. Seldom seen.

Value: $350-600 (Holsters, cuffs & spurs.)

DE-10

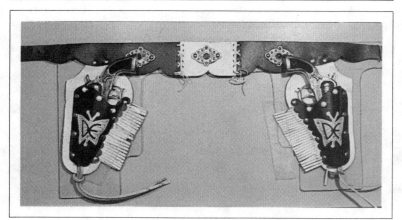

Dale Evans

Classy- 1960 era. Similar to DE-9 except in green and white leather with fringe, silver conchos and DE butterflies. Set includes nickel Buzz Henry guns with dark green grips. Rare set. Classy #2977

Value: $700-1300 (Set including guns.)

DE-11

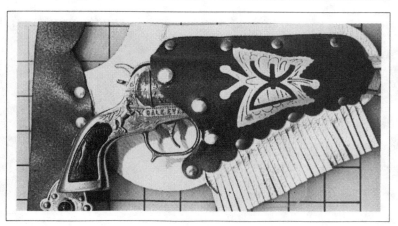

Dale Evans

*Classy-*1960 era. Close-up detail of DE-11. Note the white fringe, DE butterfly cut-out, white jewels and large silver concho with green jewel. Classy #2977 originally came with R-60 Roy Rogers 8" guns. Buzz Henry guns added by dealers.

DE-12

Dale Evans

Classy- 1960, era. Extremely rare set sold as Classy Model 2906-DE with Lone Star black finish Apache guns. Tan leather with name on belt loop. Sold primarily by mail order catalogs. Seldom seen set.

Value: $350-600 (Set with guns.)

DE-13

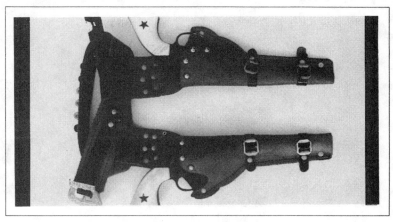

Dale Evans

Classy- 1960 era. Close-up detail of name embossed on holster loop of DE-13 set above. Also note similar holster set RR-73 in the Roy Rogers' section.

DE-14

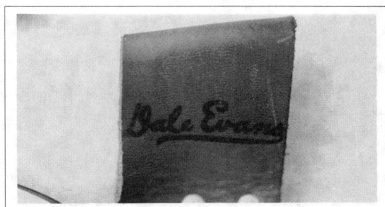

Dale Evans

Classy- 1960 era. Full color box for Dale holster set Model 2977 shown in DE-11.

Value: $200-350 (Box only)

DE-15

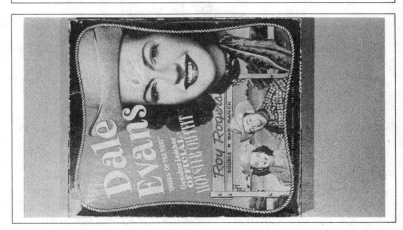

Dale Evans

Unknown- 1950-55 era. Possibly a holster box made by L-H or Halco. Rare early box in orange and dark brown. Note the wording, "Queen of the West" on box.

Value: $300-450 (Box only)

DE-16

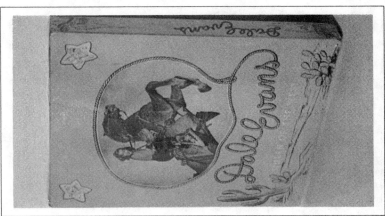

Sergeant Preston

Marx- 1947-55 era. Secondary western character. Very rare pressed steel clicker with red jewels & braided lanyard cord. Leather flap holster with gold lettering. Gold toy Mountie badge.

Value: $75-125 (Holster & gun)

SP-1

Sergeant Preston

Marx- 1947-55 era. Close-up detail of Sgt. Preston lettering and red jewel. Reverse side stamped "Yukon Mountie." Rare toy.

SP-2

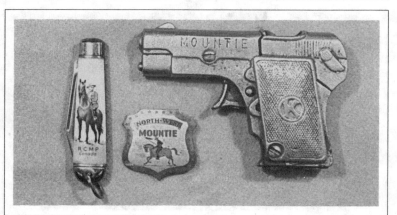

Sergeant Preston

Kilgore- 1940 era. Not western-style , but included to complete items intended for Canadian market. Unusual cast iron auto stamped Mountie. Note: R.C.M.P. knife & Northwest Mountie badge. Rare toys.

Value: $65-150 (Gun only)

SP-3

Sergeant Preston

Kilgore- 1940 era. Similar to above, cast iron "Border Patrol" auto with group of toy badges. Possible Sgt. Preston items.

Value: $55-135 (Gun only)

SP-4

Tombstone Territory

Classy Prod.- 1958 era. Rare double holster set in black & white leather with silver conchos & turquoise jewels. Box is blue & black. Generic guns are die cast Cowboy Kings by Stevens. Unusual set.

Value: $200-325 (Box, holsters & guns)

TT-1

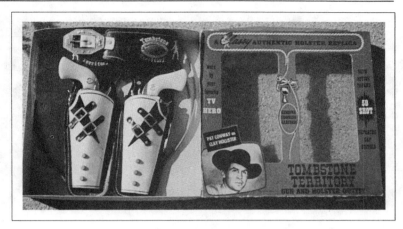

Tombstone Territory

Harvel-Kilgore Sales, Bolivar, TN.- 1958-59 era. Single holster in black and white leather. Clay Hollister artwork in white on gun belt. The gun is a die cast generic Kilgore with stag grips.

Value: $65-135 (Holster & gun)

TT-2

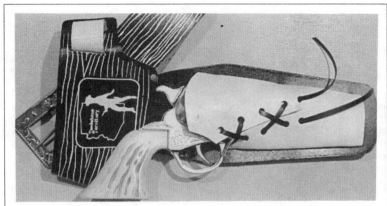

Tom Mix

Unknown- 1933. 1st model, black wooden 9 " gun that breaks open. Nail latch with revolving cylinder. Signature & TM logo rubber stamped on white grips. Made by many contractors and very fragile. Rare.
(Photo courtesy Hake's Americana, PA.)
Value; $145-250

TM-1

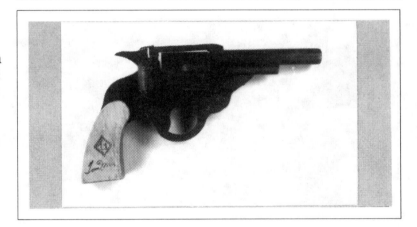

Tom Mix

Unknown- 1936. 2nd model black wooden 9" gun that doesn't break open. Has signature & TM logo rubber stamped on white grips. Seldom seen and a rare toy.
(Photo courtesy Hake's Americana, PA.)

Value: $145-250

TM-2

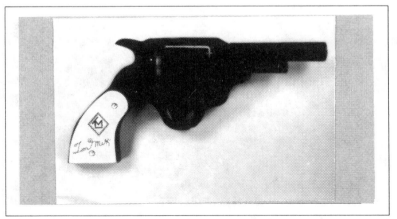

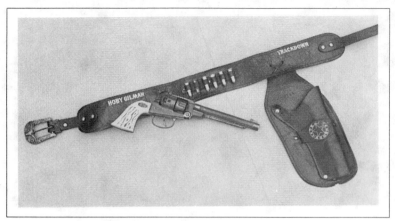

Trackdown - Hoby Gilman

Classy Prod.- 1958-59 era. Black leather with white lettering and a Texas Ranger badge. Also came as a double holster set. The gun is a L-H Texas Ranger with stag grips. Very rare character set.

Value: $145-285 (Holster & gun)

TD-1

Trackdown - Hoby Gilman

Classy Prod.- 1958-59 era. Detail of TD-1. Note the Texas Ranger badge on cross strap. A variety exist with names on holster straps & badges on belt. Classy also used generic LATCO guns in some sets.

TD-2

Wagon Train

Halco- 1957-62. Boxed set for a double holster. Features Major Adams & Flint McCullough on the front cover. See set WT-2 below for box contents.

WT-1

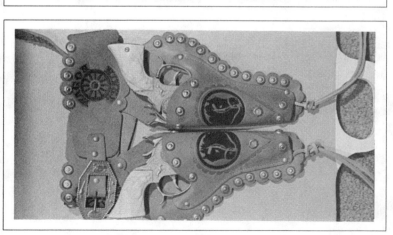

Wagon Train

Halco- 1957-62. Double set in tan leather with silver studs and embossed name, wagonwheel and horseheads in black. The guns are 9" nickel by Leslie-Henry. Box WT-1 above.

Value: $275-450 (Box, holster & guns.)

WT-2

Wagon Train

Halco- 1957-62. Box for a double holster set shown below in WT-4.

WT-3

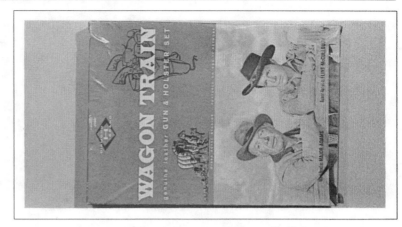

Wagon Train

Halco- 1957-62. Double holster set in tan, tooled leather with embossed name, wagon wheel and Major Adams on holster strap. Long barrel Leslie-Henry guns in nickel with white horsehead grips.

Value: $200-425 (Box, holsters & guns)

WT-4

Wagon Train

Halco- 1957-62. Similar to WT-4 except black & tan tooled leather, buckle holster straps, silver conchos & turquoise insets. L-H 9" nickel guns with white grips.

Value: $185-400 (Holsters & guns)

WT-5

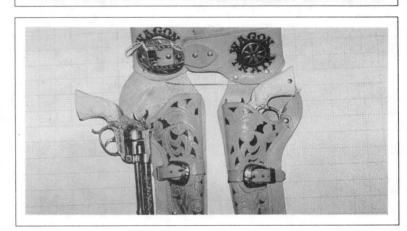

Wagon T. - Flint McCullough

Leslie-Henry- 1957-62. Very rare holster in black leather with white lettering & large silver buckle. L-H antique bronze .44 gun with revolving cylinder accepting bullets.

Value: $165-350 (Holster & gun)

WT-6

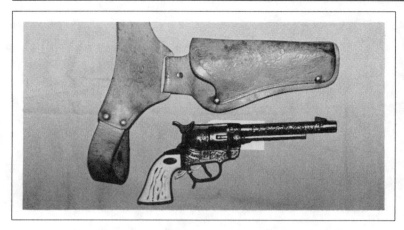

Wagon Train

Leslie-Henry- 1957-62. Simple gunfighter-style holster in tan tooled leather with embossed lettering. L-H .44 in antique bronze finish with stag grips.

Value: $125-285 (Holster & gun)

WT-7

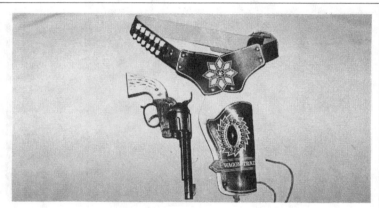

Wagon Train

Halco- 1957-62. Unusual & rare holster in black & tan leather with gold & white art, silver studs & turquoise jewels. Gun is the rare Halco .45 revolving cylinder in antique bronze finish with stag grips.

Value: $235-425 (Holster & gun)

WT-8

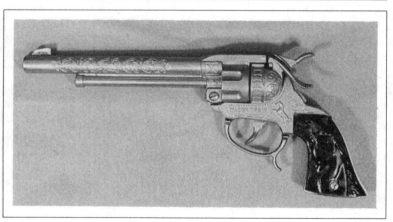

Wagon Train

Leslie-Henry- 1957-62. Very rare long barrel in nickel with fantastic transparent amber horsehead grips. All long barrel L-H guns are quite rare. L-H also made the more common 9" Wagon Train model.

Value: $145-275 (Long) $100-225 (Short)

WT-9

Wagon Train

Leslie-Henry- 1957-62. Large .44 model in antique bronze finish with the revolving cylinder that accepts bullets. Some have the ricochet sound. Stag grips.

Value: $125-245

WT-10

Wagon Train

Halco/L-H- 1957-62. Very rare and large Halco .45 in nickel finish with revolving cylinder that accepts bullets. Stag grips.

Value: $175-350

WT-11

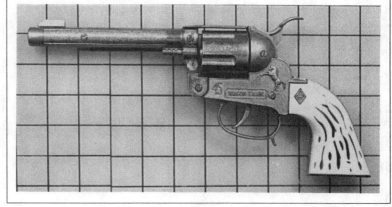

Wagon Train

Halco- 1957-62. Similar to WT-11, except in the more common antique bronze finish. Revolving cylinder that accepts bullets. Stag grips with Diamond "H" logo.

Value: $165-335

WT-12

Wagon Train

Halco- 1957-62. Unusual brown & black box with a Halco Marshal gun in nickel finish has white grips with black star inserts. The Marshal also produced in the rarer antique bronze finish. Rare box.

Value: $225-345 (Box & gun)

WT-13

Wagon Train

Leslie-Henry- 1957-62. Rare Winchester rifle with Wagon Train artwork. Plastic and metal lever action cap shooter in brown & black. Unusual rifle.

Value: $125-235

WT-14

Wagon Train

Leslie-Henry- 1957-62. Extremely rare toy. This 5-in-1 is most unusual & in the original box. Has a regular L-H .44 in the antique bronze plus a barrel extension, a detachable stock, carbine forend & scope

Value: $400-650 (Box & complete set)

WT-15

Wagon Train

Leslie-Henry- 1957-62. Detail of WT-15. Note the scope and forend fits into the butt stock. This gun accepts bullets and has the "Zing" ricochet sound. Among the rarest of character sets.

WT-16

Wanted-Dead or Alive

Marx- 1958-61. Small plastic & metal cap rifle, Josh Randall's Mares Laig. Unusual cut-down Winchester rifle. Rare character toy gun. 1st Model, only 14" in length.

Value: $85-175 (Rifle & display card)

WA-1

Wanted-Dead or Alive

Marx- 1958-61. Larger 17 1/2" plastic & metal cap rifle. On display card with holster and bullets. Rare toy gun. 2nd model with rapid-fire lever action.

Value: $100-200 (Card, holster & gun)

WA-2

Wanted-Dead or Alive

Marx- 1958-61. Largest 19" Mares Laig in plastic & metal that shoot caps. Holster and belt made from black vinyl. Large bullets. 3rd model also ejects shells. Rare, large box in black, red and brown art.

Value: $135-275 (Box, gun & holster)

WA-3

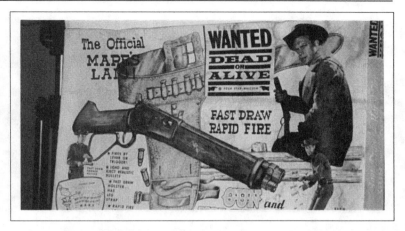

Wanted-Dead or Alive

Marx- 1958-61. Detail of gun and holster from boxed set WA-3. This is the larger 19" 3rd model that ejects shells. Note the black gun belt and holster with large brass color shells. Rare variation.

WA-4

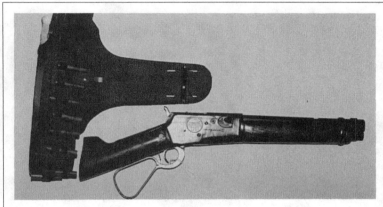

Wanted-Dead or Alive

Esquire Novelty- 1958-61. Large 19 1/2" non-licensed "Riflegun" by Actoy that shoots caps and ejects shells. Has Actoy pony on frame. Original box has black & yellow artwork. Large gun belt & holster.

Value: $100-225 (Box, gun & holster)

WA-5

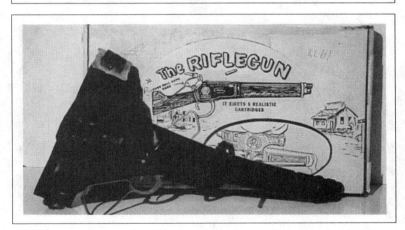

Wanted-Dead or Alive

Esquire Novelty- 1958-61. Detail of WA-5 showing tan vinyl holster with bullets & leg strap. Unusual. No mention of Mares Laig or Wanted-Dead or Alive on the set.

WA-6

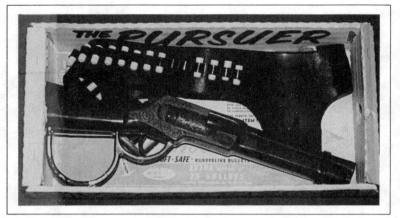

Wanted-Dead or Alive

Rayline Plastic Products- 1958-61. Unusual & rare toy gun is another non-licensed rifle called the "Pursuer." This toy shoots safe, soft, rubberlike bullets! With the original display box & holster. Engraved.

Value: $100-175 (Box, rifle & holster)

WA-7

Tales of Wells Fargo

Esquire Novelty- 1957-62. Original box in black & orange with agent Jim Hardie on the front. Includes 11" Actoy guns and a tan & dark brown, tooled leather holster.

Value: $250-375 (Box, guns & holster)

WF-1

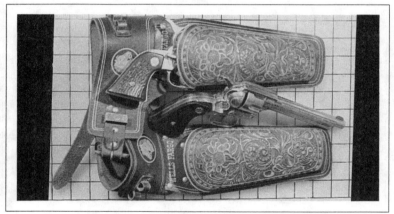

Tales of Wells Fargo

Esquire Novelty- 1957-62. Similar to WF-1, except holster in black & tan leather with a pair of Nichols' .38 Stallions with black stag grips.

Value: $100-235 (Holsters & guns)

WF-2

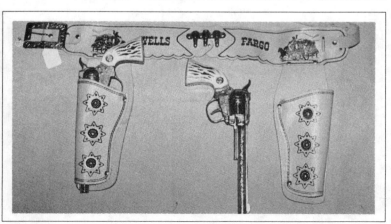

Tales of Wells Fargo

Esquire Novelty- 1957-62. Large double set in light tan leather with brown artwork & small silver conchos. Guns are Actoy long barrels, die cast in polished nickel, with stag grips having pony medallions.

Value: $150-325 (Guns & holsters)

WF-3

Tales of Wells Fargo

Unknown- 1957-62. Very large holsters in black & white tooled leather with silver snap cross straps. Lettering and strong box embossed in white on gun belt. No guns.

Value: $100-175

WF-4

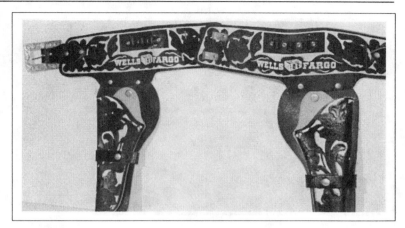

Tales of Wells Fargo

Esquire Novelty- 1957-62. Rare single set in black leather with silver bullets and white lettering. Unusual snap allows the gun to be held firmly or sit on the strap top for fast draw. Actoy long barrel gun.

Value: $135-250 (Holster & gun)

WF-5

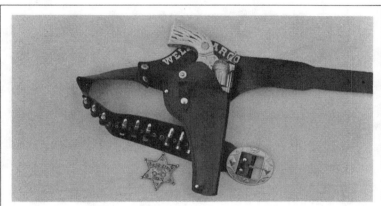

Tales of Wells Fargo

Actoy- 1957-62. Long barrel 11" die cast in the dull nickel finish with stag grips & pony medallions. Engraved repeater. Also found in the rarer antique bronze finish.

Value: $85-165 (Ant. bronze add $20)

WF-6

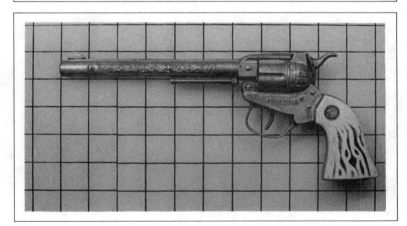

Tales of Wells Fargo

Actoy- 1957-62. Similar to WF-6 above, except in the rare polished nickel finish. Grips are ivory-white with the very small grooved stag.

Value: $95-175

WF-7

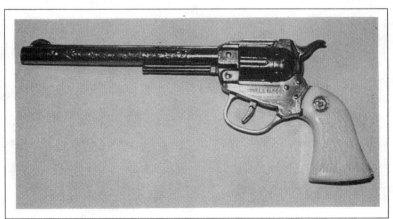

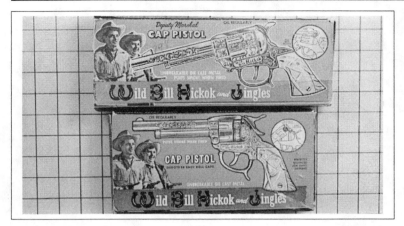

Wild Bill Hickok

Leslie-Henry- 1951-58 Rare boxes showing Wild Bill & Jingles. *Top:* Rare box for the 10 1/2" pop-up cap box model. *Lower:* A box for a normal 9" model.

Value: $35-85 (Top) $25-65 (Lower)

WB-1

Wild Bill Hickok

Leslie-Henry- 1951-58. Nearly identical pair of nickel guns. *Top:* Rarer with large horse on frame & large lettering. *Lower:* Small horse & small lettering. Both guns have butterscotch tan horsehead grips.

Value: $85-165 (Either variety)

WB-2

Wild Bill Hickok

Leslie-Henry- 1951-58. Very rare gold finished die cast with black horsehead grips. Note this is the large horse variety. There is a gold gun with transparent red grips.

Value: $125-200 (Gold)

WB-3

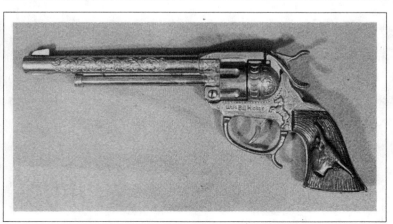

Wild Bill Hickok

Leslie-Henry- 1951-58. Very rare long barrel die cast with rare Marshal, steerhead copper grips. I believe this variety comes from Canada. This gun was found there.

Value: $135-250 (Long barrel & copper)

WB-4

Wild Bill Hickok

Leslie-Henry- 1951-58. Three rare pop-up cap box guns. *Left:* Polished nickel with transparent amber grips & star insert. *Middle:* Nickel with white horsehead grips. *Right:* Dull nickel & copper grips.

Value: $125-265 (Any variety)

WB-5

Wild Bill Hickok

Leslie-Henry- 1951-58. Very rare pop-up cap box variety in gold finish with tan butterscotch grips. Note that the grip screw has a square hole, which I believe denotes Canadian manufacture by L-H.

Value: $150-300 (Gold)

WB-6

Wild Bill Hickok

Buzz Henry- 1951-58. Extremely rare gun and seldom seen. A 7 1/2" nickel die cast with white horsehead & checkered grips. This may have been made in Canada. It also exists in the rarer gold finish.

Value: $135-250 (Gold $25 additional)

WB-7

Wild Bill Hickok

G. Schmidt- 1951-58. Extremely rare gun, may be a factory prototype. Similar to small frame Schmidt guns. "C-K Deputy" on frame. Scroll copper grips have Wild Bill Hickok & Jingles lettering. "C-K" ??

(Also see C-K Deputy-TG-73)

Value: $125-200 (Possibly Canadian)

WB-8

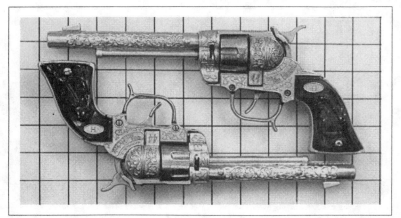

Wild Bill Hickok

Leslie-Henry- 1951-58. A pair of L-H .44s. *Top:* Nickel with revolving cylinder that accepts bullets. Transparent amber horse head grips. *Lower:* Rare, gold finish with black horsehead grips. Also uses bullets.

Value: $100-185 (Nic) - $125-225 (Gold)

WB-9

Wild Bill Hickok

Leslie-Henry- 1951-58. Close-up detail of L-H .44 model. Note fine engraving, the name and "H" oval medallion.

WB-10

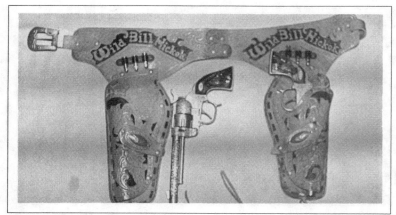

Wild Bill Hickok

Leslie-Henry- 1951-58. Highly tooled, tan leather double set. Large silver oval conchos and bullets. Pair of L-H .44 guns with transparent amber grips.

Value: $225-450 (Holsters & guns)

WB-11

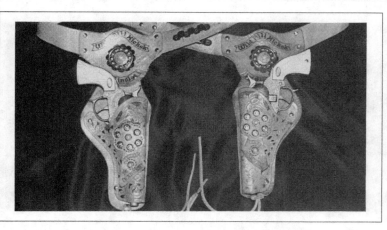

Wild Bill Hickok

Unknown- 1951-58. Unusual double set in the gunslinger-style with tooled tan leather, silver studs, large conchos and red jewels. L-H .44s in nickel with white horsehead grips. Rare style holsters.

Value: $245-475 (Holsters & guns)

WB-12

Wild Bill Hickok

Esquire Novelty- 1951-57. Tan leather double holster set with black embossed horseheads & names. Silver bullets. The guns are the rare L-H pop-up cap box variety with white horsehead grips.

Value: $265-550 Holsters & pop-up guns

WB-13

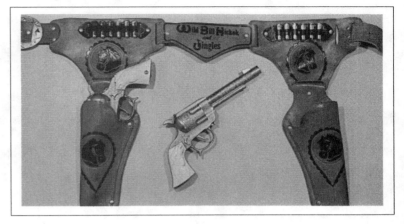

Wild Bill Hickok

Unknown- 1951-57. Large ornate double set in russet & black tooled leather with large silver conchos, studs and buckles. Name on gun belt around silver conchos. Six red bullets. No guns.

Value: $125-235 (Holsters only)

WB-14

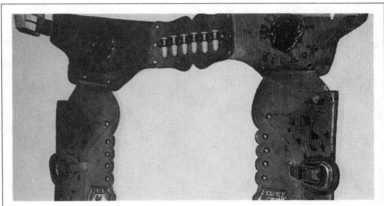

Wild Bill Hickok

Leslie-Henry- 1951-57. A rare gunslinger-style holster in black & tan leather with silver studs & diamond conchos with red jewels. Embossed art & name. 6 bullets. The gun is a L-H .44 in nickel finish.

Value: $185-300 (Holster & gun)

WB-15

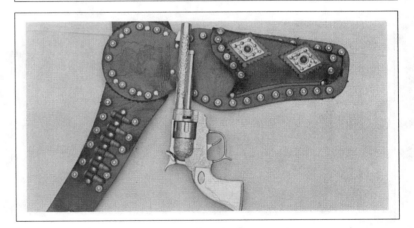

Wild Bill Hickok

Leslie-Henry- 1951-57. Similar gunslinger-style to WB-15, except in rare white & turquoise leather with silver conchos, studs and buckles with turquoise jewels. Perhaps a cowgirl set. Gun is pop-up L-H.

Value: $200-350 (Holster & pop-up gun)

WB-16

Wyatt Earp

Leslie-Henry- 1955-61. Nickel finish die cast 9" with white horsehead grips.

Value: $75-165

WE-1

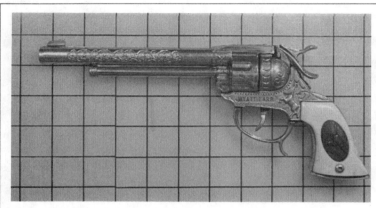

Wyatt Earp

Leslie-Henry- 1955-61. Very rare long barrel die cast. Note square hole screws. The grips are white with unusual steerhead insert. Possibly made in Canada.

Value: $100-250

WE-2

Wyatt Earp

Kilgore- 1955-61. Seldom seen die cast. It has white-tan horsehead grips. This gun came in nickel and the rarer gold finish.

Value: $65-145 (Nic) $75-165 (Gold)

WE-3

Wyatt Earp

Actoy- 1955-61. Rare die cast in nickel finish with white stag grips having pony medallions. Large gun with lanyard ring and engraving.

Value: $75-165

WE-4

Wyatt Earp

G. Schmidt- 1955-61. Very rare DC pistol has a ribbed long barrel with minimal engraving and checkered copper grips. In polished nickel finish. Featured in 1959-60 Nerlich & Company Holiday catalog.

Value: $175-350

WE-5

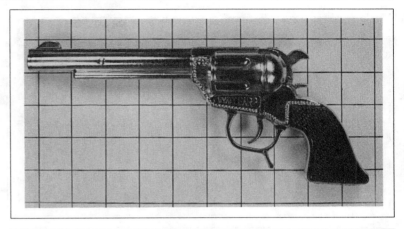

Wyatt Earp

G. Schmidt- 1955-61. Detail, close-up of WE-5 showing the name on the frame. It is believed that this variety was only sold in Canada. Also appears in the Eaton's 1959 Christmas catalog.

WE-6

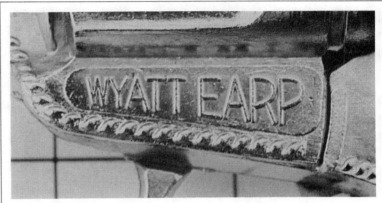

Wyatt Earp

Hubley- 1955-61. Long barrel "Buntline Special" die cast in nickel finish with canyon brown (swirl-purple) steerhead grips with star medallion.

Value: $85-175

WE-7

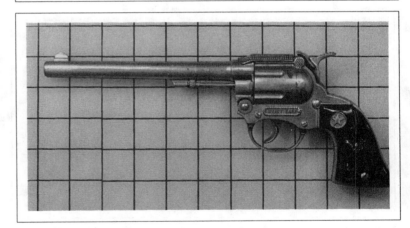

Wyatt Earp

Service Mfg. Co., Yonkers, NY- 1955-61. This gun is absolutely identical to WE-7 but is stamped Service Mfg. It appears that this gun was produced under contract. Rare. Turquoise steerhead grips.

Value: $100-200

WE-8

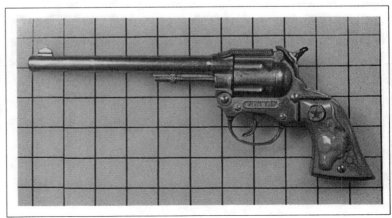

Wyatt Earp

Actoy- 1955-61. Unusual die cast in polished nickel finish with stag grips and pony medallion. Lanyard ring. The short barrel variety.

Value: $65-150

WE-9

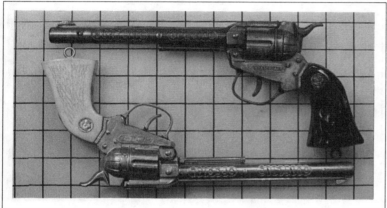

Wyatt Earp

Actoy- 1955-61. Pair of Buntline Specials. *Top:* Rare antique bronze with black stag grips. Lower: Nickel finish with white stag. Both have pony medallions and lanyard rings.

Value; $85-175 (Either finish)

WE-10

Wyatt Earp

G. Schmidt- 1955-61. Extremely rare gun is fully scroll engraved, has a rib barrel & the reduced size, copper, steerhead grips. This variety was apparently made for the Canadian market.

Value: $275-450

WE-11

Wyatt Earp

G. Schmidt- 1955-61. Close-up detail of WE-11. Note the rare and unusual scroll engraving, name on the side plate and the copper steerhead grips. A very rare gun. Appears in both the Eaton's and Nerlich Company 1959-60 catalogs.

WE-12

Wyatt Earp

B.C.M., England- 1955-61. Large revolving cylinder Buntline Special from their Outlaw series. Dark finish with beautiful Indian Chief white grips. Rare gun with extra long barrel. Also in nickel finish.

Value: $125-245 (Gun & box)

WE-13

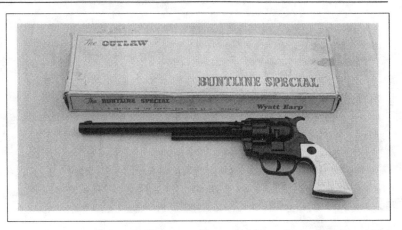

Wyatt Earp

L.I. Die Casting Inc., NY- 1955-61. Nearly identical to Hubley guns & made under contract. Short barrel with engraving. Steerhead grips and Service-V medallion. Rare variety.

Value: $100-200

WE-14

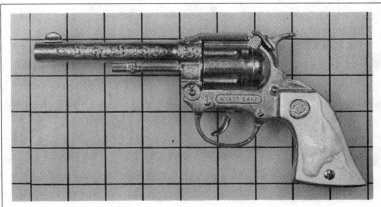

Wyatt Earp

Young Premium Co., CA- 1955-61. A very rare, extra long 18 1/2" Buntline Special. Plastic & metal clicker in gun metal finish, engraved with checkered grips. This was offered as a toothpaste premium.

Value: $85-175

WE-15

Wyatt Earp

Young Premium Co., CA- 1955-61. Detail, close-up of WE-15. Note the very fine scroll engraving and checkered grips with Wyatt's signature. Gun came with a vinyl holster with name & star on front.

WE-16

Wyatt Earp

Crescent Toys, Eng.- 1960. Unusual "Buntline Special" .38 in the dark finish that has ivory-style grips with horse & rider. There is a nickel variety of this gun also.

Value: $75-145 (Nickel or dark finish)

WE-17

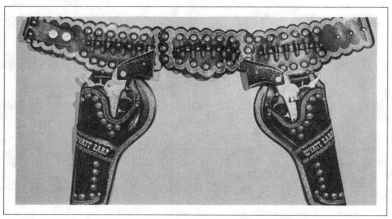

Wyatt Earp

Esquire Novelty Co.- 1955-61. Double set in black leather with gold & red artwork, silver studs, buckles & red bullets. Guns are Nichols Stallion .41-40s with black stag.

Value: $125-255 (Holsters only)

WE-18

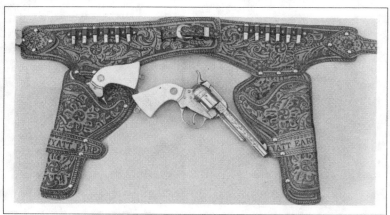

Wyatt Earp

Esquire Novelty Co.- 1955-61. Large double set in black and gold floral tooling. Silver studs, buckles & bullets. Pair of the short barreled Actoy nickel guns. Nice.

Value: $225-400 (Holsters & guns)

WE-19

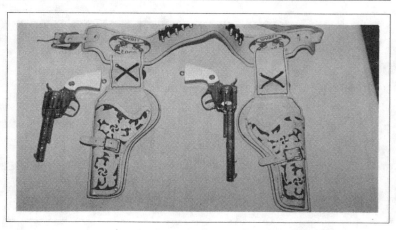

Wyatt Earp

Esquire Novelty Co.- 1955-61. Unusal set with two sizes of holsters in tan & brown tooled leather. Right holster has an Actoy Buntline Special, left has the short barrel variety. Both in nickel finish. Rare set.

Value: $225-435 (Holsters & guns)

WE-20

Wyatt Earp

Unknown- 1955-61. Exremely rare red & white set with matching cuffs & spurs. It has silver studs, conchos & red jewels. A pair of extremely rare nickel G. Schmidt guns. Probably intended for a cowgirl.

Value: $400-700 (Set with Schmidt Earps)

WE-21

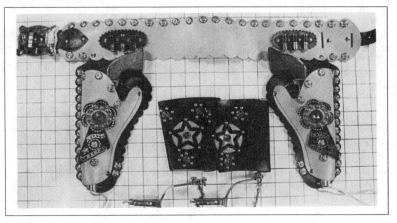

Wyatt Earp

Unknown- 1955-61. Russet brown leather set with fringe, silver conchos with red jewels, buckles & lettering. Red bullets.

Value: $85-165 (Holsters only)

WE-22

Wyatt Earp

Unknown- 1955-61. Black & white leather set is tooled & has steerheads and name with crossed guns embossed. Unusual set.

Value: $100-225

WE-23

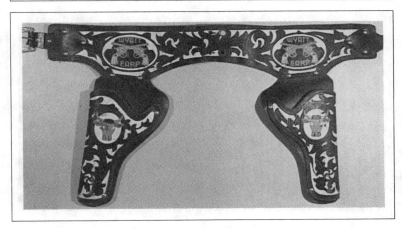

Wyatt Earp

Halco- 1955-61. Large black leather set with white artwork, silver conchos & red jewels. Silver bullets & buckles. Guns are Halco revolving cylinder Marshals in the antique bronze finish.

Value: $235-450 (Holsters & guns)

WE-24

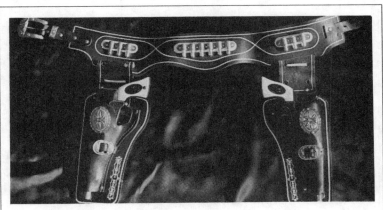

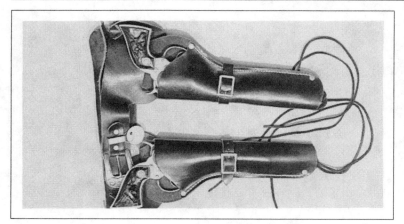

Wyatt Earp

Hubley- 1955-61. Extremely rare, long holsters in black leather for the Hubley Buntline Special guns. Very plain gunfighter style. Most unusual variation.

Value: $200-425 (Holsters & guns)

WE-25

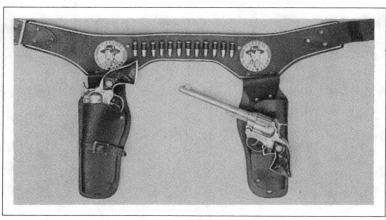

Wyatt Earp

Hubley- 1955-61. Similar to black gunfighter-style in WE-25, except has artwork circles above each holster. Pair of Hubley Buntline Specials. Unusual set.

Value: $200-425 (Holsters & guns)

WE-26

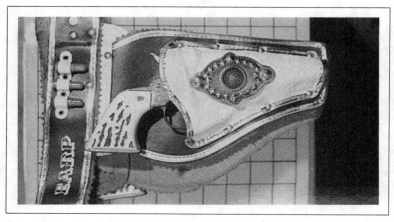

Wyatt Earp

Halco- 1955-61. Very small single holster in white & black leather with silver concho and red jewel. Generic late-style gun.

Value: $35-125 (Holster & gun)

WE-27

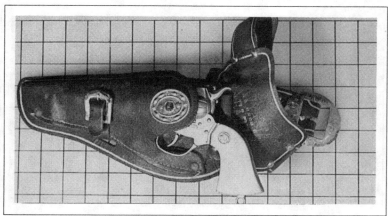

Wyatt Earp

Halco- 1955-61.Very small, left-handed holster in black leather with gold art & lettering. Silver buckle & concho with red jewel. Short barreled Actoy in nickel finish.

Value: $85-165 (Holster & gun)

WE-28

Wyatt Earp

Esquire Novelty Co.- 1955-61. Small gunfighter-style holster in tan leather with
brown artwork. Gun is the short barreled
Actoy in nickel with stag grips.

Value: $85-175 (Holster & gun)

WE-29

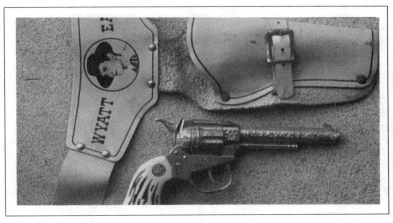

Wyatt Earp

Halco- 1955-61. Large single, gunfighter-
style in black leather with silver concho,
large buckle & red jewels. 12 bullets. Has
Hubley Buntline Special long barrel gun.

Value: $100-235 (Holster & gun)

WE-30

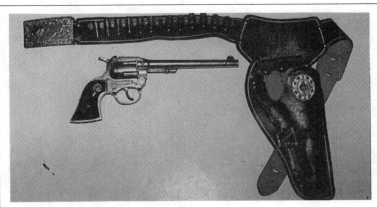

Wyatt Earp

Esquire Novelty Co.- 1955-61. Large gunfighter-style in black leather with gold
and red artwork. Gold conchos and 12
bullets. Beautiful set. Has Actoy Buntline
Special long barrel in nickel finish. Rare.

Value: $150-325 (Holster & gun)

WE-31

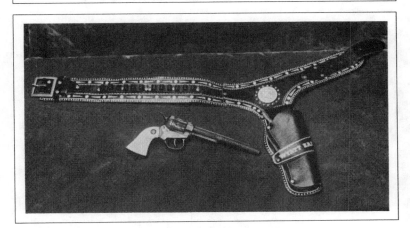

Wyatt Earp

Esquire Novelty Co.- 1955-61. Large single
holster in tan leather with brown artwork. Silver buckles, conchos and red
jewel. Hubley Buntline Special long barrel gun in nickel finish.

Value: $100-235 (Holster & gun)

WE-32

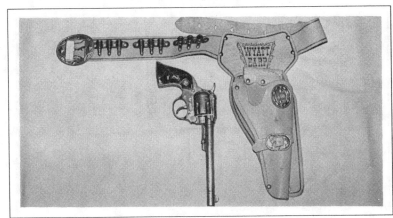

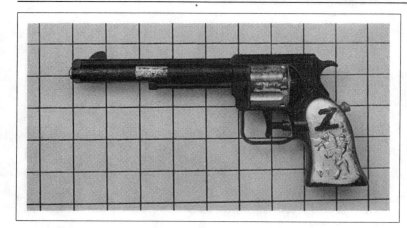

Zorro

Unknown- 1957-60. Unusual water pistol in black, silver and red plastic. Name on barrel with rider and rearing horse on grips.

Value: $25-45

Z-1

Zorro

Daisy Mfg. Co.- 1960 era. Full color box for Official Shooting Outfit. Unusual & seldom seen set. Contents shown below in Z-3.
(Photo courtesy Hake's Americana, PA)

Value: $125-300 (Box & contents)

Z-2

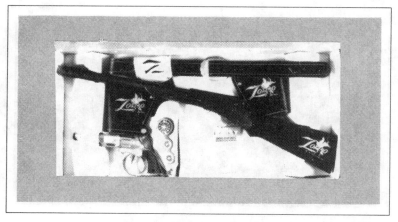

Zorro

Daisy Mfg. Co.- 1960 era. Black & white holster & wrist cuffs with silver conchos & white art of horse & rider. Double barrel pop gun with name on stock. Pistol is Hubley Pioneer, but some have a Coyote.
(Photo courtesy Hake's Americana, PA)
Value: $125-300 (Box and contents)

Z-3

Zorro

Unknown- 1957-60 era. Unusual set that includes mask, whip, lariat and ring. A rare set seldom found intact on display card.

Value: $65-150 (Complete on card)

Z-4

Agent Zero

Mattel- 1965-68. Snubnose .38 Shootin' Shell. Secret Frontier Defender in black finish with gold revolving cylinder. Grips are walnut grained with Agent Zero decal on left grip top. Dura-hide holster.

Value: $75-145

TG-1

Alan Ladd

*G. Schmidt-*1952-53. Pair of very rare die cast guns in polished chrome with copper stag grips. "AL" circle medallions. Name on frame. Related to movie Shane.

Value: $150-325

TG-2

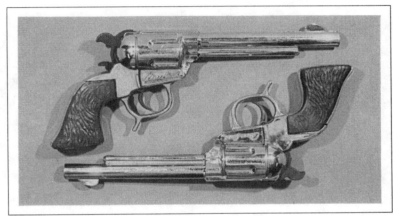

American

Kilgore- 1940-45. Classic cast iron toy. *Top:* 1st model has one piece cast iron cylinder. *Lower:* 2nd model with two piece pressed steel cylinder. Has beautiful engraving and eagle on ivory-like grips.

Value: $300-575 (1st) $275-500 (2nd)

TG-3

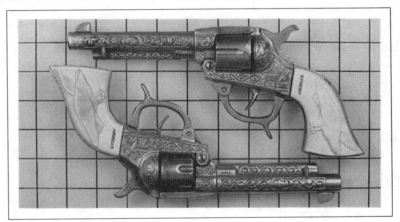

American - Dummy

Kilgore- 1940-45. Very rare cast iron 1st model with a dummy hammer. This variety cannot fire a cap.

Value: $325-600

TG-4

American

Kilgore- 1940-45. Unusual finish on a 2nd model cast iron. The entire gun was dark finished except for the cylinder, trigger and hammer. The raised engraving was polished bright nickel. Rare variation.

Value: $275-500

TG-5

Apache

Lone Star, Eng.-1955-65. Pair of die cast guns with revolving cylinders. *Top:* Rare nickel finish & silver star. *Lower:* Normal black finish. Listed in the Sears & Classy Prod. catalogs 1960. Also in Daisy boxes.

Value: $65-125 (Nic) - $50-100 (Black)

TG-6

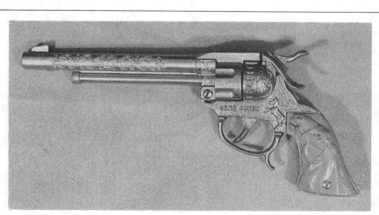

Arizona

Wicke, Germany (?)- 1980. Rare gold die cast with revolving cylinder. Has Indian Chief grips similar to Lone Star. Wicke Co. purchased Lone Star in the 1980s.

Value: $95-175 (Gold)

TG-7

Gene Autry

Leslie-Henry- 1955-60 era. Very rare die cast has the extra long barrel. Research indicates these were made in Canada. Light orange grips. Same as GA-25. (More Gene Autry guns in Western Characters.)

Value: $175-250

TG-8

Bango

Stevens- 1938-40. Cast iron. *Left:* The 2nd model in nickel with raised horsehead grips & jewel. *Center:* 1st model in dark finish small grips, no jewel. *Right:* Nickel 1st model with small grips, no jewel.

Value: $65-150 (All varieties)

TG-9

Bango

Stevens- 1938-40. Cast iron. *Left:* The 3rd model in nickel & engraved. *Middle:* 3rd model engraved with black grips & red jewel. *Right:* 1st model nickel with small red grips and no jewels.

Value: $75-155 (3rd model engraved)

TG-10

Bango

Stevens- 1938-40. Rare cast iron 1st model in dark finish with extremely rare eagle grips. These grips were apparently made in this patriotic style during WW II.

Value: $100-175 (Gun with eagle grips)

TG-11

Bango

Stevens- 1938-40. Detail, close-up of the grips on gun TG-11 above. Note the fine checkering, eagle and U.S.A. Absolutely beautiful, and very rare grips. I know of only three original examples!

TG-12

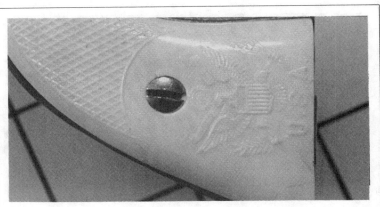

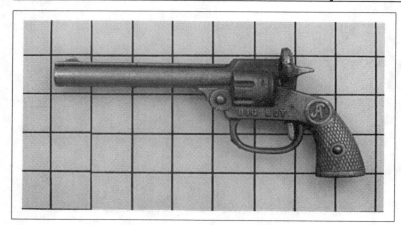

Big Boy

Andes- 1920 era. Cast iron single shot has large hammer for mammoth caps. Andes guns are rather rare.

Value: $65-100

TG-13

Big Buck

Kilgore- 1960-65. Unusual die cast, single shot, in nickel finish with full engraving. Sculptured grips are cherry red.

Value: $25-55

TG-14

Big Chief

Stevens- 1960 era. Die cast repeater in nickel finish & full engraving. Beautiful Indian Chief ivory grips. This box is very rare.

Value: $50-120 (Gun) - $35 (Box)

TG-15

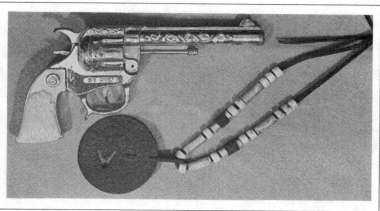

Big Chief

Stevens- 1960 era. Later style with painted finish. Found with a kid's Indian bead necklace that has a Victor trap-plate for the large medallion. Great accessory!

Value: $35-100 (Gun only)

TG-16

Big Horn

Kilgore- 1940 era. Classic cast iron with a revolving cylinder. Top: Rare 1st model with C.I. cylinder. Lower: 2nd model with two piece, pressed steel cylinder. A classic western gun that is very desirable.

Value: $350-600 (1st) - $300-500 (2nd)

TG-17

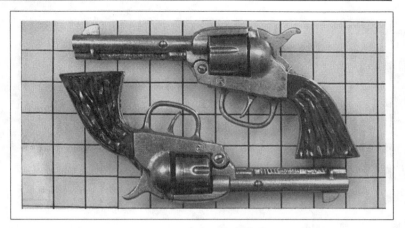

Big Horn

Kilgore- 1940 era. One of the rarest boxes is this one in red, white & blue for the Big Horn. There is no explanation for its rarity, as the gun was very popular. The pair of guns are 2nd models.

Value: $150-200 (Box only)

TG-18

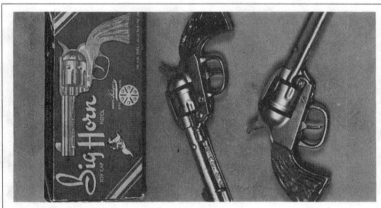

Big Horn

Kilgore- 1940 era. Very rare cast iron 1st model, in completely polished nickel. It is beautiful! It has molasses-brown swirl stag grips. Seldom seen variety.

Value: $400-650

TG-19

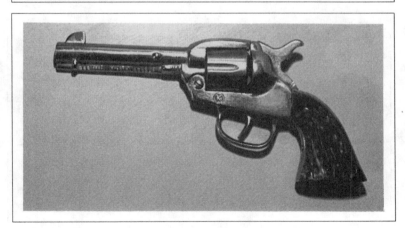

Big Horn

Kilgore- 1940 era. This extremely rare 1st model variety is in the blue finish. The hammer and trigger are nickel. Grips are ivory stag. It's among the rarest of blue finished toy guns.

Value: $400-750

TG-20

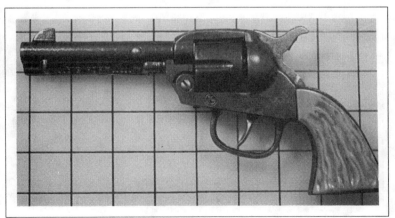

Big Horn

Kilgore- 1940 era. Extremely rare variety is this 1st model, in polished nickel, with dummy hammer! All dummy guns are quite rare. The grips are dark brown and black swirl.

Value: $425-700 (Polished - dummy)

TG-21

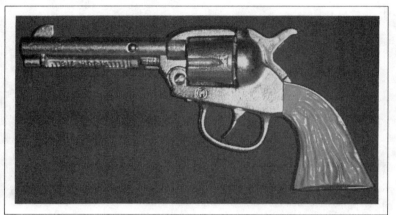

Big Horn - Roy Rogers

Kilgore- 1940 era. Perhaps the rarest variety is this 1st model with Roy Rogers very lightly etched on the frame under the cylinder. It can be found on either side. Red stag grips. (Long Tom gun also)

Value: $750-1,000 (Roy Rogers etched)

TG-22

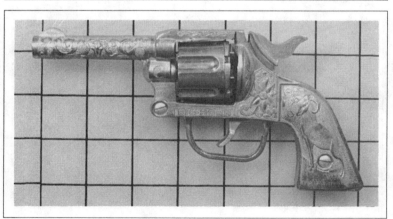

Big Horn

Kilgore- 1950-60. Engraved die cast with revolving cylinder. All metal. Photo is of a 2nd model. The 1st model has a lanyard ring on bottom of the grip.

Value; $45-100 (Either model)

TG-23

Big Injun Hammerless

Ives- Pre 1900. Very rare and early cast iron single shot. Unusual and quaint toy.

Value: $200-350

TG-24

Big Scout

Stevens- 1930 era. Rare long barrel cast iron single shot. All long barrel guns are quite difficult to find due to their fragile nature.

Value: $125-200

TG-25

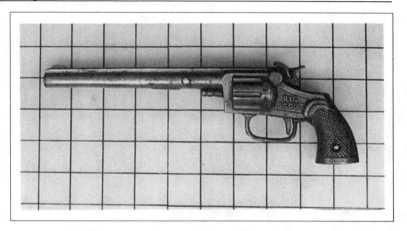

Big Scout

Stevens- 1940. Cast iron completely engraved single shot. *Top:* Regular hammer. *Lower:* The rare dummy hammer variety. Both have white grips.

Value: $60-100 - $85-125 (Dummy)

TG-26

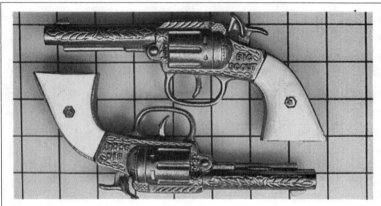

Big Scout

Stevens- 1940. *Top:* Dark finish Big Scout. White horsehead grips. *Lower:* A nearly identical Stevens cast iron gun is this Hi-Ho in the dark finish with no engraving. Virtually the same mold.

Value: $60-100 (Big Scout dark finish)

TG-27

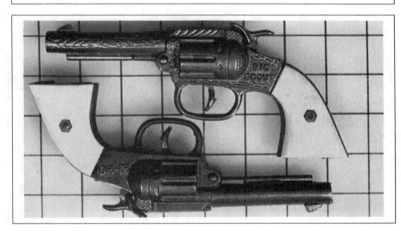

Big 6

Kilgore- 1920 era. Unique, ugly, but very rare, cast iron repeater in the blue finish. Many safeties, spur trigger with unusual opening system as half the barrel hinges.

Value: $150-325

TG-28

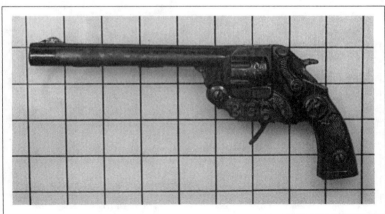

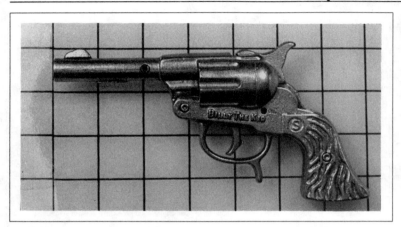

Billy The Kid

Stevens- 1950. One of the last cast iron guns made. A rather rare small repeater. The stag grips on many guns are painted black. Nickel finish.

Value: $100-165 (See character section)

TG-29

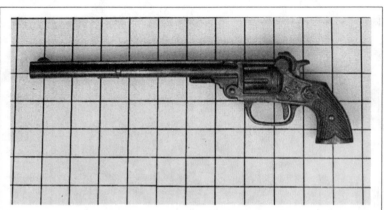

Black Jack

Kenton- 1930 era. Very rare cast iron long barrel single shot. Possibly named after General "Black Jack" Pershing. All long barrel toy guns are rare due to their fragile nature.

Value: $200-350

TG-30

Brave

Nichols- 1962. Small 6" die cast single shot in the polished nickel. Gun is all metal with stag grips and the Circle "N" medallion cast into the metal.

Value: $30-65

TG-31

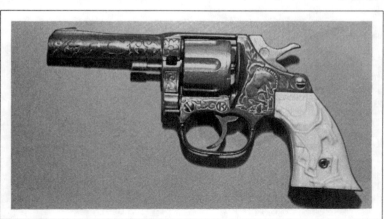

Bronco

Kilgore- 1950 era. Rare 1st model die cast in nickel with revolving cylinder. Shorter barrel has engraved mountain lion, and frame has a bucking horse. White grips have saddle and boots. Low front sight.

Value: $75-135

TG-32

Bronco

Kilgore- 1950-55 era. 2nd model die cast in nickel with revolving cylinder. Longer barrel engraved with two horseheads and frame has pine trees. Black grips with a bucking horse. High front sight.

Value: $65-125   (See Bronco- TG-346)

TG-33

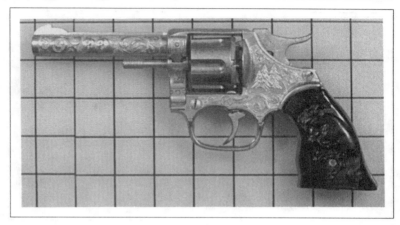

Buc-a-roo

Kilgore- 1940 era. Cast iron single shot. *Top:* 2nd model with wide hammer in the nickel finish with red grips. *Lower:* Rarer 1st model with narrow hammer in dark finish with white-pearl grips.

Value: $75-150 (Either variety)

TG-34

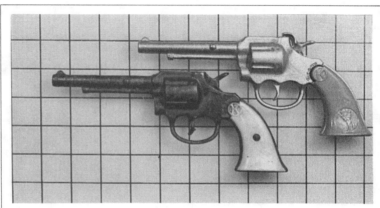

Buc-a-roo

Kilgore- 1940 era. Very rare 2nd model cast iron with a dummy hammer. Rather than the normal wide hammer, this has an extremely narrow ridge down the center that prevents the firing of caps.

Value: $100-185 (Dummy)

TG-35

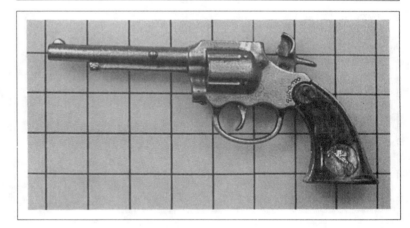

Buc-a-roo

Kilgore- 1940 era. This rare and unusual variety has a ribbed barrel and a different style wide & low hammer. Note beautiful white and purple swirl grips. Gun also has a small trigger. Nickel finish.

Value: $100-175

TG-36

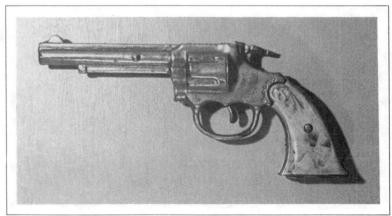

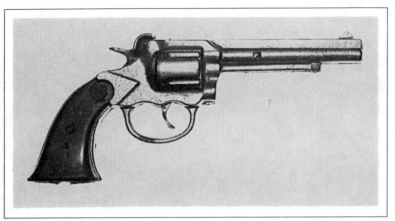

Buc-a-roo (Unmarked)

Kilgore- 1940 era. Extremely rare variety that is similar to the Buc-a-roo in TG-36, except this one is unmarked. Nickel finish with ribbed barrel and raised cast triangle above the red grips. Wide hammer.

Value: $100-185

TG-37

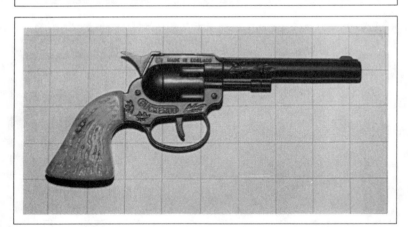

Buckeroo

Actoy- 1960 era. Small, engraved die cast in dull nickel with white grips and pony medallion. Unusual single shot.

Value: $25-65

TG-38

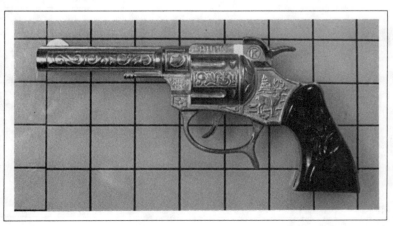

Buckeroo

Lone Star, Eng.- 1960-70 era. Black finish die cast repeater with red stag grips. Later-style cap gun.

Value: $35-75

TG-39

Buck

Kilgore- 1955-60 era. Unusual die cast single shot in engraved nickel. Black deerhead grips.

Value: $30-65

TG-40

Buck

Kilgore- 1955-60. Similar to TG-40, except in polished nickel finish with ivory-tan color grips. Engraved single shot die cast.

Value: $30-65

TG-41

Buck'n Bronc

G. Schmidt- 1950 era. The very rare, small frame die cast repeater. Similar to Dale Evans, BB Deputy & Roy Rogers. Copper stag grips. Nickel finish. Buck'n Bronc on both sides of frame. Ribbed barrel.

Value: $85-150

TG-42

Buck'n Bronc

G. Schmidt- 1950-55. Normal 10" die cast in chrome finish with stag copper grips. 2nd model has smaller name on front of frame. Round barrel no rib. No engraving. Rare original box in red & black.

Value: $85-150 (Box- $45)

TG-43

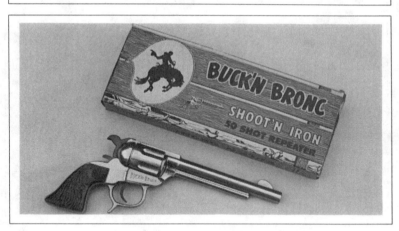

Buck'n Bronc

G. Schmidt- 1950-55. very rare 1st model which has large lettering covering entire side frame. Gold finish, engraved, short barrel with black horse & rider on black grips. Very rare box in gold & black.

Value: $150-275 (Gold) (Box- $100)

TG-44

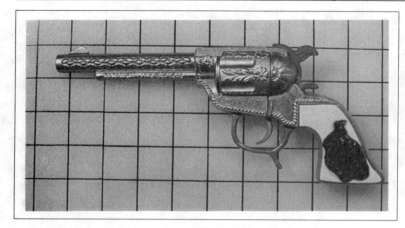

Buck'n Bronc

G. Schmidt- 1950-55. 2nd model short barrel, engraved, in chrome finish with unusual white grips and black horse. The gun has a dummy style hammer to prevent firing caps. Rare variety.

Value: $100-165 (Dummy hammer)

TG-45

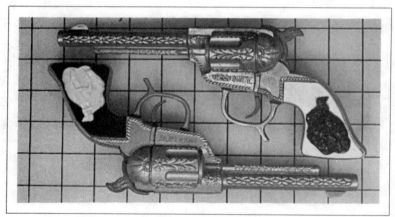

Buck'n Bronc

G. Schmidt- 1950-55. Very rare gold guns with short barrels. *Top:* Identical to 1st model TG-44. *Lower:* 1st model in gold finish with unusual copper stag grips. Note: Engraving & large lettering.

Value; $150-275 (Gold finish)

TG-46

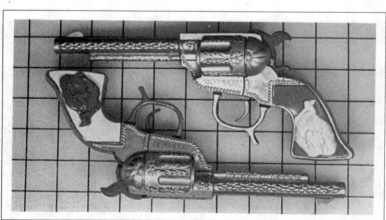

Buck'n Bronc

G. Schmidt- 1950-55. Pair of short barrels, engraved & in nickel finish. 2nd models with small lettering. *Top:* Unusual white grips with black horse. *Lower:* Unusual black grips with white horse.

Value: $ 85-150

TG-47

Buck'n Bronc

G. Schmidt- 1950-55. Pair of 2nd model die cast with short barrels, engraved and nickel finish. *Top:* Red grips with white horse. *Lower:* White grips with red horse. Usual grips on the guns are stag copper.

Value: $85-150

TG-48

Buck'n Bronc

G. Schmidt- 1950-55. Long barreled 2nd
models. *Left:* Chrome, no engraving, has
white stag. *Center:* Ribbed barrel, nickel,
engraved, slick black grips. *Right:* Chrome
with no engraving and white slick grips.

Value: $85-150 (Any variety)

TG-49

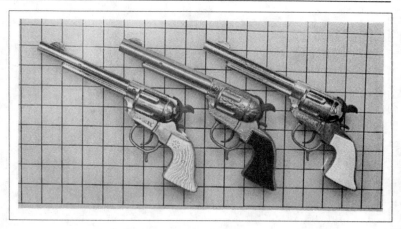

Buck'n Bronc

G. Schmidt- 1950-55. Long barreled 2nd
models. *Top:* Polished chrome, with no
engraving. Black grips with black horse.
*Lower: R*ib barrel, nickel finish, engraved
with checkered copper grips.

Value: $85-150 (Either variety)

TG-50

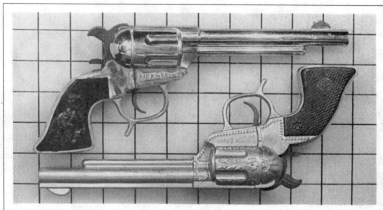

Buck'n Bronc

G. Schmidt- 1950-55. Long barreled 2nd
models. *Top:* Dull nickel with no engraving. Stag copper grips with BB medallion.
Lower: Polished chrome with no engraving. Stag grips and flower medallions.

Value: $85-150 (Either variety)

TG-51

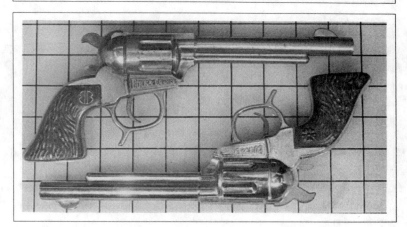

Buck'n Bronc

G. Schmidt- 1950-55. Long barreled 2nd
models. Top: Rib barrel with engraving
and slick black grips. Lower: BB Marshal
in dull nickel with painted stag grips.

Value: $85-150

TG-52

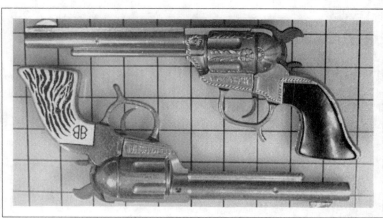

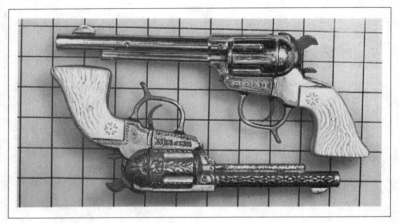

Buck'n Bronc

G. Schmidt- 1950-55. 2nd models. *Top:* A long barreled in polished chrome with no engraving and white stag grips. *Lower:* Short barrel with engraving & dull nickel finish. White stag grips.

Value: $85-150 (Either variety)

TG-53

Bulls Eye

Kenton- 1950-51. Cast iron. *Left:* A late model with silver painted finish and red grips. *Center:* Black finish & white grips. *Right:* Nickel finish & red grips. All guns are engraved with hat & spur grips. Rare.

Value: $125-225 (Any variety)

TG-54

Bulls Eye - Gene Autry

Kenton- 1950-51. Unusual cast iron in dark finish and red-orange "Gene Autry" grips. Found this way at a yard sale. Not surprising as both this gun & Gene short barrel engraved guns are nearly identical.

Value: $125-225

TG-55

Bulls Eye

Kenton- 1950-51. Extremely rare cast iron dummy in nickel finish with red grips. This is the only known dummy variety of this gun.

Value: $225-450

TG-56

Bulls Eye

Stevens- Pre 1900. Extremely rare early cast iron toy. Single shot, spur trigger, engraved, skeleton grip and nickel finish. Seldom seen.

Value: $325-550

TG-57

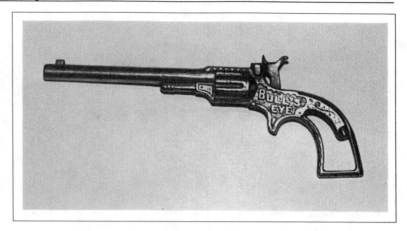

Bulls Eye - 50

Daisy- 1961. Rare die cast in dark finish. Name is on the barrel and has Daisy on frame. Identical to a Nichols Cowhand. The wood grained grips have circle Daisy medallions. Daisy stamped brass bullet.

Value: $55-100

TG-58

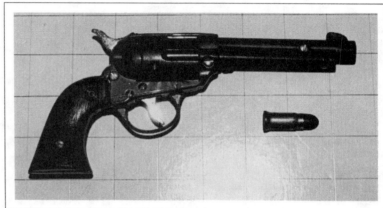

Bunt-Line

Lone Star, Eng.- 1960 era. Die cast long barrels. Top: Dull nickel, engraved with stag notch-bar grips. Lower: Chrome plated, engraved with green-gray swirl horsehead grips. Wyatt Earp inspired.

Value: $75-135

TG-59

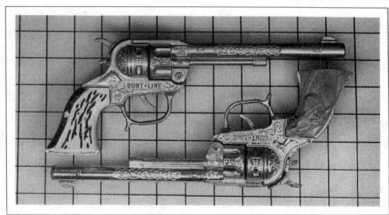

Cavalry

Ideal- 1900-10. Extremely rare, early cast iron in beautiful nickel finish. Ribbed barrel, spur trigger and checkered grips.

Value: $350-500

TG-60

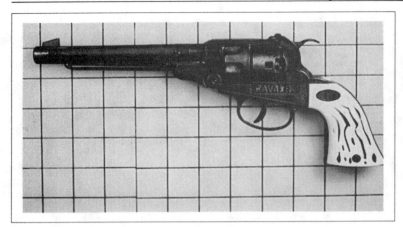

Cavalry

Leslie-Henry- 1955-60. Unusual die cast in antique bronze finish with a revolving cylinder. Stag grips with "H" oval medallion. Also found in nickel finish.

Value: $65-125

TG-61

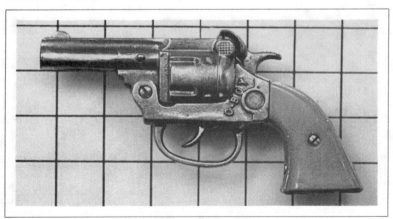

C-Boy

Kenton- 1940. Rare cast iron 1st model, with a red jewel in raised cast side plate. Early pearl grips with red rearing horse & rider. Nickel finish.

Value: $125-235

TG-62

C-Boy

Kenton- 1940. Rare cast iron 1st model with raised circle side plate. Nickel finish. Orange grips.

Value: $125-225

TG-63

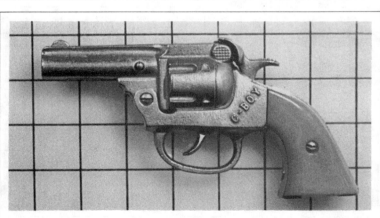

C-Boy

Kenton- 1940. Rare cast iron 2nd model with flat side plate in nickel finish. Grips are red-orange.

Value: $125-225

TG-64

Challenge

Stevens- Pre-1900. Rare, early cast iron toy with quaint engraving, spur trigger, and scroll grips. Large single shot.

Value: $225-400

TG-65

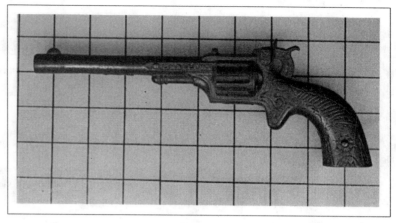

Champion

Kilgore- 1960. Unusual die cast is a fast-draw model. Grip has spring-wind timer that is released by lever on inside of grip. A seldom seen variety. Engraved nickel with black grips.

Value: $45-100

TG-66

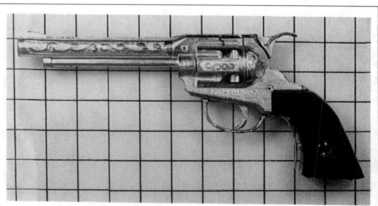

Champion

Leslie-Henry- 1950-55. Die cast named for Gene Autry's horse Champion. *Top:* A 1st model with a heavy frame in polished nickel with white horsehead grips. *Lower:* 2nd model with dull nickel finish.

Value: $75-165

TG-67

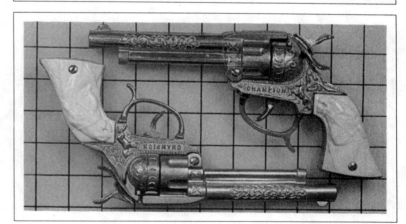

Champion

Leslie-Henry- 1950-55. *Top:* Very rare 2nd model in nickel finish with a dummy hammer with long spur. *Lower:* Rare 1st model in the gold finish with the black horsehead grips. Long spur hammer also.

Value: $100-200 (Either variety)

TG-68

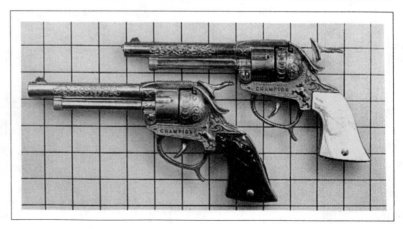

Cheyenne

Hamilton- 1955-60. Unusual die cast in dull nickel finish with the smooth white grips. "CS"- "Cheyenne Shooter" logo in gold on grips. This repeater also found in polished nickel.

Value: $55-120

TG-69

Chief

Hubley- 1960. Small 7" die cast single shot in nickel finish. All metal casting is completely engraved with scroll grips.

Value: $25-45

TG-70

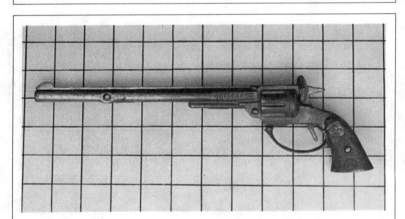

Chieftain

National- 1920 era. Rare extra long barrel cast iron. Single shot for mammoth caps. Checkered grips.

Value: $200-325

TG-71

Cisco Kid

Lone Star, Eng.- 1955. Die cast in polished chrome. Repeater with the red horsehead grips with silver star medallion. Name in circle on side frame.

Value: $65-130

TG-72

C-K Deputy

G. Schmidt (?)- 1950-55. Rare small frame die cast repeater in nickel with copper grips. Left side C-K Deputy. Right side Kwik-Draw. Right grip Wild Bill Hickok. Left grip Jingles. Unusual toy gun.
(See Character gun-WB-8)
Value: $125-200

TG-73

Cody .45

Lone Star, Eng.- 1975. Die cast repeater in polished chrome with black steerhead grips. Engraved Buffalo Bill Cody model with box. See character section.

Value: $35-75 (Gun & box)

TG-74

Colt- Cap & Ball

Marx- 1961. Plastic & metal, shooting shell cap gun. Civil war commemorative came in North-South sets. Blue finish with ivory grips.

Value: $65-135

TG-75

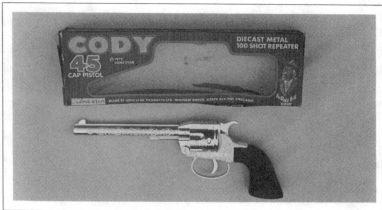

Colt- Cap & Ball

Marx- 1961. Pair of plastic & metal C. W. models. *Top:* Clicker gun in black & silver with walnut plastic grips. *Lower:* Gun is revolving cylinder, cap shooter. Black, silver & brass with walnut plastic grips.

Value: $35-75 (Clicker) $55-125 (Cap)

TG-76

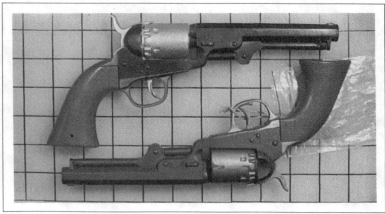

Colt .38

Hubley- 1960 era. Die cast with revolving cylinder & bullets. Engraved in dull nickel with stag grips & star medallion. Also found in polished nickel finish. Hard to find model.

Value: $135-250 (Either finish)

TG-77

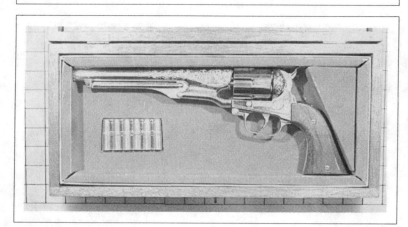

Colt .45 & Colt .44

Hubley- 1959-65.Both, large die cast with revolving cylinders & bullets. Engraved. *Top:* Colt .45 nickel, gold cylinder & ivory grips. *Lower:* Rarer Model 1860 .44 cal. in dull finish with ivory grips.

Value: $85-175 (.45) $100-225 (.44)

TG-78

Colt .45

Hubley -1960. Special Hubley presentation model in polished nickel with genuine cherry grips. Gun is in a special cherry box. Perhaps one-of-a-kind. Rare.

Value: $150-300 (Gun & box)

TG-79

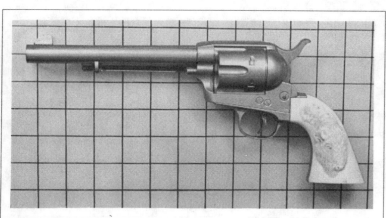

Colt .45 Peacemaker

Marx- 1960-65. Full size plastic & metal clicker with superb, buffalo-head, ivory grips. Metallic silver finish.

Value: $50-100

TG-80

Colt .45 Peacemaker

Marx- 1960-65. Full size plastic & metal clicker. Metallic silver finish with olive green grips having U.S. Army in gold. It may be a factory prototype model. Rare.

Value: $50-100

TG-81

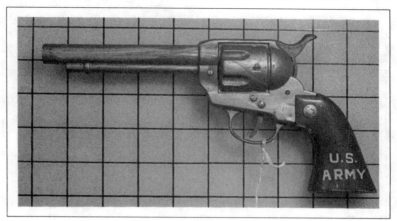

Colt .45 Peacemaker

Marx- 1960-65. Full size plastic & metal clicker. Black finish with unusual horse & rider ivory grips.

Value: $50-100

TG-82

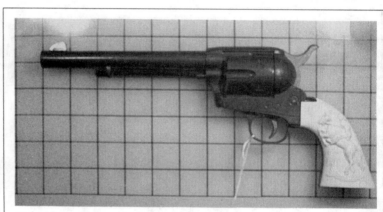

Colt .45 Peacemaker

Marx. 1960-65. Smaller frame metal and plastic clicker in black finish with ivory steerhead and rope grips.

Value: $35-75

TG-83

Colt .45 Peacemaker

Marx- 1960-65 Pair of factory prototypes. *Top:* Small frame Wyatt Earp Special with extra long barrel, black with horsehead white grips. *Lower:* Lone Ranger large frame in black with eagle white grips.

Value: $100-165 (Earp) $125-185 (L.R.)

TG-84

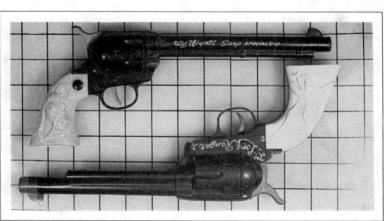

Colt .45 Peacemaker

Hubley- 1960-65. Full size flat-top version in metal & plastic. Cap shooter in black finish with walnut plastic grips. Unusual toy gun.

Value: $55-100

TG-85

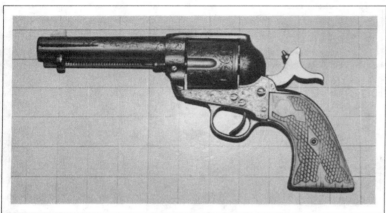

Colt .45 Peacemaker

Revell- 1950 era. All plastic model kit. Engraved in metallic blue finish with checkered ivory grips. Non-working display model in full size.

Value: $35-65

TG-86

Colt .45 Peacemaker

Marx- 1960-65. Small frame all plastic water pistol in metallic silver finish. The grips have a cowboy with sheriff's badge. Also in various plastic colors.

Value: $20-45

TG-87

Colt Six Shooter 44-40

L.S. Co., Japan- 1980. Full size plastic gun with full working mechanism. Gun has metal finish with black checkered grips and Colt horse medallions.

Value: $35-75

TG-88

Colt Special

Nichols- 1957. Small 7" die cast repeater in nickel finish with black stag grips.

Value: $50-100

TG-88-C

Columbia

Stevens- Pre 1900. Very rare, early cast iron single shot for mammoth caps. Scroll engraved grips.

Value: $250-400

TG-89

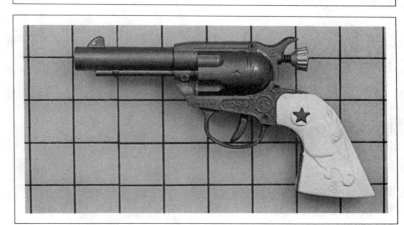

Cork .45

Lone Star, Eng.- 1970. Die cast single shot cork shooter. Plunger operated. Gun has metallic blue finish with white horse-head grips and red star medallion.

Value: $30-45

TG-90

Corporal

Ideal Modell,Ger.- 1970-75. Pair of chrome plated die cast repeaters. Both guns have engraving and slick black handles.

Value: $25-55 (Each)

TG-91

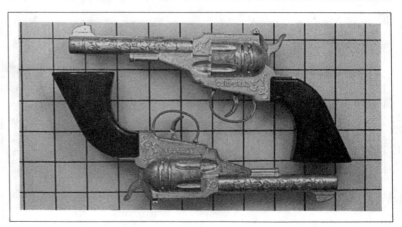

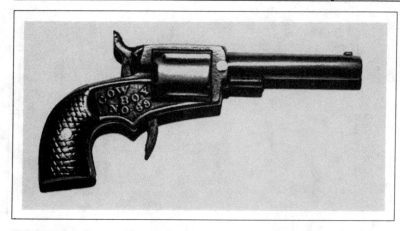

Cowboy No. 69

Unknown- 1880 era. Extremely rare, early cast iron single shot cap pistol. Perhaps the earliest toy gun to use the name cowboy. Checkered grips. Size about 6".

Value: $250-450

TG-92

Cowboy

Ives- 1890 era. Rare, early cast iron single shot. Checkered grips.

Value: $150-300

TG-93

Cowboy

Unknown, England- 1900 era. Early cast iron single shot. One of the first foreign toy guns to have the word cowboy.

Value: $125-200

TG-94

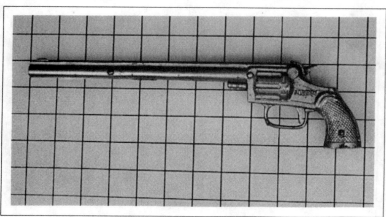

Cowboy

Stevens- 1930 era. Quite rare cast iron has an extra long barrel. 12" length. All long barrels are rare, but this model is seldom encountered. Nickel finish.

Value: $200-350

TG-94C

Cowboy

Hubley- 1940 era. C.I repeater. *Top:* This nickel gun has a painted red star and checkered grips with plain oval. *Lower:* A blue-black finish with checkered pearl-type grips with Colt horse logo in oval.

Value: $85-165 (Either finish)

TG-95

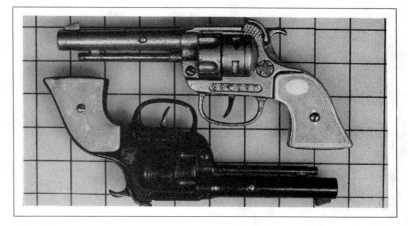

Cowboy

Hubley- 1940 era. C.I. repeater. *Top:* This is a rare polished nickel with plain oval. *Lower:* Rare green-blue finish and brown-molasses checkered grips with Colt oval.

Value: $100-185 (Pol.) $95-175 (G-B)

TG-96

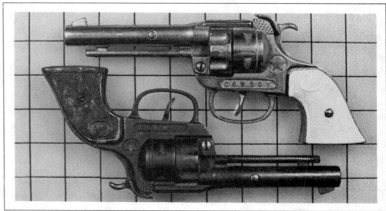

Cowboy

Hubley- 1940 era. Rare cast iron in nickel finish with the dummy hammer. A very seldom seen variety of this model. White checkered grips with plain oval.

Value: $125-225 (Dummy)

TG-97

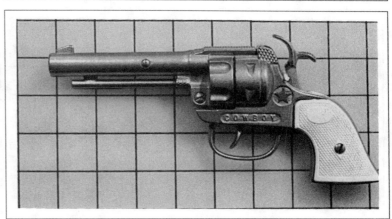

Cowboy

Hubley- 1950 era. Perhaps the most popular western toy gun. *Top:* D.C. in nickel finish with white steerhead grips. *Lower:* Rare dark finished D.C. with white and black steerhead grips.

Value: $85-185 (Nic) $100-200 (Black)

TG-98

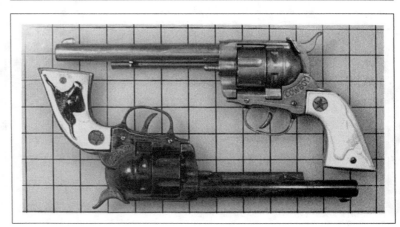

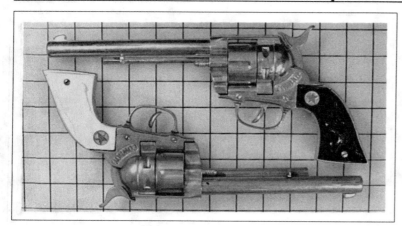

Cowboy

Hubley- 1950 era. *Top:* Very rare D. C. Cowboy Classic in gold finish with black steerhead grips. *Lower:* D.C. in dull nickel finish with white steerhead grips.

Value: $175-350 (Gold) $85-185 (Dull N.)

TG-99

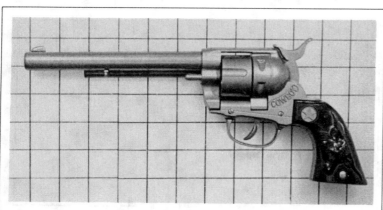

Cowboy

Hubley- 1950 era. Three rare models. *Left:* rare prototype in antique bronze. *Center:* Satin gray finish. *Right:* Pale metallic blue finish. All have exceptional swirl colored grips from Hubley's prototype shop.

Value: $165-325 (Any finish variety)

TG-100

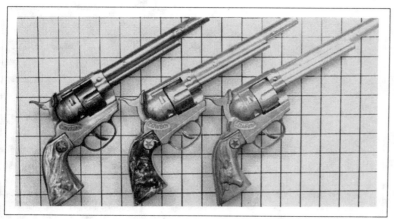

Cowboy

Hubley- 1950 era. Rare prototype in satin black finish with black & red swirl, steerhead grips.

Value: $165-325 (Satin black)

TG-101

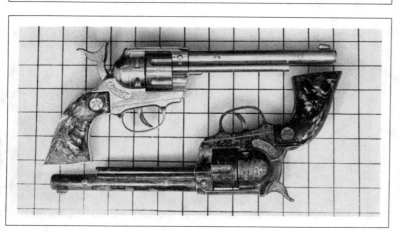

Cowboy

Hubley- 1950 era. Pair of rare "dummy" varieties. Top: Nickel finish with green & white swirl steerhead grips. Lower: Black finish with black & orange swirl steerhead grips. D.C. dummy guns are rare.

Value: $165-325 (Either finish)

TG-102

Cowboy Joe

Lone Star, Eng.- 1980. Pair of small die cast, single shot guns in chrome finish with red horsehead grips and silver stars.

Value: $20-35 (Each)

TG-103

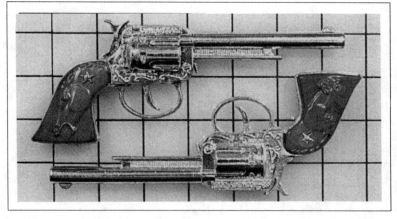

Cowboy, Jr.

Hubley- 1955-60. Unusual die cast. 1st model with opening latch on side of barrel. Lanyard ring and braided cord. Has revolving cylinder & white steerhead grips.

Value: $65-100

TG-104

Cowboy, Jr.

Hubley- 1955-60. 2nd model with friction close latch. Revolving cylinder with lanyard ring and braided cord. Purple-black swirl steerhead grips.

Value: $65-100

TG-105

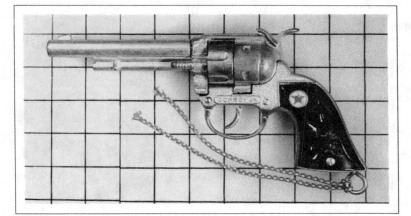

Cowboy, Jr.

Hubley- 1955-60. Rare variety 2nd model in gold finish with black steerhead grips and no lanyard ring.

Value: $85-145 (Gold)

TG-106

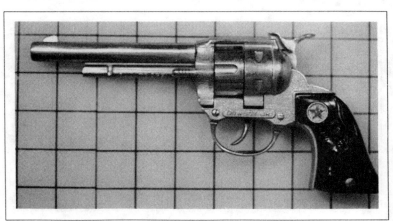

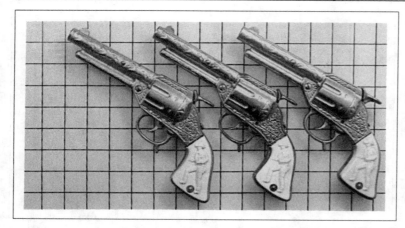

Cowboy King

Stevens- 1940. Classic C.I. *Left:* 1st model with long plain hammer in nickel finish. *Middle:* 1st model in the rare gold finish. *Right:* 2nd model with reinforced hammer spur in nickel. Unusual toy guns.

Value: $165-350 (Either model)

TG-107

Cowboy King

Stevens- 1950-55. *Top:* Rare long barrel D.C. repeater in nickel. Engraved with stag grips. *Lower:* Shorter D.C. in chrome finish with pearl swirl grips with circle S medallions.
Value: $ $85-165 (Long) $65-125 (Short)

TG-108

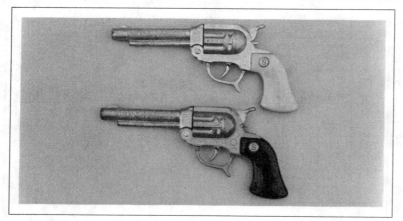

Cowboy King

Stevens- 1950-55. D.C. with longer ejector rods & hammer variation. *Top:* Rare gold finish with pearl grips. Lower: dull nickel finish with black grips. Both have circle S medallions.

Value: $75-150 (Gold) $65-135 (Nickel)

TG-109

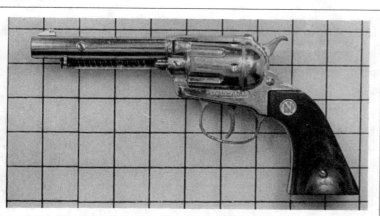

Cowhand

Nichols- 1961. D.C. repeater in polished nickel finish with black, wood-grained grips with circle N medallions.

Value: $50-95

TG-110

Cowhand

G. Schmidt- 1950-55. D.C. repeaters. *Top:* Rib barrel, engraved, with checkered copper grips & rare red jewel. *Lower:* Similar to above except rare dummy hammer and the grips have a small flower.

Value: $75-150 (Reg) $100-185 (Dummy)

TG-111

BB Cowhand

G. Schmidt (?)- 1955-60. Very rare variety similar to Schmidt guns has a short barrel with no engraving. Nickel finish with turquoise blue steerhead grips. Circle "D" medallion possibly Daisy Ltd., Canada.

Value: $125-185

TG-112

Cowman

Nichols- 1960. Die cast repeater in the polished nickel with black stag grips and circle N medallions.

Value: $50-95

TG-113

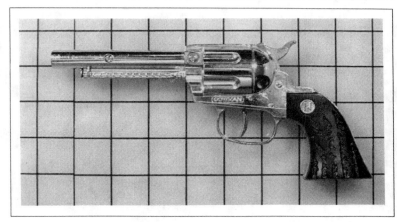

Cowpoke

Lone Star, Eng.- 1960. Die cast 9" repeater in the dull gray nickel finish. Has Notch-Bar stag grips. Also found in a long barrel version.

Value: $75-150

TG-114

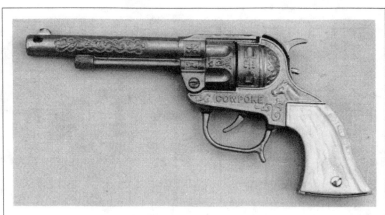

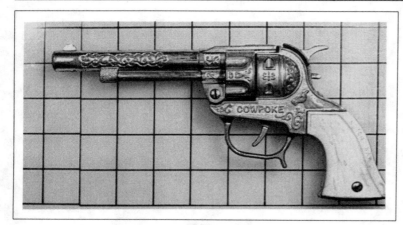

Cowpoke

Lone Star, Eng.- 1960. Die cast repeater in polished chrome with the Notch-Bar stag grips. Also found in long barrel version.

Value: $75-150

TG-115

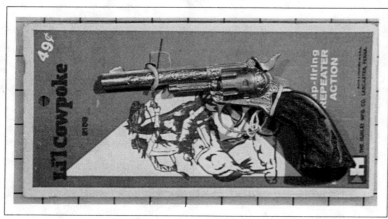

Li'l Cowpoke

Hubley- 1960 era. Small 6 1/2" die cast in nickel finish with engraving and black stag grips. Single shot. Original card is marked $.49.

Value: $10-25 (Gun & card)

TG-116

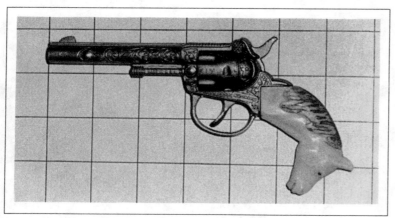

Cowtyke

Hubley- 1960 era. Identical to above gun TG-116, except the one-piece stag grips have been replaced with a sculptured tan & white horsehead. Unique variation in '63 Sears catalog, in a "Pee Wee" gun set.

Value: $40-85

TG-117

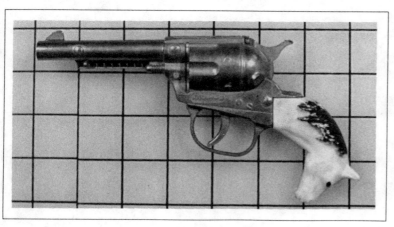

Cowtyke

Hubley- 1960 era. Larger, 7" die cast variety with no engraving in nickel finish with a black & white sculptured horsehead grip. Single shot. Rarer variety.

Value: $50-100

TG-118

Cowtyke

Hubley- 1960 era. *Left:* Engraved small TG-117. *Center:* Large model, no engraving & prototype Puma head in full color. *Right:* Smaller model with engraving and prototype black Panther in color. Rare

Value: $125-200 (Either prototype gun)

TG-119

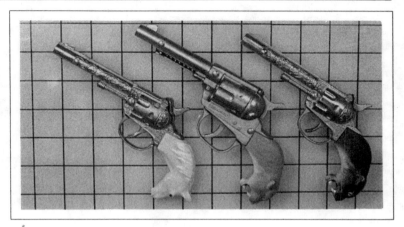

Cowpoke, Jr.

Lone Star, Eng.- 1960. Small, all metal, 8" die cast in dull nickel finish with Notch-Bar stag grips. Engraved. It might be difficult to notch the metal grips! Unusual toy gun.

Value: $50-85

TG-120

Coyote

Hubley- 1960 era. Small die cast repeater in nickel finish. All metal with engraving. Checkered grips painted black. Can be found in some Zorro & small toy Civil War holster sets.

Value: $50-85

TG-121

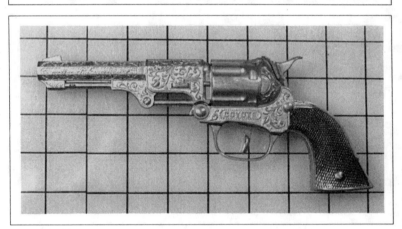

Custer

Kenton- 1930 era. Long barrel cast iron single shot. One of the more difficult to find western character guns. Exists in the normal cast iron or blue finish.

Value: $225-350

TG-122

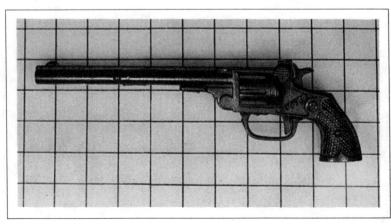

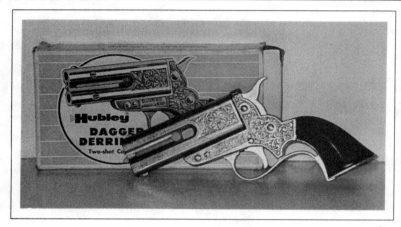

Dagger Derringer

Hubley- 1960 era. Unusual die cast over-under derringer with bullets. Beautiful engraving with slick black grips. Has a small red dagger that can be pushed-out between barrels. Nickel finish with box.

Value: $75-165 (Gun & box)

TG-123

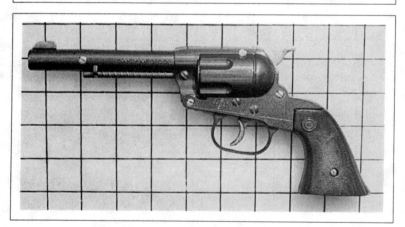

Daisy

Nichols-Kusan- 1964. 9 1/2" repeater that is similar to Nichols Mustang 250. Nickel finish with stag grips. Daisy on frame and top of grips. Unusual variety.

Value: $45-85

TG-124

Daisy

Nichols-Kusan- 1960-62. 10" repeater in Steel-Blu with brown wood-grain grips. Daisy on barrel & logo on frame & grip medallion. Similar to Nichols Cowhand.

Value: $50-100 (Steel-Blu)

TG-125

Daisy 250

Nichols-Kusan- 1964. Rare 10" die cast in Steel-Blu finish with one-piece brown stag grips with Daisy cricle medallions. Daisy on frame. Similar to a Nichols 250 Tophand. Lone Star made one similar. (?)

Value: $50-100 (Steel-Blu)

TG-126

Daisy Model 61

Nichols- 1961. Nearly identical to Nichols Model 61. Daisy on gun and logo medallion on grips. Steel-Blu and silver finish with walnut plastic grips. Has revolving cylinder with bullets. Very rare toy gun.

Value: $200-325

TG-127

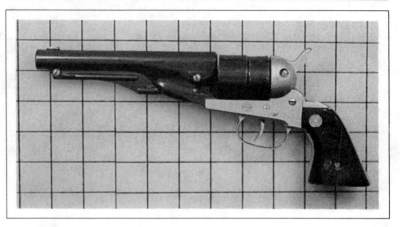

Daisy .38

Nichols- 1960 era. Both identical to the Nichols .38 Stallions. *Top:* Rare antique bronze finish with white stag. *Lower:* In Steel-Blu with walnut grained grips. Both have name & Daisy logo medallions.

Value: $85-175 (Either model)

TG-128

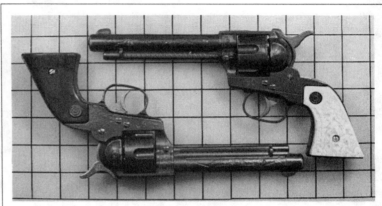

Daisy "Spittin Image"

Nichols- 1960 era. Rare Daisy boxes for both varieties of their "Spittin Image" Peacemakers. *Top:* Daisy Bullseye with 2-piece bullets. Lower: "Daisy Kid" model with the special, secret twirling trigger!

Value: $35-75 (Boxes only)

TG-129

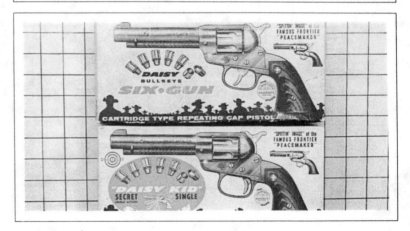

Daisy "Spittin Image"

Nichols- 1960 era. Steel-Blu with walnut wood-grained grips & Daisy medallions. *Top:* Daisy Bullseye with revolving cylinder & bullets. *Lower:* "Daisy Kid" is very similar but has special twirling trigger.

Value: $85-175 (Bul) $100-200 (Twirling)

TG-130

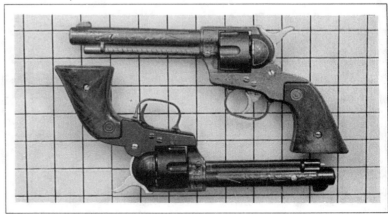

Daniel Boone

Kilgore- 1930 era. Very rare cast iron repeater for a western frontiersman. Note small bullet for front sight. Quaint and unusual, early toy gun.

Value: $200-400

TG-131

Davy Crockett

Leslie-Henry- 1955. Top: Rare L-H 9" die cast in nickel with white grips. Lower: Buzz Henry 8" die cast in nickel with the white grips. Both are seldom seen. Also see character section.

Value: $175-350 (L-H) $150-325 (Buzz)

TG-132

Davy Crockett

G. Schmidt- 1955. Very rare die cast gun in dull gray finish with copper stag grips. One of the rarest character guns. Also see character section.

Va;lue: $200-350

TG-133

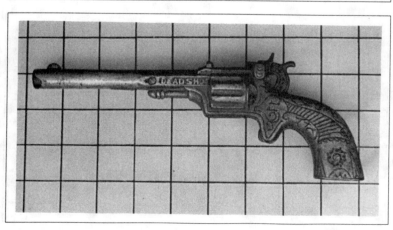

Deadshot

Stevens- 1890 era. Rare, early cast iron single shot. Scroll engraved grips. Spur trigger.

Value: $225-400

TG-134

Defender

Ideal- 1900 era. Early cast iron single shot. Has beautiful basketweave engraved grips. Spur trigger western-style toy gun.

Value: $250-350

TG-135

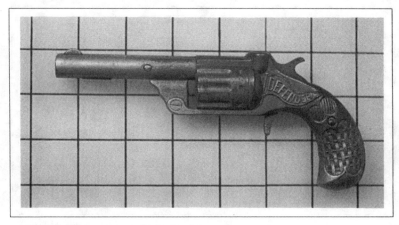

BB Deputy

G. Schmidt- 1950-55. Unusual small frame die cast repeaters in polished nickel. Top: Ribbed barrel, no engraving with copper stag grips. Lower: Identical to gun above except has the white stag grips.

Value: $65-125 (Either variety)

TG-136

Deputy

Kilgore- 1955-60 era. All metal die cast with revolving cylinder. Nickel finish with full engraving and metal grips. Uses disc caps.

Value: $45-85

TG-137

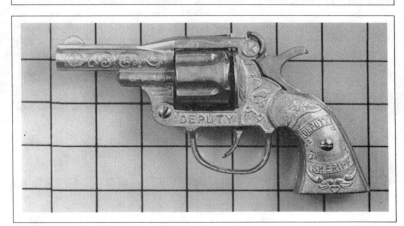

Deputy

Hubley- 1960 era. Unusual nickel die cast repeater with ribbed barrel and all metal, Tiffany-style grips. Release latch on ejector rod. Push-button variety exists. Also see character section.

Value: $65-120

TG-138

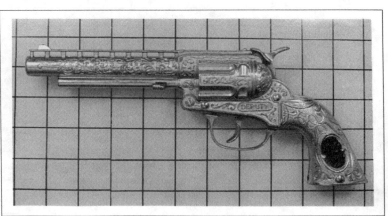

Dude

Kenton- 1940 era. Rare cast iron repeater. Top: Dark finish with white horse & rider grips. Lower: Nickel finish with rarer red horse and rider grips.

Value: $100-150 $125-175 (Red horse)

TG-139

Dude

Kenton- 1940 era. Very rare cast iron gun in the dummy variety. Note the dummy plate on this dark finish gun with yellow ivory horse & rider grips.

Value: $135-200

TG-140

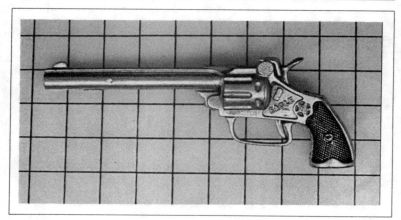

Eagle

Hubley- 1935. Cast iron long barrel, single shot for mammoth caps. Nickel with black grips. Uncommon toy gun.

Value: $125-200

TG-141

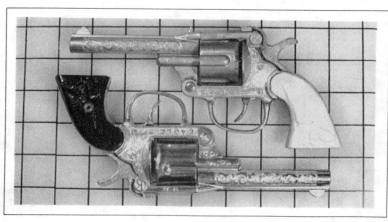

Eagle

Kilgore- 1950-55. Die cast revolving cylinder. Top: Engraved nickel finish & white eagle grips. Lower: Rare, engraved gold finish & black eagle grips.

Value: $65-125 (Nic) $85-150 (Gold)

TG-142

Fanner .45

Mattel- 1959-62. Pair of large die cast in polished nickel finish with tan stag grips. This gun has a revolving cylinder and is a "Shootin' Shell" variety. Difficult to find and very desirable western toy gun.

Value $150-325 (Each)

TG-143

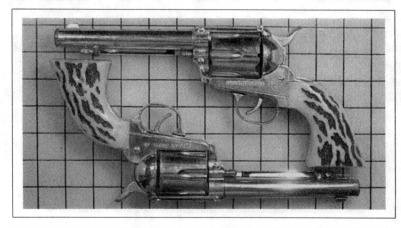

Fanner .45

Mattel- 1959-62. Similar to TG-143 above except has a gold plated cylinder. These large Fanners look great in large holster sets.

Value: $165-350 (Gold cylinder variety)

TG-144

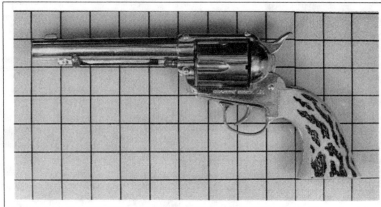

Fanner 50

Mattel- 1959. Early experimental model in blue finish with stag grips. Possibly the first attempt at a "Shootin' Shell" gun. Non-revolving cylinder. See TG-146.

Value: $200-350 (Exp. model)

TG-145

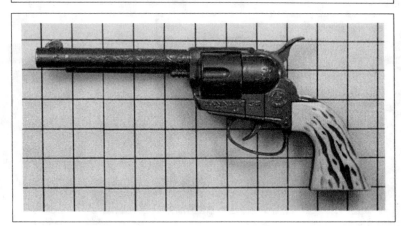

Fanner 50

Mattel- 1959. Detail of TG-145. Note the spring-loading mechanism on the left side. Rare variation and may be a factory prototype.

TG-146

Fanner 50

Mattel- 1959-65. Die cast in chrome finish with revolving cylinder that accepts bullets. In unusual display box with the original instruction booklet.

Value: $100-225 (Gun & box)

TG-147

Fanner 50

Mattel- 1959-65. Gun shown in TG-147. Note the barrel scroll engraving and the beautiful tan stag grips. Accepts the solid variety of Mattel bullets. Revolving cylinder model.

Value: $85-185

TG-148

Fanner 50

Mattel- 1959-65. Detail of TG-148. Note the revolving cylinder that accepts bullets & the cap sprocket mechanism. The side plate reminds the owner to use only perforated caps and oil after ten rolls.

TG-149

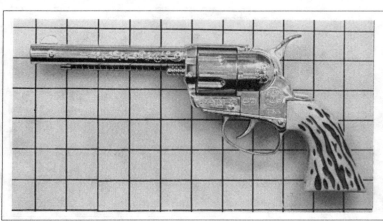

Fanner 50

Mattel- 1959-65. Similar to TG-148 above except this gun has no revolving cylinder & doesn't accept bullets. Chrome plated with engraving & stag grips.

Value: $55-135 (No revolving cylinder)

TG-150

Fanner 50

Mattel- 1962. Cowboy in Africa model in chrome finish with white Impala head grips.

Value: $60-140

TG-151

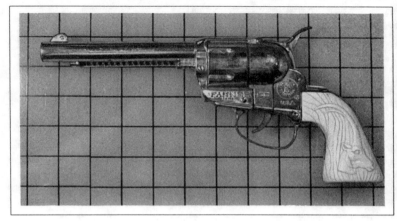

Fanner 50

Mattel- 1962. Similar to TG-151 but in the black finish with white Impala head grips.

Va;ue: $65-145

TG-152

Fanner 50

Mattel- 1960. Planet of the Apes model in antique bronze finish with black Impala head grips. Seldom seen variety.

Value: $70-150

TG-153

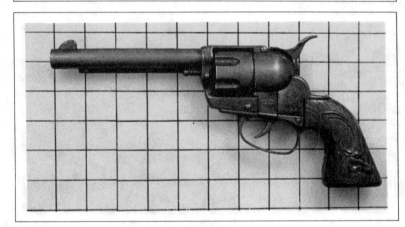

Fanner 50

Mattel- 1965-68. Agent Zero model in the black finish, engraved with walnut style grips & decal. Rare model with longer barrel & non-revolving cylinder. Shown with the rare original display box.

Value: $100-185 (Gun & box)

TG-154

Fanner 50

Mattel- 1965-68. Detail of TG-154 showing the Agent Zero decal on the walnut grip in the medallion recess. Agent Zero was a secret frontier defender!

TG-155

Fanner 50 (.38)

Mattel- 1965-68. Rare snub-nose .38 variety of the Agent Zero model. Revolving cylinder "Shootin' Shell" model. *Top:* Has the black finish & gold cylinder. *Lower:* Has black finish with black cylinder.

Value: $75-145

TG-156

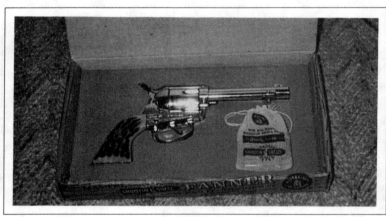

Fanner Shootin' Shell

Mattel- 1959-65. Smaller 9" die cast with revolving cylinder that accepts bullets. Chrome plated with stag grips. Shown with original box and bag of Shootin' Shell bullets.

Value: $85-150 (Gun & box)

TG-157

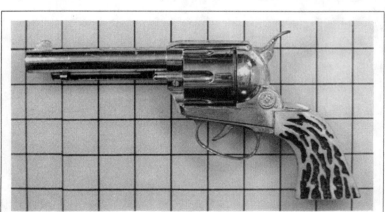

Fanner Shootin' Shell

Mattel- 1958-65. Gun shown in TG-157. Notice the quality finish and stag grips. Collectors suspect that a jewel is missing from right grip, but this is for loading a bullet into the Shootin' shell case.

Value: $75-145 (Gun only)

TG-158

Fargo Express

Kilgore- 1945 era. Extremely rare cast iron & pressed steel. Research indicates utilizing remaining parts after WW II, or producing a toy of less weight for shipping. Revolving steel cylinder and eagle grips.

Value: $ 650-950

TG-159

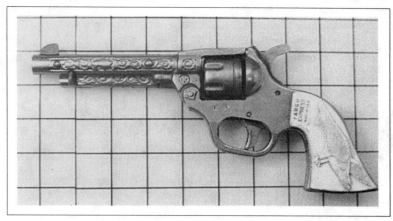

Federal No. 2

Federal- 1920 era. Rare cast iron repeater is a charming toy interpretation of a six shooter. Checkered grips.

Value: $75-150

TG-160

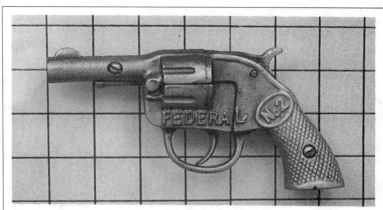

Fenix   (Phoenix ?)

Unknown- 1950-60 era. Reverse of gun is stamped Texan, Jr. Light alloy cap gun is a copy of a Hubley Texan, Jr. Left grip is steerhead with star. History of Mexican manufacture. See reverse below.

Value: $35-75

TG-161

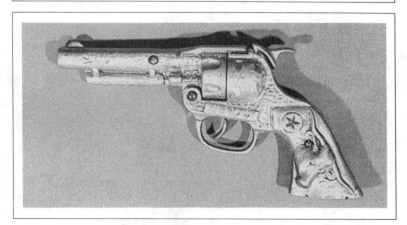

Texan, Jr.

Unknown- 1955-60 era. Reverse view of TG-161 shown above. Note the steerhead grip with Colt horse medallion. Crude casting and workmanship.

TG-162

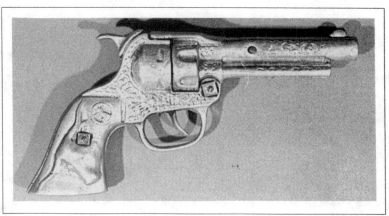

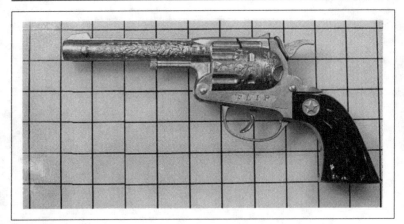

Flip

Hubley- 1960 era. Unusual, engraved, die cast repeater with black stag grips. "Flip" was the sidekick of "Kelly" in the TV show "Overland Trail". Also see character section.

Value: $40-85

TG-163

.44 Cal.

Kenton- 1930 era. Cast iron 7 1/2" single shot. 1st model with small and narrow hammer. Checkered grips. Rather rare. Circle S-W medallions.

Value: $125-250

TG-164

.44 Cal.

Kenton- 1930 era. Nearly identical to TG-164 above except, 2nd model with wide hammer. Seldom seen toy gun. Circle S-W medallions.

Value: $125-250

TG-165

45

Stevens- 1910 era. Extremely rare cast iron single shot. Early, & most charming, attempt to produce a toy western Colt 45 revolver. This 6" gun is seldom seen.

Value: $150-300

TG-166

45 Cal.

Balantyne Mfg. C., IL.-1950 era. Unusual pressed steel repeating cap gun. Grips are white horse & rider. Revolving cylinder. 3 models: No name, Roy Rogers and the Buffalo Bill. Only difference is the grips.

Value: $100-200

TG-167

45 Smoker

Product Eng.-1950-60. Large die cast gun is all metal. Insert barrel into bag of white powder & cock hammer to fill. Add a cap & fire! Powder will look like smoke. Grip is checkered & painted black. Dull gray.

Value: $45-85

TG-168

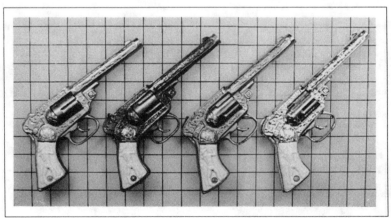

49-ER

Stevens- 1940 era. Strange looking, hammerless-style C.I. with revolving cylinder. White grips have covered wagon & cowboy. Engraved nickel with dark cylinder & original box. Rather rare classic toy.

Value: $150-350 (Gun & Box)

TG-169

49-ER

Stevens- 1940 era. Four finish variations that appear in this model. *Left to right:* 1st-Nickel finish. 2nd-Antique Bronze is quite rare. 3rd-Pale gold finish also rare. 4th-Silver chrome paint-type of finish is very late and virtually unknown.

Value: $125-275 (Nik) $150-325 (Other)

TG-170

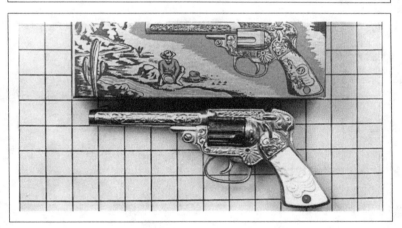

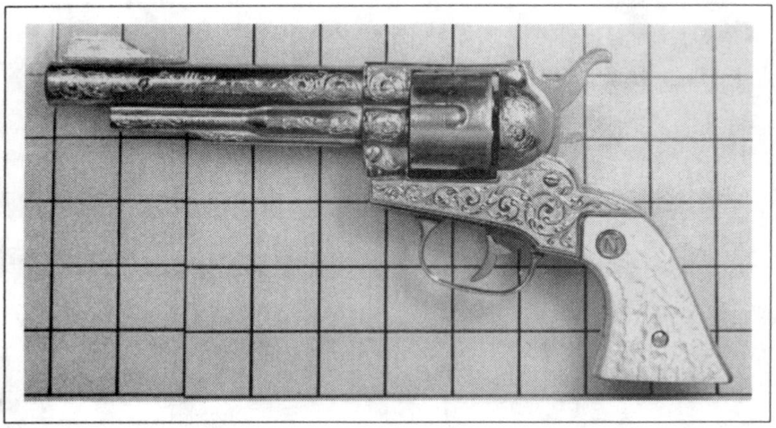

41-40 Stallion

Nichols- 1958-60 era. Large die cast with flip-out revolving cylinder & bullets. The engraving is exceptional on this toy. In the nickel finish with stag grips. One of the more difficult D.C. toys to find.

Value: $150-300

TG-171

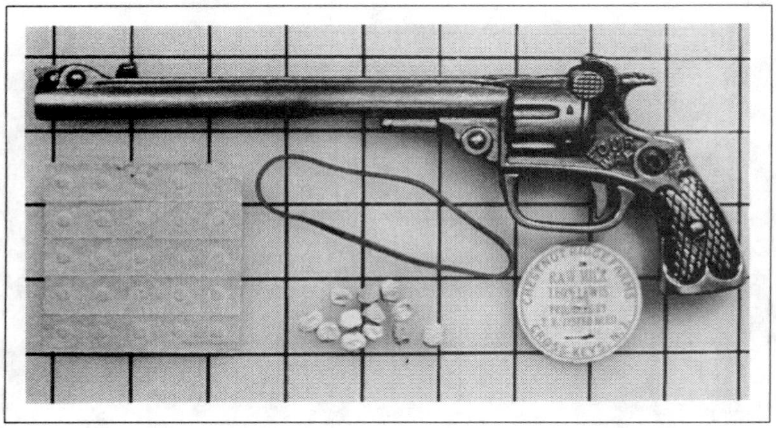

Four Way

Kenton- 1930 era. Extremely rare cast iron. Mechanically designed to shoot; caps, peas, milk bottle tops and rubber bands! A mere handful are known to exist. Nickel finish & painted black grips.

Value: $300-550

TG-172

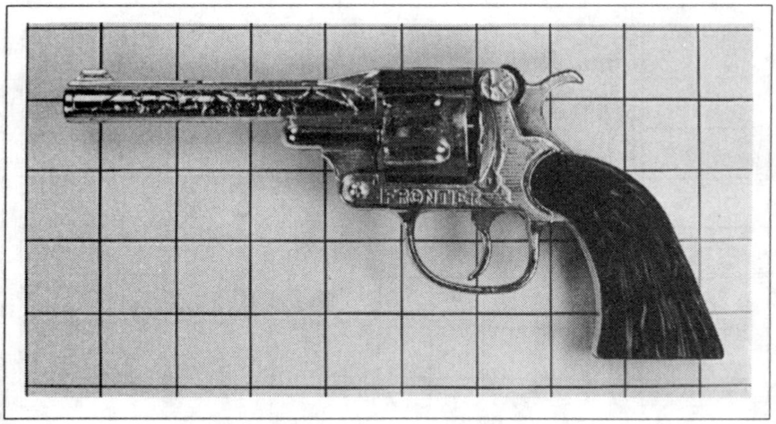

Frontier

Kilgore- 1960 era. Nickel die cast with revolving cylinder. Engraved with black stag grips. Disc caps.

Value: $65-125

TG-173

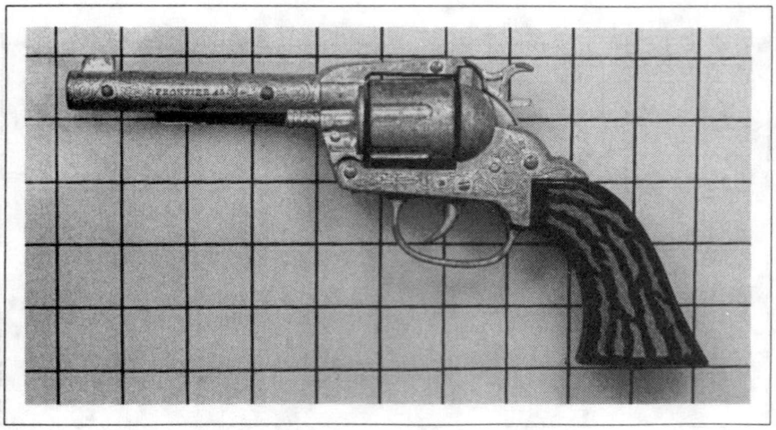

Frontier .45

American West- 1965-70 era. Die cast with revolving cylinder in dull nickel. It is engraved with black & tan stag grips.

Value: $35-75

TG-174

Frontier .44 Cal.

Unknown- 1965-70. Unusual plastic and metal cap gun. Colt Sheriff model with 3" barrel. Beautiful engraving in black finish with white stag and gold sheriff badge as medallion. Also with 6" barrel.

Value: $35-75

TG-175

Frontier .44 Cal.

Unknown- 1965-70. Detail of TG-175 to show reverse side with unusual side-opening access for cap loading. This may have been made by Marx.

TG-176

Frontier .45

British Cast Metals, Eng.- 1960-70. 10 1/2" Die cast with a revolving cylinder and engraving in black finish with Indian Chief white grips. Also in nickel finish.

Value: $65-150

TG-177

Frontier Smoker

Product Engineering Co. Oregon- 1950-60. Unusual gun that shoots caps and smoke powder. Shown with original box, bag of special powder and instruction sheet. One variation does not shoot caps.

Value: $75-150 (Gun, box & contents)

TG-178

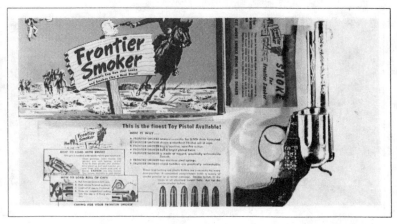

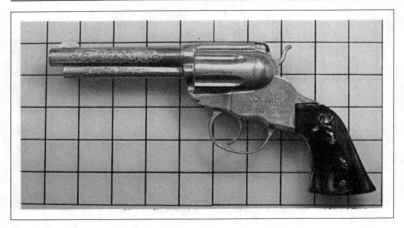

Frontier Smoker

Product Engineering Co.Oregon- 1950-60. Die cast that shoots caps and smoke powder. Nickel finish with engraving and black horsehead grips. Variation exists that does not shoot caps. Seldom seen toy.

Value: $65-135 (Either model)

TG-179

Gabriel

Hubley/Gabriel- 1966-70. Repeating die cast gun in dull nickel with engraving and one-piece stag grips. Gabriel became the owner of Hubley in 1966.

Value: $20-35

TG-180

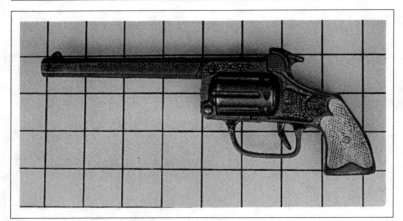

Gat

Hubley- 1935. Unusual & rare cast iron is a repeater. The barrel tips down to cock the hammer. Blue-bronze finish with ivory painted grips.

Value: $125-225

TG-181

Gene Autry

Kenton- 1951 era. Unusual polished nickel finish long barrel with the hat & spur grips usually found on engraved models. This gun was found this way in a linen drawer. See G. Autry in character section.

Value: $175-300 (Polished model)

TG-182

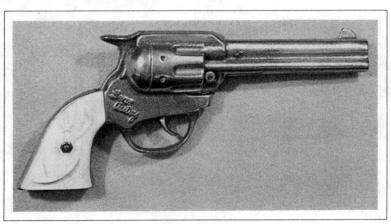

Giant

Kilgore- 1935 era. Extremely rare cast iron in highly polished nickel. Single shot has checkered grips. Has the original factory salesman's sample tag attached. This is a very elusive toy gun. Polished for sales.

Value: $225-450

TG-183

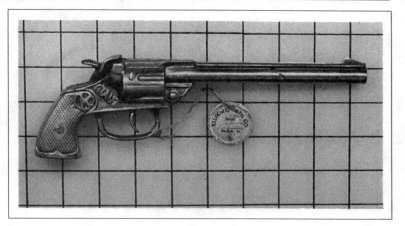

Giant

Unknown, Eng.- 1945-50. Large cast iron with fluted barrel and checkered grips. A nickel finished single shot that is seldom seen.

Value: $125-250

TG-184

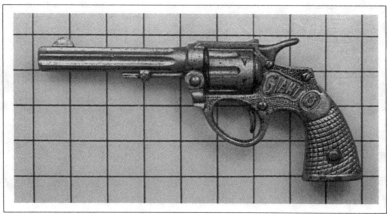

Giant

Unknown, Eng.- 1940-50. Similar to above TG-184, except in the blue-black painted finish.

Value: $125-250

TG-185

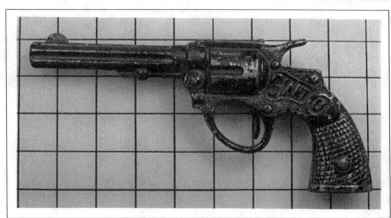

Gray Ghost

Lone Star, Eng.- 1957 era. One of the rarer die cast character guns. Nickel gun with engraving & smooth silver plastic grips. See character section also.

Value: $150-300

TG-186

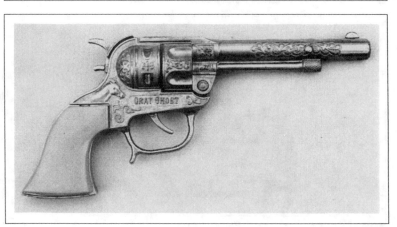

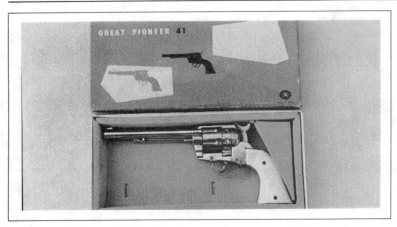

Great Pioneer .41

Modern Toys, Japan- 1965-75 era. Rare die cast in polished nickel with slick white grips. This is a near duplicate of the Hubley Ric-O-Shay. Revolving cylinder, bullets & presentation box.

Value: $100-165

TG-187

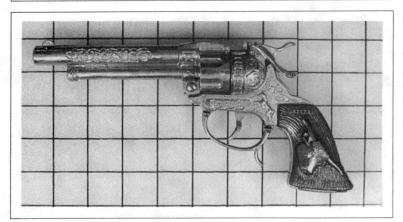

Grizzly

Kilgore- 1955-60. Large 10 1/4" die cast, engraved with special black Grizzly bear grips. This variation has superb gold finish. Also in nickel. Both variations have black grips. Revolving cylinder. Very rare.

Value: $125-250 (Gold) $100-200 (Nic)

TG-188

Gunsmoke

Leslie-Henry- 1955-75. Nickel die cast with the rarer copper steerhead & Matt Dillon grips. Came in long barrel. See the character section also.

Value: $95-185 (Short) $125-220)(Long)

TG-189

Gunsmoke Fanner

Lincoln Indus., Ltd., N. Zealand-1960-65. An exact replica of a Hubley Texan .38. Even the display box is identical in both design & color. Name under the cylinder. Engraved nickel & white steerhead grips.

Value: $100-185 (Gun & box)

TG-190

Gunfighter

Lone Star, Eng.- 1960-70. Chrome plated die cast repeater with cherry-red horsehead grips. Engraved frame & cylinder. Also available in the black painted finish with red grips.

Value: $45-110 (Chrome or black)

TG-191

Halco

Hubley- 1965-70. Contract gun for Halco. Die cast repeater in nickel with 2-piece white & tan stag. An identical gun exists called Ranger. Late model gun.

Value: $30-75

TG-192

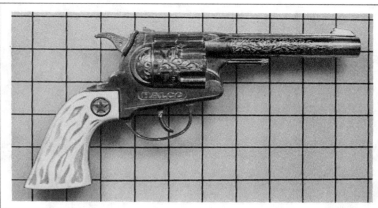

Halco

Hubley- 1965-70. Unusual die cast models for Halco with saw-handle grips in wood grained brown and white finish. Nickel finish with no engraving. Repeaters.

Value: $20-45

TG-193

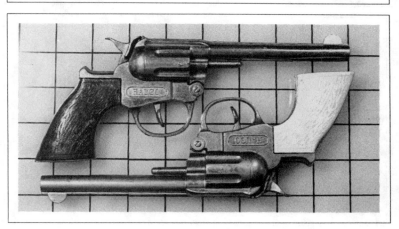

H-BAR-O

Kilgore- 1925-30 era. Cast iron single shot in the dark finish. The H-BAR-O was the name of radio star, Bobby Benson's Texas ranch. Show's sponsor was Hecker's Oats cereal. Thus "H-O". See character section.

Value: $50-95

TG-194

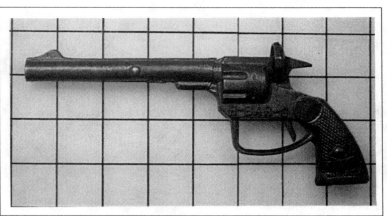

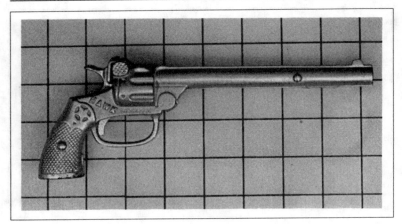

Hawk

Hubley- 1930-40 era. One of the rarest long barreled cast iron single shots. This nickel finished gun shoots mammoth caps. Only a handful are known to exist.

Value: $200-350

TG-195

Hero

Stevens- 1940 era. 5 1/4" cast iron single shot in nickel with rope engraving on the barrel. All metal with cowboy on grips. For mammoth caps.

Value: $35-85

TG-196

Hero

Stevens- 1940 era. Identical to TG-196, except in the rare dummy variety. Note the hammer.

Value: $50-100

TG-197

Hi-Ho

Kilgore- 1938-40. Very rare long barrel cast iron model in polished nickel finish. Wide hammer repeater with brown-tan swirl grips.

Value: $125-245

TG-198

Hi-Ho

Kilgore- 1940. Cast iron repeaters in the dark blue finish. *Left:* Rare scalloped grips and early narrow hammer. *Center:* Early narrow hammer & regular grip. *Right:* A wide hammer variety with regular grip.

Value: $85-165 (Scalloped grips add $25)

TG-199

Hi-Ho

Kilgore- 1940. Variations. *Left:* dark finish, wide hammer & riveted pearl horse grips. *Center:* Nickel & press-fit red grips. *Right:* Nickel finish with riveted red horse grips.

Value: $85-165 (All models)

TG-200

Hi-Ho Jr.

Kilgore- 1940 era. Very rare variety cast iron repeater. Scalloped top grips. *Left:* Nickel, wide hammer with brown-tan swirl grips. *Right:* Blue finish with narrow hammer and pearl grips.

Value: $175-250

TG-201

HI-HO

Stevens- 1940 era. 7" cast iron single shot in nickel finish with the rare dummy hammer. Red horsehead grips. Also made in regular hammer to fire caps.

Value: $75-135 Normal hammer $15 less.

TG-202

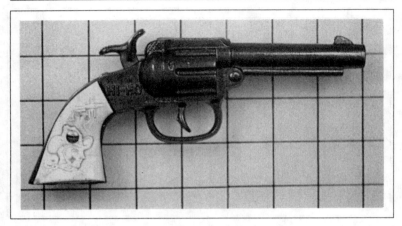

HI-HO

Stevens- 1940 era. Dark finish cast iron in the rarer dummy hammer variety. Also made in regular hammer variety. Note the white grips with the cowboy & pair of crossed guns.

Value: $75-135 Normal hammer $15 less.

TG-203

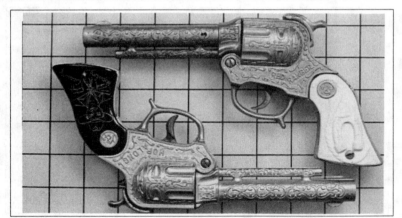

HI-Ranger

Stevens- 1940 era. Cast iron single shot in nickel finish with white horsehead grips & yellow jewel. Other color jewels used. Note the rare, and early original box.

Value: $135-200 (Gun & box)

TG-204

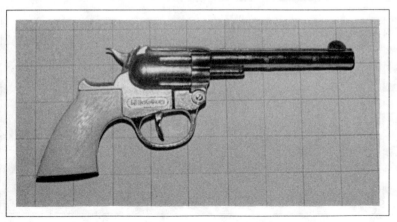

Hopalong Cassidy

Wyandotte- 1950-55. Pair of 9" die cast. *Top:* Nickel with white grips. *Lower:* Rare gold finish with black grips. All Hoppy guns are scarce. See character section.

Value: $225-400 (Nic) $250-450 (Gold)

TG-205

Hubley

Hubley- 1965-70. Nickel die cast repeater with no engraving and white wood-grained saw-handle grips. Similar to guns Hubley made for Halco. Unusual.

Value: $20-45

TG-206

Wells Fargo & Co. was a familiar part of the west. This toy strong-box is protected by a sawed-off double barrel shotgun, an Actoy Wells Fargo cap gun & a pair of Roy Rogers' G. Schmidt pistols in a beautifully tooled set of holsters by Classy. The gold pieces are candy and the badge is a Tales of Wells Fargo on the original card.

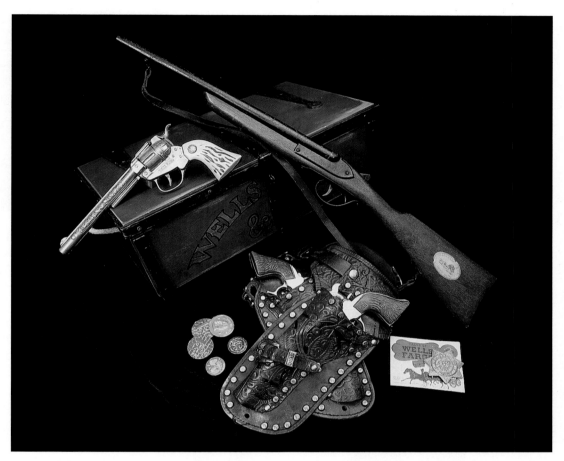

The Kilgore, cast iron & pressed steel Fargo Express is among the rarest of toy guns. Only a few have been discovered and this most unusual toy creates lots of un-answered questions. It is shown with a Kilgore CI American for comparison. Note the original Wells Fargo & Co. envelope and the toy W.F. & Co. agent's badge.

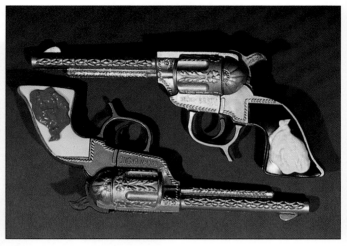

(UL) Lone Ranger CI guns by Kilgore. The group includes: Wide & narrow hammers, nickel, polished & blue finishes, engraved Ranger and a very rare dummy variety.

(UR) A pair of Geo. Schmidt Buck'n Bronc guns with short barrels, engraved frames & horse with rider grips in two rare color varieties.

(LC) Unusual Hopalong Cassidy single holster set with a cowhide covering, jewels & studs. Heart-shaped holster strap implies a cowgirl variety. Gun is a George Schmidt.

(LL) Two of the most desirable toy guns. A Kilgore CI polished Roy Rogers and a Long Tom, shown with the matching boxes. The rare Roy R. cloverleaf spurs are by Classy.

(LR) Large double holster set with jewels, studs, conchos and fringe. The guns are Hubley DC Cowboys which are among the most popular of western toy guns.

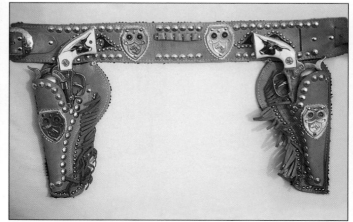

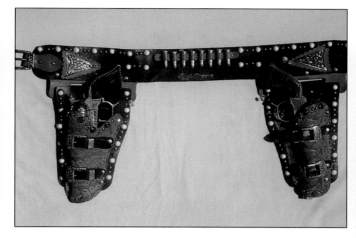

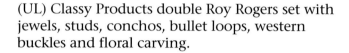

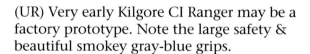

(UL) Classy Products double Roy Rogers set with jewels, studs, conchos, bullet loops, western buckles and floral carving.

(UR) Very early Kilgore CI Ranger may be a factory prototype. Note the large safety & beautiful smokey gray-blue grips.

(RC) Group of Leslie-Henry Gene Autry DC .44 models including: the nickel with solid cylinder, nickel with bullets, the rare gold model with box and antique bronze.

(LR) Extremely rare DC Roy Rogers model by Lone Star of England. Note the similarities to a Hubley CI Cowboy.

(LL) Superb Keyston Brothers double set has studs, jewels, conchos, cut-outs, fringe, bullet loops and western buckles. The guns are CI Hubley Texans with Colt logos.

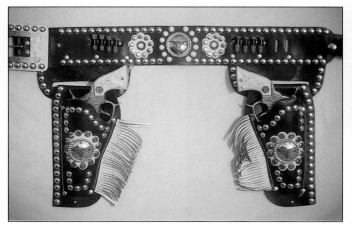

Three superb single holsters with jewels, silver studs, embossed art, fringe, cut-outs & many memories. The guns are Hubley DC Cowboys & a Nichols 41-40 Stallion.

A gleaming array of gold plated toy guns! A collection of gold guns would be most impressive & valuable. Shown are examples by: Hubley, Kilgore, Nichols, Leslie-Henry, Actoy, Stevens and Wyandotte. The rarest gun featured is the Nichols Stallion .45 Mark II with powder-blue pearlescent grips. Less than 200 of this model G-45 gun were produced in 1959.

Roy Rogers: Top gun is a Leslie-Henry in gold finish with black grips. It is a smoker model & has small holes in the cap anvil. The lower gun is by Classy with rare, two-toned gold & polished chrome. Note the beautiful floral and scroll grips in gold.

Keyston Brothers gave this double holster set the full treatment! The set contains hundreds of silver studs, ivory-like cowboy conchos, western buckles, bullet loops and many emerald green jewels which are most unusual. The running buffalo logo is on many of the rivets.

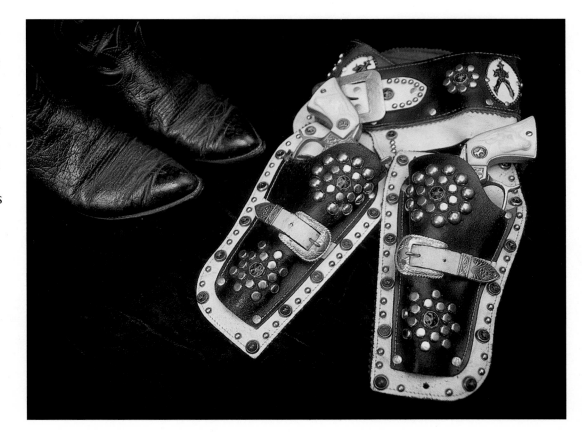

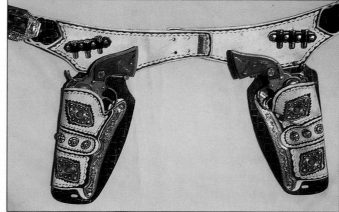

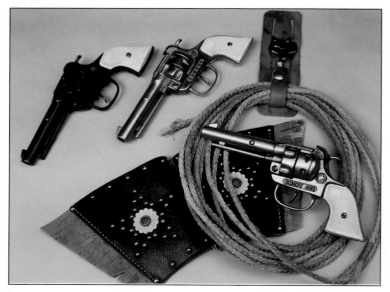

(UL) Pair of CI Stevens 49-ERs in unusual finishes. One model is in the seldom seen antique bronze and the other has the late, silver chrome paint finish.

(LC) Three Hubley CI guns that are nearly identical. A rare Smoky Joe model rests on the lariat. The two Cowboys are shown in the polished nickel and blue-black finish.

(LL) Fantastic Classy Roy Rogers holster set in black and metallic silver! Double set has jewels, studs, bullet loops and embossed artwork. DC guns are by George Schmidt.

(UR) Cowgirl double holster set with studs, turquoise jewels, metallic silver edges and bullet loops. The Hubley DC Western guns have turquoise steerhead grips.

(LR) Unusual Mattel Fanner-50 Cowboy in Africa model in black finish with the white Impala grips. Original display box.

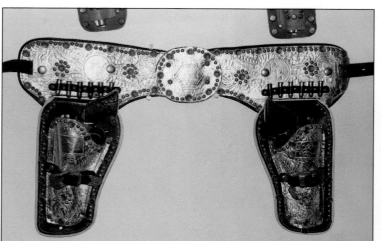

(UL) An unbelievable group of CI Kilgore Americans! Included are 1st models with CI cylinders, 2nd models with two-piece pressed steel cylinders and dummy model.

(UR) Beautiful antique bronze finishes on a Hubley late model Texan, Jr. and Hubley Western. Both of these guns are probably factory prototypes.

(RC) These beautiful gold guns are by Geo. Schmidt. Three are the short barrel Buck'n Bronc with large lettering & grip varieties. The other is a rare gold Hopalong Cassidy.

(LR) This Alan Ladd Shoot'n Iron by Geo. Schmidt is one of the rarest of all character guns. This chrome finished toy gun was produced soon after the movie *Shane*.

(LL) Charming cowgirl double holster set has red jewels, felt lining, bullets, silver studs and heart cut-outs. The guns are gold DC Texan, Jrs. by Hubley.

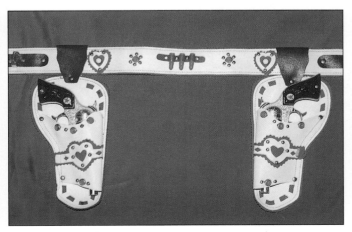

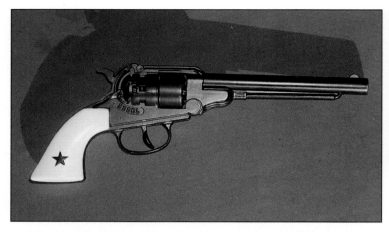

(UL) Rarely seen Rebel DC by Lone Star of England. These were distributed by Classy Products. The one shown is in black finish with ivory-type white grips.

(LC) King of the Cap Guns: A group of DC Nichols' Stallion .45s including: 1st models, Mark II models, Kusan transition, gold, steel-blu and nickel. Note grip varieties.

(LL) The rare Nichols Stallion .45 Mark II, model G-45, in the gold finish. Note the powder blue pearlescent grips and original presentation box with gold label.

(UR) Double holster set with metallic silver floral scroll fronts. Many silver studs with two adjustable buckles. The guns are 41-40 DC Stallions by Nichols.

(LR) The box for the Kilgore CI Big Horn is among the rarest! Only a few examples have survived. Shown with a rare polished Big Horn that has white stag grips.

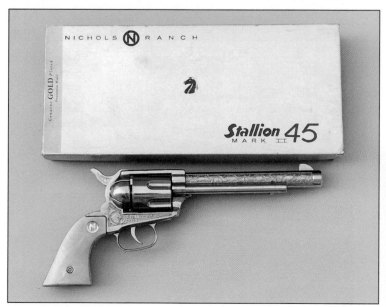

(UL) The very rare Gray Ghost DC by Lone Star of England. Nickel finish with silver metallic grips. The Gray Ghost was Major John Mosby of the 1st Virginia Cavalry.

(UR) Unusual single holster rig by Keyston Brothers has hundreds of silver studs and stars. The word "Texan" is spelled-out in tiny silver studs on both ends of the belt.

(RC) Dale Evans: Large frame G. Schmidt with red jewels. Small frame G. Schmidt. Pair of D-E butterfly spurs with six guns. All these cowgirl items are quite rare.

(LR) Very large Roy Rogers double holster set by Classy. Heavily tooled with many studs, jewels, bullet loops and metallic foil conchos. Classy Products Roy Rogers guns.

(LL) Extremely rare Daisy Model 61 made by Nichols has a mixture of steel-blu and brass with walnut-type grips & Daisy bullseye medallions.

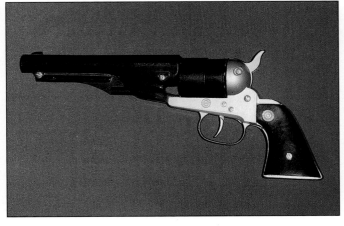

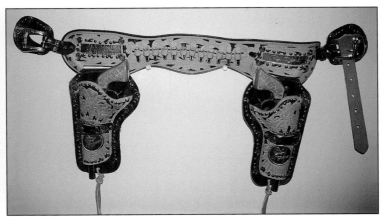

Any Hopalong Cassidy fan would be excited about this group. The Geo. Schmidt varieties include the long and short barrels, as well as, the various grips. The nickel gun by Wyandotte is the rare dummy. The smaller, gold Wyandotte is missing the ejector rod.

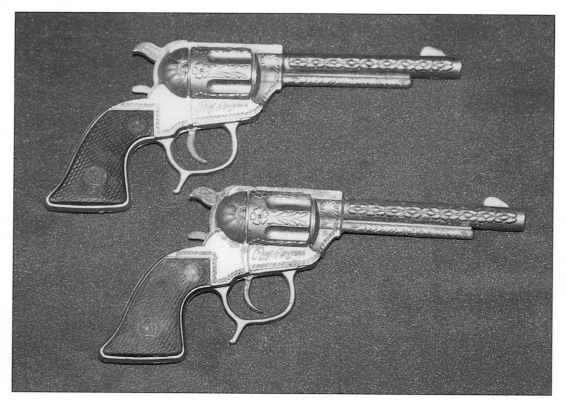

A rare and early pair of Roy Rogers guns made by Geo. Schmidt. This model has the shorter barrel and is completely engraved. A jewel is inlaid in the copper grips. These jewels can be found in red, green, yellow and blue.

A group of Roy Rogers guns by Geo. Schmidt. The varieties include long & short barrels, chrome & nickel finish and both the engraved & plain models. Grips include all the various types known to exist. Note the original price tag of $1.49 from the Western Auto store.

Perhaps the rarest of George Schmidt guns is the gold finished Hopalong Cassidy. The gold plating is 1st class and the black Hoppy busts on the black grip add to the quality.

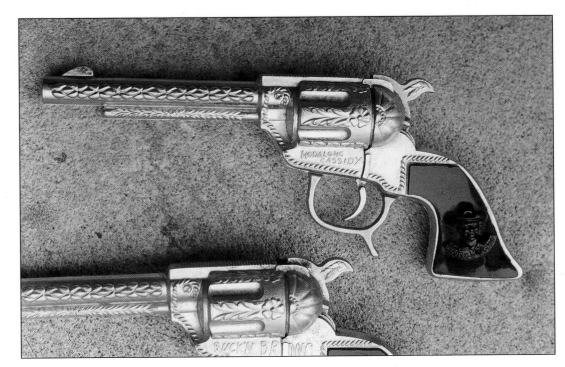

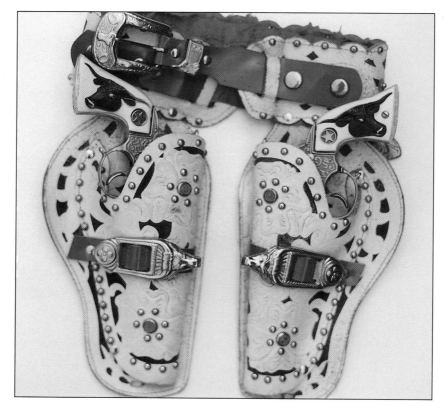

Double cowgirl holster set in red and white leather with red jewels and silver studs. Lined in red felt with tooled & cut-out decorations. Unusual steerhead holster buckles. This set made by Hubley, contains two Texan, Jrs.

Group of very popular Hubley DC Cowboys. Included are: polished nickel, antique bronze, blue-black, gold, nickel and dull blue-gray. The grips have a wide variety of swirl colors and represent some of the finest grips put on toy guns.

Very rare Roy Rogers CI guns by Kilgore. *T to B:* Polished nickel with long top strap, CI cylinder and riveted Roy grip. The polished nickel with short top strap, CI cylinder and snap-on Roy grip. The rarer Long Tom model with two piece steel cylinder and the name Roy Rogers very lightly etched on the side frame.

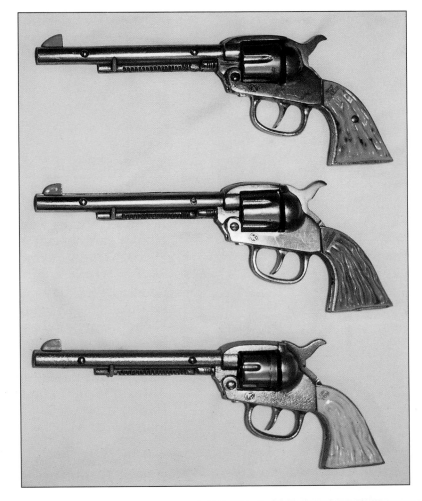

This pair of Kenton CI guns from the early 1950s, are nearly identical twins. Probably the last of the CI toy guns. The gun on the left is a Law Maker in the rarer nickel finish. The other gun is a rare Gene Autry engraved in nickel finish. Both guns share similar engraving & grips. The boxes are seldom seen, and the Gene box is among the rarest for a toy gun.

(UL) I'll raise you two bottle caps! A group of derringers for the western gambler: Note the Hubley Panther cuff gun, Dagger gun & the Halco, Nichols, Actoy & tiny Classy.

(LC) Early leather holster with an unusual stud arrangement. The gun is a Stallion 41-40 DC by Nichols. This gun has beautiful engraving and looks great in large holsters.

(LL) Antique bronze guns on Keyston Bros. vest. All are difficult to find. Rare G. Autry by L-H, Hubley Cowboy, Esq./Actoy Wyatt Earp, Halco Marshal & L-H Texas Ranger.

(UR) Top quality gunslinger double holster set with silver studs, steerhead conchos & bullets. Guns are L-H/Halco DC Marshals.

(LR) A Cowgirl double holster set in pink leather with floral tooling, silver studs, conchos, bullets and jewels. Guns are the Hubley Remington .36 models.

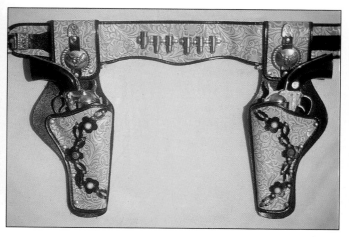

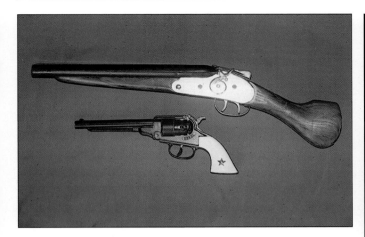

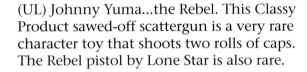

(UL) Johnny Yuma...the Rebel. This Classy Product sawed-off scattergun is a very rare character toy that shoots two rolls of caps. The Rebel pistol by Lone Star is also rare.

(UR) Keyston Brothers holster set with fine tooling, cut-outs, multi-color jewels and studs. Set has matching wrist cuffs and contains an early Kilgore CI Warrior.

(RC) Keyston Brothers large single holster with hundreds of silver studs, red jewels & cut-outs of green leather. The gun is a 1st model Nichols Stallion .45.

(LR) A very early Hoppy single holster in black leather with various size silver studs and red jewels. Hopalong on holster strap and a Wyandotte nickel pistol.

(LL) Very rare cowgirl set. This Dale Evans double holster set in red & white, has the familiar D-E butterfly logo. The guns are Buzz Henry models with red insert grips.

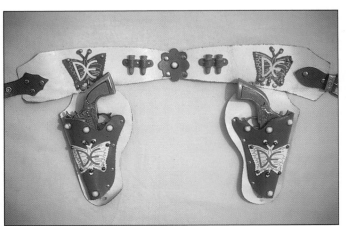

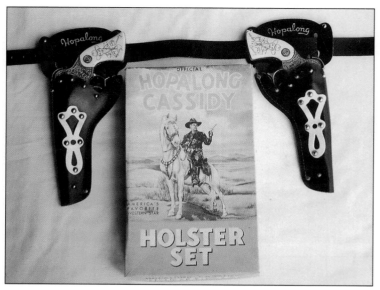

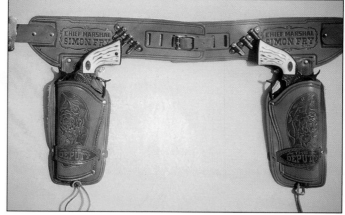

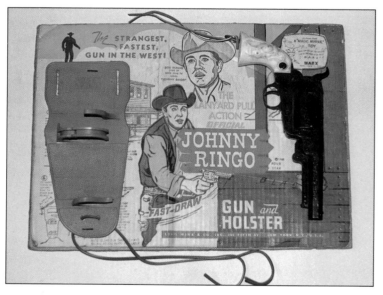

(UL) Hopalong Cassidy double holster set with the original box from Wyandotte. An unusual style that is seldom found. Both guns are by Wyandotte in nickel finished.

(UR) Simon Fry, Chief Marshal, double holster set with embossed tooling. A pair of Leslie-Henry .44 Marshal guns with the antique bronze finish are in the holsters.

(LC) Rarely seen Johnny Ringo gun and holster set on the original card. This gun is fired by pulling the string attached to the lanyard ring. Dragoon-style pistol.

(LL) Early child-size leather holster with beautiful beadwork on the front. Possibly from a western show. The gun is a rare CI Hubley Texan dummy in the dark finish.

(LR) Beautiful Hubley holster set in black and white tooled leather. The pair of guns are gold plated Hubley DC Texan Jrs.

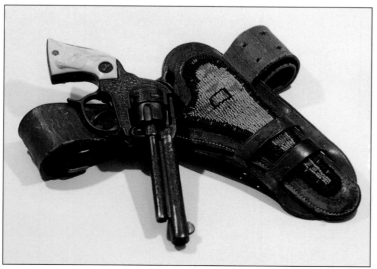

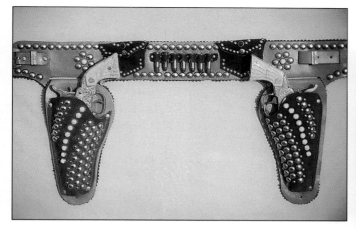

(UL) Rare double holster with an unusual arrangement of studs & jewels. Note the two small pouches for caps or coins on the gun belt. Guns are Nichols Stallion 41-40s.

(UR) Sharps saddle ring carbine, the Lone Ranger carbine & Roy Rogers rifle all made by Marx. Two rubber knives and a superb pair of fancy spurs by C-Bar-K (Corkale).

(RC) Detail photograph of the very rare CI Kenton Bull's Eye dummy variety. Note the word "Dummy" on the side plate and the hammer that can not fire caps.

(LR) Toy guns issued 1961-65 for the 100th Anniversary of the Civil War. Hubley 1860 Colt .44 & Remington .36, Nichols Model 61 chrome & steel-blu & Lone Star Apache.

(LL) Annie Oakley cowgirl holster is a very desirable set. Note Annie's logo on the top of the holster which has two shades of blue and natural buckskin with fringe.

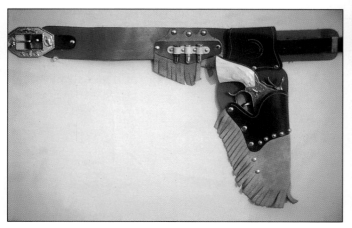

A trio of Leslie-Henry .44 models in antique bronze finish includes: a U.S. Marshal, Wagon Train and Gene Autry. The small chaps are a pair of "woolies" with leather trim & fringe. A collection of antique bronze toy guns can be both attractive and valuable.

Patriotic colors of red, white & blue are predominant in toy guns and their boxes. Their connection to fireworks & the 4th of July makes it obvious why. This group of Kenton CI Gene Autry guns all have red grips. Photo includes regular nickel, engraved, black and dummy varieties. All the boxes are difficult to find. The big rubber camp knife is a rare & early Keyston Brothers item.

The author's childhood treasures include: a CI Kenton Gene Autry, a red handled Barlow knife, wooden-match safe, skate key, bag of marbles & stag handled Kabar sheath knife. I'm most fortunate to have these items that were constant companions as I rode the imaginary range nearly 50 years ago.

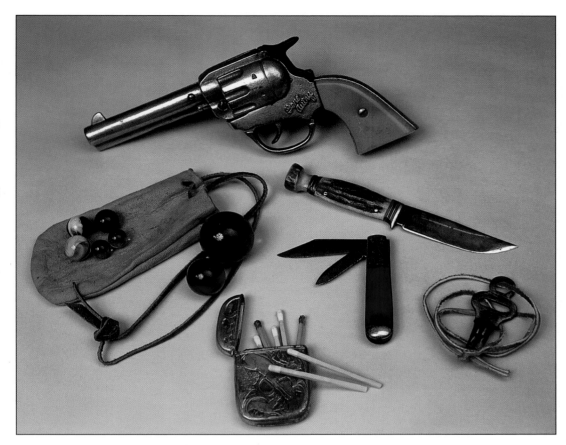

Round-up the posse! A selection of lawman-styled guns, cast iron handcuffs and badges. The guns include: CI Stevens Sheriff, Mattel Shootin' Shell Agent Zero, Marx double barrel pop gun and short barrel Frontier .44. The early handcuffs & "Tin Star" lawman badges make wonderful additions to any toy gun collection.

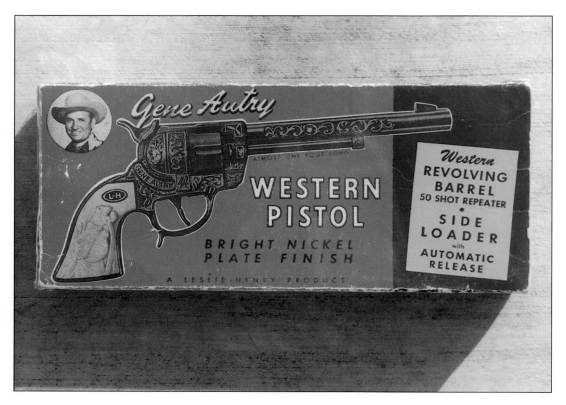

Large box for a Leslie-Henry .44 Gene Autry western pistol. Boxes for toy guns are found in limited numbers as most were discarded. The boxes for early CI guns and those having familiar western character names are most desirable and valuable.

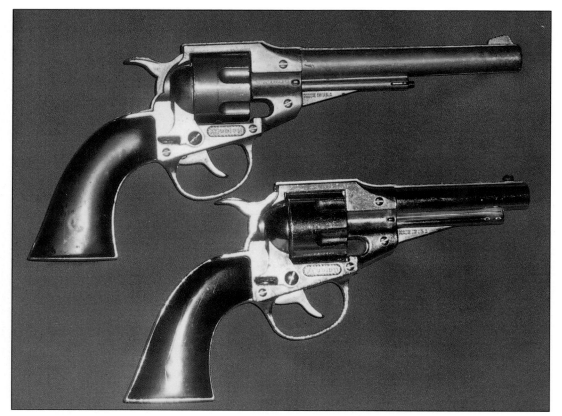

A pair of Hubley DC Remington .36 pistols with revolving cylinders and bullets. The longer barrel variety is quite rare. These were produced in the early 1960 era for the Civil War Centennial.

This Hubley 1860 Colt .44 is an unusual toy gun as it came as a kit, and had to be assembled. Gun is shown in the original box with the wooden display plaque. Early 1960s.

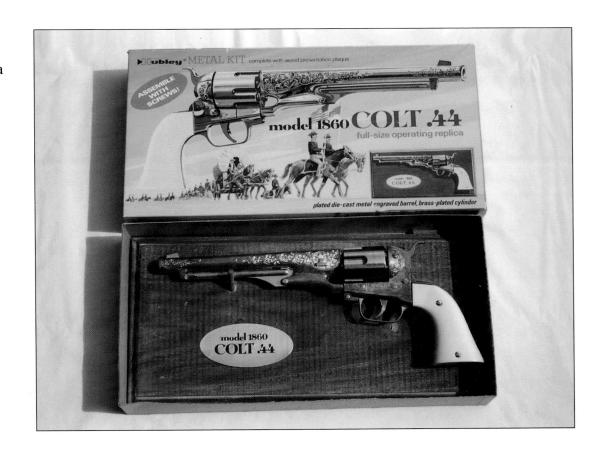

This Planet of the Apes is an unusual Mattel Fanner 50 model. The gun has an antique bronze finish & black Impala grips. 1960 era.

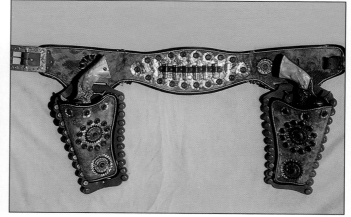

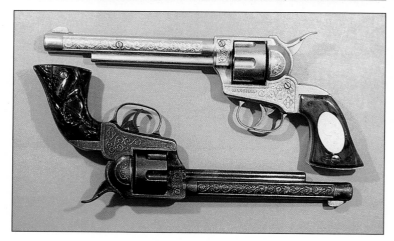

(UL) A pair of rare Leslie-Henry long barrel DC pistols. The Gene Autry was found with the orange grips and the Wyatt Earp has unusual steerhead ovals in the grips.

(UR) This cowhide covered holster with jewels, studs and conchos is possibly a cowgirl set. The guns are by Leslie-Henry and have the horsehead grips.

(LC) A pair of L-H/Halco Marshals with the revolving cylinders & bullets. Both have transparent amber grips, and the nickel gun has an ivory inset oval.

(LL) Rustler .45 by Crescent, Cowhand by unknown maker, Hubley DC Texan with a revolving cylinder but no lever & extremely rare Schmidt engraved Earp & Maverick.

(LR) This early holster is made of very thin leather and has a snap top, fringe, a star concho and belt. It was intended for a long barrel toy like this Hubley 101 Ranch.

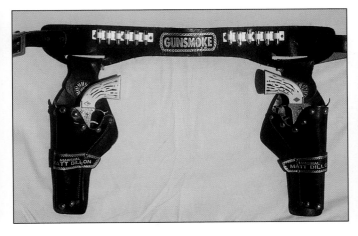

(UL) Gunsmoke-Marshal Matt Dillon large holster set for the very rare Halco .45 guns with the revolving cylinders. This pair in the nickel finish are Matt Dillon models.

(UR) Davy Crockett rubber frontier knife in the original cowhide covered sheath with leather fringe. The sheath attaches to a holster set.

(RC) Extremely rare pair of cast iron Gene Autry spurs. Most spurs are die cast metal. The pair matches a Keyston Bros. holster, so it is assumed they also made the spurs.

(LR) Set of Deputy jailer's keys by Jim-Lu Products of Washington, DC. They have a large keeper ring and are shown with their original box.

(LL) Wagon Train-Major Adams large holster set in tooled leather. The guns are Leslie-Henry .44 Wagon Train models in the antique bronze finish.

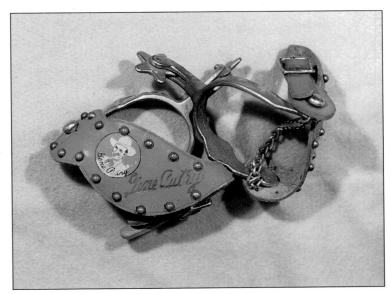

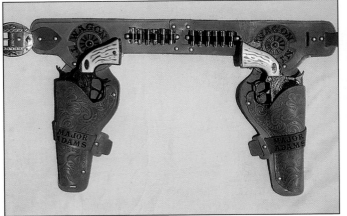

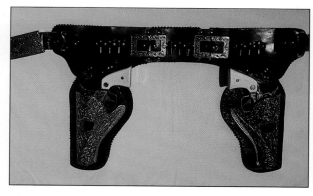

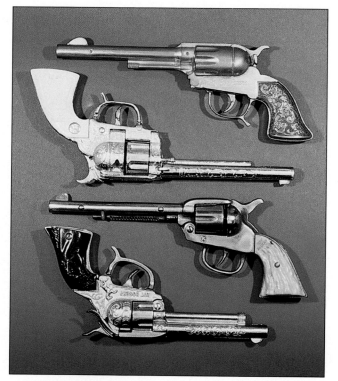

(UL) Indian-style decorations: Winchester by Mattel with studs, beads & feathers. A rubber knife & sheath with studs. Beaded holster. Stevens Big Chief gun. Tomahawk.

(UR) Very fancy holster set in tooled black leather with scroll, metallic gold fronts. It has bullets and gold buckles. The guns are Stallion .38s by Nichols.

(LC) Roy Rogers guns: Classy 2-tone gold with scroll grips. Lone Star with Indian Chief grips. Polished Kilgore CI with long top strap. Leslie-Henry 49er model in gold.

(LL) Ready for the matinee! A Lone Ranger clicker with celuloid grips, a bottle of milk, a new pad, some Mary Janes, Bazooka gum, a box of popcorn and a movie ticket.

(LR) A superb Roy Rogers double holster by Classy with tooling, jewels, conchos, hundreds of RR studs and large buckle. DC guns by Kilgore with revolving cylinders.

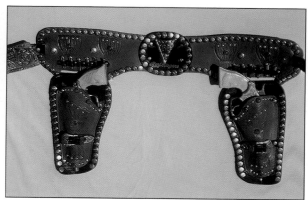

Hubley

Hubley- 1968-70. Die cast 8 1/2" repeater with engraving in nickel finish. One piece black stag grips. Side opening.

Value; $20-45

TG-207

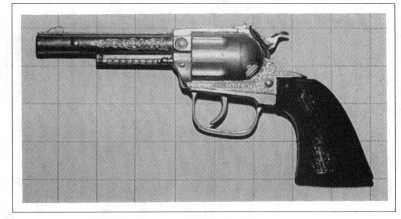

Hubley

Hubley- 1965-70. Large 10" die cast in nickel finish with engraving and one piece tan and white grips. Side opening. Similar to late Marshal guns.

Value: $25-50

TG-208

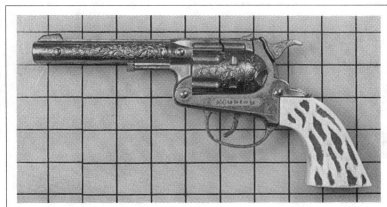

Hubley

Hubley- 1965-70. Pair of 10" die cast guns. Top: Similar to TG-208 except in chrome finish with black & white stag. Lower: Chrome finish & one piece black and white steerhead grips. Late guns.

Value: $25-50

TG-209

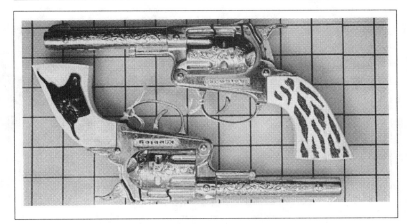

Indian

Kenton- 1930 era. Single shot cast iron in the blue-black finish. Difficult to find. It was also offered in nickel and a metallic bronze-green finish.

Value: $125-200

TG-210

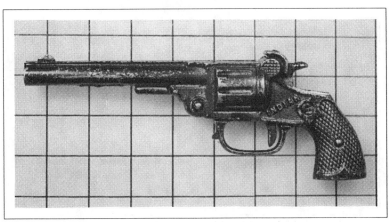

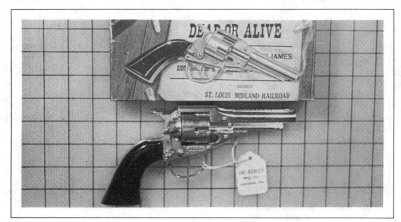

Jesse James

Hubley- 1960. Rare boxed set includes a Remington .36 short barrel with revolving cylinder. The gun is not marked Jesse James, just the box. Contains a wanted poster.

Value: $65-150 (Gun, box & poster)

TG-211

Johnny Ringo

Marx- 1960 era. Rare dragoon-style die cast in black finish with white steerhead grips. Fires by the lanyard ring thong. See character section.

Value: $50-125

TG-212

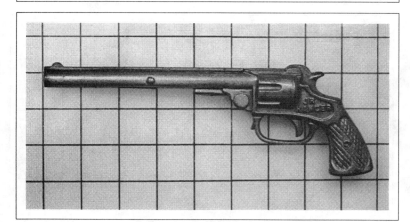

Jr. Ranger

Kenton- 1928 era. Extremely rare cast iron gun that is a solid casting with no moving parts. One of the rarest long barreled toy guns. Only a few exist.

Value: $325-450

TG-213

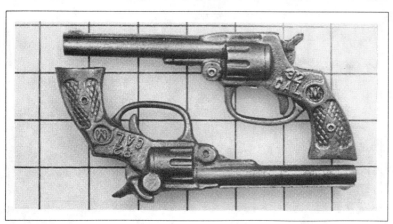

Jr. Ranger .32 Cal

Mordt- 1928 era. Pair of cast iron single shot guns *Top:* 1st model with small, narrow hammer. *Lower:* 2nd model with large, wide hammer. Seldom seen toys.

Value: $85-165

TG-214

Jr. Ranger .38 Cal

Mordt- 1928 era. Rare cast iron single shot. 2nd model with large, wide hammer in the dark finish. 1st model has small, narrow hammer.

Value: $95- 175

TG-215

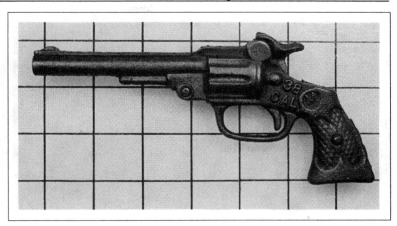

Jr. Ranger .44 Cal

Mordt- 1928 era. Rare 1st model cast iron with a small, narrow hammer. Single shot in the dark finish.

Value: $95-175

TG-216

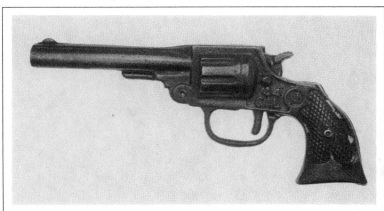

Jr. Ranger .44 Cal

Mordt- 1928 era. Rare 2nd model cast iron with a large, wide hammer. Single shot in dark finish with white painted grips.

Value: $95-175

TG-217

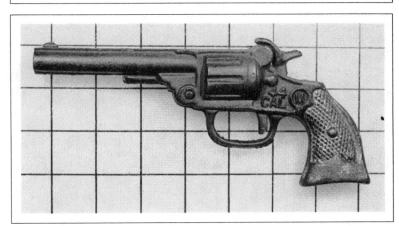

Jumbo

Stevens- 1890 era. Rare early cast iron has quaint engraving. Possibly named for the large elephant in P.T. Barnum's Circus. It is one of the rarer long barrel toy guns.

Value: $175-300

TG-218

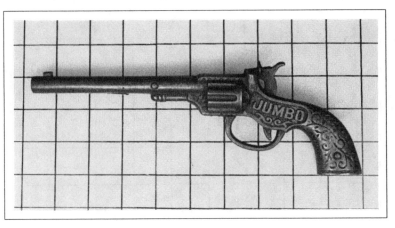

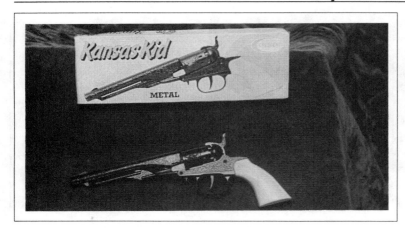

Kansas Kid

Crescent, Eng- 1970 era. Die cast 10 1/2"
with engraving and dark finish. Ivory
grips. Original box.

Value: $45-100 (Gun & box)

Tg-219

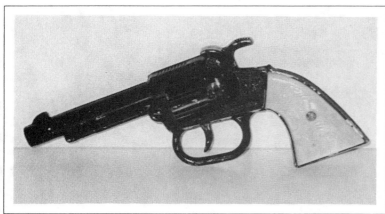

Keen Shot

Acme- 1945-50. Solid cast iron with ivory
cowboy bust grips. Non-working toy gun
in blue finish. Rare. 5" length.

Value: $45-85

TG-220

Keen Shot

Callen Mfg. Co., Haywood, IL- 1950 era. A
die cast, similar to TG-220, but this is a
single shot cap gun. Identical cowboy
bust ivory grips. Dark black finish. Rare.
Also all metal, with cast checkered grips.

Value: $30-65

TG-221

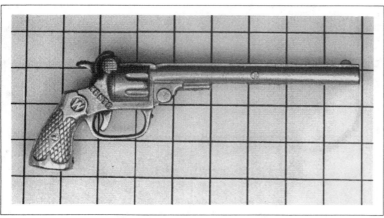

Kento

Kenton- 1935 era. Rare cast iron single
shot with long barrel. Nickel finish with
checkered grips. Shoots mammoth caps.

Value: $175-250

TG-222

King

Stevens- 1900 era. Cast iron single shot with long barrel. Nickel finish with the quaint, early-style floral engraving. Rare.

Value: $85-175

TG-223

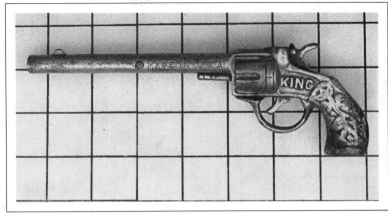

Kit Carson

Kenton- 1930 era. Cast iron single shot in nickel finish that shoots mammoth caps. Long barrel toy gun that is seldom seen.

Value: $100-175

TG-224

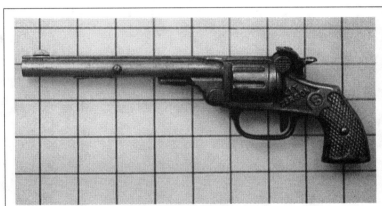

Kit Carson

Kenton- 1930 era. Cast iron gun similar to TG-224, except in the blue-black finish.

Value: $100-175

TG-225

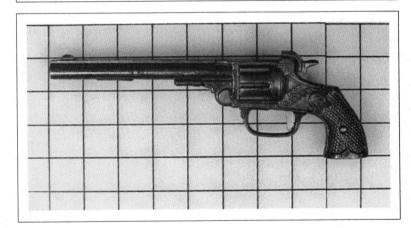

Kit Carson

Kilgore- 1955-60 era. Die cast repeaters. *Top:* 10" nickel finish with beautiful engraving & black bust grips. *Lower:* 8" nickel finish engraved with white bust-grips.

Value: $50-85 (Top) $30-65 (lower)

TG-226

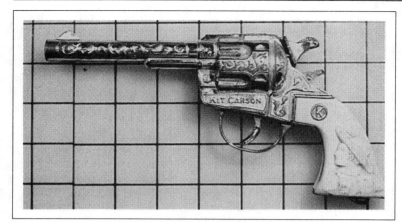

Kit Carson

Kilgore: 1955-60 era. Die cast repeater in the rarer gold finish with white bust grips. Also found with black grips.

Value: $45-80 (Gold)

TG-227

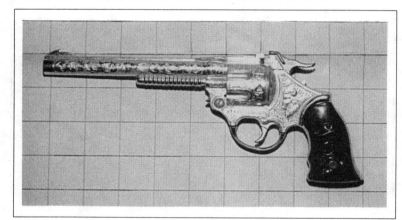

Kit Carson

Kilgore- 1955-60. Die cast repeater in the rarer gold finish. This gold plating by Kilgore is very high quality. The grips are black with a bust of Kit Carson.

Value: $65-125 (Gold)

TG-228

Klondike .44

Nichols- 1961. Extremely rare die cast repeater with revolving cylinder & bullets. Steel-Blu with walnut grained grips and circle "N" medallions. Note bottom of ejector rod is similar to a 41-40.

Value: $185-275

TG-229

Klondike .44

Nichols- 1961. Klondike .44 was a short-lived NBC TV show. Detail of lettering on the frame. Gun is similar to a Stallion .38 with some features of the 41-40 gun. Some had real wood grips which are also found on other Nichols' models in 1961-62. Many collectors believe these rare grips are home-made replacements.
TG-230

Larami

Unknown, Macau- 1990. Large 12" metal and plastic electronic noise maker. Black finish with gold hammer and trigger guard. Ivory checkered grips. Unusual.

Value: $10-15

TG-231

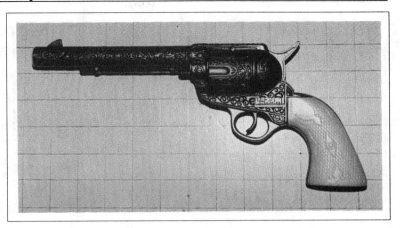

Laredo

Kilgore- 1960-65 era. Rare die cast similar to a Pinto. Chrome finished repeater has one piece tan & brown stag grips. It has minimal engraving.

Value: $20-45

TG-232

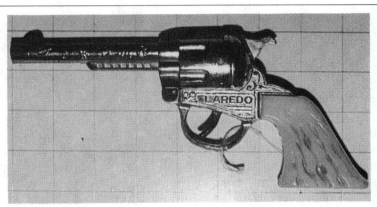

Lasso 'Em Bill

Kenton- 1930 era. Rare cast iron with the revolving cylinder that accepts bullets. Single shot. *Top:* Blue with white grips & blank medallions. *Lower:* plain cast iron with red grips & S-W medallions.

Value: $150-250

TG-233

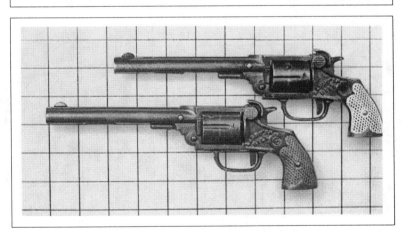

Lasso 'Em Bill

Kenton- 1930 era. Rare cast iron single shots. *Top:* Plain cast iron with red grips & blank medallions. *Lower:* Blue finish with red grips and blank medallions.

Value: $150-250

TG-234

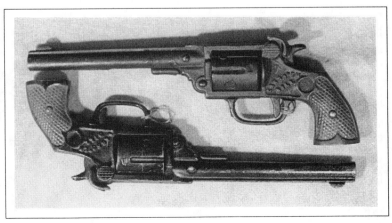

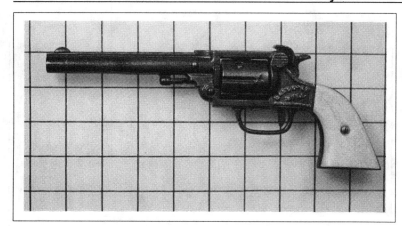

Lasso 'Em Bill

Kenton- 1930-35 era. Extremely rare model with blue finish. Has pearl grips similar to early Gene Autry guns and there are no medallions. Only example known to exist.

Value: $300-500

TG-235

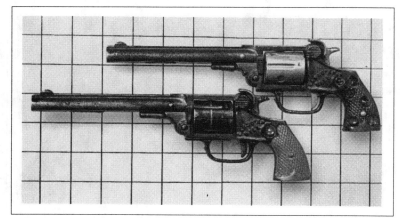

Lasso 'Em Bill

Kenton- 1930 era. Rare cast iron single shots. *Top:* Among the rarest varieties is this blue finish with nickel cylinder and 10 red jewels on the grips. *Lower:* Blue finish with red grips & jewel in circles.

Value: $250-450 (10 Jewels) $175-275 (L)

TG-236

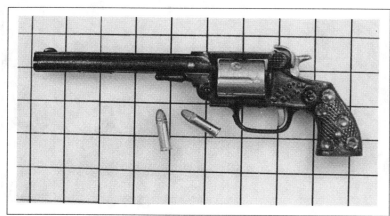

Lasso 'Em Bill

Kenton- 1930.Same gun shown in the photo above TG-236. Note the 2 bullets that fit in the cylinder. Both are .32 RF in nickel by Remington. Also note the tiny holes drilled in the bottom of each.

TG-237

Lasso 'Em Bill

Kenton- 1930 era. Extremely rare variety. Blue finish with 10 red jewels in the grip. S-W medallions, nickel cylinder, hammer & trigger. Note this is a dummy variety.

Value: $300-500 (Dummy with jewels)

TG-238

Lasso 'Em Bill Jr.

Kenton- 1930. Rare short barrel variation is 6 3/4" cast iron, single shot. Revolving cylinder in blue finish with the S-W grip medallions. Seldom seen model.

Value: $175-275

TG-239

Lasso 'Em Bill

George Schmidt- 1950 era. Unusual die cast repeater in polished chrome finish with painted white and brown copper stag grips. "LB" on grips.

Value: $75-145

TG-240

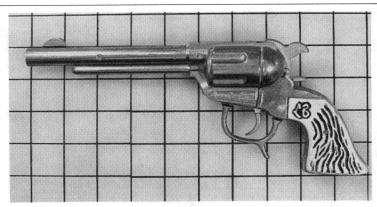

Law Maker

Kenton- 1950-51.One of the last cast iron guns. Due to lower production they are not very common. Engraved in the silver paint finish with white hat & spur grips. Nearly identical to G. Autry engraved.

Value: $125-235 Box- $75-125

TG-241

Law Maker

Kenton- 1950-51. Three variations of cast iron repeaters. *Left:* Quite rare nickel finish. *Center:* Rare silver paint finish. *Right:* the most common variety in black finish. Grips identical, white hat & spur.

Value: $125-235 $165-300 (Nickel)

TG-242

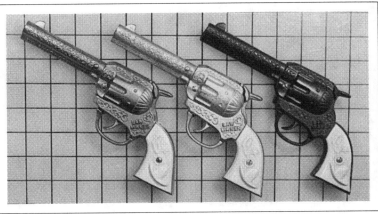

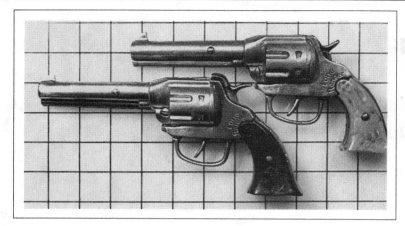

Lone Ranger

Kilgore- 1938-40 era. Cast iron repeaters. Top: 1st model with small, narrow hammer in nickel and blue swirl grips. Lower: 2nd model with large wide hammer in nickel with maroon swirl grips. Both are friction open. Also see character section.

Value: $165-325 (1st) $150-300 (2nd)
TG-243

Lone Ranger

Kilgore- 1940 era. Detail of the 3rd model cast iron that has the push lever- type release on the right. The one shown is in the black finish with pearl grips. The 3rd models have large wide hammers.

Value: $150-285

TG-244

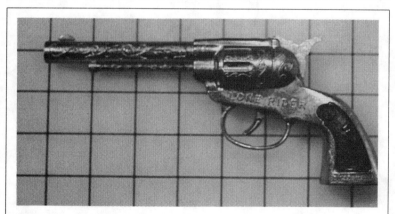

Lone Rider

Buzz Henry- 1950 era. Die cast single shot with engraving & insert grips in red. Also with white or black grips. Lettering is in the block-style.

Value: $30-65

TG-245

Lone Rider

Buzz Henry- 1950 era. Die cast similar to above, except in the rarer black finish & script-style lettering on the frame. Grips are insert-type with white rearing horse.

Value: $35-75

TG-246

Long Boy & Longboy

Kilgore- 1920 era. Rare long barrel cast iron. Top: Long Boy (2 words) in nickel finish. Lower: Longboy (one word) in cast iron no plating. Both shoot mammoth caps.

Value: $135-200

TG-247

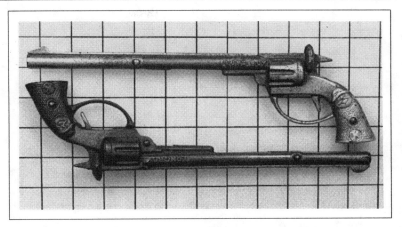

Longhorn

Leslie-Henry- 1960 era. Unusual die cast with pop-up cap box. Engraved in polished nickel finish with white horsehead grips. On an original Halco display card. Note price of $.98.

Value: $125-215 (Gun & card)

TG-248

Longhorn

Leslie-Henry- 1960 era. Similar to TG-248 above, except in the dull nickel finish The engraving is exceptional. Note that most pop-up cap boxes are broken due to the fragile hinge. Mint guns are rare.

Value: $125-200

TG-249

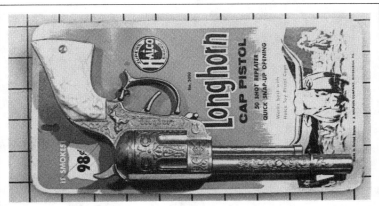

Long Tom

Kilgore- 1938-45 era. Perhaps the most desirable classic cast iron gun. *Top:* A 1st model with C.I. cylinder in nickel finish. *Lower:* 2nd model with the 2-piece steel cylinder. Both have revolving cylinders.

Value: $375-650 (1st) $300-550 (2nd)

TG-250

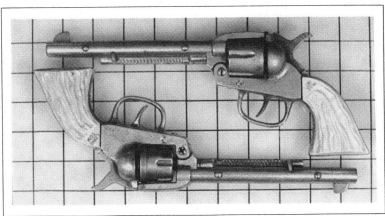

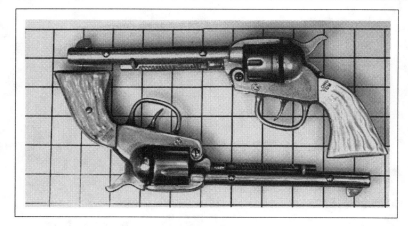

Long Tom - Roy Rogers

Kilgore- 1938-45 era. Very rare variations. *Top:* Rare 2nd model Long Tom with Roy Rogers etched on side plate. *Lower:* 1st model Roy in polished nickel with riveted Roy Rogers grips. See Roy section.

Value: $850-1,300 (Either variety)

TG-251

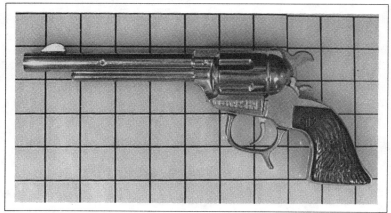

Marshal (BB)

G. Schmidt- 1950-55. Die cast repeater in polished chrome with copper stag grips with "BB" (Buckin' Bronc) medallions.

Value: $75-150

TG-252

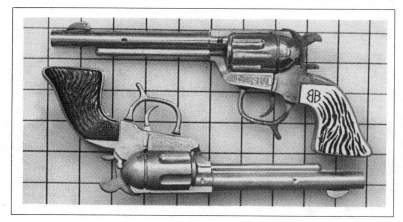

Marshal (BB)

G. Schmidt- 1950-55. Die cast repeaters. *Top:* Chrome finish with brown & white painted copper stag. *Lower:* Dull nickel finish with copper stag grips. Both have "BB" medallions.

Value: $75-150

TG-253

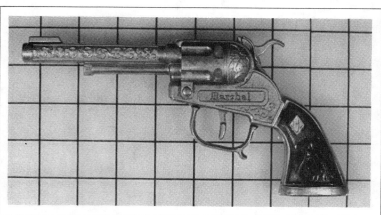

Marshal (Halco)

Leslie-Henry- 1960-65. Die cast repeater in nickel finish with engraving. Inset transparent amber horsehead grips with the diamond "H" medallion. L-H made guns very similar for both Gabriel and Halco.

Value: $35-70

TG-254

Marshal (Halco)

Leslie-Henry- 1955-60. Desirable die cast with revolving cylinders and bullets. *Top:* Nickel finish, engraved with transparent amber grips & star ovals. *Lower:* Antique bronze finish with transparent amber horsehead grips. Note solid brass bullets.

Value: $85-175 (Either with bullets)
TG-255

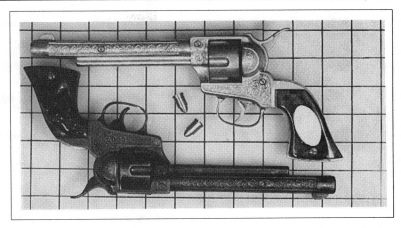

Marshal (Halco)

Leslie-Henry- 1955-60. Die cast similar to above, except in a copper finish with the white grips having copper flower ovals. Rare variation.

Value: $100-200

TG-256

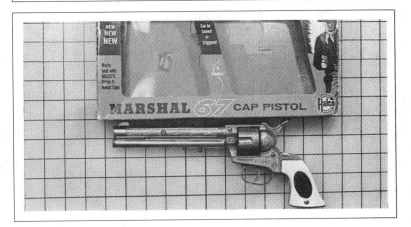

Marshal 6 & 7 Shooter (Halco)

Leslie-Henry- 1955-60. One of the most unique & rare die cast guns. Nickel with revolving cylinder & bullets. Extra shotgun barrel under regular barrel with the seventh shot, for after you fired 6 shots!

Value: $165-300 (Gun & original box)

TG-257

Marshal 6 & 7 Shooter (Halco)

Leslie-Henry- 1955-60. Gun shown in TG-257. Note nickel finish, fine engraving & diamond "H" logo on frame. *Caution:* the small brass, cap holder at the end of the shotgun barrel is usually missing!

Value: $150-275 (Gun complete)

TG-258

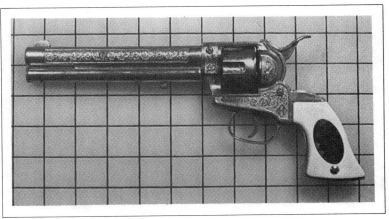

Marshal

Hubley- 1960-65. Die cast repeater in the nickel finish with fine engraving. Side opening. 2-piece steerhead grips with star medallions.Late model cap gun.

Value: $35-85

TG-259

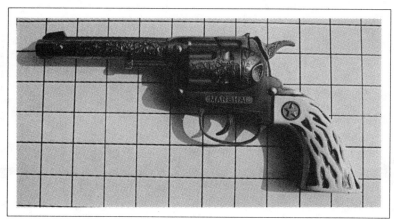

Marshal

Hubley- 1960-65. Similar to above but last model made. Has antique bronze finish with 2-piece brown & tan stag grips with star medallions.

Value: $45-95

TG-260

Marx 6 Shooter

Marx- 1955-60 era. Rarely seen die cast repeater with a revolving cylinder. Black finish with plastic walnut grips. Breaks open to load disc caps. Marx logo on the frame.

Value: $35-85

TG-261

Matt Dillon .45 Gunsmoke

Halco- 1955-75. Rare & very large die cast has revolving cylinder & bullets. Seldom seen character gun. Note the name and diamond "H" medallion in this detail. See character section under Gunsmoke.

Value: $175-325

TG-262

Maverick

Lone Star, Eng. 1960 era. Rare long barrel engraved, die cast in dull nickel finish with tan stag, notch bar grips. The ridge down the grips was for keeping track of the bad guys with a notch!

Value: $100-185

TG-263

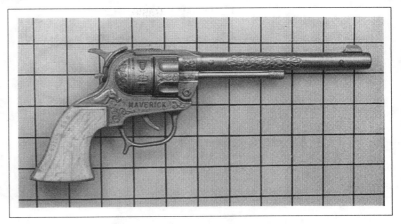

Maverick

Leslie-Henry- 1960. All long barrel L-H guns are rare. Nickel finish with engraving. Transparent amber grips with 4 leaf clover in the oval. See character section.

Value: $100-250

TG-264

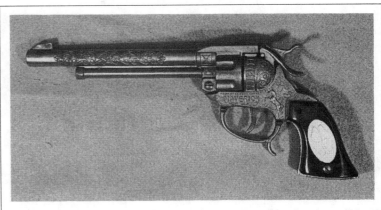

McCloud

Pilen, Spain- 1960-65. Foreign die cast with revolving cylinder & brown grips. Not western-style, but intended for TV market of Marshal McCloud. Nice box.

Value: $85-150 (Gun & box)

TG-265

Me & My Buddy

Marx- 1930-45. An unusual pressed steel clicker with an animated cowboy that resembles Tom Mix. The trigger activates the cowboy. If I don't get you, my buddy will! Black with a full color cowboy.

Value: $75-125 (Gun & box)

TG-266

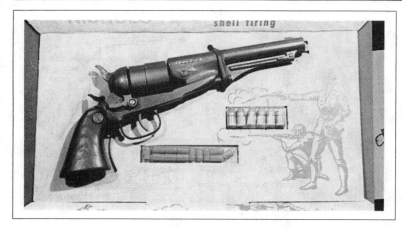

Model 61

Nichols- 1960-61. Die cast gun. Civil War Centennial model with revolving cylinder & bullets. Steel-Blu finish and walnut grained grips. In original display box and shooting shells. Rare die cast.

Value: $200-350 (Gun & box)

TG-267

Model 61

Nichols- 1960-61. Similar to above. *Top:* The rarer polished nickel finish with the black wood-grained grips. *Lower:* Steel-Blu & walnut grips. Circle N medallions.

Value: $225-375 (Nic) $175-300 (Blu)

TG-268

Model 61 - Daisy

Nichols- 1961-62. Contract die cast gun. 1st model, Steel-Blu & brass. Shell firing with black stag grips. No Dasiy name or logo on frame. Blank circle medallion on grips. Very rare variation. Civil War gun.

Value: $200-325

TG-269

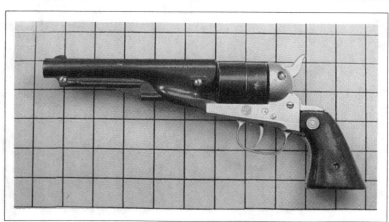

Model 61 - Daisy

Nichols- 1961-62. Similar to above except 2nd model, Steel-Blue & brass with walnut-grained grips. Daisy name & logo on frame. Daisy bullseye medallion on grips. These varieties are rare Nichols & Daisys.

Value: $200-325

TG-270

Mohawk

Hubley- 1930. Cast iron single shot is one of the few Indian name related toy guns. This long barrel is seldom seen. Nickel finish with checkered grips and the star medallion.

Value: $125-250

TG-271

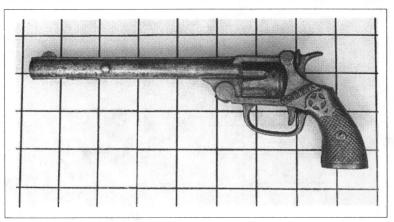

Mohican

Dent- 1925 era. Another Indian named, cast iron single shot. Shoots mammoth caps. All Dent toy guns are rather scarce. Nickel finish and checkered grips having circle "D" medallions.

Value: $85-150

TG-272

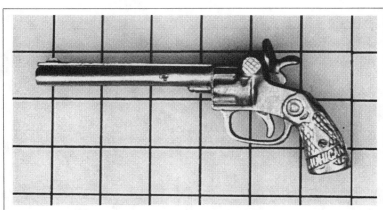

Mordt

Mordt- 1930 era. Rare cast iron single shot guns for caps and darts, in the dark finish. *Top:* Checkered grips are cast in metal. Lower: Very rare variety has pearl insert grips with rivet.

Value: $135-200 $235-400 (Pearl insert)

TG-273

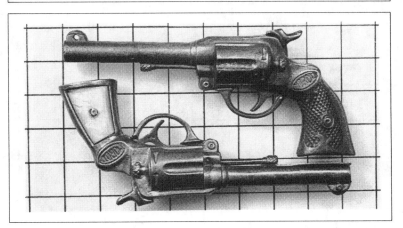

Mordt

Kenton- 1930-35 era. Unusual long barrel gun is a single shot, cast iron with nickel finish. Grips are checkered with the S-W medallions.

Value: $125-200

TG-274

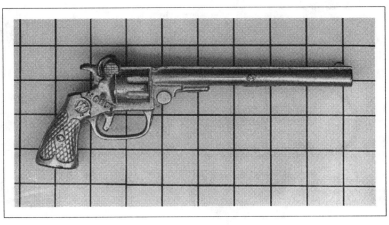

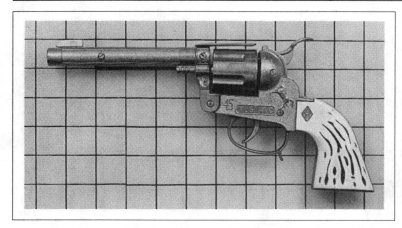

Mustang

Halco- 1955-60. Rare name variation of this large .45 die cast with the revolving cylinder and bullets. Stag grips with the diamond "H" medallions.

Value: $135-225

TG-275

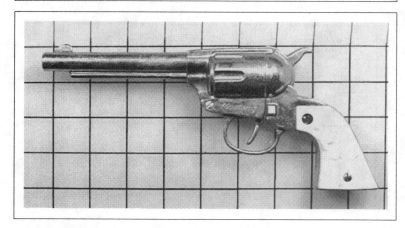

Mustang

Nichols- 1947. 1st model die cast repeater has plain grips with horse and steerhead. Nickel finish with push button release.

Value: $65-100

TG-276

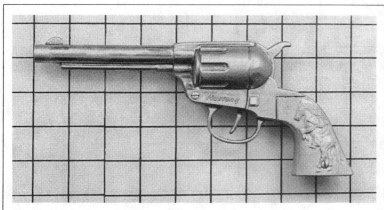

Mustang (Silver)

Nichols- 1948. 2nd model repeater in the nickel finish with the addition of the red jewel to top of the grips. Other features identical to gun above. Name changed to Silver Mustang in 1948.

Value: $65-100

TG-277

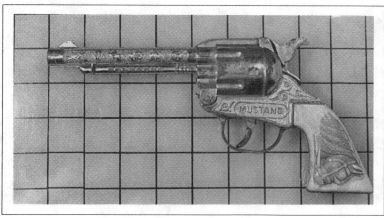

Mustang

Kilgore- 1960 era. Die cast repeater in the chrome finish with engraving. Has white and tan horsehead grips.

Value: $30-75

TG-278

Mustang

Kilgore- 1960 era. Pair of die cast presentation guns in special wood-grained and blue box. Both guns gold plated with white and red horsehead grips. Priced as a set.

Value: $100-200 (Pair in box)

TG-279

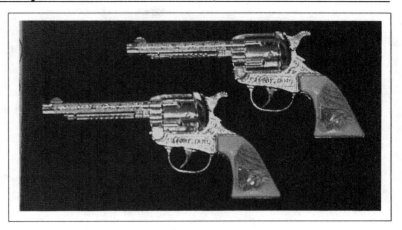

Mustang 500

Nichols- 1959. Pair of large die cast, 500 shot, engraved repeaters with stag grips. *Top:* vacuum metalized aluminum finish. *Lower:* Steel-Blu finish. Look great in the larger holster sets! Hard to find model.

Value: $125-250 (Alum) $150-285 (Blu)
(Gun in Alum. with gold trigger & hammer-$25+)
TG-280

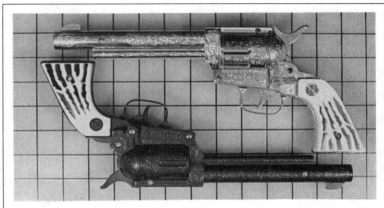

Mustang 250

Nichols- 1964. One of the last guns made by Nichols. 9 1/2" die cast engraved in unusual copper-like finish and stag grips. Also made in nickel finish and stag grips.

Value: $45-100 (Cpr) $35-75 (Nic)

TG-281

Nat'l

National, N.Y.C.- 1945-50. Single shot die cast with cast iron hammer & trigger. It is in the dull nickel finish with checkered grips. Similar to Stevens C.I Hero.

Value: $20-35

TG-282

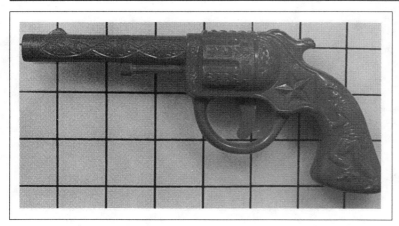

Nevadan

Esquire Novelty Co., NJ-1950. Red plastic clicker with beautiful engraving, having a cowboy on the grips. Early, post WW II toy gun. Found in other colors.

Value: $15-25

TG-283

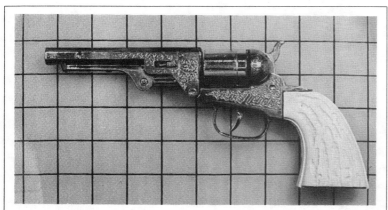

Nichols

Nichols-Kusan (?)- 1965 era. Civil War die cast repeater that tips down to open. It is nickel with engraving & white stag grips. Unusual gun with Nichols name. Rare.

Value: $45-100

TG-284

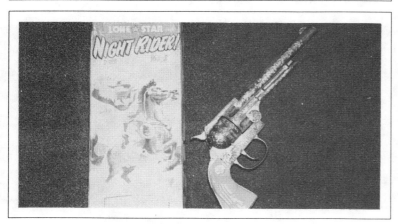

Night Rider

Lone Star, Eng.- 1965 era. 10 1/2" die cast repeater in nickel finish with engraving. Red horsehead grips. Full color box. Rare.

Value: $75-165 (nic) $85-175 (Blu) $20 (Box)

TG-285

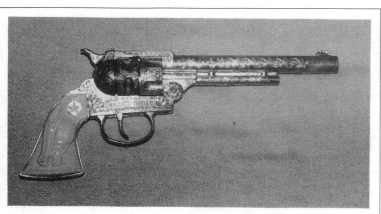

Night Rider

Lone Star, Eng.- 1965 era. Identical to TG-285 above, except in the rarer gold finish with black horsehead grips.

Value: $100-185 (Gold)

TG-286

OKE

Kilgore- 1930 era. Rare cast iron single shot in blue finish with checkered grips & circle K medallion. Possibly a nickname for a cowpoke from Oklahoma. Note large safety! Shoots mammoth caps.

Value: $85-150

TG-287

Old Ironsides

National- 1920 era. Unusual long barrel cast iron named for the old square rigger ship U.S. Constitution. All long barrels are rarely found. National was located in Boston where the ship is anchored.

Value: $135-200

TG-288

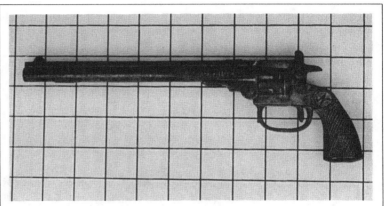

101 Ranch

Hubley- 1930. Cast iron long barrel. This was a touring Wild West Show. *Top:* Gun has a wide rounded hammer. *Lower:* Gun has a very narrow hammer with rounded flange. Rare long barrel.

Value: $165-250 (Either variation)

TG-289

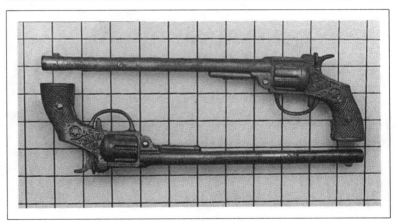

One Shot

Kilgore- 1960-65. Small 4 1/2" single shot die cast in chrome finish that has unusual stippled engraving and grip. Seldom seen toy gun.

Value: $20-40

TG-290

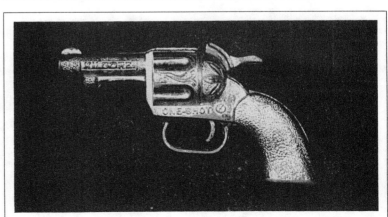

Outlaw - Buntline

British Cast Metals, Eng. -1955-60. Extra long barrel, 14" die cast in black finish with Indian Chief grips. Revolving cylinder. It is also found in the chrome finish.

Value: $125-245 (Gun & box)

TG-291

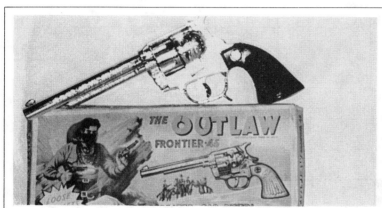

Outlaw - Frontier .45

B.C.M, Eng.-1960-70. Die cast repeater in gold finish, engraved with a revolving cylinder that accepts bullets. Has black Indian Chief grips. Full color box. Gun is 10 1/2". Similar to Hubley D.C. Cowboy.

Value: $85-175 (Gold gun & box)

TG-292

Paladin

Halco- 1957-63. Large die cast with revolving cylinder & bullets. Stag grips with diamond "H" medallions. Nickel finish, but also found in antique bronze. See character section.

Value: $175-325

TG-293

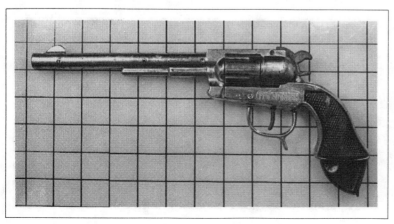

Pathfinder

G. Schmidt- 1950 era. One of the 1st guns made by Schmidt. Rare DC with revolving cylinder, checkered copper grips with a secret compartment and compass! Also identical, marked Davy Crockett. Nickel.

Value: $235-400.

TG-294

Patrol

G. Schmidt- 1950-55. Seldom seen die cast repeaters with the checkered copper grips. *Top:* Gun has polished chrome finish. *Lower:* A rare copper finished variety.

Value: $65-125 (Chr) $85-150 (Cpr)

TG-295

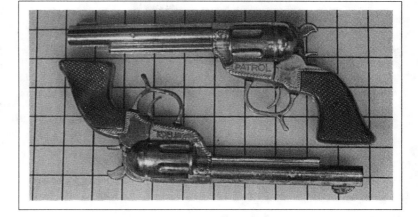

Pawnee Bill

Stevens- 1940. C.I. gun named for Maj. G. W. "PB" Lillie, western showman. Quaint engraving with horsehead grips cast onto gun. This variety is in a beautiful gold finish. Also found in nickel finish.

Value: $135-250 (Gold) $100-225 (Nic)

TG-296

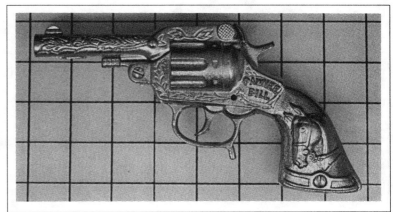

Peacemaker

Stevens- 1940. Cast iron repeater in gold finish with black horsehead grips and original box. Engraved.

Value: $135-250 (Gold gun & box)

TG-297

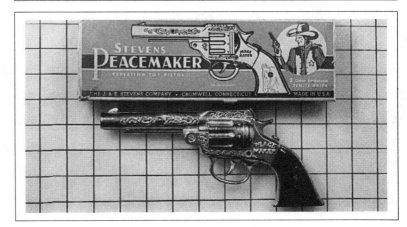

Peacemaker

Stevens- 1940. Very rare variety of this cast iron gun in an antique bronze finish with white horsehead grips.

Value: $120-200

TG-298

Peacemaker

Stevens- 1940. A rarer variety is this dark finish with black horsehead grips. Guns, made by Stevens, are seldom seen in this dark finish.

Value: $120-200

TG-299

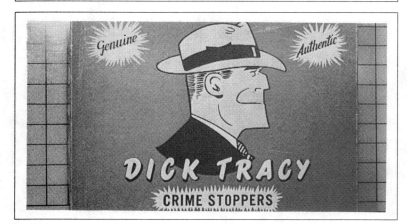

Peacemaker

Stevens- 1940. Very rare variety cast iron gun is a dummy in the nickel finish with black horsehead grips. Note there is no anvil for the hammer to strike! It can not fire caps.

Value: $150-250

TG-300

Peacemaker - Dick Tracy

Stevens- 1940. Yes, Dick Tracy in a western book! This original full color box has a western gun inside. Early set by Classy Products of N.Y. Entire mint set discovered as photographed. See TG-302 below.

TG-301

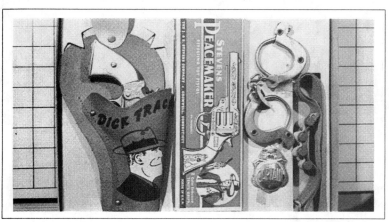

Peacemaker - Dick Tracy

Stevens/Classy- 1940. Note that box has a cast iron Peacemaker, holster, belt, badge bullets and hand-cuffs. Dick Tracy is certainly a peacemaker. Unusual & rare set.

Value: $175-325 (Box & entire contents)

TG-302

Pecos Bill

Mondial, Italy- 1955-65 era. An unusual die cast repeater in blue finish with ivory grips that have full color artwork of a cowboy. Revolving cylinder.

Value: $45-100

TG-303

Pecos Kid

Lone Star, Eng.- 1965. Die cast repeater in chrome finish with engraving and one-piece plastic walnut grips. Could be more recent.

Value: $35-75

TG-304

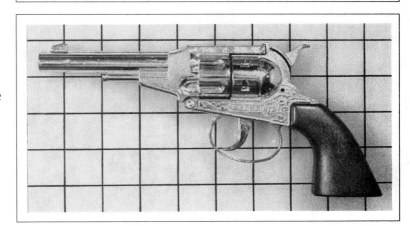

Pinto

Stevens- 1945 era. Cast aluminum with a cast iron hammer & trigger. Unusual gun is a single shot with checkered and steer-head red grips. WW II era toy gun. Rare.

Value: $75-125

TG-305

Pinto (Halco)

Leslie-Henry- 1960-65. Die cast repeater in nickel finish with engraving and insert white horsehead grips. Has diamond "H" medallions.

Value: $35-70

TG-306

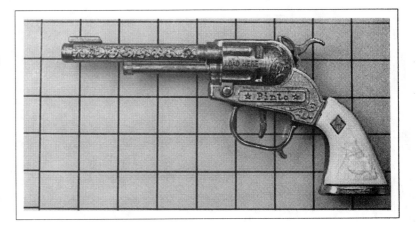

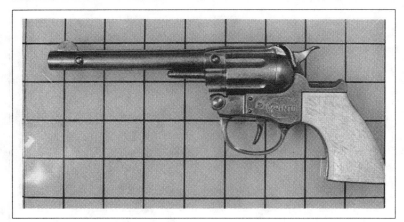

Pinto

Hubley- 1965-70. Die cast repeater in nickel finish with no engraving. Has saw-handle grips in white wood-grain.

Value: $20-45

TG-307

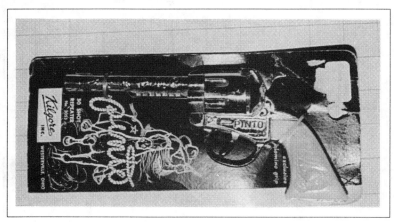

Pinto

Kilgore- 1960 era. Die cast repeater in chrome finish with engraving. Has white and tan horsehead grips. On the original display card.

Value: $35-85 (Gun & card)

TG-308

Pioneer

Stevens- 1950-55 era. Die cast single shot similar to the C.I. Billy the Kid which is one of the last C.I. guns made. Gun is in nickel with black painted grips. Original box is red and white. Rare die cast toy.

Value: $75-135 (Gun & box)

TG-309

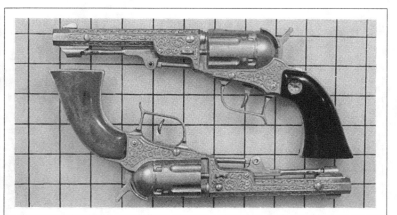

Pioneer

Hubley- 1950. Pair of die cast repeaters in nickel finish with super engraving. *Top:* Rare 1st model with black grips and inset compass. *Lower* 2nd model with orange-amber swirl grips. Loading lever operates.

Value: $85-165 (1st) $65-125 (2nd)

TG-310

Pioneer

Hubley- 1950. Unusual dark finish model. The original plastic grips were replaced with real walnut by the original owner's father. Seldom seen dark variety.

Value: $65-125

TG-311

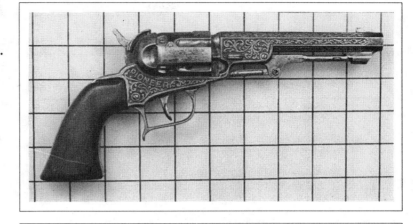

Plainsman

C. Ray Lawyer Co., Calif.- 1950 era. Rare die cast 1st model with the top opening mechanism. Revolving cylinder, in nickel finish with engraving. Slick white grips. A Dodge Melton design. Unusual toy.

Value: $75-150

TG-312

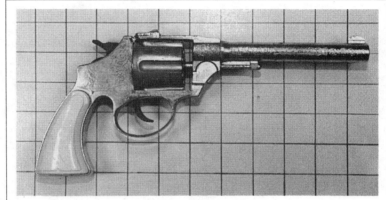

Plainsman

C. Ray Lawyer Co., Calif.- 1950 era. Detail of TG-312 above. Note the opening latch and fine engraving. Name on frame. This gun was quite complicated & unpopular. A number of variations exist

TG-313

Plainsman

National Metal & Plastic Toy Co.- 1950 era This variety does not break open & has a sliding cylinder-type of mechanism. The lettering is different. Nickel finish with slick white grips. Unusual toy gun.

Value: $75-150

TG-314

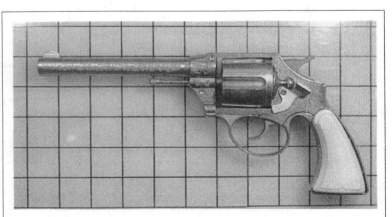

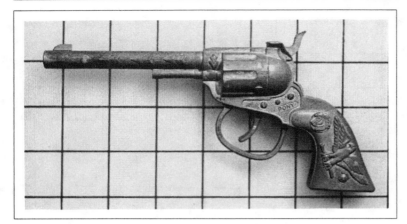

Pony

Esquire-Actoy- 1955 era. Small 7" die cast in dull nickel finish. All metal toy gun with a patriotic eagle on the grips with a pony medallion. Single shot.

Value: $20-45

TG-315

Pony

Nichols- 1957. Small 8" die cast single shot in nickel finish. Black stag grips.

Value: $25-45

TG-316

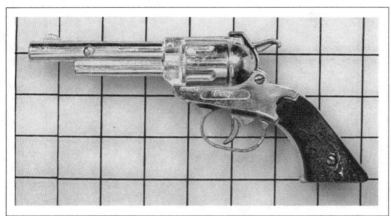

Pony Boy

Esquire-Actoy- 1960 era. Large 10" die cast repeater with engraving. This variety is in the antique bronze finish with white stag grips and pony medallion. Lanyard ring usually missing.

Value: $65-100

TG-317

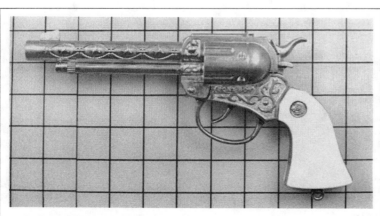

Pony Boy

Esquire-Actoy- 1960 era. Similar to TG-317 except in the nickel finish. Most of the Actoy guns are in antique bronze. All nickel varieties are rarer.

Value: $75-110

TG-318

Pony Boy

Hubley/Gabriel (?)- 1970 era. Details suggest a Hubley, but not sure. Die cast in nickel with one-piece stag grips. Late-style gun. Engraved repeater. Side opening. 10" length.

Value: $20-45

TG-319

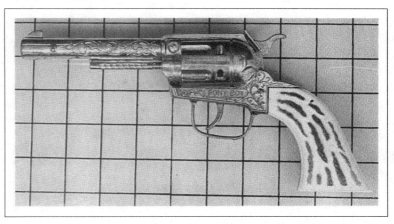

Pony Boy

Hubley/Gabriel (?)-1970 era. Similar to TG-319, except in chrome finish with one-piece black stag grips. Late-style gun. 10" length.

Value: $20-45

TG-320

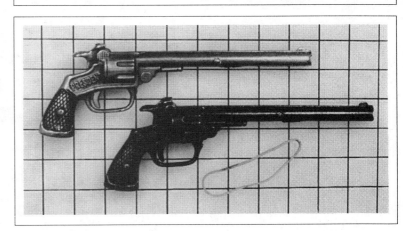

President

Kilgore- 1925 era. Pair of long barrel cast iron single shots. *Top:* Nickel finish with black painted grips. *Lower:* Rarer blue finish. Both have the notched barrel ends to fire rubber bands as well as caps. Rare.

Value: $135-225 (Either finish)

TG-321

Ramrod

Lone Star, Eng.- 1965-75. Smaller die cast in chrome finish with slick red grips & silver star medallion. Unusual toy gun.

Value: $35-85

TG-322

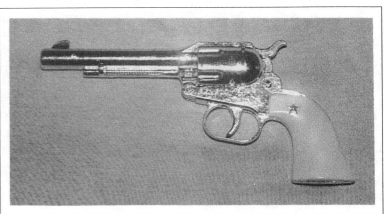

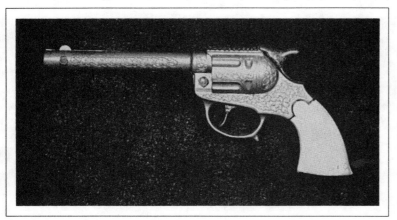

Rancher

Wyandotte- 1955. 7 1/2" DC in nickel finish with engraving. Single shot with white checkered grips. Name on grips. A seldom seen toy gun. Similar to Hoppy.

Value: $45-85

TG-323

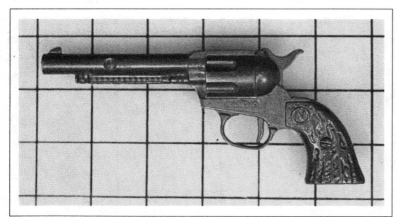

Rancho

Nichols- 1962. Small all metal die cast is a single shot in a Steel-Blu finish. The stag grips and circle "N" medallions are cast onto gun.

Value: $30-65

TG-324

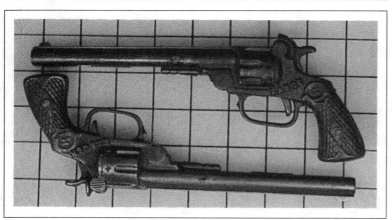

Range & Ranger

Kenton- 1925 era. Pair of rare long barrel cast iron single shots. *Top:* "Range" with checkered grips & S-W medallion. *Lower:* Very rare variation is nearly identical to a Range, but is named "Ranger." Note: "R".

Value: $100-175 $135--250 (Ranger)

TG-325

Ranger

Stevens- Pre-1900. Extremly rare cast iron single shot with quaint floral engraving. This early toy gun is seldom seen.

Value: $300-450

TG-326

Ranger

Kenton- 1920 era. Very rare small cast iron single shot. Checkered grips with no medallions. Small narrow hammer..

Value: $125-200

TG-327

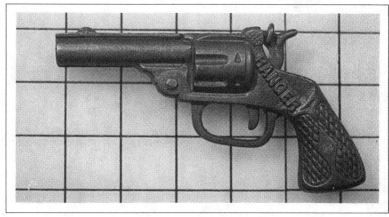

Ranger

Kenton- 1925 era. Pair of nearly identical cast iron single shots. *Top:* Black finish with tan painted checkered grips & rare star medallions. *Lower:* Black finish with brown checkered grips & no medallions.

Value: $125-185

TG-328

Ranger

Kilgore- 1920-30. *Top:* Extremely rare cast iron repeater in nickel finish with white-blue swirl grips. Early, narrow hammer. This may be a factory prototype. *Lower:* A typical Lone Ranger for comparison.

Value: $175-350

TG-329

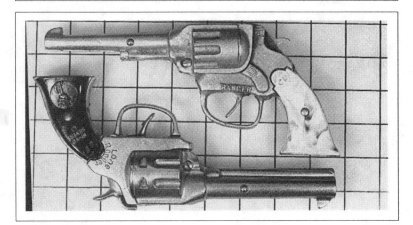

Ranger

Stevens- 1940 era. Cast iron single shot with white horsehead grips. There are a number of minor variations with grips, finishes & even alloy castings with cast iron parts. Alloy castings are rarer.

Value: $50-100 $100-150 (Alloy)

TG-330

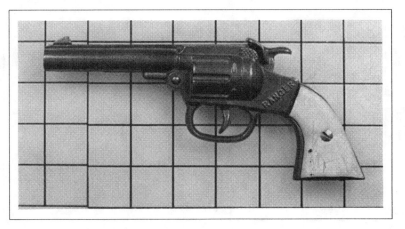

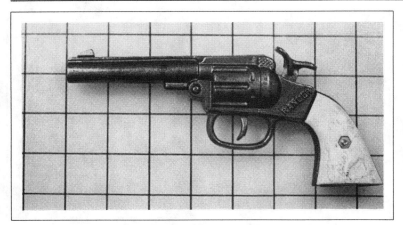

Ranger

Stevens- 1940 era. Rare cast iron variety with the dummy hammer. Has white-tan swirl, horsehead grips. Dark finish.

Value: $75-125

TG-331

Ranger

Kilgore- Pre 1940. Pair of C.I. repeaters & small ejector rods. *Top:* Gun has the dark finish with narrow small hammer & the white rearing horse grips. *Lower:* A rare gun with "no name" in polished nickel.

Value: $100-165 (1st) $145-225 (Polish)

TG-332

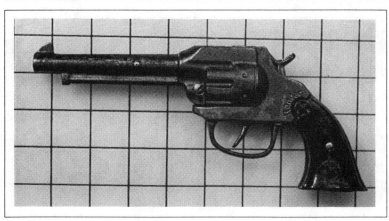

Ranger

Kilgore- Pre 1940. C.I. repeater in the blue painted finish with narrow hammer and brown-molasses swirl grips having the rearing horse in circle. Small ejector.

Value: $100-165

TG-333

Ranger

Kilgore- 1940 era. C.I. with the large wide hammer, full ejector rod & blue painted finish. Pearl grips with rearing horse in a circle.

Value: $100-165

TG-334

Ranger

Kilgore- 1940 era. Pair of C.I. with wide hammers. *Top:* Dark finish with white rearing horse in circle grips. *Lower:* Rarer polished nickel with burgundy-red rearing horse in circle grips.

Value: $100-165 $125-185 (Polished)

TG-335

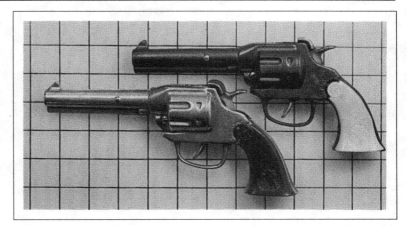

Ranger

Kilgore- 1940 era. Unusual C.I. in the full engraved version. Nickel finish with brown-reds swirl grips. Seldom seen toy.

Value: $125-200

TG-336

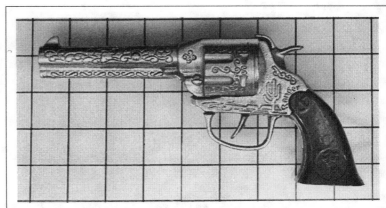

Ranger

Kilgore- 1940 era. Pair of nearly identical, rare polished cast iron guns. *Left:* Gun in the polished nickel with cherry red grips. *Right:* Engraved model in polished nickel with cherry red grips. Beautiful pair!

Value: $125-225 (Polished)

TG-337

Ranger - No Name

Kilgore- 1940 era. Extremely rare variety is this C.I. similar to Ranger engraved in nickel finish. *Note:* "no name" and the triangle cast piece above the circle "K" grip medallion.

Value: $185-275

TG-338

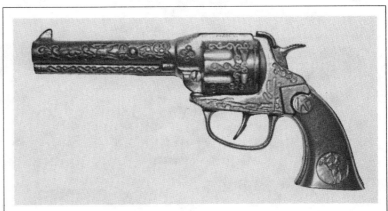

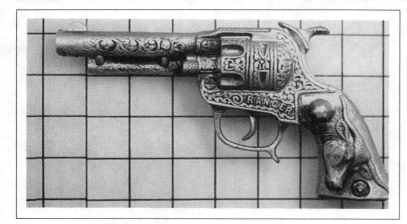

Ranger

Unknown- 1940-45 era. Light alloy copy of Hubley Texan, Jr. Clicker, does not fire caps. Steerhead grips cast on gun. This is an all metal toy gun. Very light.

Value: $25-50

TG-339

Ranger

Leslie-Henry- 1945-50. Aluminum casting of a Hubley Texan, Jr. Possibly made by Hamilton in Canada & is a single shot. It has red horsehead grips.

Value: $30-65

TG-340

Ranger

Leslie-Henry- 1945-50. Die cast single shot copy of Hubley Texan, Jr. Heavy metal & orange horsehead grips. Polished nickel finish. Probably Hamilton in Canada also.

Value: $35-75 (Polished Nickel)

TG-341

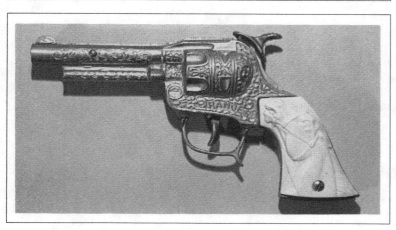

Ranger

Leslie-Henry- 1945-50. Similar to TG-341 above, except in rare gold finish with tan horsehead grips. Very heavy casting. Gun probably from Hamilton of Canada also.

Value: $45-100 (Gold)

TG-342

Ranger .44

Hamilton, Canada- 1950 era. Die cast gun is copy of the Hubley Texan, Jr. Repeater with large red opening button, engraving and white cowboy bust grips with star medallions. Rare box. Dull nickel finish.

Value: $45-100 (Gun & box)

TG-343

Ranger .44

Hamilton, Canada- 1950 era. Similar to TG-343 except in polished gold finish & light blue grips with cowboy bust & star medallions. Rare finish.

Value: $65-125 (Gold)

TG-344

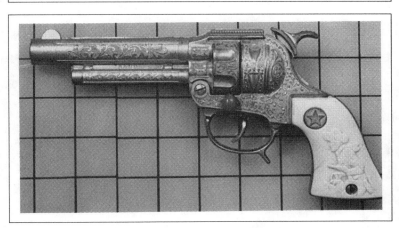

Ranger

Buzz Henry- 1950. Die cast repeater in the dull nickel finish with engraving. Large ivory horsehead grips. Note insert grips on the gun in TG-346.

Value: $50-85

TG-345

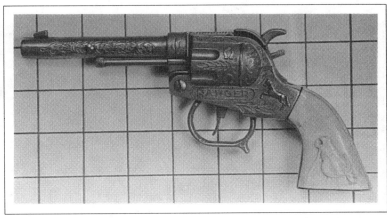

Ranger & Bronco

Buzz Henry- 1950. Similar to TG-345 but has nickel finish and ivory rearing horse insert grips. *Lower:* This gun is a rare single shot "Bronco" by *Buzz Henry* with the large, tan horsehead grips. Rare toy gun.
(Bronco) $65-100
Value: $50-85 (Ranger-Nic) Gold add $20

TG-346

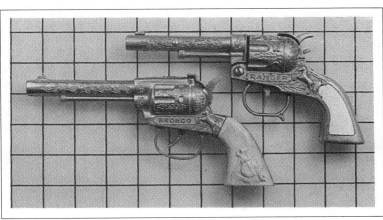

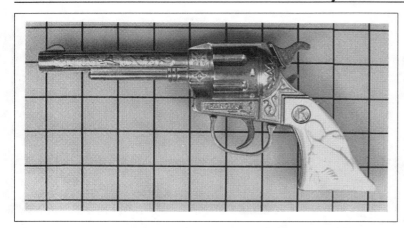

Ranger

Kilgore- 1950-55. Die cast repeater with engraving in nickel finish. White cowboy bust grips with circle "K" medallion.

Value: $35-75

TG-347

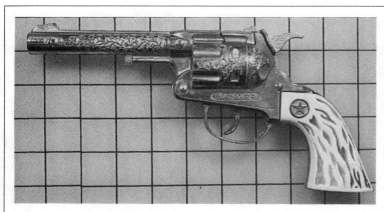

Ranger

Hubley- 1960-65. Rare die cast model has Halco on right side. Nickel finish with nice engraving and ivory & tan stag grips with star medallions. Unusual repeater.

Value: $35-80

TG-348

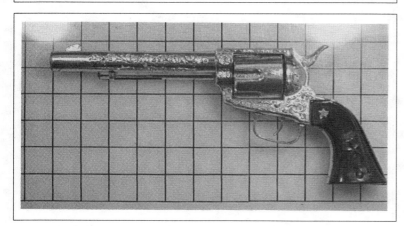

Range Rider MK II

Lone Star, Eng.- 1955-60. Large die cast with revolving cylinder & bullets. Gun is chrome finished with black grips having stars and small jewels. Copy of Nichols' Stallion .45.

Value: $145-250

TG-349

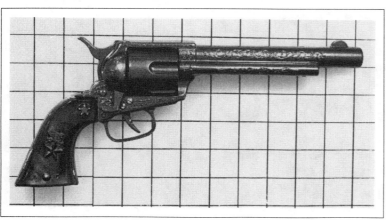

Range Rider MK II

Lone Star, Eng.- 1955-60. Similar to TG-349 above, except in the rare black finish with black grips having stars and small jewels.

Value: $150-265 (Black finish)

TG-350

Range Rider MK II

Lone Star, Eng.- 1955-60. Very rare gold finish. Seldom seen variety of this large die cast gun. Black grips have a gold star and small jewels. The engraving is very nice on all these variations.

Value: $175-285 (Gold)

TG-351

Range Rider

G. Schmidt- 1950-55. Rare die cast with ribbed barrel, minimal engraving and a nickel finish. Grips are checkered copper. Lower gun is a Cowhand for comparison.

Value: $85-175

TG-352

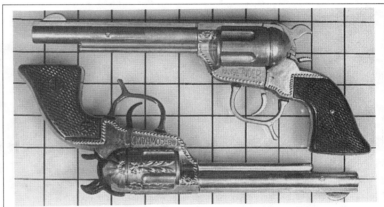

Rebel

Lone Star, Eng.- 1960 era. Die cast listed in Classy catalog. Black finish, revolving cylinder with white grips & black star. It is also found in the rarer nickel finish.

Value: $75-135 (Black)   (Nickel add $20)

TG-353

Rebel Scattergun

Classy Prod.- 1960 era. Extremely rare toy sawed-off shotgun. Uses 2 rolls of caps. Made with both brown and black stocks.

Value: $250-500 (Shotgun only)

TG-354

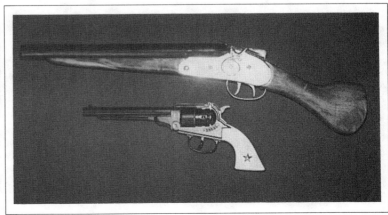

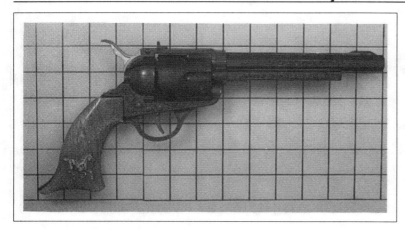

Red River- Johnny Eagle

Topper-Deluxe Corp., NJ- 1965. Plastic & metal cap gun with revolving cylinder & bullets. Has wood grained grips with the gold horse. Also has a matching rifle.

Value: $25-65

TG-355

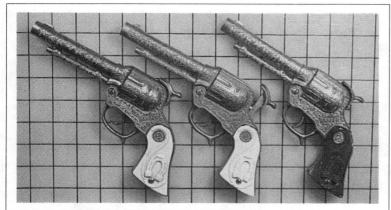

Red Ranger

Wyandotte- 1955 era. 3 die cast repeaters. *Left:* Nickel finish engraved with white grips. *Center:* Dull nickel finish with the dummy hammer, white grips. *Right:* Gold finish & black grips. "Y & • " medallions.

Value: $65-100 Dummy or gold add $35

TG-356

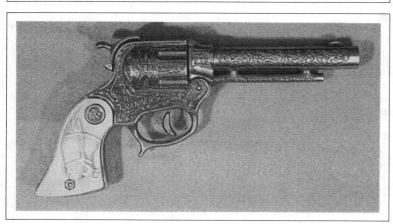

Red Ranger

Wyandotte- 1955 era. Polished nickel die cast. Note the fine engraving and horse-head grips. Reverse of grips has horse-shoe & rope. Parts used for Hoppy guns.

Value: $70-110 (Polished nickel)

TG-357

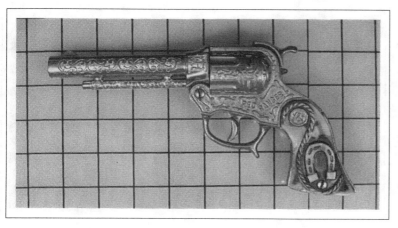

Red Ranger

Wyandotte- 1955. Rare gun in polished gold finish with unusual cherry red and gold swirl grips. Seldom seen variety of this model. "Y & •" medallions.

Value: $100-145 (Polished gold)

TG-358

Red Ranger

Wyandotte- 1955 era. Rare experimental die cast with a mechanism for smoke. It may be one-of-a-kind factory prototype. Nickel finish. Probably shoots powder.

Value: $100-150

TG-359

Red Ranger

Wyandotte- 1960 era. Die cast repeater in the large dragoon-style. Nickel finish and black grips. Engraved. Lanyard ring. Gun found in many Roy, Paladin & Cheyenne holster sets in Canadian mail catalogs.

Value: $50-95 (Nickel) $65-125 (Gold)

TG-360

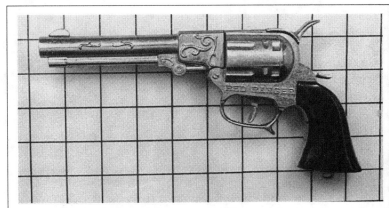

Red Ranger

Wyandotte- 1960 era. Similar to TG-360, except in the dark, dull nickel finish. Has slick black grips. Engraved. Lanyard ring. Gun made for Civil War Centennial.

Value: $45-90

TG-361

Red Ranger, Jr.

Wyandotte- 1955-60. Small die cast repeater in dull nickel finish with white horsehead grips. Engraved. Also found in the regular nickel finish and gold.

Value: $30-50 (Nickel or gold add $10)

TG-362

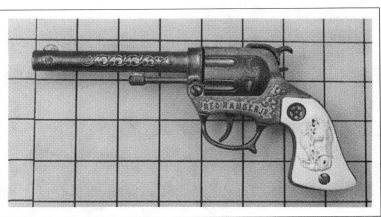

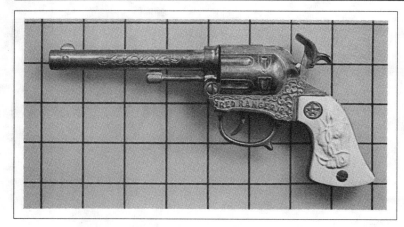

Red Ranger, Jr.

Wyandotte- 1955-60 era. Rare die cast in gold finish. Has a rare dummy hammer. This model seldom seen in gold or in the dummy variety. Engraved with the ivory horsehead grips.

Value: $50-100 (Gold dummy)

TG-363

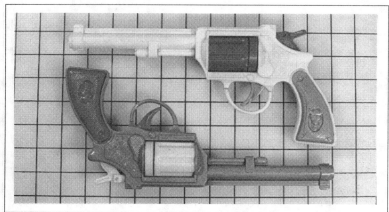

Renwal No.129

Renwal Co.- 1945-50. Unusual plastic toy guns with revolving cylinders that shoot bullets. Spring operated. Produced in a mixture of red, blue and yellow plastic. Colorful, post WW II toy guns.

Value: $25-50

TG-364

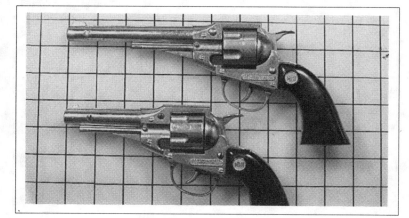

Remington .36

Hubley- 1960. Civil War model. *Top:* Rare variation with longer barrel in polished nickel & black grips. *Lower:* The common short barrel variety. Both have revolving cylinders with bullets. "H" medallions.

Value: $85-175 (Long) $50-125 (Short)

TG-365

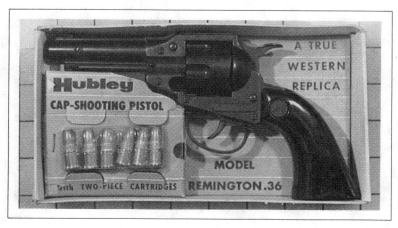

Remington .36

Hubley- 1960. Short barrel die cast cap repeater in the extremely rare black finish with black grips. Revolving cylinder with bullets. In original display box.

Value: $125-200

TG-366

Remington .36

Hubley- 1960. Rarer long barrel die cast repeater in the dull nickel finish with black grips. Revolving cylinder & bullets. The long barrel version is very elusive.

Value: $85-175 (Long barrel)

TG-367

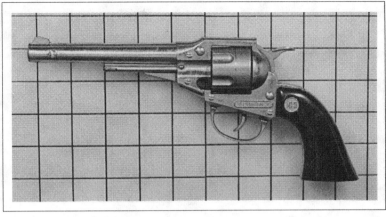

Restless Gun

Esquire-Actoy- 1957-59. Die cast repeater with engraving in nickel finish. Grips are transparent amber with a secret comparment in the bottom. See the character section.

Value: $65-145

TG-368

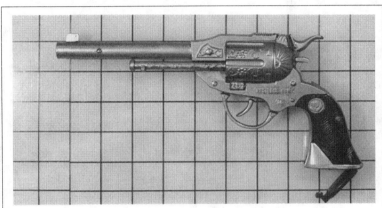

Ric-O-Shay .45

Hubley- 1960-65. Large 12" die cast with revolving cylinder, bullets, engraving & a bullet "whi-i-ine" trigger sound. Nickel finish with slick black grips. Occasionally found with white grips from a Colt .45.

Value: $75-150

TG-369

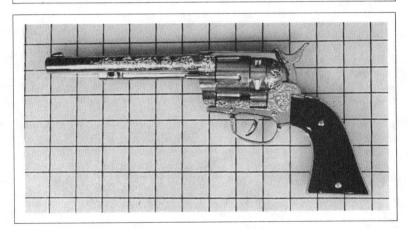

Ric-O-Shay Jr.

Hubley- 1960-65. A 10" die cast repeater with engraving and a bullet "whi-i-ine" trigger sound. Nickel finish with either black or black & white steerhead grips. A rather rare die cast variety. Display box.

Value: $75-125 (Gun & box)

TG-370

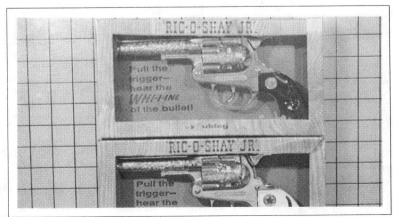

Ric-O-Shay Jr.

Hubley- 1960-65. Similar to TG-370, but this variety is in the very rare gold finish with turquoise blue grips. Probably was intended for a cowgirl. Beautiful gun in this color variety.

Value: $100-165 (Gold)

TG-371

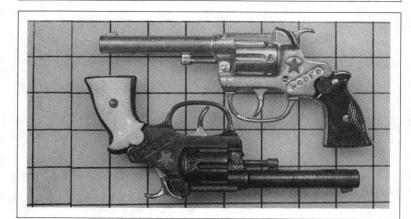

Rodeo

Hubley- 1920-25. Very rare long barrel cast iron. *Top:* 1st model with narrow hammer & dark finish. *Lower:* 2nd model with large, wide hammer in the nickel finish. All long barrels are elusive.

Value: $200-350

TG-372

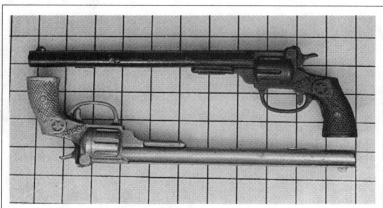

Rodeo

Hubley- 1938-50. Pre & post WW II single shots. *Top:* Cast iron in nickel finish with brown or white checkered grips. *Lower:* A die cast gun with C.I. hammer & trigger. Dark finish with white checkered grips.

Value: $50-100 (C.I.) $35-70 (D.C. part)

TG-373

Rodeo

Hubley- 1955 era. Unusual 8" die cast has beautiful engraving and Colt Bisley-type grips. Nickel single shot with white steer-head grips. Original red & white box is seldom seen.

Value: $45-80 (Gun & box)

TG-374

Rodeo

Hubley- 1955 era. *Top:* Light alloy in the satin gray finish with die cast hammer & trigger. Brown-red swirl grips. *Lower:* Gun is similar to TG-374, except in the rarer gold finish with white steerhead grips.

Value: $35-75 (Satin G.) $65-110 (Gold)

TG-375

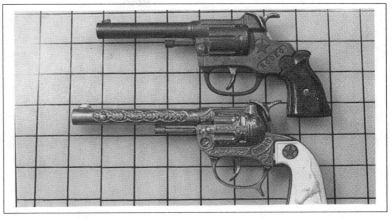

Rodeo

Hubley 1955-65. Top: Die cast completely with white checkered grips. Lower: Later die cast with engraving in nickel finish. Has amber-orange-white swirl stag grips. These are both single shots.

Value: $30-65 (Either model)

TG-376

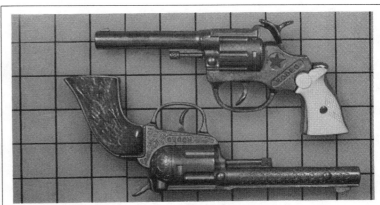

Rodeo

Hubley- 1960 era. Similar to model in TG-376, except in chrome finish with white stag grips. These were made for Daisy & are found in many holster sets sold by them about 1960. No Daisy name.

Value: $30-65

TG-377

Roy Rogers

Kilgore- 1938-45 era. Pair of very rare cast iron polished nickel guns. Note the long top strap, riveted stag grips & name on top of grips. A very desirable classic toy gun. See character section.

Value: $850-1,300 (Each)

TG-378

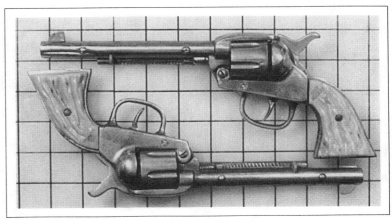

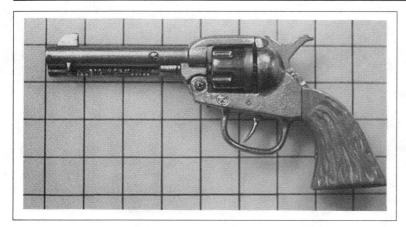

Roy Rogers - Big Horn

Kilgore- 1938-45. Very rare cast iron variation. Both Big Horns & Long Toms can be found with Roy's name etched on the side frame. This nickel finish gun has cherry red stag grips. See character guns.

Vlalue: $850-1,300

TG-379

Roy Rogers - Big Horn

Kilgore- 1938-45. Detail of TG-379 showing the lightly etched name on the left side plate under the cylinder. This type is a mystery, except that the Kilgore catalog of this era shows Roy's name on the side.

TG-380

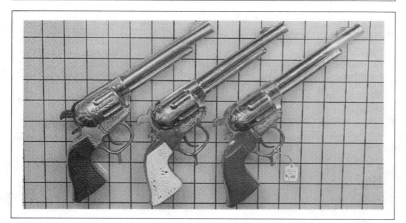

Roy Rogers

G. Schmidt- 1950-60. D.C. guns with long barrels. *Left:* Engraved, rib barrel, nickel & copper stag grips. *Center:* Chrome, no engraving, plain barrel, and white stag. *Right:* Chrome & checkered copper grips.

Value: $135-250 (Either model)

TG-381

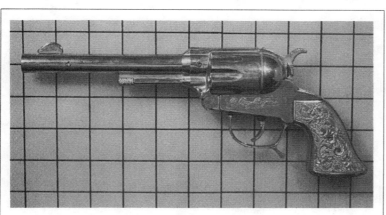

Roy Rogers

Classy- 1950-60. D.C. repeater possibly made by Latco. Chrome finish with the super floral scroll grips in the gold finish. Among the best grips put on toy guns. See Roy items in the character section.

Value: $150-300

TG-382

Ruf Rider & Unmarked

Latco-Los Angeles Toy Co.-1960 era. These are identical to Classy guns. *Top:* nickel gun with pewter floral scroll grips. *Lower:* Unmarked, has flowers where name usually appears & brass floral scroll grips.

Value: $65-125

TG-383

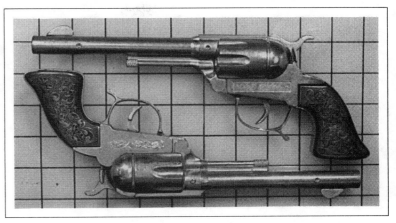

Ruf Rider

Latco- 1960 era. Rare die cast variety has a highly polished chrome finish with the copper floral scroll grips. Came in some holster sets with metallic silver fronts.

Value: $85-150

TG-384

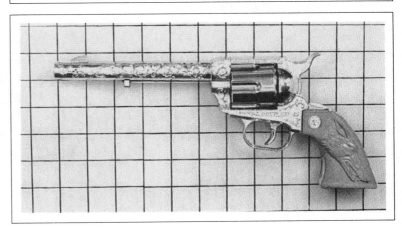

Rustler .45

Crescent Toys, Eng.- 1965-75. Large 12" die cast with revolving cylinder and bullets. Chrome finish engraved with cherry red wolf head grips. Similar to a Nichols Stallion .45.

Value: $125-235

TG-385

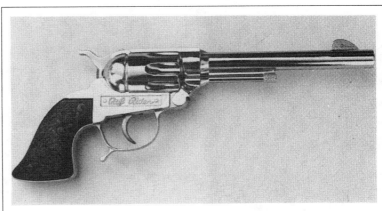

Rustler .38

Crescent Toys, Eng.- 1965-75. Small 9 1/2" die cast with revolving cylinder. Chrome finish with red wolf head grips. Engraved with top opening lever.

Value: $65-125

TG-386

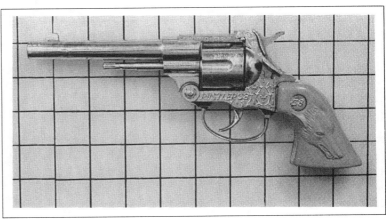

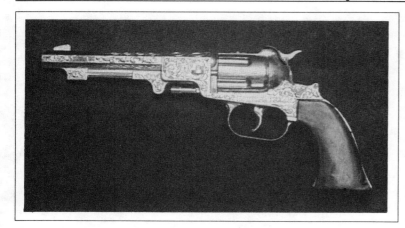

Rustler Texan

Lone Star, Eng.-1965-75. Die cast repeater in nickel finish with engraving and brown-black swirl grips. 10" gun is very similar to a Hubley Pioneer.

Value: $55-100

TG-387

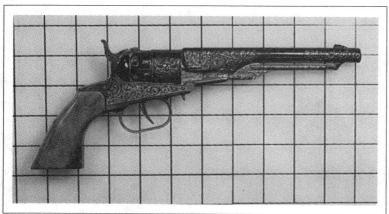

Rustler-Outlaw

Crescent Toys, Eng.- 1965-75. Die cast repeater is 11" in the dull black finish, engraved with red-black swirl grips. Similar to Kansas Kid model.

Value: $40-85

TG-388

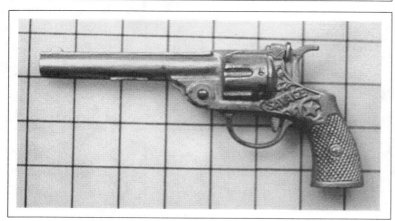

Savage

Hubley- 1925. Cast iron single shot in the nickel finish with checkered grips and star medallion. Rarely seen toy gun.

Value: $75-145

TG-389

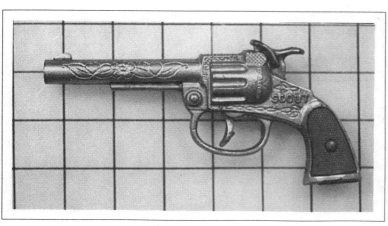

Scout

Stevens- 1940. Rare cast iron in the nickel finish and engraving. Has checkered red insert grips with rivet. Unusual variation that shoots mammoth caps.

Value: $60-100

TG-390

Sharpshooter

Kilgore- 1935 era. Very rare C.I. repeaters, engraved with white rearing horse grips & circle "K" medallions. *Left:* Gun with a nickel finish. *Right:* Blue-black finish.

Value: $135-250

TG-391

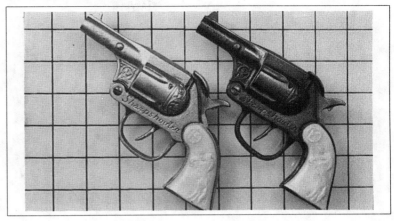

Sheik

Kenton- Pre 1930. Rare long barrel C.I. single shot guns. Top: Dark cast iron finish with checkered grips & S-W medallions. Lower: Identical except in nickel finish.

Value: $200-350

TG-392

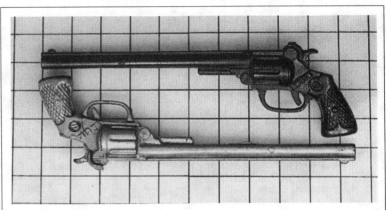

Sheik

Dent- Pre 1930. Very rare long barrel in a special finish was a salesman's sample. Note tag still attached. Checkered grips with circle "D" medallions. All Dent guns are difficult to find.

Value: $250-450

TG-393

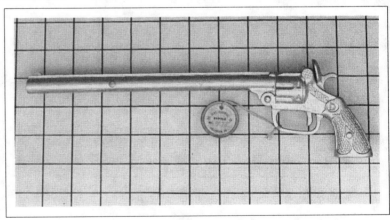

Sheriff

Stevens- 1940. Cast iron repeater in nickel finish with engraving and white horse-head grips with red jewel. Also green and yellow jewels used. Unusual box.

Value: $85-165 (Gun & box)

TG-394

Sheriff

Wyandotte- 1955. 7 1/2" die cast single shot in rare gold finish and engraving with black checkered grips. Note missing ejector rod. Bottom gun is a Hoppy for comparison. Guns are nearly identical.

Value: $65-110 (Gold)

TG-395

Sheriff

Wyandotte- 1955. *Top:* Hoppy shown for comparison. *Lower::* Sheriff in nickel finish and engraving with white checkered grips. Ejector rods often missing.

Value: $45-85 (Nickel)

TG-396

Silver Colt

Nichols- 1948. Die cast repeater in nickel finish with engraving & white rearing horse & steer head grips. 1st gun to have the circle "N" ranch medallions.

Value: $75-145

TG-397

Silver Colt

Nichols- 1948. Similar to TG-397 above, except with the black rearing horse and steerhead grips.

Value: $75-145

TG-398

Silver Pony

Nichols- 1946. The very first Nichols' cap gun! *Top:* All die cast metal single shot & rearing horse & steerhead grips. Lower: A 2nd model with black stag grips. Both of these toy guns are rare.

Value: $65-135

TG-399

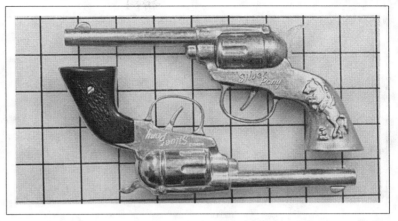

Silver Pony

Nichols-Kusan- 1965 era. Similar to a die cast Cowhand. This is a rarer model of the Silver Pony with Steel-Blu finish and white stag grips with circle N medallions.

Value: $50-100

TG-400

Sioux

Dent- Pre 1930. Rare Dent gun honoring Indians. Cast iron single shot for mammoth caps. Nickel finish with checkered grips and circle "D" medallions.

Value: $85-150

TG-401

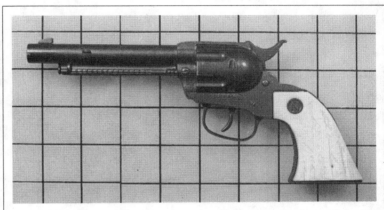

Six Shooter

Kilgore- 1938-45. CI nickel repeaters have revolving cylinders. (L-R) 1.Presssed steel cyl. & metal grips. 2. Pressed steel cyl. & brown grips. 3. Pressed steel cyl. & light blue grips. 4. C.I. cyl. & burgundy grips.

Value: $75-150 (Steel) $85-165 (Cast I.)

TG-402

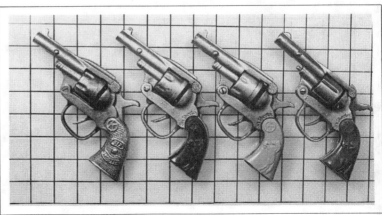

Six Shooter

Kilgore- 1938-45. Cast iron. (L-R) 1. All metal with pressed steel cyl. 2. CI cyl. & orange grips. 3. CI cyl. in blue finish & white grips. 4. Pressed steel cyl. and tan-butterscotch swirl grips. Many varieties.

Value: $75-165 (Steel) $85-165 (Cast I.)

TG-403

Six Shooter - Unmarked

Kilgore- 1938-45. Very rare cast iron variety with blank sides and no name! Has a pressed steel cylinder and light blue grips with circle "K" medallions.

Value: $100-175

TG-404

Six Shooter

Kilgore- 1938-45. Very rare cast iron with CI cylinder in nickel and the rarely seen dummy hammer that can't fire caps. The grips are swirl brown.

Value: $100-175

TG-405

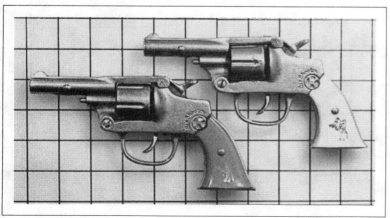

Six Shooter

Kilgore- 1940 era. Cast iron with revolving CI cylinders. *Top:* Nickel finish with pearl grips having the rearing horse in red. *Lower:* Rarer polished nickel & red-orange grips with white rearing horse.

Value: $65-145 (Nic) $85-160 (Polished)

TG-406

Smoker .45

Product Eng.-1950. Large die cast shoots smoke. Insert pistol into bag of powder, cock hammer, add cap, fire! Smoke-like powder comes from gun. All metal with black painted grips.

Value: $45-85

TG-407

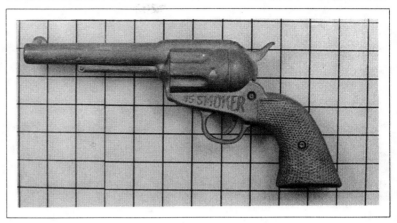

Smoky Joe

Hubley- 1945. Perhaps the last CI made by Hubley. Rather rare gun similar to the Cowboy. Nickel finish with white checkered grips. Note SJ Halco caps. Character names seldom appear on boxes of caps.

Value: $150-275

TG-408

Smoky Joe

Leslie-Henry- 1950-55. Die cast repeater in nickel finish with copper steerhead grips. Original Halco display card. Price $.98.

Value: $75-125 (Gun & card)

TG-409

Smoky Joe

Leslie-Henry- 1950-55. DC repeaters. *Left:* Nickel and small horse on frame & transparent amber grips. *Center:* Gold finish & small horse & white grips. *Right:* Nickel finish with large horse & copper grips.

Value: $65-100 (Nic) $85-135 (Gold)

TG-410

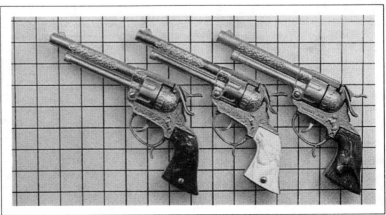

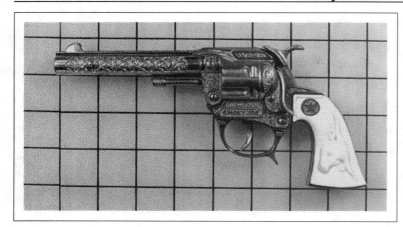

Smoky Joe

Hubley- 1950 era. Die cast repeater in the nickel finish with engraving and the top opening side lever. Colt Bisley-style grips, white with steerheads & star medallions.

Value: $55-100

TG-411

Smoky Joe

Stevens- 1955. Very rare die cast repeater in antique copper finish with engraving and slick black grips with the circle "S" medallions. Seldom seen Stevens' gun.

Value: $65-110

TG-412

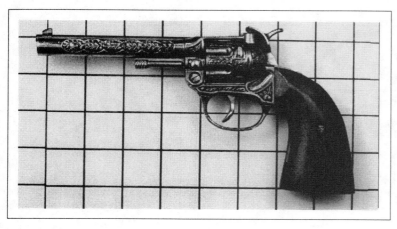

Sniper

Hubley- 1960-65 era. Unusual plastic and metal clicker with an exceptionally long 16 1/2" barrel! Unbelievable six gun! In metallic silver finish & brown grips. Also found in black-blue finish & white grips.

Value: $35-75

TG-413

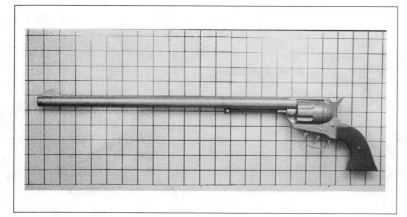

Spatz

Lunde Arms Corp., CA- 1953. Lunde Arms converted Hubley DC Rodeos with insert barrels that would shoot #6 lead shot by firing a cap. Unusual toy. Hubley name is ground off & walnut grips added. Rare.

Value: $45-100

TG-414

Special

Esquire-Actoy- 1955-60. Rare, long barrel, die cast repeater in nickel & engraved. Stag grips with pony medallions. *Lower:* This gun is a Wells Fargo model for comparison. Both guns are nearly identical.

Value: $75-145

TG-415

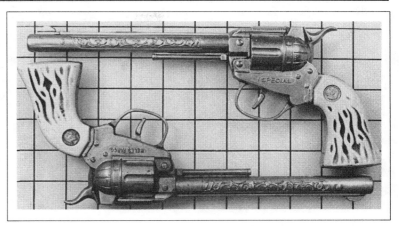

Special

Esquire-Actoy- 1955-60. Similar to TG-415 above, except this gun in nickel, has the very rare black grips with inlaid flower of turquoise & gold. Has pony medallions. The flower matches a holster set front.

(See TG-508)

Value: $85-165

TG-416

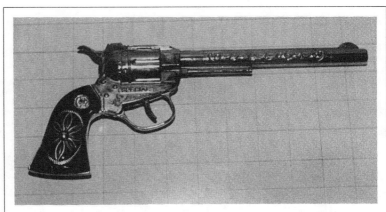

Stag

Pyro- 1950-55. A 7 1/2" plastic clicker has stag grips and engraving. Made in various colors. The one pictured is yellow.

Value: $ 10-15

TG-417

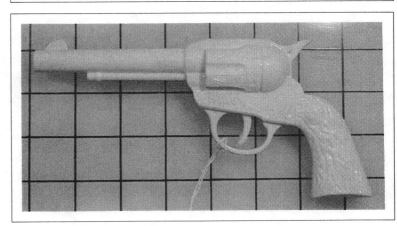

Stallion .45

*Nichols-*1950. 1st model die cast in nickel finish, engraved with revolving cylinder & bullets. White grips have a horse & steerhead with red jewel. This variety has notches around back of cylinder.

Value: $175-345

TG-418

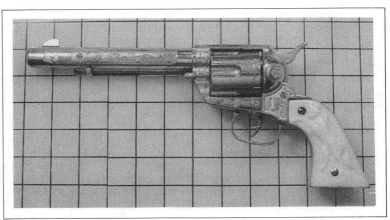

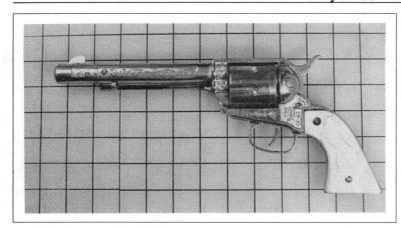

Stallion .45

Nichols- 1950. 1st model similar to TG-418, except there are no notches around the back of the cylinder. Bullets for the .45 Stallions average about $10 each.

Value: $175-345

TG-419

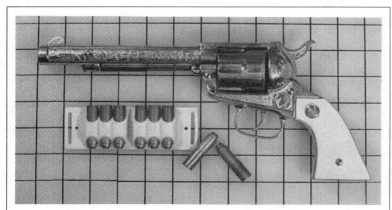

Stallion .45 Mark II

Nichols- 1957. King of the die cast guns! Nickel finish with engraving, revolving cylinder & bullets. White pearl grips with red circle "N" medallions. Came with an extra pair of black grips. Note bullet clip.

Value: $175-350

TG-420

Stallion .45 Mark II

Nichols- 1960-64. Very rare Steel-Blu variety. Identical to TG-420 except finish & walnut-type plastic grips. Some guns had wood grips stained walnut. Many throw these away, thinking they were added.

Value: $200-425 (Steel-Blu)

TG-421

Stallion .45 Mark II

Nichols- 1959. Extremely rare gold plated model. Less than 200 were produced. Boxes have a special gold label and grips are a special pearlescent blue. Many guns are recently plated, so use much caution!

Value: $750-1,200 (Original gold)

TG-422

Stallion .45 Mark II

Nichols-Kusan- 1964-70. *Top:* Kusan gun with bronze-green finish and stag grips. Medallions cast on the gun. Rare model. *Lower:* Regular Nichols' Stallion in nickel finish with unusual black stag grips.

Value: $200-350 (Bronze) $175-300 (Nic)

TG-423

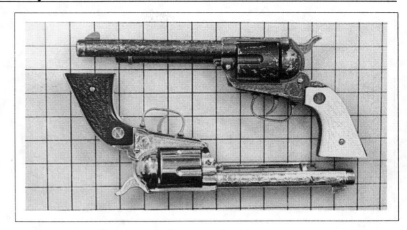

Stallion .45 Mark II

Nichols- 1957-62. Similar to TG-420 with black grips and shown with the special display box made like a wooden frame. Note bullets and plastic clip. Rare item.

Value: $200-375 (Gun & display box)

TG-424

Stallion .45 Mark II

Nichols-Kusan- 1964-70. Among the very rarest of Nichols' models. It is similar to TG-420 except in polished chrome finish & transparent pearl grips with circle "N" cast into them. Dummy bullets in cyl.

Value: $250-450

TG-425

Stallion .45 Mark II

Nichols-Kusan- 1964-70. Detail of the gun shown above. Note the dummy bullets in the cylinder. They cannot be removed. This is an exceptionally beautiful toy gun with outstanding grips!

TG-426

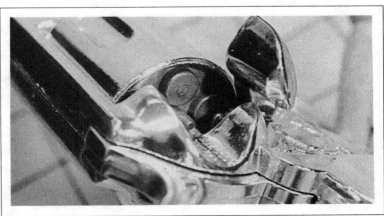

Stallion .41-40

Nichols- 1958. Large die cast with flip-out revolving cylinder & bullets. Exceptional engraving in nickel finish with stag grips in a translucent tan. One of the more elusive toy guns. Great in large holsters.

Value: $175-325 (Gun & Box)

TG-427

Stallion .41-40

Nichols- 1958. Similar to TG-427 except a normal model with regular white stag grips. Note the bullets and the circle "N" medallions.

Value: $150-300

TG-428

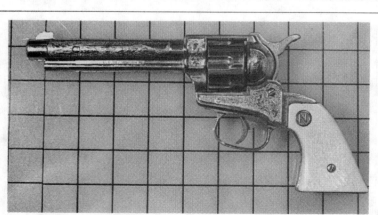

Stallion .38 Dual Set

Nichols- 1960. Unusual boxed dual set. Stallion .38 & Dynamite derringer, both in nickel finish with white grips. Small belt holster for derringer with 2 bullets.

Value: $150-235 (Dual set in box)

TG-429

Stallion .38

Nichols- 1951-60. Die cast gun. revolving cylinder with bullets in nickel finish. White stag grips with circle "N" medallions. Popular gun for kids due to size.

Value: $75-145

TG-430

Stallion .32

Nichols- 1956-60. Small die cast with the revolving cylinder and bullets. In nickel finish with engraving. White stag grips & circle "N" medallions.

Value:$35-75

TG-431

Stallion .32

Nichols- 1956-60. Similar to TG-431, but in the rarer Steel-Blu finish with black stag grips. Seldom seen in blue.

Value: $45-90

TG-432

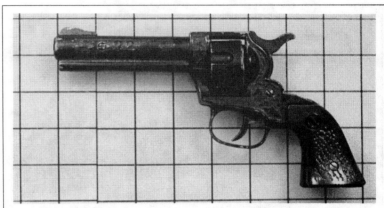

Stallion .32

Nichols- 1956-60. Similar to TG-431, but in the very rare gold finish with the blue stag grips. Note the box has the gold presentation model label. Rare variation.

Value: $85-165 (Gold gun & box)

TG-433

Stallion .22

Nichols- 1957-60. Small die cast with the revolving cylinder and bullets. Nickel finished with engraving. White stag grips with circle "N" medallions.

Value: $30-65

TG-434

Star

Hubley- 1955-65. Die cast, single shot in nickel finish with engraving. Steerhead grips cast on gun. Star medallions. Very common gun.

Value: $15-25

TG-435

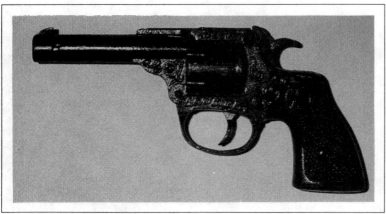

Steve Larrabee

Lone Star, Eng.- 1960. "Lone Star Rider" is a die cast gun with some Hubley Trooper details. Dark blue finish with checkered grips and star medallions. Unusual.

Value: $45-85

TG-436

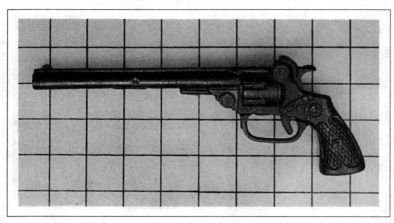

Super

Kenton- 1930 era. Rare cast iron single shot in the dark finish with checkered grips and S-W medallions. Seldom seen long barrel.

Value: $125-185

TG-437

Sure-Shot

Hubley- 1955-60. All metal die cast repeater in nickel finish, engraved with black painted steerhead grips. Star medallions. Rare box. Common toy gun.

Value: $30-65 (Gun & box)

TG-438

Target

Hubley- 1935. Unusual cast iron gun is a single shot where the barrel is tipped down to cock the hammer. Shoots mammoth caps. Rather rare toy gun.

Value: $150-275

TG-439

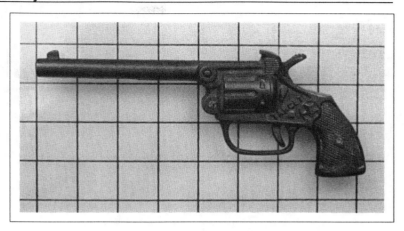

TEX

Hubley- 1950. Die cast repeater in nickel finish with engraving. Lever opening with white & black steerhead grips with star medallion. Also in rarer gold finish.

Value: $35-85 (Nic) $55-100 (Gold)

TG-440

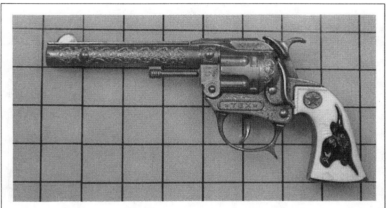

Texan

Hubley- 1940. One of the most popular cap guns ever made. CI repeater with the revolving cylinder & engraved. *Top:* Rare dark finish and Colt medallions. *Lower:* Polished nickel finish & star medallions.

Value: $100-175 (Dark or polished nic)

TG-441

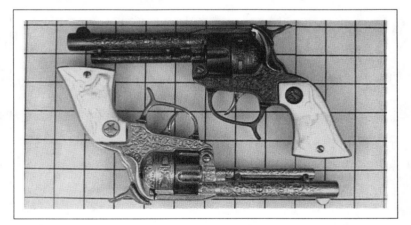

Texan

Hubley- 1940. Dummy variations. *Left:* Dark finish dummy & Colt Medallions. *Center:* Polished nickel dummy with star. *Right:* Nickel dummy with Colt. All rare!

Value: $135-225 (Dummy)

TG-442

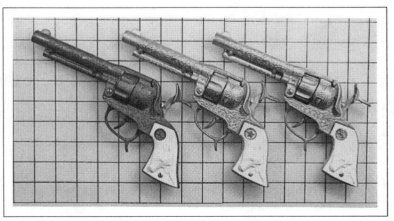

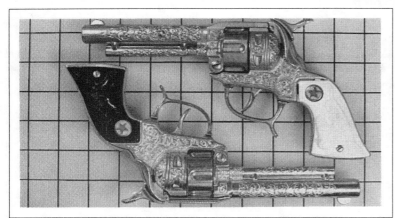

Texan

Hubley- 1950. Die cast Texan is seldom seen. Engraved with revolving cylinder & star. Top: Nickel finish with white steerhead grips. Lower: Rarer gold finish with black steerhead grips.

Value: $65-125 (Nic)　$100-175 (Gold)

TG-443

Texan

Hubley- 1950. Extremely rare die cast gun in the dummy variation. Nickel finish with white steerhead grips and star.

Value: $100-150

TG-444

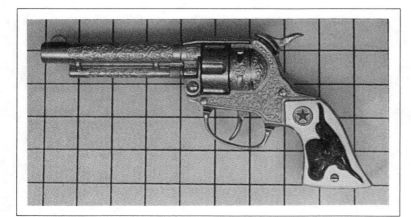

Texan

Hubley- 1955. The last model die cast of the Texan was friction-closed and had no opening lever. Rare with the revolving cylinder. Nickel, & B&W steerhead grips. Guns exist with non-revolving cylinders.

Value: $85-150 (Rev)　$65-100 (Non-R)

TG-445

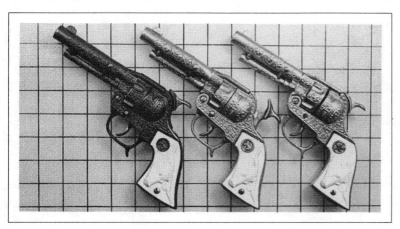

Texan Jr.

Hubley- 1940. Very popular cast iron gun. *Left:* Dark finish, engraved and Colt logo. Center: Nickel with dummy hammer and Colt. Right: Nickel finish with star medallions. White steerhead grips on all.

Value: $85-160　$125-200 (Dummy CI)

TG-446

Texan .45

Hubley- 1961. Extremely rare die cast gun produced as a special order for the 125th Anniversary of Texas. Only a handful are known to exist. Model is usually marked Colt 45 or 1860 44 Cal. Polished nickel.

Value: $150-350 (Texas 45)

TG-447

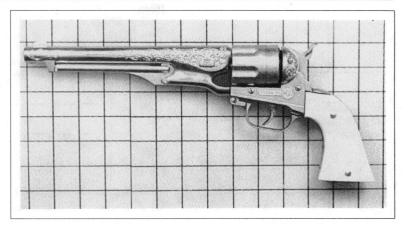

Texan 45

Hubley- 1961. Detail of TG-447 above. Note the "Texan 45" lettering, Hubley logo, engraving, polished finish and gold cylinder. Very rare.

TG-448

Texan Jr.

Hubley- 1940. Cast iron repeater in the dark finish, engraved with the very rare dummy hammer. White steerhead grips and Colt medallions.

Value: $125-200 (CI Dummy)

TG-449

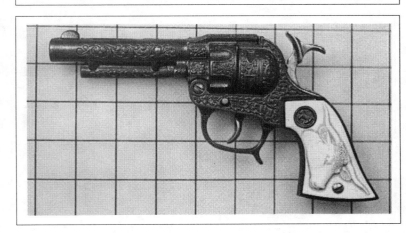

Texan Jr. - No Name

Hubley (Hamilton)- 1950.Nearly identical to Texan Jr. Possibly is a Canadian copy. Same engraving. Heavy die cast clicker. Hammer does not move. Checkered grips with star. Dull nickel finish. Unusual.

Value: $35-85

TG450

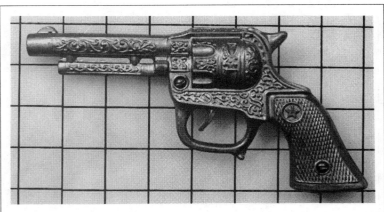

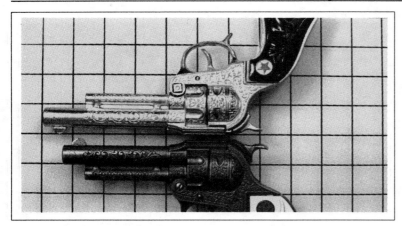

Texan Jr.

Hubley- 1950. Rarer DC variations. Note longer barrel. In 1950 Hubley added 5/8" to the Texan, Jr. *Top:* Long barrel in the gold finish with black grips. *Lower:* Dark finish alloy, shorter gun with CI parts.

Value: $75-135 $85-150 (Gold)

TG-451

Texan Jr.

*Hubley-*1950. Die cast repeater in the dull gold finish with black grips. Note box for "Gold PLated" pistol. Long barrel model. All die cast models have star medallions.

Value: $115-165 (Gold gun & box)

TG-452

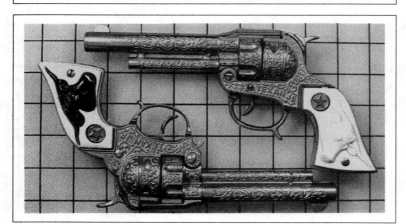

Texan Jr.

Hubley- 1950-55. Die cast models. *Top:* A nickel finish with push button & white grips. *Lower:* Nickel finish with lever in front of trigger guard with B&W grips.

Value: $75-135 (But) $35-85 (Lever)

TG-453

Texan Jr.

Hubley- 1955. Extremely rare and beautiful die cast in antique bronze with lever opener with B&W grips. Perhaps factory prototype finish.

Value: $100-150 (Antique bronze)

TG-454

Texan Jr.

Hubley- 1955. Die cast in the rarer gold finish with lever opener and turquoise blue grips. Very few lever opening models were gold plated. Perhaps intended for a cowgirl.

Value: $95-145 (Gold)

TG-455

Texan Jr.

Hubley- 1960. The later model die cast with friction opener in nickel finish with one-piece W&B steerhead grips. Gun has no medallions, no button & no lever.

Value: $35-75

TG-456

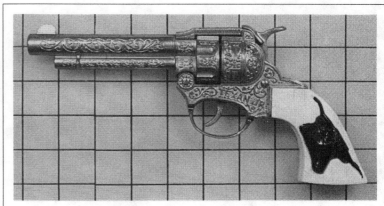

Texan Jr.

Hubley- 1960. Similar to TG-456, except in the black finish with turquoise blue & black steerhead, one-piece grips. Friction open. Unusual variation. Later model.

Value: $45-85 (Black)

TG-457

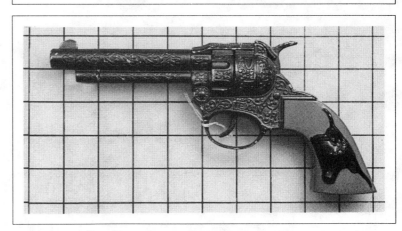

Texan Jr.

Hubley- 1960. Large 10" die cast model in nickel with half size ejector rod & button release on back of cylinder. Engraved gun with B&W steerhead grips & star logo.

Value: $50-100 (Gun & box)

TG-458

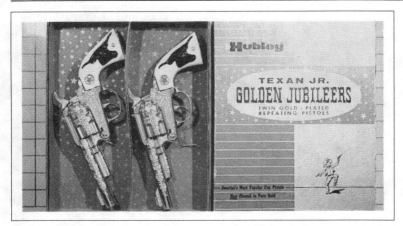

Texan Jr.

Hubley- 1960. Unusual pair similar to TG-458 except in gold finish. Note box says Golden Jubileers. Few Hubley guns came in a presentation box as a pair. Rare set.

Value: $185-275 (Gold pair in box)

TG-459

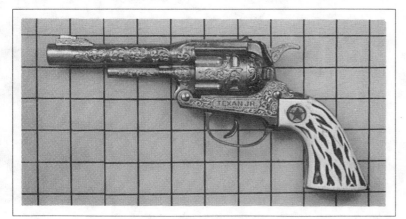

Texan Jr.

Hubley- 1960. Similar to TG-459 with the rarer polished gold finish with turquoise-blue & red swirl steerhead grips. Has gold star medallions. Beautiful toy gun.

Value: $75-125 (Gold)

TG-460

Texan Jr.

Hubley- 1960. 10" similar to TG-458 with half ejector rod, button release in a dull nickel finish with tan & white stag with red star.

Value: $40-75

TG-461

Texan Jr.

Hubley- 1960-65. 10" DC in the very rare antique bronze finish with white & black steerhead grips. Only a minimal amount of Hubley guns are in bronze. Last model with same engraving but no ejector rod.

Value: $85-135 (Antique bronze)

TG-462

Texan Jr.

Hubley- 1960-65. Last model similar to TG-462 with no ejector rod. Nickel finish with engraving & one-piece B&W steerhead grips. Normal star medallion.

Value: $40-75

TG-463

Texan

Dent- 1925. Rare long barrel cast iron. Nickel finish with checkered grips & circle "D" medallions. Like all Dent guns, it is seldom found. Single shot that shoots mammoth caps.

Value: $150-225

TG-464

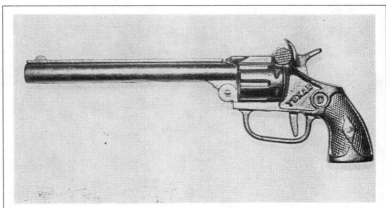

Texas

*Leslie-Henry-*1955. DC repeater variations. *Top:* 1st model with low hammer spur, large horse & lettering on frame & nickel finish. *Lower:* 2nd model with the small horse & lettering, high hammer has dull nickel finish. Both have horsehead grips.
Value: $65-125 (Either model)

TG-465

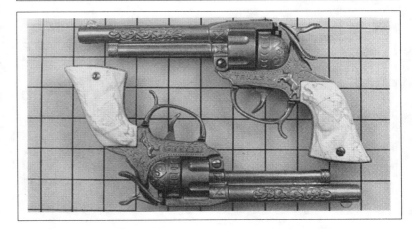

Texas

Leslie-Henry- 1955. *Top gun:* Similar to TG-465, 1st model, except has the rarer long barrel & black oval with star. All the long barrel L-H are rare. *Lower:* Rare long barrel Wild Bill Hickok for comparison.

Value: $85-150 (Long barrel Texas)

TG-466

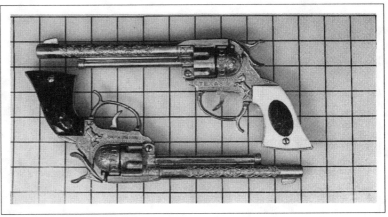

Texas

L.I. Die Castings Inc, NY- 1960. Rare DC repeater nearly identical to Hubley guns. Nickel finish with engraved barrel & the circle "T" medallions. Has chocolate brown steerhead grips. Beautiful gun.

Value: $75-125

TG-467

Texas

L.I. Die Castings Inc., NY- 1960. Similar to TG-467, except in the dull nickel finish with white steerhead grips and the "T" medallions.

Value: $65-115 (Dull finish)

TG-468

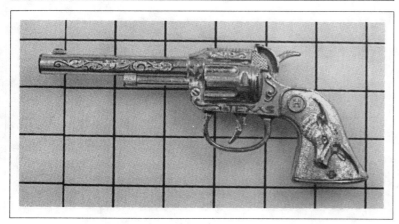

Texas

Hubley- 1965. Late Hubley die cast single shot, engraved, has metal steerhead grips with circle "H" medallions. Possibly a chrome finished contract gun for Halco.

Value: $15-25

TG-469

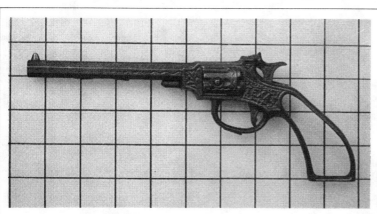

Texas Jack

Ives- Pre 1890. Extremely rare CI single shot with engraving, octagon barrel & skeleton grip. One of the earliest western toy guns. Jack was a western pulp novel character in late 1800s. (Also round brl.)

Value: $165-300 (Oct) $200-375 (Rnd)

TG-470

Texas Jack

Unknown- 1900. English copy of the Ives gun in cast iron with solid grips having scroll engraving & circle "G" medallions. Octagon barrel in nickel finish. Rare toy gun.

Value: $150-285

TG-471

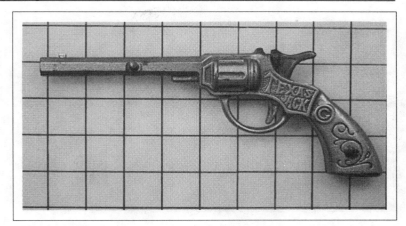

Texas Kid

Hubley/Gabriel 1965-70. Nickel die cast repeater with engraving and one-piece white steerhead grips. Unusual, late western toy gun.

Value: $15-30.

TG-472

Texas Longhorn

Leslie-Henry- 1960. Unmarked frame, die cast repeater in chrome finish. Rare long barrel variety with copper steerhead grips with Texas Longhorn lettering. Unusual.

Value: $75-125

TG-473

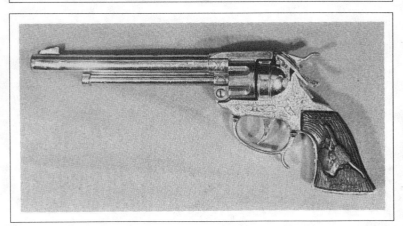

Texas Ranger

Kilgore- Pre 1930. Very rare C.I. repeater. Nickel finish with checkered grips. Note the bullet for front sight! Only a handful exist of this model.

Value: $275-500

TG-474

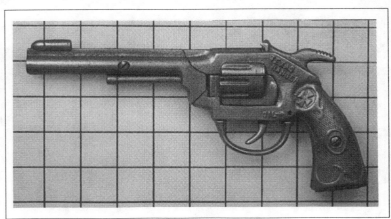

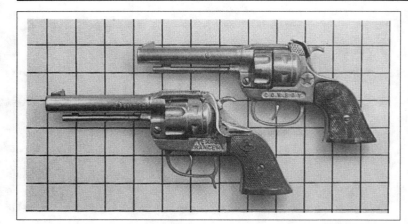

Texas Ranger - Colt .45

Hubley- 1940. Extremely rare CI repeater with obvious similarites to this Cowboy. *Lower:* Polished nickel finish, side opening lever, revolving cylinder, spur on the trigger guard, brown grips & Colt logo.

Value: $200-350 (Texas Ranger- Pol)

TG-475

Texas Ranger - Colt .45

Hubley- 1940. Detail of TG-475. Note the polished finish, frame lettering, Colt .45 on barrel, revolving cylinder & lever. Gun is probably a Hubley factory prototype as no other has surfaced. Very rare.

TG-476

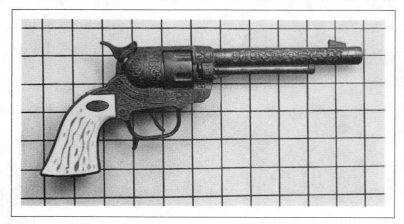

Texas Ranger

Leslie-Henry- 1955. Rare DC .44 model in antique bronze finish, engraved & has a revolving cylinder. Seldom seen. A few of these have been discoverd as parts for a western lamp & have cord holes drilled.

Value: $125-200 (With no lamp holes)

TG-477

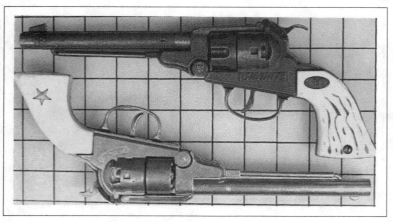

Texas Ranger

Leslie-Henry- 1960. Rarely seen DC with a revolving cylinder & antique bronze finish. Stag grips with "H" ovals. Has similar details to the Lone Star Apache gun shown in the photograph.

Value: $65-125 (Texas Ranger)

TG-478

Texas Ranger

Leslie-Henry- 1960. Detail of gun TG-478. Note the rare "Texas Ranger" lettering, revolving cylinder and the "H" oval grip medallion. White and tan stag grips.

TG-479

Texas Ranger

Leslie-Henry- 1955. 1st model DC with no barrel engraving, has extra large opening lever, dark finish with transparent amber horsehead grips. Unpopular toy gun.

Value: $45-85

TG-480

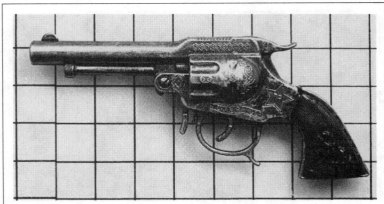

Texas Ranger

Leslie-Henry- 1955. *Top:* 1st model, no barrel engraving, large lever in polished nickel finish with amber grips. *Lower:* A 2nd model in nickel with engraved barrel, small lever & white horsehead grips.

Value: $45-85 (Either model)

TG-481

Texas Ranger

Leslie-Henry- 1955. Similar 2nd model to TG-481 except, in rarer antique bronze finish. Rare original box in blue & yellow colors. One-piece box. Grips are white.

Value: $75-125 (Bronze gun & box)

TG-482

Texas Ranger

Leslie-Henry- 1955. 1st model DC with no engraving, large lever & in the very rare gold finish with black horsehead grips. The 2-piece box has different art in blue & gold that reads "Bright Gold Finish."

Value: $75-125 (Gold gun)

TG-483

Texas Ranger

Leslie-Henry-Wilkes-Barre, PA.- 1960. Die cast repeater, engraved with stag insert grips & diamond "H" medallions. Third L-H address. Also: Scarborough Junction, Ontario, Canada & Mount Vernon, NY.

Value: $25-50 (Gun & display card)

TG-484

Texas Ranger

Leslie-Henry- 1955. 8 1/2" nickel die cast with engraving & opening lever. Brown and white stag grips with diamond "H" medallions.

Value: $35-65

TG-485

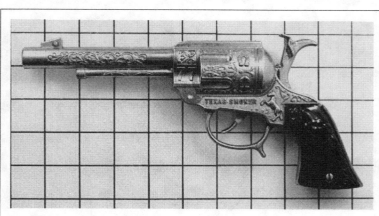

Texas Smoker

Leslie-Henry- 1950-55. Unusual & rare die cast in nickel with engraving and black steerhead grips. Shoots white powder to imitate smoke! One of the rarer western or L-H toy guns.

Value: $100-225

TG-486

Texan .38

Hubley- 1955. 10 1/2" die cast in a nickel finish, engraved with revolving cylinder & bullets. Shown with a rare display case & clip of bullets. White and black steerhead grips. Seldom seen toy gun.

Value: $125-200

TG-487

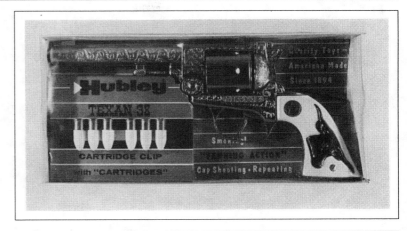

Texan .38

Hubley- 1955. *Top:* Similar to TG-487 but in the very rare gold finish & turquoise blue steerhead grips & red star medallions. Lower: Similar, but in chrome-type finish with white steerhead grips.

Value: $150-250 (Gold) $125-200 (Chm)

TG-488

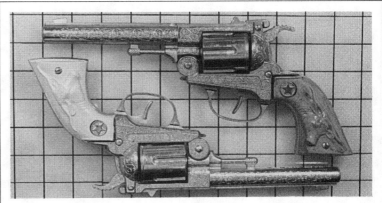

Texan .38

Hubley- 1955. Similar to TG-487 except in the dull nickel finish with the reddish brown and tan stag grips. Later model.

Value: $100-150

TG-489

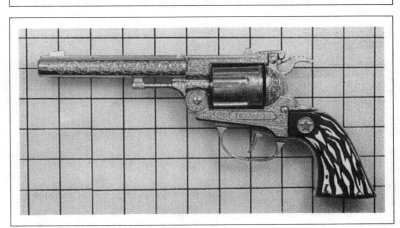

The Forty Five

National- Pre 1930. Rather rare and ugly toy gun. Cast iron repeater that requires much imagination to be a western-style six gun! Buntline-style, long barrel toy.

Value: $100-225

TG-490

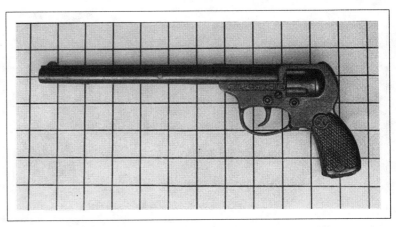

The Law West of the Pecos

Unknown- 1936. Non-working, solid cast iron gun. Copy of a Colt Peacemaker. A rather unusual and rare toy.

Value: $145-235

TG-491

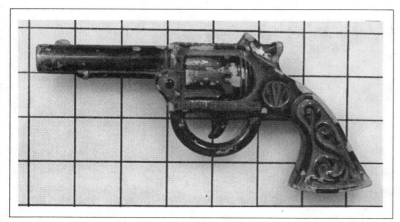

.38 Repeater

Best Co.- 1940-45. Rare WW-II toy gun in multi-color plastic. Note the victory "V" in the circle behind the cylinder. Gun is a clicker & the hammer is also a whistle!

Value: $15-25

TG-492

Thundergun

Marx- 1955-60. Huge, 12 1/2" die cast is engraved & shoots two rolls of caps! *Top:* Nickel finish with superb, buffalo head ivory grips! *Lower:* Black finish & brown and black swirl grips.

Value: $125-225

TG-493

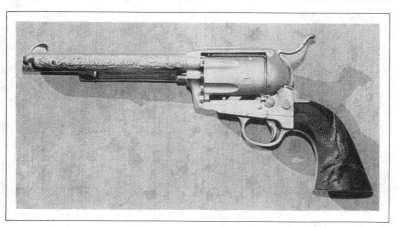

Thundergun

Marx- 1955-60. Similar to TG-493, except in the dull gray finish that has beautiful chocolate brown flying eagle grips. Marx grips are among some of the finest ever put on toy guns.

Value: $110-200

TG-494

Tom Mix

Unknown- Mid 1930s. Ralston Cereal premium, wooden guns by various contractors. Painted black with stained or painted grips. Logo & name is rubber stamped on grips. Revolving cylinder. Gun opens.

Value: $150-250

TG495

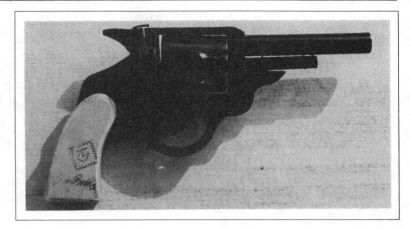

Tom Mix

Unknown- Mid-1930s. 2nd model wooden gun. This variation does not open. It has a revolving cylinder and rubber stamped paper grips. Rarely found toy. The hand labor generates many varieties.

Value: $175-275

TG-496

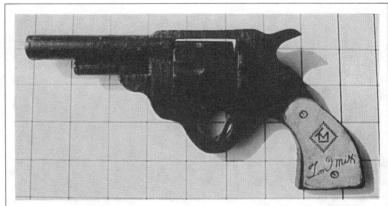

Top Gun Jr.

Hubley- 1960-65. Nickel 8" die cast with no engraving. A repeater with white stag grips. Later cap gun. Side-opening.

Value: $20-35

TG-497

Top-Hand 250

Nichols- 1960. Die cast repeater in polished nickel with black woodgrain grips having circle "N" medallions.

Value: $60-115

TG-498

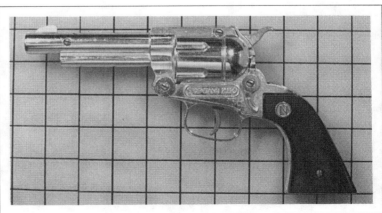

Top-Hand 250

Nichols- 1960. Similar to TG-498, except in the Steel-Blu finish with brown wood-grain grips and circle "N" medallions. A rarer variation of this model.

Value: $75-125

TG-499

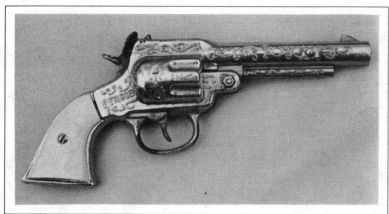

Trigger

Stevens- 1950-60. Rare die cast repeater in polished nickel with engraving and white cowboy and crossed guns grips. A dull finished variety is more common. See also, character section under Rogers.

Value: $75-125 (Polished nickel)

TG-500

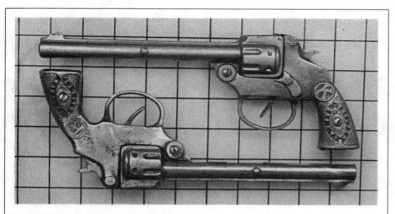

Trooper Safety

Kilgore- 1920-30. Cast iron repeaters in nickel finish with long barrels. *Top:* Gun has a safety under the cylinder. *Lower:* No safety on frame. Both guns have the name on the grips.

Value: $100-175

TG-501

Trooper Safety

Kilgore- 1930. Unusual & rare cast iron toy gun repeater with a crank to fire at a rapid rate! Long barrel in the dark finish. Cranks usually missing, but reproduction ones are available.

Value: $125-225

TG-502

2 in 1

Stevens- 1930. Dual fire-power cast iron. Single shot cap gun plus a rubber band shooter! When cap is fired so is the rubber band. Nickel finish with black checkered grips. Rare long barrel toy gun.

Value: $135-225

TG-503

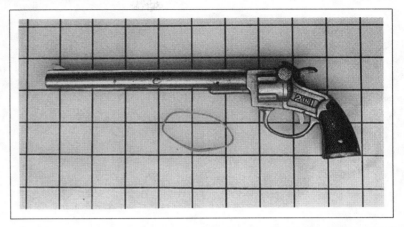

2 in 1

Stevens- 1930. Similar to TG-503 except in the normal dark finish. Note the small rubber band catch in front of the hammer. This drops down when the trigger is pulled, firing the cap and a rubber band.

Value: $135-225

TG-504

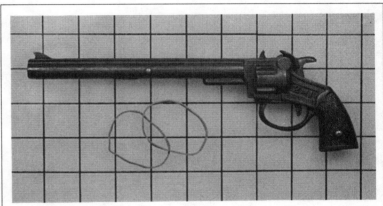

Two Time

Kenton- Pre 1930. Cast iron single shot cap shooter and rubber band gun. Nickel finish and fires similar to TG-504 above. All the long barrel guns are rarer.

Value: $115-200

TG-505

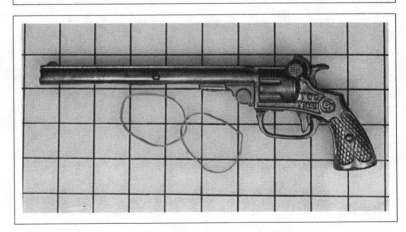

2 in 1

Hubley- 1960-65. Unusual D.C. repeater in nickel finish with white stag grips and red painted star. Gun comes with an extra barrel extension to make either a short or long barrel variation. Common.

Value: $25-65

TG-506

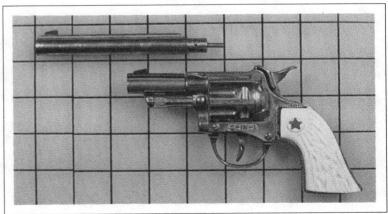

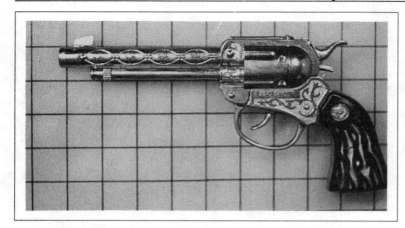

250 Shot

Esquire-Actoy- 1955-60. 10" die cast uses large rolls of 250 caps! Engraved with black stag one-piece grips and the pony medallions. Rare gold finish.

Value: $85-135 (Gold)

TG-507

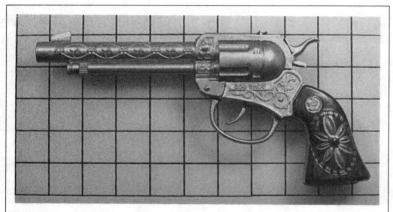

250 Shot

Esquire-Actoy- 1955-60. Similar to TG-507, except in nickel finish and unusual black, turquoise & gold floral grips. The nickel variety also found with plain stag grips. The floral grips match a holster set.
(See TG-416)
Value: $65-100 (Floral grips add $15)

TG-508

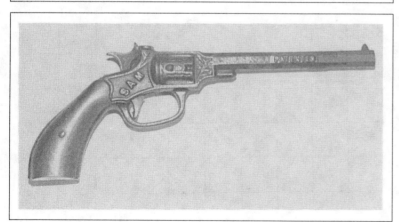

Uncle Sam

Ives- 1880. Extremely rare cast iron single shot. 9 1/4" early and quaint-style toy. It is similar to the Texas Jack.

Value: $350-500

TG-509

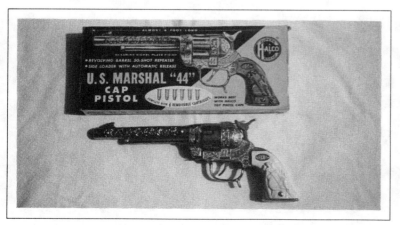

U.S. Marshal .44

Leslie-Henry- 1955. Large die cast with a revolving cylinder that accepts bullets. Engraved nickel with white horsehead grips with "H" ovals. 11 1/4" length with original box.

Value: $125-200 (Gun & box)

TG-510

U.S. Marshal .44

Leslie-Henry- 1955. Similar to TG-510, but in the antique bronze finish and the stag grips with "H" ovals. Revolving cylinder with six solid copper bullets.

Value: $100-185

TG-511

U.S. Marshal .45

Crescent Toy Co., Eng.- 1960-70. A nickel die cast repeater with engraving & lever opener. Red grips with horse & rider and circle "45" medallions. Unusual toy gun.

Value: $65-125

TG-512

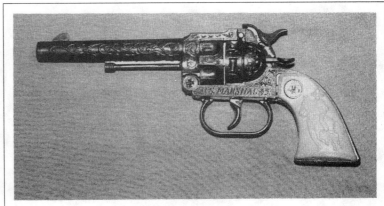

Unmarked - Marshal .44

Leslie-Henry (or perhaps Roth)- 1960-80. This gun may be newer model. Similar to TG-511 except no name on the frame & the bronze finish is painted on. Quality is far inferior to early L-H toy guns.

Value: $15-50

TG-513

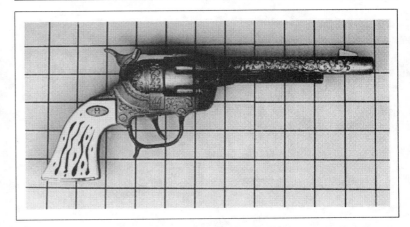

Unmarked

Leslie-Henry (or perhaps Roth)- 1960-80. These may be newer models. Similar to Apache. *Top:* Gold finish no name with stag grips. *Lower:* Chrome no name with black stag grips. Both have revolving cyl.

Value: $15-50

TG-514

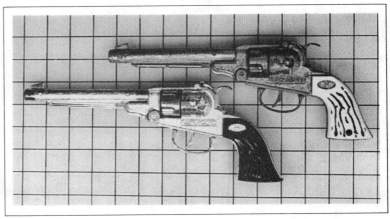

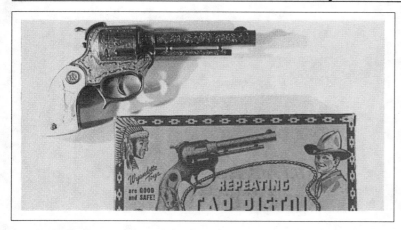

Unmarked

Wyandotte- 1955. Engraved, nickel finish die cast repeater with no name. Similar to Hoppy and Red Ranger guns. Hard to find as parts are used to restore Hoppy guns. Very rare original box. Y&• logo.

Value: $45-100 (Box $35 additional)

TG-515

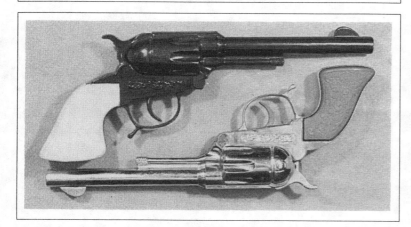

Unmarked

Wyandotte- 1955. Similar to TG-515 but in the dull nickel finish. White grips with horsehead, horseshoe and rope. Has "Y&•" medallions.

Value: $40-85

TG-516

Unmarked

Classy- 1960. Pair of no name repeaters in DC. Top: Black finish with one-piece white stag grips. Lower: Chrome finish & floral scroll pewter grips. Seldom found as they provide parts for Roy R. guns.

Value: $45-85 (Blk) $65-125 (Chrm)

TG-517

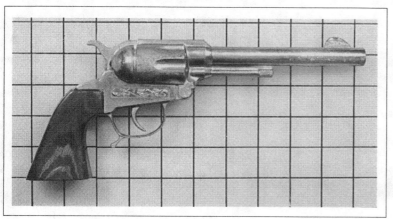

Unmarked

Classy- 1960. Similar to TG-517 except in nickel finish with brown woodgrained grips. These are found in the Civil War, North- South holster sets. Rarer variety.

Value: $65-135

TG-518

Unmarked

Leslie-Henry- 1960. Pair of no name guns in chrome finish. Rare long barrels with minimal engraving. *Top:* Has the copper steerhead grips with Longhorn. *Lower:* black stag grips. Possibly newer models.

Value: $35-85   (Copper grips add $15)

TG-519

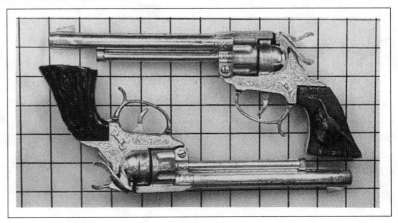

Unmarked

Leslie-Henry- 1960. Rare long barrel die cast in gold finish with stag grips and no medallions. Possibly newer model.

Value: $40-90 (Gold)

TG-520

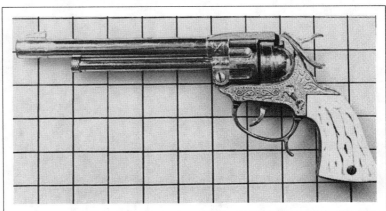

Unmarked

Leslie-Henry- 1960. Rare long barrel die cast in dull nickel finish with black stag grips. Possibly newer model.

Value: $35-85

TG-521

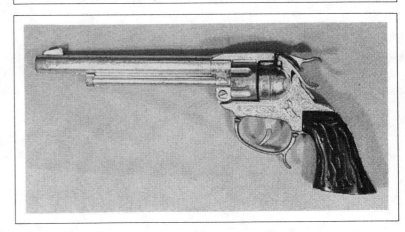

Unmarked

Leslie-Henry- 1950. Early, heavy frame die cast with engraving only on barrel. A rare variety in nickel finish with white horsehead grips. Also found in gold finish.

Value: $100-185

TG-522

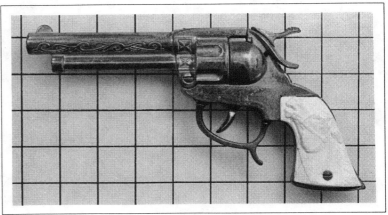

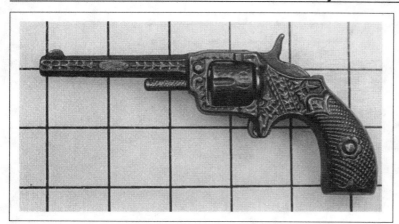

Unmarked

Unknown- 1880 era. Rare cast iron with a revolving cylinder, engraving and checkered grips. Spur trigger model.

Value: $85-165

TG-523

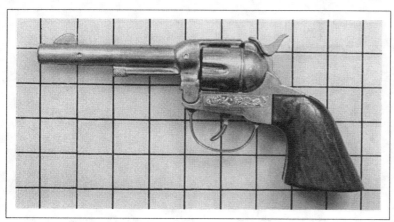

Unmarked

Classy- 1960. 9" die cast repeater, short barrel in nickel finish with scroll engraving on frame. Brown, woodgrained grips. Rare variation.

Value: $35-85

TG-524

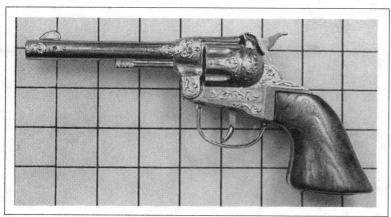

Unmarked

Classy- 1960. Smaller 8 1/4" die cast with engraving in chrome finish with brown, woodgrained grips. Rare variation.

Value: $30-75

TG-525

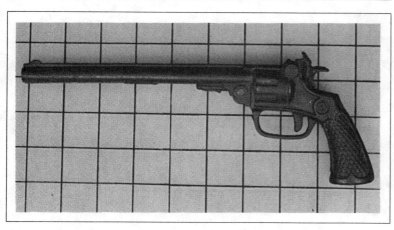

Unmarked

Kilgore- 1930. Large cast iron long barrel with checkered grips and the circle "P" medallions. One of the rarer long barrel guns.

Value: $145-275

TG-526

Unmarked

Dent & Kenton- 1925 era. Pair of cast iron long barrel single shots in nickel finish. Note both are nearly identical 8 7/8". *Top:* Dent with circle "D" logo. *Lower:* A rare Kenton with "S-W" logo.

Value: $75-125 (Either company)

TG-526-A

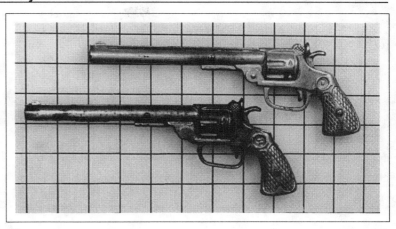

Unmarked

Kenton- Pre-1920. Very rare long barrel in cast iron that shoots mammoth caps. All long barrels are difficult to find. 11 1/2" S-W circle medallions.

Value: $165-275

TG-526-B

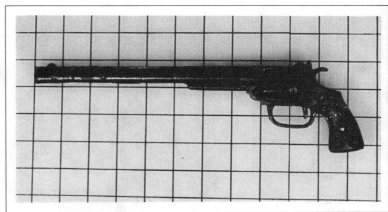

Unmarked

Kilgore- 1930. 6 1/2" cast iron single shot with a "P" logo in the dark finish. Rarely seen model.

Value: $50-85

TG-527

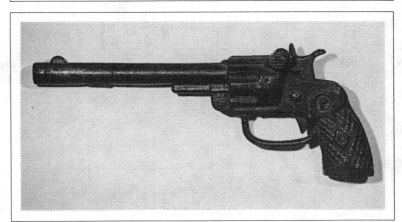

Unmarked

Stevens (?)- 1945-50. An unusual 9" cast light alloy. Probably Stevens. Solid non-working toy gun. Has an Indian on right grip and cowboy on the left. Blank logo.

Value: $25-45

TG-528

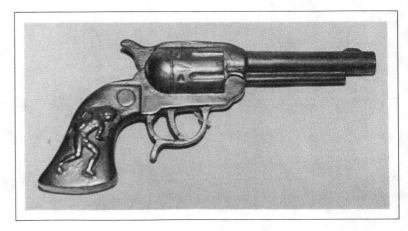

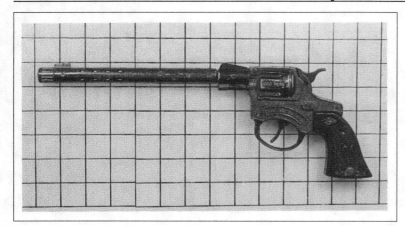

Unmarked

Halco- 1965. Die cast contract repeater in black finish with a 7" barrel extension to make a long barrel model. Unusual toy gun and seldom seen.

Value: $35-75 (Gun & barrel extension)

TG-529

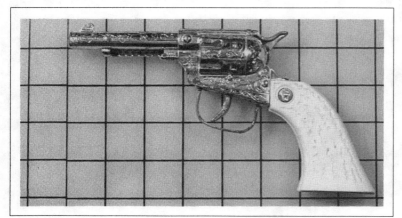

Unmarked

Hubley/Gabriel- 1970. 8" later model die cast repeater with engraving has chrome finish. Grips are one-piece stag with Indian Chief circle medallions. Possibly a more recent foreign made model.

Value: $15-25

TG-530

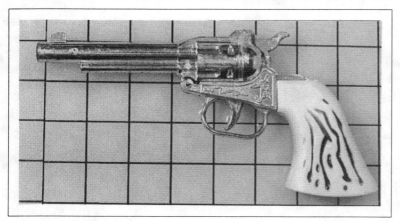

Unmarked

Leslie-Henry (?)- 1970-80. Recent die cast gun in chrome finish, engraved with one-piece stag grips. Offered in a recent Western Man Frontier series.

Value: $15-25

TG-531

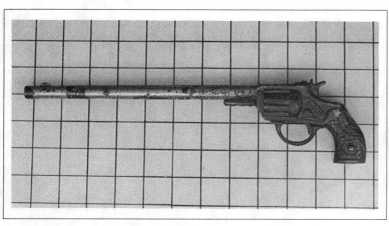

Victor

Stevens- 1924. Very rare long barrel cast iron. Single shot in nickel finish. Quaint scroll and floral engraving. Very limited number exist.

Value: $200-425

TG-532

Wagon Train

Leslie-Henry- 1957-62. Pair of die cast repeaters engraved in nickel finish. Top: Rare long barrel variety with white grips & horseshoe ovals. Lower: Regular length barrel in white grips with star ovals.

Value: $145-275 (Long) $100-225 (short)

TG-533

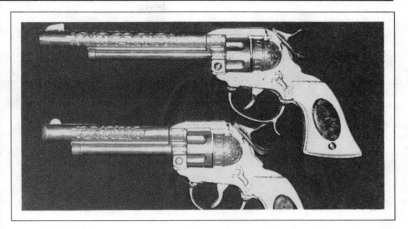

Wagon Train

Leslie-Henry- 1957-62. *Top:* Rare long barrel repeater in dull nickel with transparent amber horsehead grips. *Lower:* Gene Autry rare long barrel for comparison. See western character section.

Value: $135-250 (Long with dull finish)

TG-534

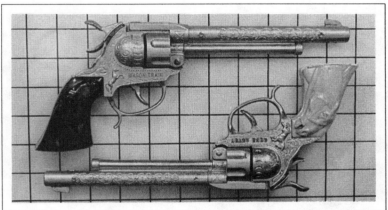

Warrior

Kilgore- 1926. Rare cast iron repeater in nickel finish. Checkered grips with cross medallions. Classic early gun with quaint toy gun appeal.

Value: $135-245

TG-535

Wells Fargo

Esquire-Actoy- 1957-62. Long barrel die cast repeater in engraved nickel finish. Stag grips with pony medallions. Also in bronze. See western character section.

Value: $85-165

TG-536

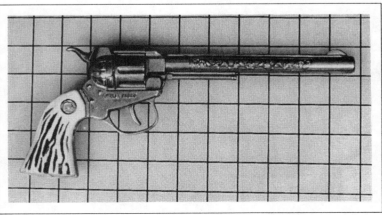

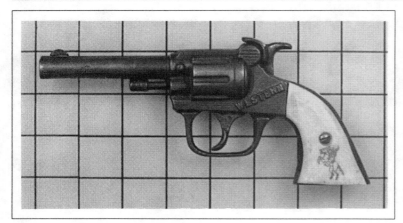

Western

Kenton- 1938. Early cast iron with dark finish and rearing horse & rider artwork on pearl grips. Single shot.

Value: $45-100

TG-537

Western

Kenton- 1939. Similar to TG-537, except in nickel finish with the rare dummy hammer variation. Blank pearl grips.

Value: $65-125 (Dummy)

TG-538

Western

Kenton- 1950. Very rare late model in the engraved version and nickel finish. Red grips with horse & rider artwork. Also in a dummy variety ($35 additional).

Value: $85-165

TG-539

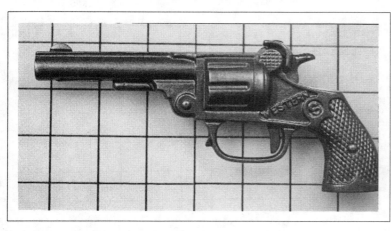

Western

Kenton- 1930 era. Cast iron single shot in the dark finish. Shoots mammoth caps. A rarer dummy version is shown in the detail of TG-541. S&W medallions.

Value: $35-85

TG-540

Western

Kenton- 1930 era. Detail photo showing a very rare dummy variety. Note from this top view that the right side casting will not allow the hammer to cock. I have never seen this type of casting before.

Value: $85-150

TG-541

Western

Hubley- 1960. Die cast repeater in nickel finish with white steerhead grips & star medallions.

Value: $35-70

TG-542

Western

Hubley- 1960. Similar to TG-542, except in the very rare antique bronze finish & white and black steerhead grips. Gun is possibly a factory prototype finish.

Value: $65-125

TG-543

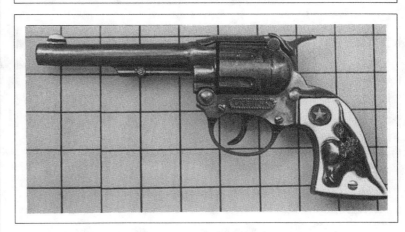

Western

Hubley- 1960. Similar to TG-542, except in the very rare gold finish & turquoise blue steerhead grips. Probably intended for a cowgirl.

Value: $65-125

TG-544

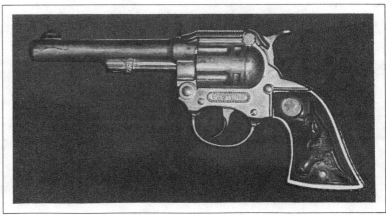

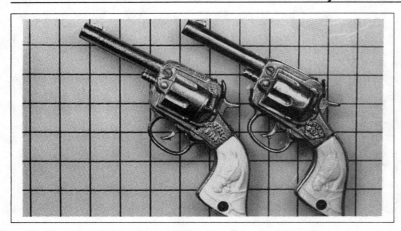

Western Boy

Stevens- 1940. *Right:* The CI Western Boy repeater in polished nickel with white horsehead grip and red jewel. *Left:* This nearly identical gun is a Buffalo Bill for comparison. Almost the same mold.

Value: $145-250

TG-545

Western Boy

Stevens- 1940. Similar cast iron to TG-545 but in the rarer painted silver finish. The grips are black horsehead with the green jewels. Unusual finish.

Value: $145-250

TG-546

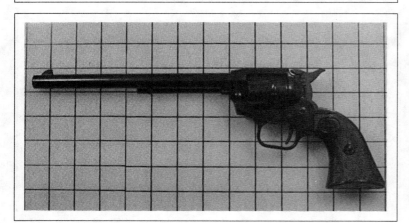

Western Haig - Buntline

Haig, San Gabriel, CA.- 1960 era. Plastic & metal accurate copy of a Colt. Black with checkered grips. Fires caps & small BBs. A rod pushes a BB down the 8" barrel & a cap propels it. Unusual toy gun.

Value: $75-150

TG-547

Westerner

Hamilton- 1955-60. Seldom seen die cast repeater in dull nickel finish with slick black grips.

Value: $35-65

TG-548

Western Man

Roth American Inc.,PA- 1965-70. Die cast .44 similar to L-H with no name. Painted antique bronze finish. Appears that Roth made guns from Leslie-Henry molds in Wilkes Barre, PA.during the mid 1960s.

Value: $25-50 (Gun on display card)

TG-549

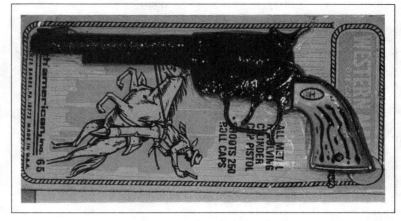

Westo

Kenton- 1935-40. Cast iron single shot in the rare dummy hammer variety. Dark finish with white painted grips and red jewel. Also in regular model for caps.

Value: $85-165 (Dummy) $55-100 (Reg)

TG-550

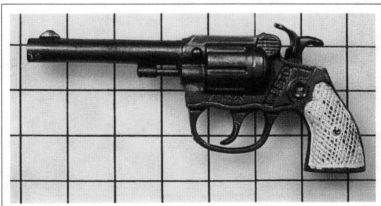

Wild Bill Hickok .44

Leslie-Henry- 1951-58. Large .44 model in die cast with nickel finish. Has revolving cylinder that accepts small solid copper bullets. Engraved with the white horse-head grips & "H" ovals.

Value: $100-185

TG-551

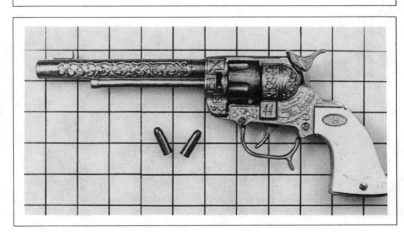

Wild Bill Hickok

Leslie-Henry- 1951-58. Nearly identical die cast pair of 9" guns. *Top:* Frame has large horse & lettering. *Lower:* Has small horse & lettering. Both have butterscotch horsehead grips. See character section.

Value: $85-165 (Either variety)

TG-552

Wild Bill Hickok

Leslie-Henry- 1951-58. Matching pair of die cast repeaters in nickel finish. Copper grips have steerhead & U.S. Marshal-Wild Bill Hickok on them. These grips are the rarer variety. See character section.

Value: $100-185 (Each - copper grips)

TG-553

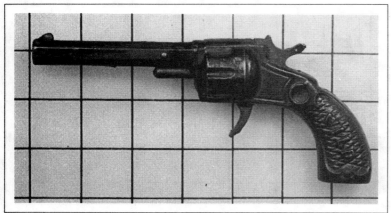

Wild West

Ives- 1890. Early and very rare octagon barrel single shot cast iron. Name on the grips. Spur trigger in dark finish. Seldom seen toy gun.

Value: $150-275

TG-554

Wild West

Ives- 1890. Early and rare cast iron single shot engraved with name on the grips. A quaint and unusual toy gun.

Value: $150-275

TG-555

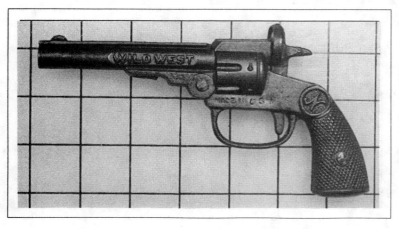

Wild West

National- 1930. Cast iron single shot for mammoth caps. Name is on the barrel. Checkered grips & circle "N" medallions.

Value: $75-150

TG-556

Wild West

Kenton- 1925 era. Very rare long barrel CI guns. *Top:* Lettering on the frame has no ridge around area. *Lower:* The rarer gun with the ridge around frame & lettering. Both toy guns shoot mammoth caps.

Value: $150-250 (No R) $185-325 (Ridge)

TG-557

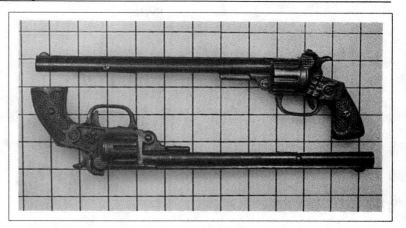

Winner

Hubley- 1960-65. Rare plastic & metal repeater similar to a Texan Jr. Has a lever opener. Hammer, trigger and anvil are in metal. Metallic silver color & black steerhead grips. Late & unusual toy gun.

Value: $75-165 (Gun & box)

TG-558

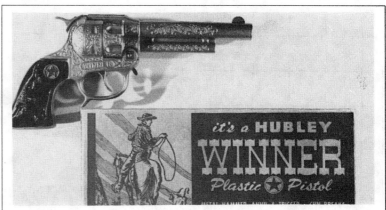

Wyatt Earp

Leslie-Henry- 1955-61. Die cast long barrel in nickel finish with black steerhead oval on grips. Square hole screws suggest gun was made in Canada. Rare variety. Also see character section.

Value: $100-250

TG-559

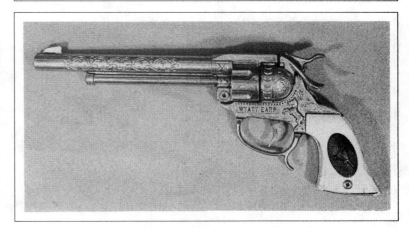

Wyatt Earp

Hubley- 1955-61. Buntline Special die cast in nickel finish with brown-red swirl steerhead grips. See character section.

Value: $85-175

TG-560

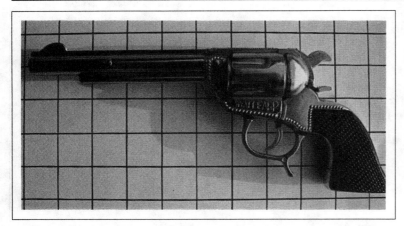

Wyatt Earp

G. Schmidt- 1955-61. Very rare die cast in nickel finish and checkered copper grips. Research indicates this model was made in Canada. See character section.
Value: $175-350

TG-561

Wyatt Earp

Kilgore- 1955-61. Die cast repeater in gold finish with horsehead white & tan grips. Also see the character section.

Value: $75-165 (Gold)

TG-562

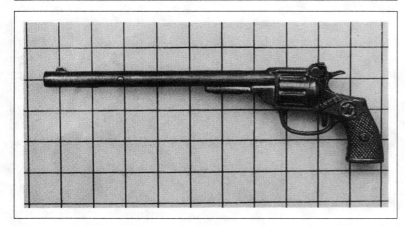

Yankee

Hubley- 1925. Rare long barrel cast iron single shot for mammoth caps. Grips are checkered with star medallions. All long barrel guns are seldom found.

Value: $200-425

TG-563

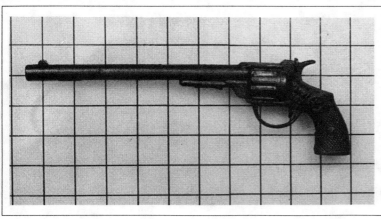

Yankee Boy

Hubley- 1930. Rare long barrel cast iron single shot. Checkered grips with the star medallions.

Value: $200-425

TG-564

Annie Oakley

Daisy- 1956. Bang or pop rifle. 32" lever action in silver & gold with blue sling & Annie's logo on stock. Rather rare cowgirl toy gun. Came with a canteen-$4.98.

Value: $85-175 (Rifle & canteen)

R-1

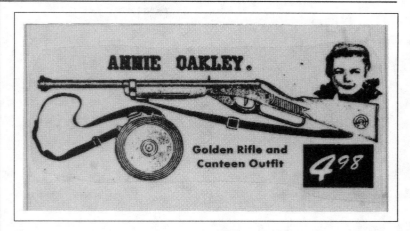

Buffalo Bill

Leslie-Henry- 1957 era. Die cast cap gun is 26" with scope and sling. Probably made in Canada. Plastic stock has magazine to store extra caps in the butt. $1.95.

Value: $50-85

R-2

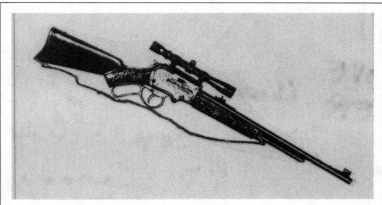

Cheyenne Saddle Carbine

Daisy- 1959. Pop-bang rifle with bullet whine sound! Saddle ring with thong. Suede leather stock boot. 32" long.

Value: $45-85

R-3

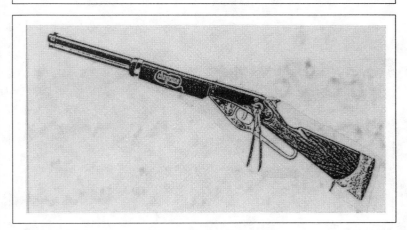

Colt 6 Shooter Rifle

Mattel- 1960 era. Shootin' shell with a revolving cylinder. Extra bullets on stock. One of the rarer Mattel guns. 31" length.

Value: $85-200

R-4

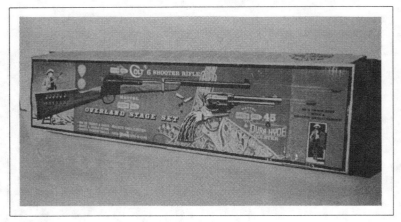

Colt 6 Shooter-Overland Set

Mattel- 1960 era. Overland Stage Set. Rare set includes the Colt 6 Shooter rifle, the .45 Shootin' Shell revolver & Dura-Hide fast draw holster. In full color box.

Value: $350-600 Complete set & box

R-5

Cowboy in Africa Rifle

Mattel- 1962. Plastic & metal 26" rifle. It has a "Tommy gun" style drum and is a clicker or noise maker. Very unusual toy gun and seldom seen.

Value: $45-100

R-6

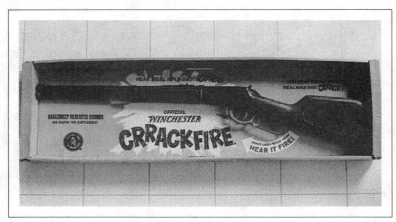

Crrackfire! Rifle

Mattel- 1960 era. Winchester lever action rifle in plastic & metal. Realistic rifle fire sound. Shown in original display box.

Value: $85-165 (Rifle & box)

R-7

Crrackfire! Rifle

Mattel- 1960 era. Similar to R-7 above, except this model has a working scope mounted on the top. Same mechanism and sound.

Value: $65-125

R-8

Daisy Pop Gun

Three early, lever action, nickel plated, pop rifles. 1920 era. *Top:* Daisy. *Center:* King. *Lower:* American Tool Works. Three of the earlier lever action, western-styled toy rifles.

Value: $35-100 each

R-9

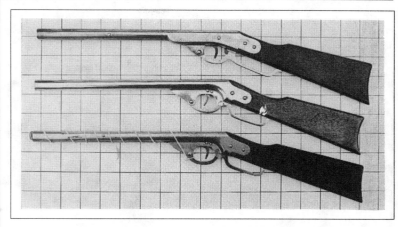

Davy Crockett

Daisy- 1955. Smoke & bang rifle 35" long in blue finish with leather boot & name on the stock. Came with leather fringed plastic powder horn. Shown with a rare L-H 9" DC cap gun. Seldom seen set.

Value: $100-225 (Rifle & powder horn)

R-10

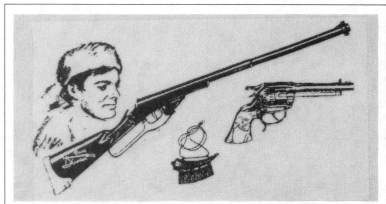

Davy Crockett

Leslie-Henry- 1955. Plastic & metal lever action Winchester. Cap shooter 26" in length. Rare toy rifle and Crockett toy.

Value: $75-150

R-11

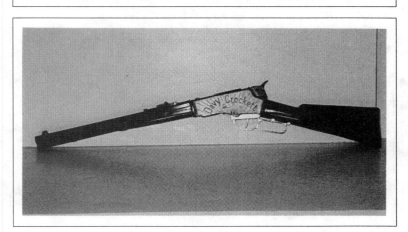

Davy Crockett

Parris Mfg.- 1955. Pressed steel & wood , 24" lever action rifle. Pop/cork shooter. Name printed on stock. Seldom seen.

Value: $30-65

R-12

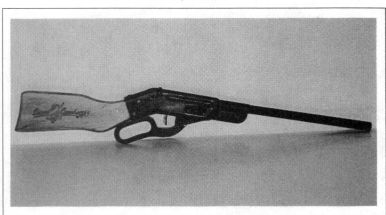

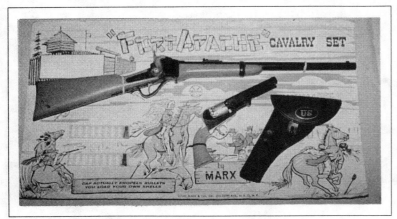

Fort Apache Set

Marx- 1960 era. Civil War Sharps carbine & Colt pistol on original card. Cap and shootin' shell models. Plastic and metal. A very rare and impressive carbine. 27"

Value: $150-300 (Entire display card)

R-13

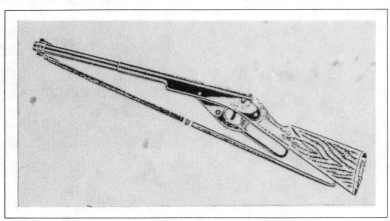

Frontier Scout Rifle

Daisy- 1959. Metal with plastic stock. 32" smoker and loud bang model with sling. Also available with 11" golden scope.

Value: $25-65

R-14

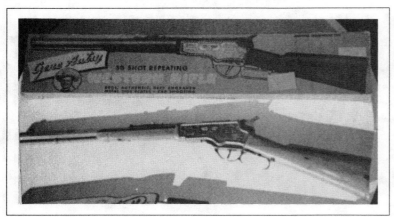

Gene Autry Ranch Rifle

Leslie-Henry- 1950-55. Flying "A" Ranch rifle. Metal & plastic cap shooter with the original L-H box. Very rare. Engraved side plates. Only box known to exist.

Value: $125-300 (Rifle & box)

R-15

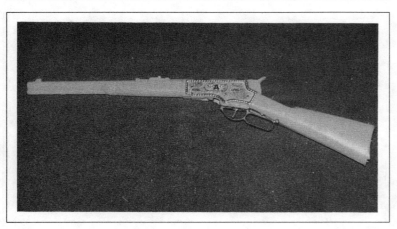

Gene Autry Ranch Rifle

Leslie-Henry- 1955-60. Similar to R-15, except rifle is all red plastic rather than the normal brown stock-black barrel. Has silver side plates with Flying "A" Ranch.

Value: $85-175 (Rifle)

R-16

Indian Scout Rifle

Mattel- 1959. 30" metal and plastic rifle. Remington Rolling Block style. Shootin' shell and caps. Shown with original box. Beautiful toy rifle.

Value: $145-250 (Rifle & box)

R-17

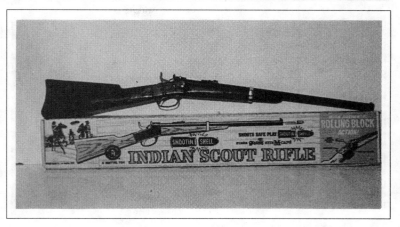

Indian Scout Rifle- Bandolier

Mattel- 1959. Original box for the Indian Scout set including a rifle and bandolier with rifle scabbard. Seldom seen box.

Value: $ 175-275 (Box-rifle-bandolier)

R-18

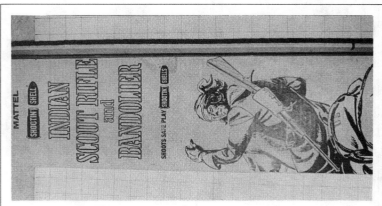

Indian Scout Rifle

Mattel- 1959. The Rolling Block, Shootin' Shell rifle shown with the suede leather bandolier strap, rifle scabbard & bullets. Authentic replica toy rifle.

Value: $85-165 (Rifle) $30-75 (Bandolier)

R-19

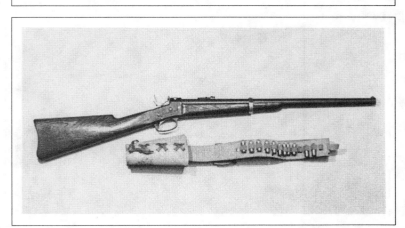

Johnny Eagle-Red River Rifle

Topper-Deluxe Corp., NJ- 1965. Large 36" Winchester-style, lever action cap rifle. Brown & black plastic & metal. Horse in gold on stock. Name in red on forend. A red feather should be attached to barrel.

Value: $65-135

R-20

Johnny Eagle-Red River Rifle

Topper-Deluxe Corp.- 1965. Detail of R-20. The 3-dimensional gold horse found on the butt stock of the rifle. Note the wood grained stock and rifle butt plate. This rifle is not very common or popular.

R-21

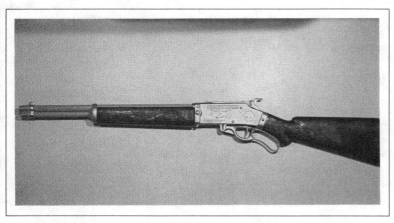

Kelly's Rifle

Hubley- 1960. Overland Trail rifle is metal and plastic cap shooter. Kelly was played by William Bendix. This box with his photo is quite rare.

Value: $75-150 (Box only)

R-22

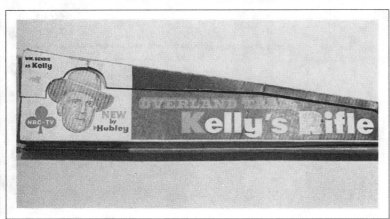

Kelly's Rifle

Hubley- 1960. Plastic stock had simulated carving. Engraved metal receiver with his name. The barrel is metal. Has shamrock decal on the right side of butt stock.

Value: $85-175

R-23

Kelly's Rifle

Hubley- 1960. Detail of the metal receiver on Kelly's rifle R-23. Note the name and fine engraving of steerhead and vines. The Hubley logo is within the rope circle.

R-24

Lone Ranger Rifle

Marx- 1950s era. Silver plastic & metal. Deluxe Winchester rifle with checkering, engraving, octagon barrel and pistol grip. Name on stock. Cap shooter in original box. 25" length.

Value: $85-200 (Rifle) $35-75 (box)

R-25

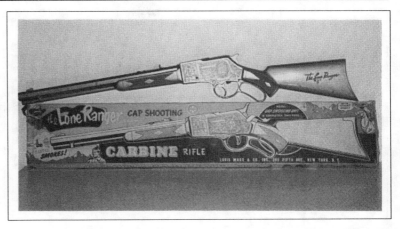

Lone Ranger Deluxe Rifle

Marx-1950s era. Very rare Winchester 33" lever action deluxe rifle with engraving & checkering. Plastic with metal barrels & cap shooting mechanism. Name is on stock in gold. Rare carrying case in color.

Value: $125-250 (Rifle) $50-125 (Case)

R-26

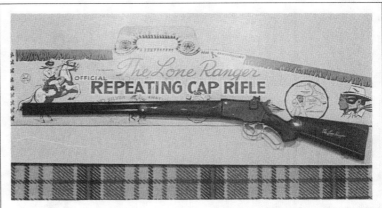

Lone Ranger Carbine

Marx- 1950s era. Extremely rare carbine. All plastic clicker-style. Metallic silver & walnut. Engraved. Also found in a model with a fake scope. One of the rarer toy character rifles. 23" length.

Value: $85-150

R-27

Lone Ranger Carbine

Marx- 1950s era. Detail of R-27. Note the name in gold and the beautiful Indian Chief carved in the butt stock. Receiver is scroll engraved. Stock is checkered.

R-28

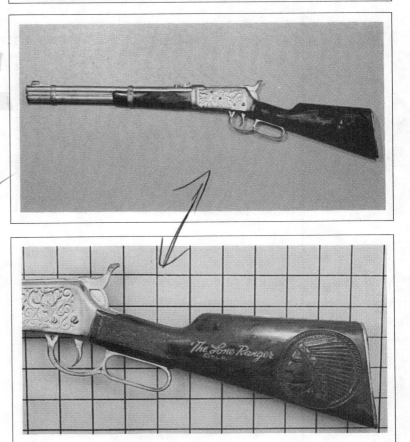

Lone Ranger Deluxe Rifle

Marx- 1950s era. Detail of rifle R-26. Note the fine engraved receiver, checkered stock and rear peep sight. Marx quality & realism is second to none. Top quality craftsmanship!

R-29

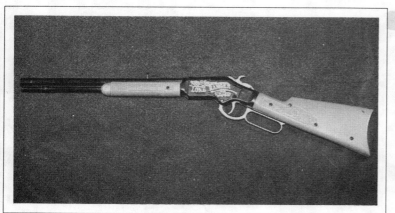

Lone Ranger

Mattel- 1960 era. 26" Shootin' Shell rifle. The Lone Ranger models have a metallic silver decal with red and black artwork on the butt stock. No other identification is on the rifle. Rare Mattel model.

Value: $85-165

R-30

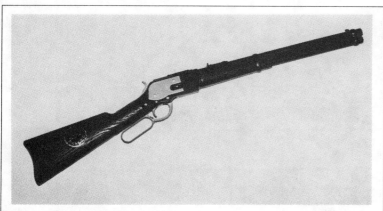

Lone Ranger Rifle

Gabriel- 1970s. Winchester '73 octagon barrel rifle. Cap shooter. with name on side of receiver. Plastic & metal. Black, silver & tan.

Value: $65-125

R-31

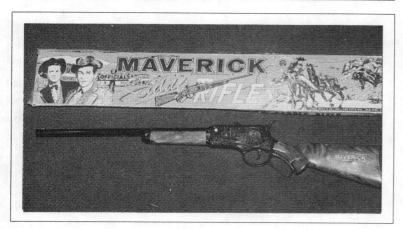

Maverick Rifle

Marx- 1959 era. Black & brown all plastic clicker rifle. Engraved receiver, half magazine with checkered stock. Name is in gold on stock. 27" length. Original box.

Value: $85-135 (Rifle) $50-125 (Box)

R-32

Minute Man Rifle

Kilgore- Mid 1930s. Very rare cast iron repeating cap shooter. Seldom seen toy and even rarer original box! Nickel finish with red painted wood stock.

Value: $225-450 (Gun) $85-175 (Box)

R-33

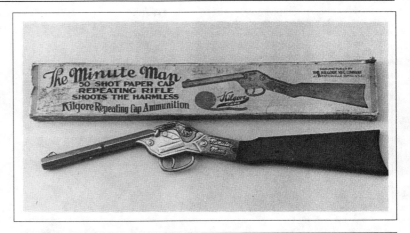

Model 95 Rifle

Nichols- 1961. Among the rarest of rifles and Nichols' toys. Cap-activated shell-firing carbine. Copy of a Winchester Model 95. Plastic & metal. Listed as Daisy Rough Rider rifle in 1967 Eaton catalog, Canada.

Value: $175-375 (Rifle) $30-65 (Box)

R-34

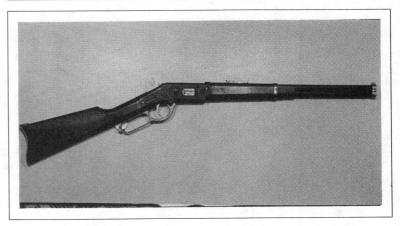

Mustang Rifle

MAM, Italy- 1970 era. Heavy DC & wood Winchester '73 carbine. Cap shooting lever action. Saddle ring. Engraved. Very realistic toy is 33" long. Unusual toy gun.

Value: $75-150

R-35

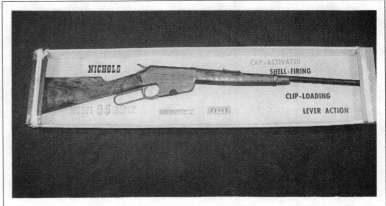

Pancho Villa Cowboy Rifle

F. J. Strauss Co., NY- 1970 era. Die cast & plastic with revolving cylinder. 24" cap shooter. Unusual toy and seldom seen.

Value: $35-75

R-36

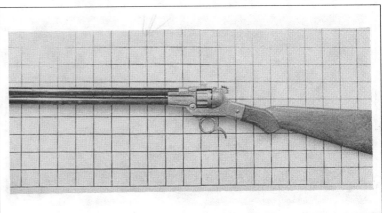

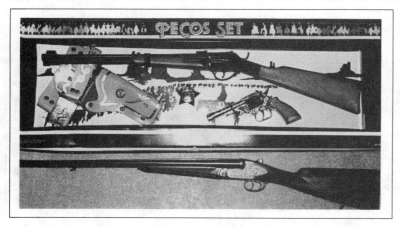

Pecos Rifle

Lone Star, Eng. ?- 1970 era. Plastic and metal rifle with revolving cylinder. Cap shooter. Perhaps made in England by Lone Star. Shown in box with pistol and holster set.

Value: $35-85 (Set)

R-37

Rin Tin Tin & Rusty Rifle

Marx- 1960 era. Identical to R-26 except for name on stock. Very rare variation of a cap shooting rifle. Deluxe Winchester in brown and black. Name in gold.

Value: $100-185

R-38

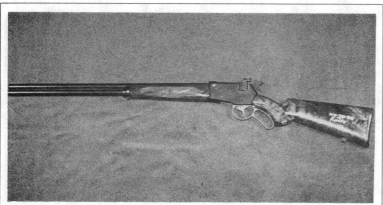

Rocky Mountain Rifle

Marx- 1956. Plastic & metal cap rifle with magnifying scope. 30" Winchester lever action & checkered stock. Metal barrel.

Value: $65-100

R-39

Roy Rogers Rifle (center)

*Marx-*1950. *Top:* Rin Tin Tin R-38. *Center:* Roy Rogers Winchester Deluxe Model 71. A beautifully engraved rifle with sling. Name in gold on stock. *Lower:* Similar Winchester 71 is a Gabriel paper-popper.

Value: $125-250 (Roy) $50-100 (Gabriel)

R-40

Roy Rogers

Marx- 1950 era. Silver plastic and metal. Deluxe Winchester with checkering, engraving, octagon barrel & pistol grip. Name on stock. 25" cap shooting rifle.

Value: $100-250

R-41

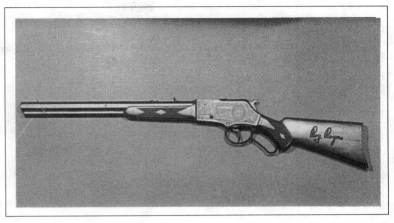

Roy Rogers

Marx- 1950s. Detail of receiver engraving of rifle R-41. Note the buffalo, scrolls and horse and rider. Marx rifles have exceptional engraving and artwork.

R-42

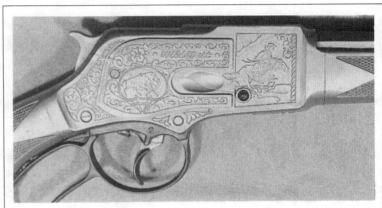

Rifle-Carbine Wagon Train

Leslie-Henry- 1957 era. 5 in1 set. Antique bronze L-H .44 with barrel extention, a detachable stock, carbine forend & scope in original box. Extremely rare toy gun.

Value: $400-750 (Complete set with box)

R-43

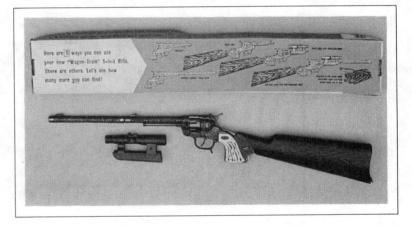

Rifleman-Ring Rifle

Hubley- 1958. "Flip Special" metal & plastic 32" cap rifle. Very desirable character rifle. Due to twirling many have broken or damaged butt stocks. Popular rifle.

Value: $150-350

R-44

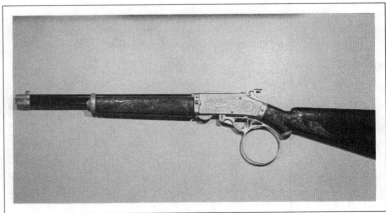

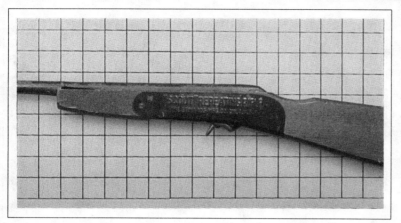

Scout Repeating Rifle

Edwards Mfg Co., OH- 1920s. Rare & early repeating cap rifle made of cast iron and pressed steel with wood stock. 26" long.

Value: $35-75

R-45

Scout Rifle

Hubley- 1960 era. Metal and plastic cap rifle. Carved dark brown stock, receiver engraved. Shown with the original box. Many stock varieties.

Value: $65-150 Rifle   Box-$65

R-46

Scout Rifle

Hubley- 1960 era. Detail of Scout receiver engraving. Note the name.

R-47

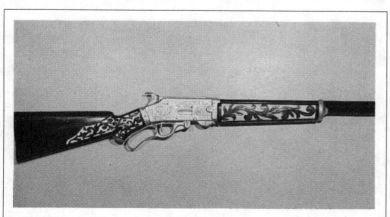

Scout Rifle

Hubley- 1960 era. Scout variation with black stock and light color behind stock carving.

Value: $75-165

R-48

Scout Rifle

Hubley- 1960 era. Cowgirl model with the white stock and dark color behind carving. A rather rare variety of this toy.

Value: $100-225

R-49

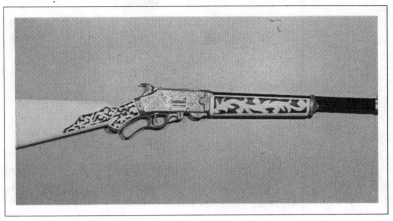

Scout Rifle

Hubley- 1960 era. Buckskin tan variety. Slightly darker behind carving. Unusual stock variety. Hubley apparently tried a wide variety of stock colors on the Scout.

Value: $65-150

R-50

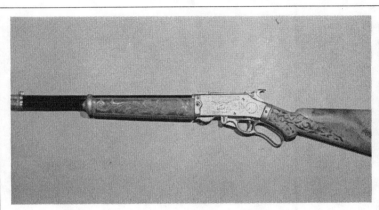

Sharps Carbine

Marx- 1960 era. Superb replica! Shootin' shell and cap rifle. Metal & plastic in black and walnut. Saddle ring. Very rare. Shown with tan leather cartridge pouch with "CS" in an oval & 6 bullets inside.

Value: $150-285

R-51

Sheriff's Rifle

Parris Mfg. Co.- 1950 era. Pressed steel and wood lever action rifle. Pop & cork shooter. 31" in length. Model #11.

Value: $15-30

R-52

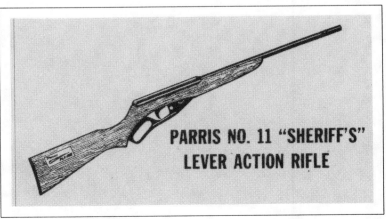

PARRIS NO. 11 "SHERIFF'S" LEVER ACTION RIFLE

Sportsman Rifle

Hubley- 1960 era. Metal & plastic cap gun with engraved receiver and checkering. It is a take-down model with scope. Shown in original box.

Value: $50-125 Rifle   Box-$25

R-53

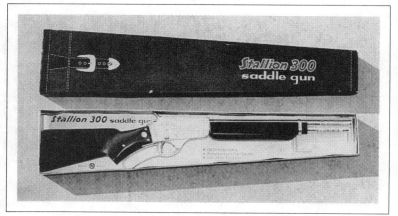

Stallion 300 Saddle Gun

Nichols- 1958. Plastic & DC metal lever action that loads cartridges. Cap firing. A single shot that ejects the cartridges. The gun shown in leather-like display box.

Value: $100-225 (Boxed)

R-54

Stallion 300 Saddle Gun

Nichols- 1958. Detail of receiver engraving on rifle R-54 above. Note the deer & running cowboy. The Circle "N" ranch medallion is inset in the stock.

R-55

Texas John Slaughter Rifle

Daisy- 1959. Unusual cap shooting rifle is 32" long and seldom seen character toy gun. Plastic and metal. Engraved gold-tone receiver with checkered stock.

Value: $35-85

R-56

Texas Ranger

Leslie-Henry- 1962 era. Lever action, cap shooting, Winchester carbine. Has large loop lever with rapid shooting catch. 34" length. Plastic and metal. Rare toy rifle.

Value: $65-135

R-57

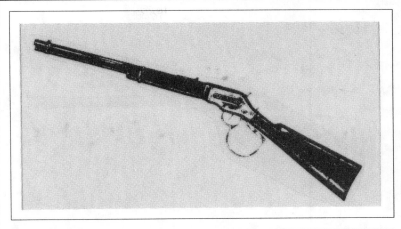

Texas Ranger

Leslie-Henry- 1962. Lever action, cap shooting, Winchester rifle with octagon barrel. Smaller 27" length. Called "Flip lever" carbine, even though it has small lever. Metal & plastic.

Value: $45-85

R-58

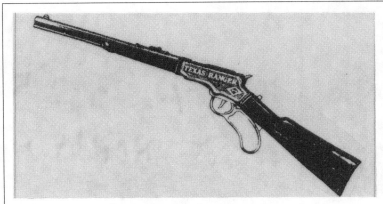

Thunderbird Indian Rifle

Daisy- 1960s. Metal & plastic smoker & bang model. Very colorful in red, black and gold Indian decoration. Shown with original box and Indian head-dress. Rare.

Value: $75-165 (Rifle & box)

R-59

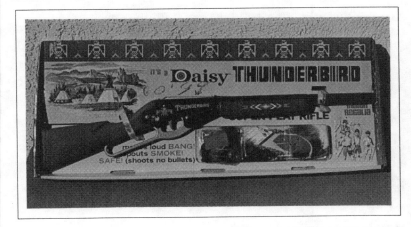

Thundergun Carbine

Marx- 1960 era. Large 35" Winchester carbine in metal and plastic. Fires large rolls of Thundercaps! Engraved silver side plates. A model exists with gold plates. It is shown with rare box. Rare toy carbine.

Value: $125-225   Box $45

R-60

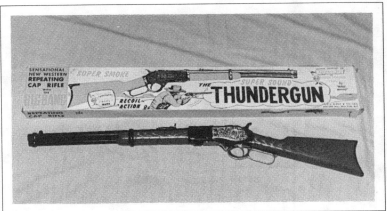

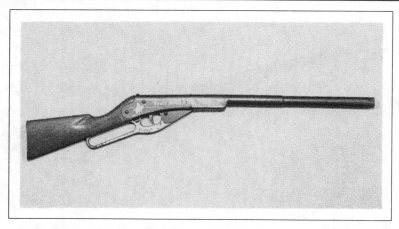

Trail Boss Rifle

Daisy- 1960 era. Metal & plastic smoker & bang model. Gold tone lever, art work and name. 32" length. Plastic walnut stock.

Value: $35-75

R-61

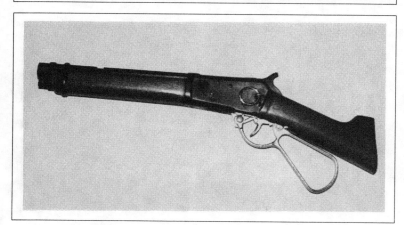

Wagon Train Rifle

Leslie-Henry- 1958. Winchester Lever action rifle with octagon barrel. Plastic & metal cap shooter. Large lever. Name and picture on the receiver frame.

Value: $85-165

R-62

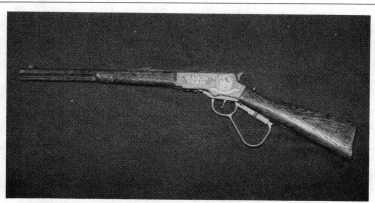

Wanted Dead or Alive

Marx- 1958-61. The 17 1/2" plastic and metal cap rifle. Cut-down Winchester Model '92 carbine. Has the rapid fire lever action. Saddle ring.

Value: $75-145

R-63

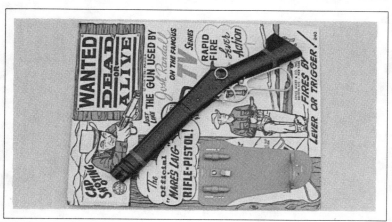

Wanted Dead or Alive

Marx- 1958-61. The smaller 14" model in plastic and metal. Cap shooter with saddle ring. On original display card. Price sticker on back-$1.79.

Value: $85-175 (Rifle & display card)

R-64

Wild West Rifle

Marx- 1960 era. Plastic & metal cap rifle. 25" round barrel with button magazine. Fake scope mounted on receiver.

Value: $35-85

R-65

Winchester Carbine

Mattel- 1960 era. Shootin' Shell cap rifle. Fires and ejects shells. 26" long metal & plastic. With the original full color box.

Value: $85-245 (Gun & box)

R-66

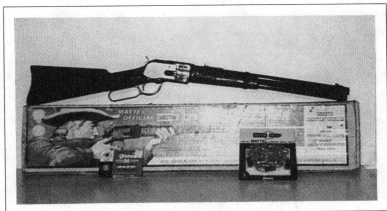

Winchester Carbine

Mattel- 1960 era. Shootin' Shell cap rifle. Fires and ejects shells. 26" metal and plastic. Black & brown with metal side-plates.

Value: $50-165

R-67

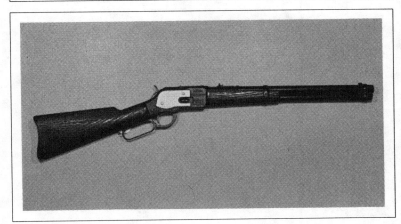

Winchester Carbine

Mattel- 1960 era. Similar to R-67, except the original owner decorated it as an Indian carbine. It has brass tacks, leather wrapping, beads, fur & feathers. Beautiful with matching rubber knife & sheath.

Value: $100-225 (One-of-a-kind)

R-68

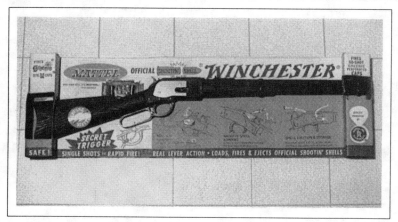

Winchester Carbine

Mattel- 1960 era. Shootin' Shell carbine on the original display card with loading and firing directions. Note the "Secret Trigger" graphics.

Value: $75-200 (Gun & display box)

R-69

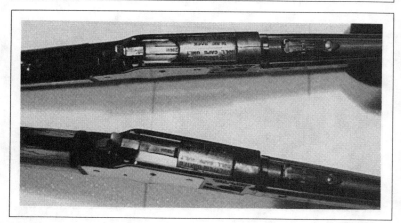

Winchester Saddle Gun

Mattel- 1960 era. Large 33" cap rifle that loads and ejects metal bullets. Shown with the original box that has bandolier enclosed.

Value: $100-275 (Rifle, bandolier & box)

R-70

Winchester Saddle Gun

Mattel- 1960 era. Detail of R-70 showing the 2nd model on top and the 1st model on the bottom. Ist have straight backs on the dust cover. 2nd models have arched dust covers and rapid fire levers. See R-72

Value: $65-150 (Same for either model.)

R-71

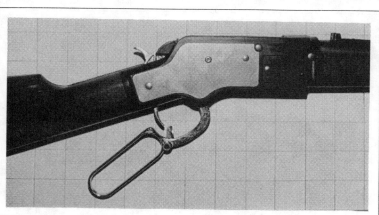

Winchester Saddle Gun

Mattel- 1960 era. Detail of R-70 showing the "rapid fire" trigger lever found on the 2nd model rifles. 1st models have a plain lever with no trigger catch.

R-72

Winchester Carbine

Coibel- Spain- 1970-80 era. Large lever action cap carbine is made of heavy die cast and is very high quality. Beautiful toy of more recent manufacture.

Value: $45-125

R-73

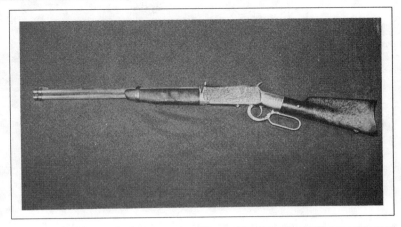

Winchester Carbine

Coibel- Spain- 1970-80 era. Detail of R-73. Note the extra fine engraving of the two bears on the pewter-like receiver. The lever has a rapid fire mechanism for the trigger.

R-74

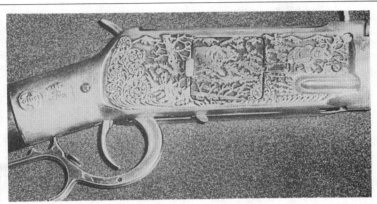

Winchester Rifle

Marx- 1955-60 era. Large 34" cap rifle is similar to an octagon barrel Winchester model '86 rifle. Ejects shells. Plastic and metal. Has richochet sound. Beautiful toy rifle.

Value: $85-165

R-75

Winchester Rifle

Marx- 1955-60 era. Detail of rifle R-75. The left side of the receiver is engraved with a rifle-totting cowboy, mounted on a horse, and a charging grizzly bear! The small lever opens the cap box.

R-76

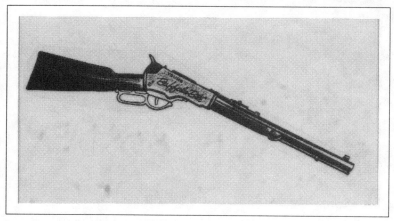

Young Buffalo Bill Rifle

Leslie-Henry- 1959 era. Die cast & plastic, cap shooting rifle. Octagon barrel with checkered stock. Name engraved on the receiver. 26" length. Shown in 1959 mail order catalog from Canada.

Value: $65-135

R-77

Scabbard

Halco- 1955. Rifle scabbard for use on a bicycle or slung over the shoulder. Made of leather with cut-outs and silver conchos. Large strap in original box. $1.50.

Value: $85-175 (Scabbard & box)

R-78

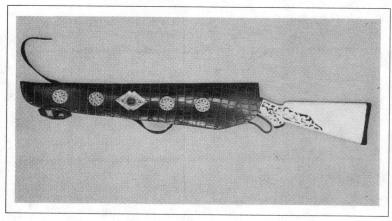

Scabbard

Hubley- 1960. Scabbard for the Hubley Scout rifle. Alligator-type leather with large silver conchos and red jewels. Strap for bike or carrying.

Value: $65-150

R-79

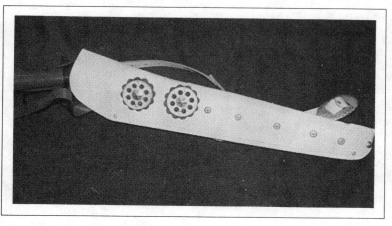

Scabbard

Esquire Novelty Co.- 1960 era. Perhaps for a cowgirl. This scabbard is made of white leather with red leather cut-outs, silver conchos and studs with turquoise jewels.

Value: 75-165

R-80

Indian Scout Rifle Scabbard

Mattel- 1960 era. Suede leather rifle scabbard with numerous bullet loops to hold extra ammo! Strap fits over the shoulder. Came with rifle sets , but could also be purchased separately.

Value: $35-85 (Bullets about $1 each)

R-81

Bike Rifle Scabbard

Classy Prod.- 1960 era. Buckskin-type tan leather with silver studs & stars. Has straps to attach to a bicycle. Smaller size for shorter rifles.

Value. $35-85

R-82

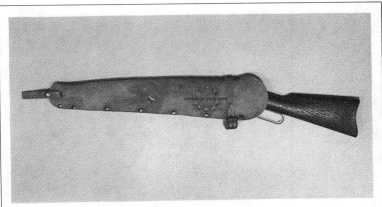

Bike Rifle Scabbard

Classy Prod.- 1960 era. Detail of R-82. The lettering is in dark brown. Note the ten silver stars and straps to attach to the bicycle bars. A nearly identical scabbard exists with Roy Rogers and Trigger on it.

Value: $35-85 $100-185 (Roy Rogers)

R-83

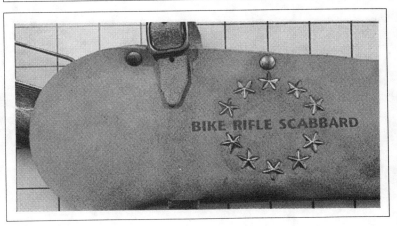

Rifle Scabbard

Hubley-Halco- 1960 era. Beautiful heavy leather with 3-D silver Conestoga wagon and silver conchos. Superb quality! For bicycle use or over the shoulder. Russet.

Value: $85-165

R-84

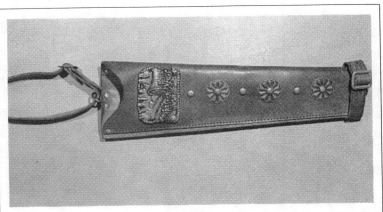

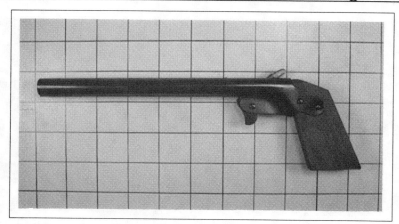

Bronco

Daisy- 1930 era. 10 1/2" blued steel pop and cork pistol. Grip is wood painted red. Also called a No. 12 dueling pistol.

Value: $15-25

P-1

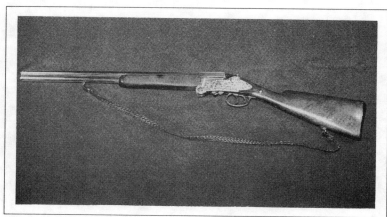

Browning Over-Under

Coibel, Spain- 1970-80. High quality copy of Browning Shotgun. Fine engraving & a heavy die cast toy gun. A cap shooter with a leather sling.

Value: $25-75

P-2

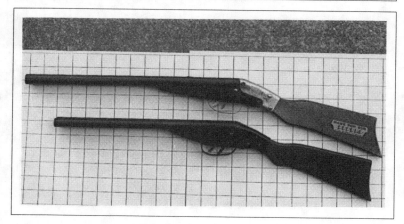

Chads Valley Double Barrel

Marx, British- 1925-40. *Top:* 24" pop gun in black steel, nickel receiver & wood stock. Marx decal on stock. *Lower:* Chads Valley, British made 21" double pop gun. Both British made guns share similarities.

Value: $35-75

P-3

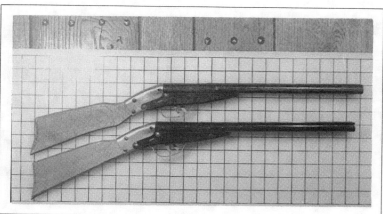

Chads Valley Double Barrel

Chads Valley, British- 1925-40. Nearly a matching pair of English double barrels! Black steel, nickel receivers & varnished wood stocks. Pop guns. Lower gun is a 1/2" shorter. Beautiful toy shotguns.

Value: $35-75

P-4

Chads Valley Single Shot

Chads Valley, British- 1930-50. Black steel single shot cork shooter & pop gun with orange stained wooden stock. "Made in England" stock decal. Shown with original cork and string still attached.

Value: $20-45

P-5

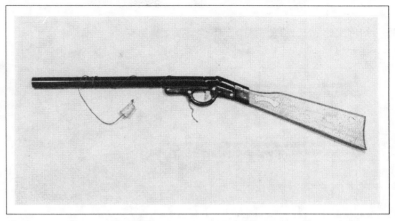

Chads Valley Single Shot

Chads Valley, British- 1930-50. *Lower:* Pop gun in black steel, nickel receiver and red painted stock. *Upper:* A *Wyandotte* dart shooting pump gun. Black steel with the pump forend and stock of wood.

Value: $20-45

P-6

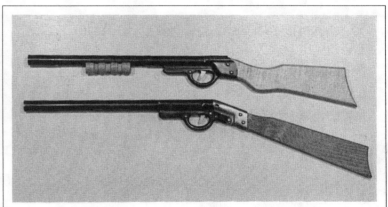

Cork Shooters

Unmarked- 1910-1920 era. Cork shooters found in early game sets. Used to shoot cardboard soldiers, Indians, birds, crows, big game animals, etc. Crudely made and all are about 13". Steel with wood stocks.

Value: $25-65

P-7

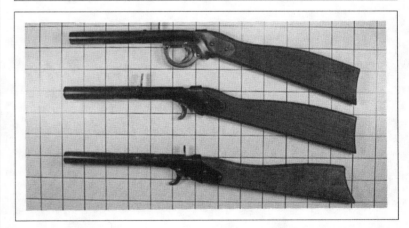

Daisy Cork Gun

Daisy- 1908. Very early 15" nickel plated cork gun. Barrel marked "Little Daisy No. 10 - Daisy Mfg. Co." Pat. Dates for U.S., France, Great Britain and Germany. Rare. Steel with wood stock. Break action.

Value: $50-100

P-8

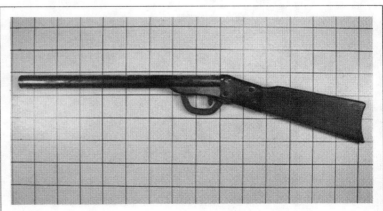

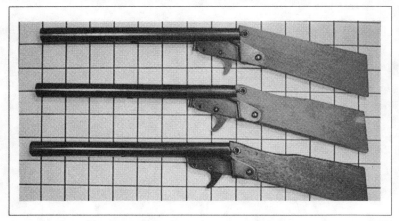

Daisy Pop Guns-No. 70 Little

Daisy- 1930-40. *Top to Bottom:* 1. Very early with straight stock. 2. Slight curve to stock. 3. Full curve comb on top. All three have natural wood, or red painted stocks and pressed steel construction.

Value: $15-35

P-9

Daisy Pop Gun - Model 65

Daisy- 1950 era. *Top:* Model 65 pop gun in black steel with a red plastic stock. *Lower:* Daisy Rocket Dart shooter in black steel with red plastic forend & stock. You push dart in the end of barrel. Rare toys.

Value: $30-65

P-10

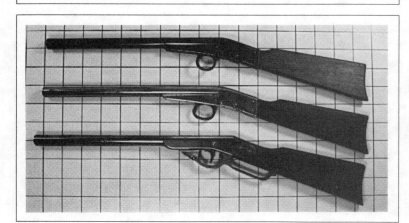

Daisy Pop Guns

Daisy- Pre-1920. *Top:* No. 7 pop break-action, blue with ring trigger. *Center:* No. 10 Little Daisy in nickel finish with a ring trigger. *Lower:* No. 10 Little Daisy in nickel with a cocking lever. Wood stocks.

Value: $30-75 (Lever # 10 is rarer)

P-11

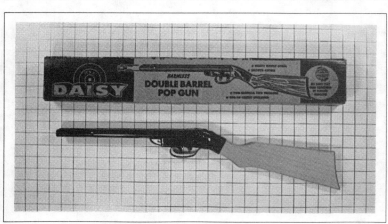

Daisy Pop Gun - Model 930

Daisy- 1950-55. Double barrel pop gun in black steel is 24", has wood stock. Shown with rare original box. Plymouth, Mich. address.

Value: $75-125 (Gun & box)

P-12

Daisy Pump - Model 16 Pop

Daisy- Pre 1920. Very early pump action pop gun. Trigger and guard are decorative and don't operate. Tiny sling and swivels. Stock & forend of real walnut! A superb little gun. 25" gun had a bayonet.

Value: $65-125

P-13

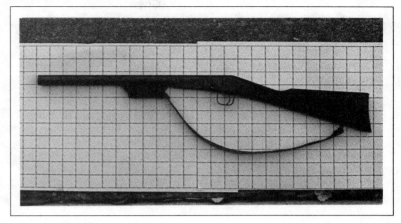

Daisy Double Barrel Guns

Daisy- 1955-60. *Top:* 22" pop gun in an antique bronze color with wood stock, is stamped Plymouth, Mich. *Lower:* 21" is a cork shooter. Metallic bronze finish with black stock. Stamped Rogers, Ark.

Value; $25-50

P-14

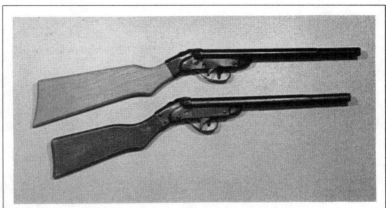

Daisy Western Set

Daisy- 1959-60. Boxed set with a Model 930 cork shooter in bronze finish with wood stock. Set includes western holsters with Hubley DC Rodeo guns. Note the bag of corks between the two pistols.

Value: $85-150 (Complete set in box)

P-15

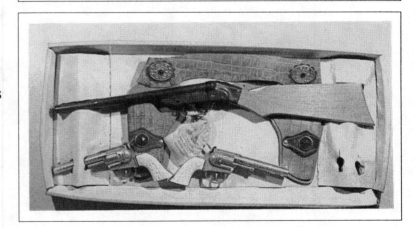

Dandy Pump Pop Gun

Dandy-Markham Co., Plymouth, MI- 1920. Large 28" pump action pop gun in black enamel paint and varnished wood stock. This ad is from the 1920 era. I wonder how many girls wanted a gun? Note $.48

Value: $45-100

P-16

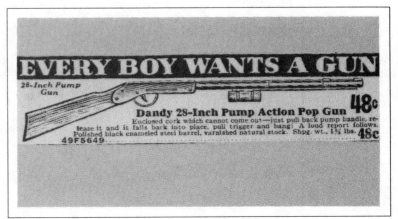

EVERY BOY WANTS A GUN

28-Inch Pump Gun

Dandy 28-Inch Pump Action Pop Gun 48c
Enclosed cork which cannot come out—just pull back pump handle, release it and it falls back into place, pull trigger and bang! A loud report follows. Polished black enameled steel barrel, varnished natural stock. Shpg. wt., 1¾ lbs. **48c**
49F5649

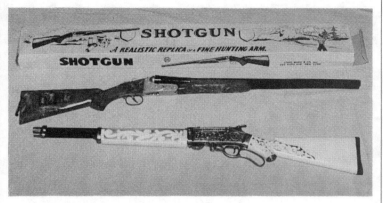

Double Barrel Shotgun

Marx- 1960 era. Metal & plastic double barrel cap shooter with dummy shotgun shells to load. Engraved receiver with the stock checkered. Lower gun is a Hubley Scout rifle covered in the rifle section.

Value: $100-165 (Gun & box)

P-17

Dragnet Double Barrel

Knickerbocker- 1955. A Western Lawman style sawed-off double barrel. Metal and plastic cap shooter. Loads shells. Has the Dragnet logo. Not a true western toy gun but appropriate style.

Value: $100-165

P-18

Dragnet Shotgun

Knickerbocker- 1955. Detail of receiver to show the Dragnet name. I have never seen this model with a western sheriff or character's name. It would have been a logical toy shotgun.

P-19

Dragnet Shotgun

Knickerbocker- 1955. Detail of Joe Friday's Badge 714 in gold on the left side of the butt stock. This shotgun is rather rare & a nice addition to a Lawman collection.

P-20

Fox Double Barrel

Ansley H. Fox- 1928-30. Top quality toy made by a real gun company. This blued metal double barrel shotgun has a varnished stock & shoots round wooden balls from two metal shells. Rare toy.

Value: $350-600 (Gun with two shells)

P-21

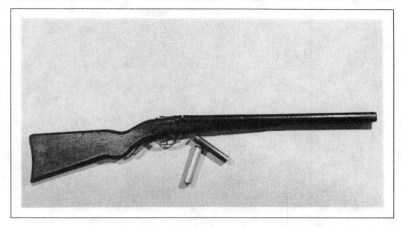

Fox Double Barrel

Ansley H. Fox- 1928-30. Detail photo of the receiver bottom showing the A.H. Fox Gun Co.,Phila. PA. U.S.A. stampings. This quality toy is also sought by collectors of real Fox double barrel shotguns. The wooden balls came in a small bag.

P-22

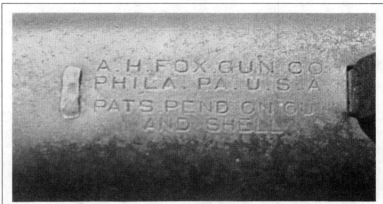

Gene Autry Double Barrel

Marx, Britain- 1950-60. A rare souvenir of Gene's Western Show at Empress Hall, in London. Double barrel pop gun made by Marx of Britain. A rare character pop gun that is seldom seen. Only a few exist.

Value: $225-350

P-23

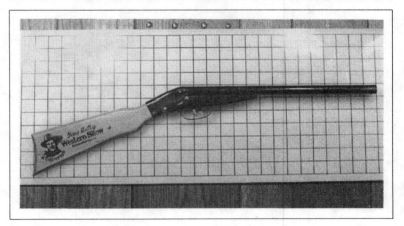

Gene Autry Double Barrel

Marx, Britain- 1950-60. Detail of the art work on the stock. Two varieties do exist, one is in black ink, and the other in dark brown. Three of those known, have been found in Canada. Note Gene's image and "Empress Hall- London" on the stock.

P-24

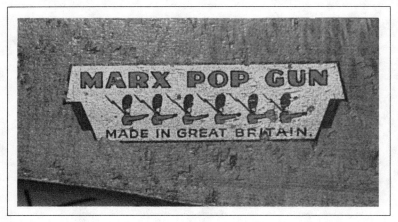

Gene Autry Double Barrel

Marx, Britain- 1950-60. Detail of the Marx decal on the left side of some Gene Autry souvenir pop guns. Note the row of British soldiers and "Made in Britain" type. Colors are black, red & gold. Some have a simple banner that reads "Made in Britain."

P-25

Gene Autry Pop Gun

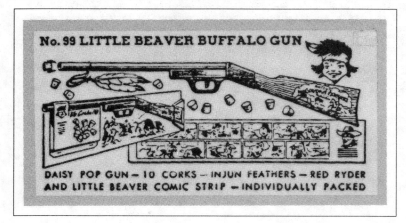

West Hollywood Craft Shop, CA.- 1950 era. Wooden souvenir pop gun sold at some Rodeos and Western Shows. Gene's name in black rope lettering on the butt stock. Sliding handle makes a pop!

Value: $100-225

P-26

Little Beaver Buffalo Gun

Daisy- 1951. No. 99 Buffalo Cork Gun in black metal with wood stock. Came with 10 corks and feathers tied to barrel. Very rare character gun. Few toys have Indian connections. 19" long. See decal below.

Value: $125-235

P-27

Little Beaver Buffalo Gun

Daisy- 1951. Detail of the full color stock decal. Note Little Beaver and the Daisy Plymouth, Mich., USA address. The gun is black and the stock is painted red. Very rare cork gun.

P-28

Markham Pop Gun

Markham, Plymouth, MI- 1920. *Top*: A 15"
nickel plated pop gun. *Center*: A King No.
19, 1930 blued automatic 17" pop gun.
Lower: A King No. 15 Safety Lever pop
gun is 17" in nickel finish, about 1914.

Value: $35-85 (Markham rarer)

P-29

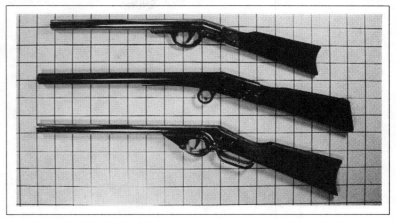

Marx Double Barrel Cork Gun

Marx- 1955-60. Black metal 30" pop and
cork shotgun with plastic stock. One of
the last Marx guns. Shown with original
box is quite rare. Most pop guns came
un-boxed.

Value: $45-85 (Gun & box)

P-30

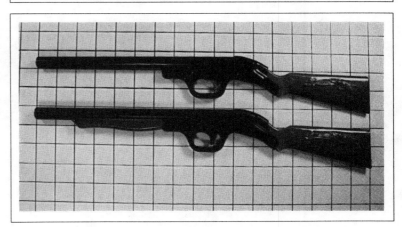

Red Ryder Dart Guns

Daisy- 1950. Similar to Model 65 but has
Red Ryder logo on plastic stock. Black
metal with either red or brown plastic
stock. Lower gun has forend. Darts are
pushed into barrel to cock. Rare.

Value: $45-85

P-31

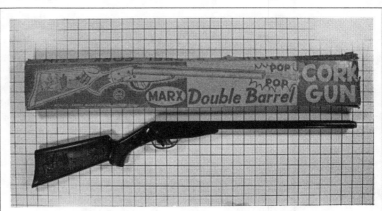

Red Ryder Dart Guns

Daisy- 1950. Detail of P-31 showing the
raised artwork of the Red Ryder logo and
the cowboy shooting a leaping Mountain
Lion. Detail cast into the plastic stock.

P-32

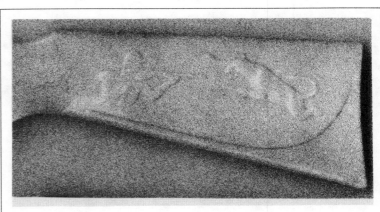

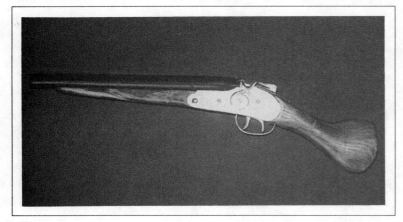

Rebel Scattergun

Classy Prod.- 1960. Perhaps the rarest toy shotgun and character gun. Shoots two rolls of caps. Made with either a black or brown plastic stock. Very desirable toy.

Value: $285-500

P-33

Shotgun Slade Over/Under

Esquire Novelty-Actoy- 1960 era. Very rare character gun is a combination rifle and shotgun. Loads shells & fires caps. Metal and plastic. Black and brown color. 30".

Value: $150-265

P-34

Shotgun Slade

Esquire Novelty-Actoy- 1960 era. Detail of the character name on the receiver of the shotgun-rifle. Right side has the typical Actoy Pony medallion. One of the rarest of the western character toy guns.

P-35

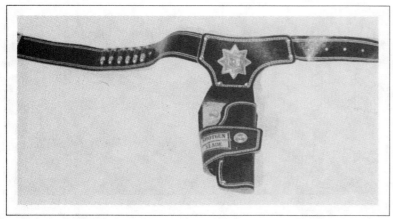

Shotgun Slade

Esquire Novelty-Actoy- 1960 era. This is among the rarest of holsters & scabbards. A rig in black leather to carry the rifle-shotgun. Gold borders & art with a silver concho. Only a few exist.

Value: $150-245

P-36

Wells Fargo Guard's Gun

Eureka-Brevete, France- 1955 era. Unusual black metal and wood stocked, dart, shot gun. Sawed-off type 27" gun with leather sling and paper label. Rare toy gun and one of the few double barreled dart guns!

Value: $100-175

P-37

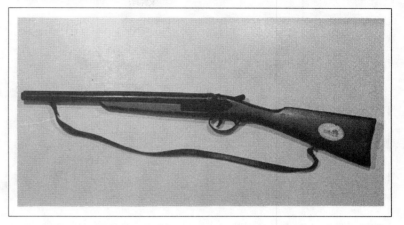

Wells Fargo Guard's Gun

Eureka-Brevete, France- 1955 era. Research indicates these were imported by Esquire Novelty Co. Detail of the paper label on the stock showing stage coach and Wells Fargo & Co.- Guard's Gun lettering in 2 colors. Rare western toy shotgun.

P-38

Wells Fargo Shotgun

Marx- 1959 era. Plastic and metal double barrel shotgun. Shoots caps and loads 2 shells. Shown with rare "Tales of Wells Fargo" marked box. Decal on stock Rare.

Value: $150-275 (Gun & box)

P-39

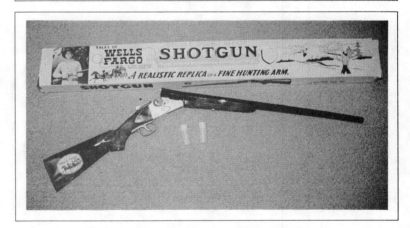

Wells Fargo Shotgun

Marx- 1959 era. Detail of the stock decal with a stagecoach and lettering in black, red and yellow. Note: Dale Robertson as agent Jim Hardie on box. Even though a real shotgun was popular with guards & western lawmen, few were popular toys.

P-39-A

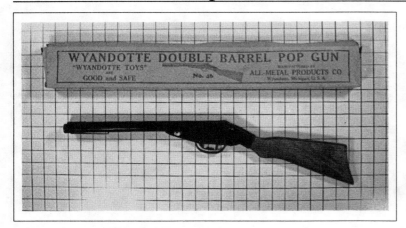

Wyandotte Double Pop Gun

Wyandotte All Metal Products Co.- 1940-50 Double barrel pop gun in black metal with varnished wood stock. Shown with a rather rare early-style box.

Value: $65-100   (Gun & box)

P-40

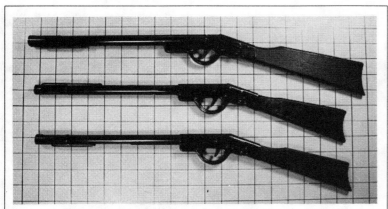

Wyandotte Single Shot Pop

Wyandotte- Late 1920s. Black painted metal guns with wood stocks. Three guns differ in size from 17' to 22" in length. One stock has red stain, others natural. Folding the butt stock cocks all guns.

Value: $ 35-65

P-41

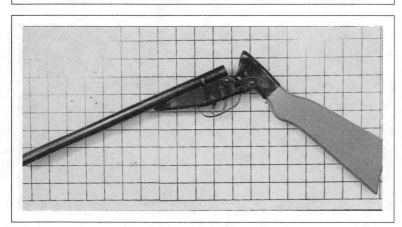

Wyandotte Double Barrel

Wyandotte- 1940 era. Extremely rare gun looks like any typical pop gun. However, cocking it, by folding the butt stock does nothing! The gun is a clicker and triggers act as one unit. Only a few exist. 22" .

Value: $65-125

P-42

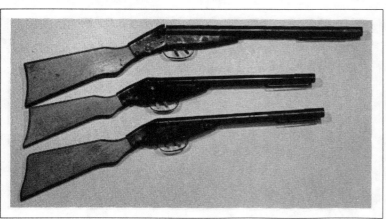

Wyandotte Double Barrel Pop

Wyandotte- 1930-50 era. 3 black painted metal guns with wood stocks. Two have orange stain. They vary by length from 21' to 25'. All make a pop sound! The varieties of these toy guns are endless!

Value: $35-85

P-43

Wyandotte Double Barrel Pop

Wyandotte- 1940 era. Rare, extra long 28"
black painted metal with wooden stock. I
have seldom seen leather slings on toy
guns made by Wyandotte. Unusual pop
gun.

Value: $65-135

P-44

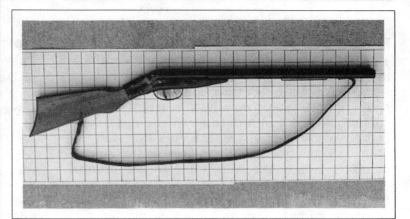

Wyandotte Pump Cork Ball

Wyandotte- 1927. Rare & unusual pump
action gun that shoots round cork balls.
Shoots 5 corks with one loading! Black
metal with wood stock. Balls about 5/8".
Gun is 34" long. Difficult to find toy.

Value: $75-165

P-45

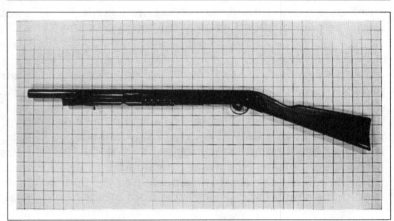

Wyandotte Double Cork Gun

Wyandotte- 1935-40. Double barrel cork
shooter is large 28" length. Black painted
metal with wood stock & painted recoil
pad. Gun is a clothing store promotional
toy. Rare with this connection.

Value: $85-185 (With advertisement)

P-46

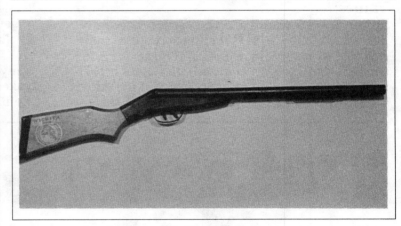

Wyandotte Double Cork Gun

Wyandotte- 1935-40. Detail of the label
on the butt stock of gun P-46. Note:
"Wichita Brand" with an Indian Chief in
red art. Type reads: "Texas Boys Shirts-
Pants-Play Suits-Wichita Falls." I assume
these were gifts when you purchased an
item of apparel. Great advertising toy!

P-47

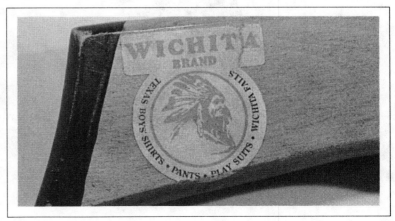

Holsters:

The demand for high quality toy holsters continues to escalate well beyond the cost of real and antique western examples. First class holster sets with gleaming metal studs, colorful faux jewels, metal conchos, leather cut-outs, fringe, fake bullets, fancy buckles and western character names are eagerly sought by collectors of toys and real western memorabilia. Obviously, the value is directly proportional to condition, the amount of decoration and the familiarity of the character name. Holsters made of synthetic materials such as: dura-hide, neolite and vinyl, or those with minimal decoration, generic names or poor quality have very limited appeal and value.

Many holsters were made by small unknown companies who employed women workers to sew and decorate thousands of holsters for the larger distributors. Most were made oversized to accomodate a wider range of gun sizes. It is easy to understand that large, medium and small toy guns would all fit into a larger holster. This was a critical factor as distributors and catalog companies purchased the guns from many sources and the holsters from others.

Values:

All the holsters featured in this section have only one value quoted. This is for an excellent to mint example with very limited wear, no tears, broken stitches or missing decorations. The values listed with each holster do not include any of the guns shown with them.

Holster Manufacturers:

Halco, Leslie-Henry, Classy Products, Hubley, most mail-order catalog companies and Esquire Novelty were major purchasers of sets. This list contains known makers of quality holster sets.

Tex-Tan, Yoakum, TX. • Classy Products, Woodside, NY & Los Angeles, CA. • Keyston Brothers Co., San Francisco, CA. • Pla-Master, NY • Hubley, Lancaster, PA. • S-Bar-M Service Manufacturing Co., NY. • Yankiboy-Sackman Bros., NY. • Wornova Co., NY. • Kilgore, Westerville, OH. • Grafton & Knight, MA. • Buckaroo Holsters-Ellman-Whiting Co., Detroit, MI. • Carnell Mfg., Brooklyn, NY. • Cisco Kid Leather Co., Los Angeles, CA. • Esquire Novelty, Jersey City, NJ. • Rodeo King Holsters, Los Angeles, CA. • Leslie-Henry, Mt. Vernon, NY. • Western Boy-R&S Toy Co., NYC. • State Ranger Holsters-R&S Toy Co., NYC. • Tumble Weed Togs, Arcadia, CA. • Halco-J. Halpern Co, Pittsburgh, PA. • Butler Brothers • Sargeant Ready Co. MA. • Indian Leather Works, Buffalo, NY. • Bashlin Industries, Grove City, PA. • Betty Leach Inc., Asheboro, NC. • Chancy Toy & Novelty Co., Brklyn, NY. • All Metal Products, Wyandotte, MI. • Harvell-Kilgore, TN. • Nichols, Jacksonville, TX. • Boyville Co. • Rangeland Holsters-C. Lawyer Co., Berkley, CA. • Mattel, CA. • Geo. Schmidt Co., Los Angeles, CA. • Feinberg & Henry Mfg. Co., NY. • Smallman & Sons, NY. • C-Bar-K Corkale Mfg. CA.

Many sets were made by saddle and real gun holster makers. Few examples are marked, so identification is difficult. Boxed sets offer the best identification.

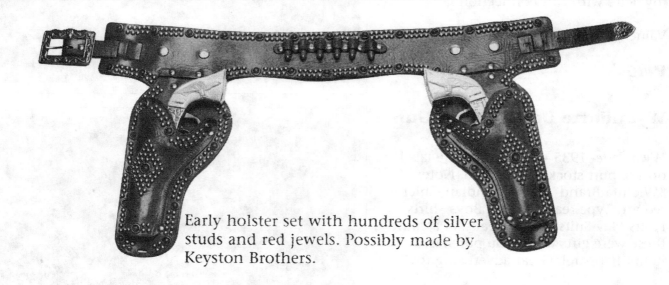

Early holster set with hundreds of silver studs and red jewels. Possibly made by Keyston Brothers.

1. Early small leather in tan & brown with snap. $15

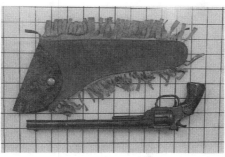

2. Soft leather with fringe for long barrels with snap. $45

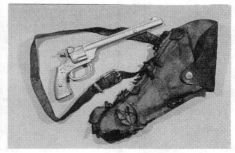

3. Soft leather, fringe, star cut out, snap & belt. Early. $45

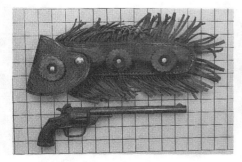

4. Tan leather, fringe, cut outs, studs, snap. Long barrel. $75

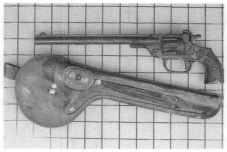

5. Russet leather, narrow, studs, concho, jewel & cut out. $65

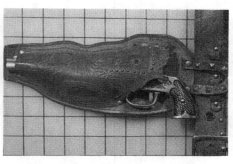

6. Tooled horse, studs, jewels, loop top & belt. Early. $100

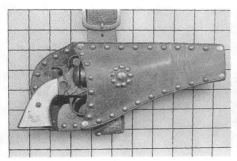

7. Early tooled horse & rope, bullets, belt with loop. $85

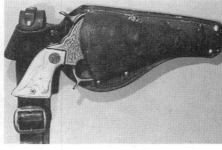

8. Tooled Lone Star Ranger. Has loop top, belt & bullets. $85

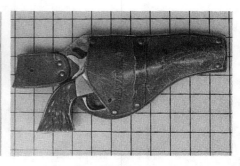

9. Lone Star Ranger, cowboy & cross strap. Loop top. $65

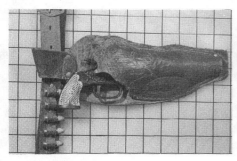

10. Pouch-style. Silver studs & concho. Belt. Loop back. $85

11. Loop top. Studs & jewels. Tooled cross straps. Belt. $100

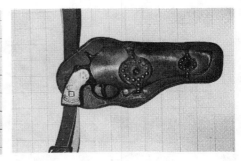

12. Loop top. Studs & jewels. 2 cross straps. Belt. $75

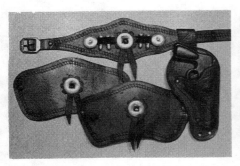

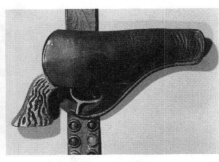

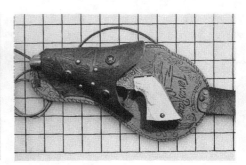

13. Early set & cuffs. Stamped borders. Conchos & belt. $125

14. Small very plain. Jewels are multi-color. Loop top. $65

15.Texas Ranger. Loop top. Red jewels, studs & star. $45

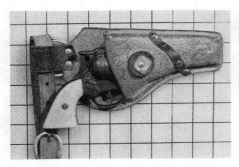

16. Rough leather, cut-out, belt loop top & cross strap. $45

17. Small, tooled, star concho, coins, jewels & bullets. $65

18. Studs, jewels, cut-outs, edge laced, cross strap & belt. $85

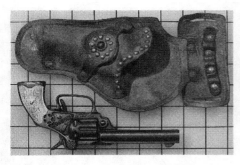

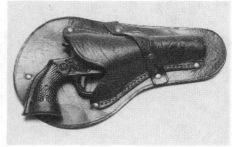

19. Small with studs, jewel on cross strap, bullet loops. $50

20.Early pouch-type with loop. Tiny silver studs make star. $75

21.Jr. Ranger. Tooled buffalo & star. Cut-outs on strap. $85

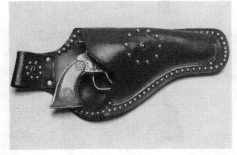

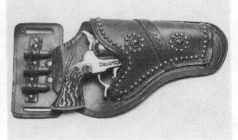

22. Early style with silver studs & red jewels. Loop top. $85

23. G. Aurty decal. Border is stamped. Jewels & studs. $100

24. Small with silver studs, red jewels, tooled straps. $65

25. Lone Star Ranger. Tooled horse, rider, studs & strap. $65

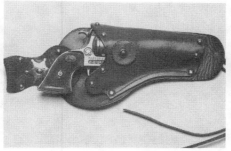

26. Star Ranch badge. Cut-out, jewel & studs. Early. $75

27. Floral tooled. Green jewels, studs, horseshoe loop top. $75

28. Large unusual deep top, red jewels, cross strap, jewels. $100

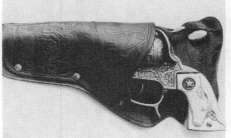

29. The Texan. Floral tooled & belt loop. Large, early. $65

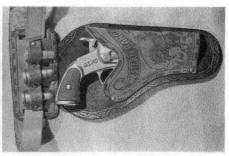

30. Small Western Ranger with horse & rider. Bullets. $45

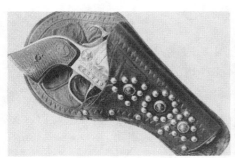

31. Large tooled with jewels & silver studs. Loop top. $75

32.Tooled Buckaroo with horse & rider. Stamped border. $50

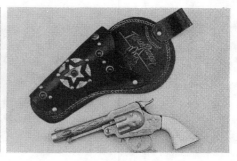

33. Texas Ranger. Jewels, studs & star cut-out. Loop top. $65

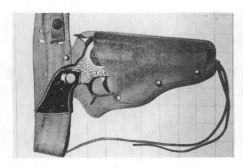

34. Plain large holster with few silver studs. Belt. $65

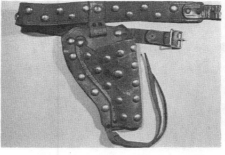

35. Early holster with large size silver studs. Loop top. $100

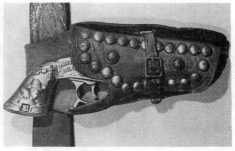

36. Full loop with large studs & large jewels. Cross strap. $75

37. Red Ranger with cowboy & decorative borders. $30

38. Broncho Bill box lid for set number 39.

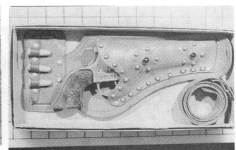

39. Broncho Bill, jewels, studs, bullets, belt & stars. $125 Set

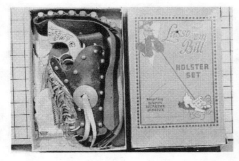

40. Lasso 'em Bill. Fringe, studs & large silver concho. $145 Set

41. Broncho Bill box lid for a double set number 42.

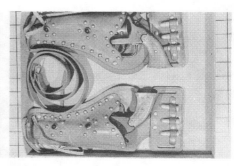

42. Similar to No. 39 but with two holsters. $175 Set

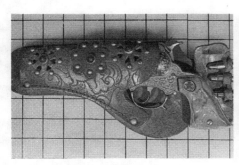

43. Tooled, heart cut-outs, jewels & studs. Bullets. Large. $65

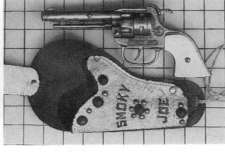

44. Smoky Joe with red jewels & studs. Loop top. $50

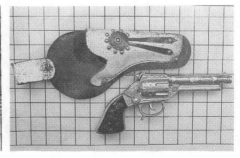

45. White & black. Cut-outs & jewels, silver studs. Loop. $50

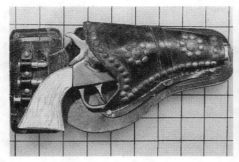

46. Black, green jewels, silver studs, bullets. Cross strap. $65

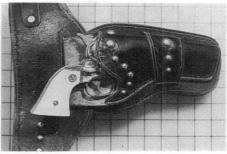

47. Black, full loop gunfighter. Silver studs, cross strap. $135

48. Patriotic, flag, God Bless America. Laced American. $150

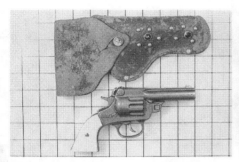

49. Patriotic eagle flap holster. Colored jewels & studs. $75

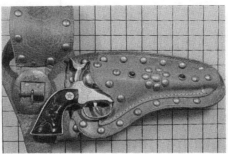

50. Large, tooled horses. Jewels & studs. Gunfighter-style. $145

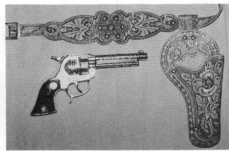

51. Large, early, fully tooled, jewels & studs. Loop top. $145

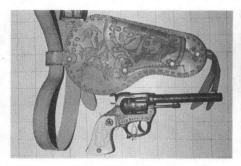

52. Rodeo-Red Ranger. Borders & cowboy, studs top loop. $65

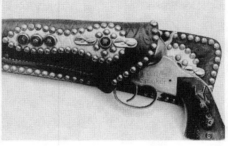

53. Large, heavy tooling, paint, jewels & many studs, $75

54. Large, wide loop. Jewels & studs, straps, cuffs & belt. $175

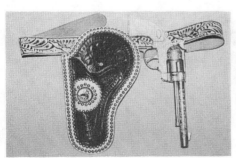

55. Large heavy tooling. Many silver studs & concho. $145

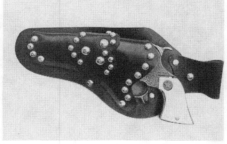

56. Large black & silver studs. Heart shape strap. Loop. $75

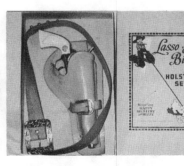

57. Large simple set. Cross strap & belt. Boxed. $145 Set

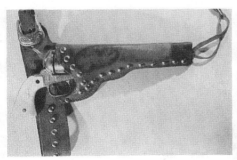

58. Large narrow holster with silver studs. Belt. $125

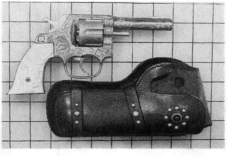

59. Large, black with red jewel & silver studs. Straps. $75

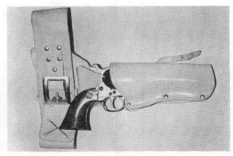

60. Simple gunfighter holster & belt. Tan leather. Daisy $85

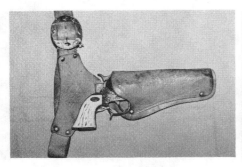

61. Wagon Train tooled holster in gunfighter-style. $125

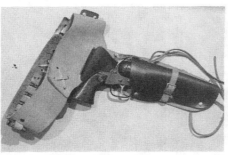

62. Black & tan gunfighter set. Bullet loops-strap. Daisy $100

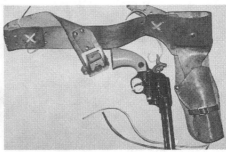

63. Russet gunfighter set. With adjustable belt. Daisy $100

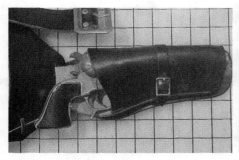

64. Black gunfighter set. With adjustable belt. Medium. $95

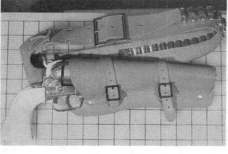

65. Large Colt .45. Tan, bullets, two straps. Adjustable. $145

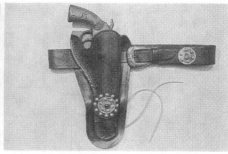

66. Earlier large loop. Stamped, concho, studs & jewels. $135

67. Old, large loop. Bead work on front. Straps & belt. $200

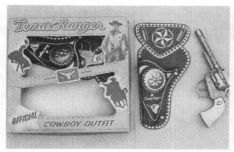

68. L-H Texas Ranger set in box with concho & artwork. $35

69. Black gunfighter set with-blue jewels & studs. $125

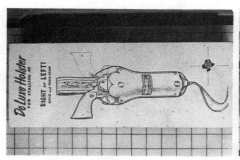

70. Box lid for Nichols reverse large set for Stallion .45. $100

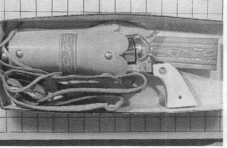

71. Contents H-70. Note gun can face right or left. Tan. $100

72. S Bar M large gunfighter set in black with cut outs. $125

73. Keyston Bros. lock set with tooling, conchos, fringe. $100

74. Detail of lock with logo. It locks into trigger guard. Rare.

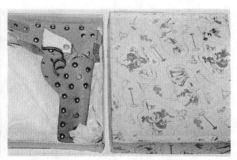

75. Large reverse draw. Russet with studs & jewels. $125 Box.

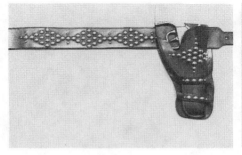

76. Early large loop. Dark with diamond stud pattern. $150

77. Boyville left hand in black. Many small silver studs. $100

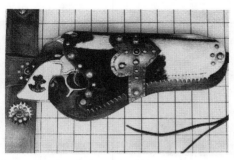

78. Hoppy set. B&W cow-hide front. Heart strap, jewels. $250

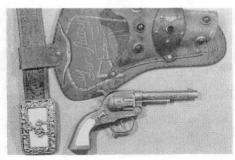

79. M.A. Henry-G. Autry. Tan & orange jewels, studs, art. $85

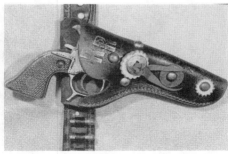

80. Classy-R Rogers. Early small black set, concho, bullets. $150

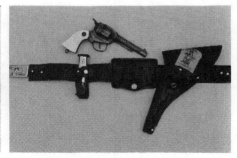

81.Esquire-Rin-Tin-Tin set in black with art. $150 (complete)

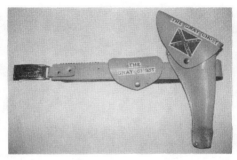

82.Rare Gray Ghost C.W. set & ammo pouch. Gray color. $165

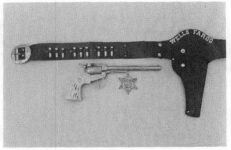

83. Wells Fargo 2 stage holster. Fast draw or secured. $165

84. Rare Trackdown-Hoby G. set, bullets, Ranger star. $165

85. Wild Bill Hickok gunslinger has studs, jewels, concho. $150

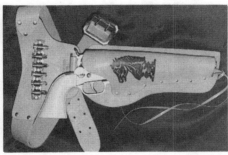

86. Large tan gunfighter with a Paladin chess piece art. $135

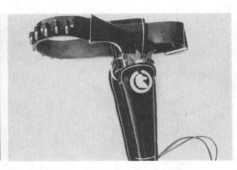

87. Large black loop & Paladin 3-D chess piece. Bullets. $125

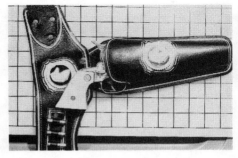

88. Black gunfighter, borders & 3-D Paladin medallions. $145

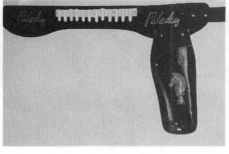

89. Large gunfighter, lettering, & Paladin 3-D medallion. $145

90. Paladin large loop, gold art & studs. 3-D chess piece. $145

91. Multi-color cut-outs, jewels studs & 3-D wild cat head. $65

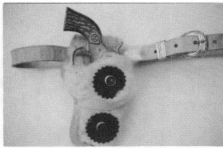

92. Small wooly front. Concho & jewels. Belt. $25

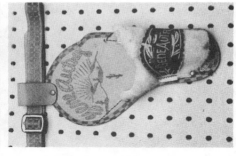

93. M.A. Henry-G. Autry wooly front & stamped artwork. $100

94. Gunfighter set in cow-hide fronts & conchos, studs. $125

95. Daisy- Elfego Baca set with canteen. B&W '59 Rare. $145

96. Kilgore fast draw set. Tan & light strap. Boxed. $65

97. Classy C.W. Rebel set. Gray with Confederate flag. $100

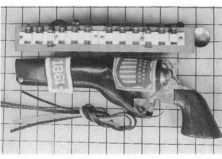

98. Classy C. W. Yankee set has Union shield. $100

99. Cavalry flap U.S. holster is C.W. style. 3-D concho. $85

100. L. Ranger. Boxed set with dark art on tan-jewel. $100-165

101. Small Deputy set. Black with silver concho, jewel. $15

102. Kilgore cardboard display holder for D.C. Big Horn. $10

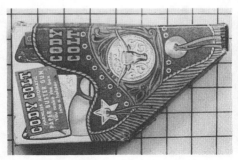

103. Cardboard package for the Cody Colt paper popper. $10

104. Box lid for Hubley set 105 on the right for Texan Jr.

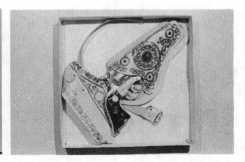

105. Small with printed art, & large concho-jewel. Boxed $35

106. Cowboy King set. Gold & silver conchos-flap badge. $150

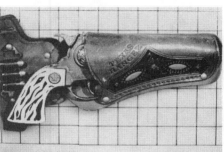

107. Texas Ranger. Tooled and painted. Jewels, bullets. $100

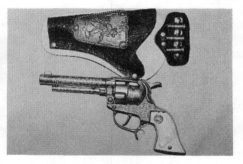

108. Real Texan 3-D metallic front. B&W with bullets. $50

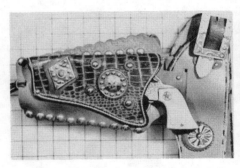

109. Alligator pattern. Silver studs & conchos. Loop. $75

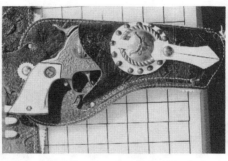

110. Tooled B&W with concho & studs. Cut-outs. Belt. $125

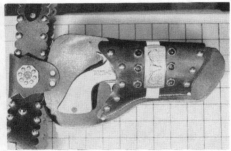

111. Top loop, blue jewels, stud & 3-D steerhead concho. $100

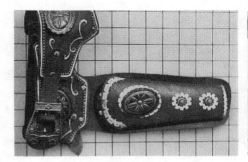

112. Multi-color art & silver conchos. R-L type holster. $95

113. Tooled, cut-outs, silver 3-D horsehead, studs, loop. $85

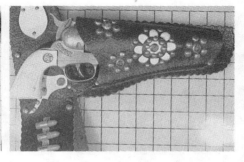

114. Large gunfighter set. Cut-outs, jewels , studs. $150

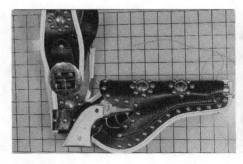

115. Large gunfighter set. Studs & white edging. S Bar M. $150

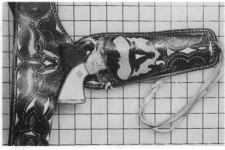

116. Large gunfighter set. Multi color cut-outs. Stitching. $135

117. Tooled gunfighter set, R-L style holster. Bullets. $125

118. Tooled black & tan. Silver star & studs. Strap. Loop. $65

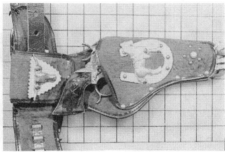

119. Loop top, wooly covering, silver horse, cow & studs. $125

120. Large gunfighter set. Multi color jewels, studs tooled. $135

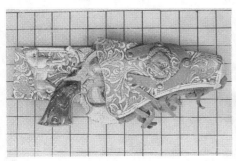

121. Loop printed art, fringe & 3-D silver horses, jewels. $35

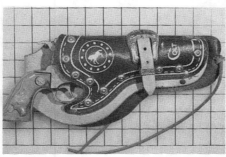

122. Hubley Colt .38 loop holster with artwork & studs. $45

123. Large gunfighter set. Fringe cut outs, jewels, studs. $100

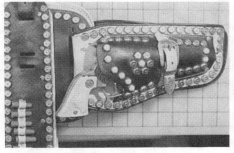

124. Gunfighter set B&W with studs, bullets & jewels. $150

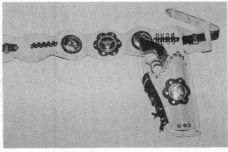

125. Tan & black. Fringe, studs, jewels & conchos. Large. $145

126. Large tooled set, studs and scalloped edge. B & tan. $150

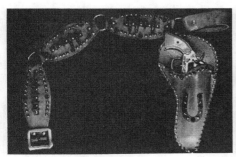

127. Unusual multi piece belt. Studs, jewels, cut-outs. $150

128. Large tooled set, conchos & studs. Scalloped edge. $150

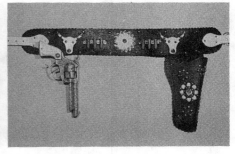

129. Early tooled set. Cut-outs, jewels, studs, bullets. Blk. $150

130. Heavy large set. Scalloped, jewels, studs, bullets. Tan. $165

131. Earlier large set. Has many studs & jewels. Tan. $165

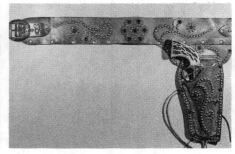

132. Superb large set. Cut-outs, many studs & jewels. $200

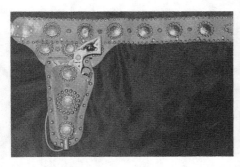

133. Large superb set. Jewels & large conchos, studs. Tan. $200

134. Black Hoppy. Large multi-color jewels, studs, name. $350

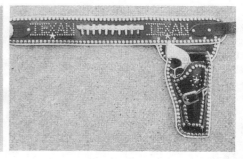

135. Large Texan set. Hundreds of studs. Stars & edging. $225

136. Russet set, has multi-color jewels, studs loop style. $200

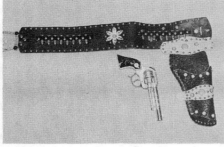

137. B&W large, cut-outs, studs & jewels. Bullets. Tooled. $185

138. Russet large set. Fringe & silver studs. Knife sheath. $250

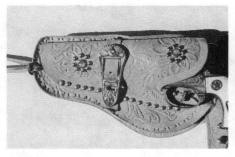

139. Large, tan, tooled with red jewels & studs. Buckles. $100

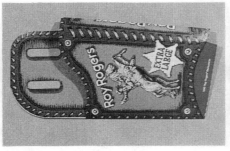

140. Roy Rogers, cardboard for large order of french fries! Free!

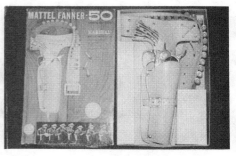

141. Mattel Marshal-gunfighter has 18 bullets & strap. $95 Box

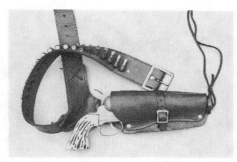

142. Mattel Marshal-gunfighter has 18 bullets. Fast-draw. $85

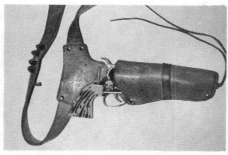

143. Mattel Deputy-gunfighter has 4 bullets no buckle. $65

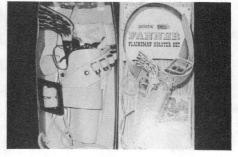

144. Mattel Plainsman. Smaller for Shootin' Shell. $85 Boxed

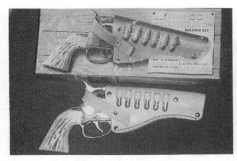

145. Mattel Fanner - Crossdraw bullets on front. Unusual. $85

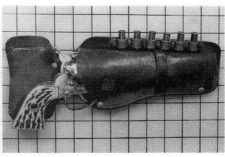

146. Mattel Fanner - Crossdraw bullets on side. Unusual. $85

147. Mattel Swivelshot, trick holster. Bullets. Tan. $125 Box

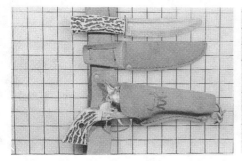

148. Mattel Buffalo Hunter in suede, has a knife sheath. $125

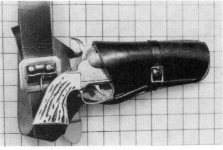

149. Mattel gunfighter series in black with strap. $100

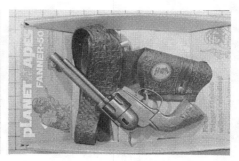

150. Mattel Planet of the Apes. tooled Black Dura-Hide. $25

151. Mattel Agent Zero. Brown tooled Dura-Hide. $15

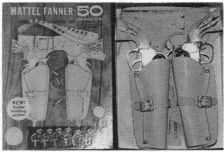

152. Mattel Fanner set. Cross straps, 10 bullets. $165 Box.

153. Mattlel Frontier set. Laced cross straps. Bullets. Rare $185

154. Mattel tooled gunfighter. Embossed steerheads. Tan $165

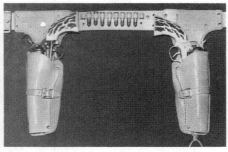

155. Mattel Vigilante set. For large 45s. 10 bullets. Tan $185

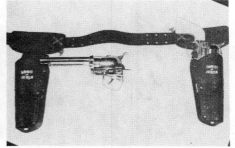

156. Mattel Cowboy in Africa. Black Dura-Hide double. $45

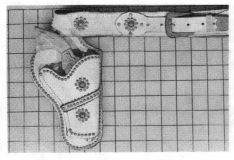

157. White, red jewels, gold studs & cross straps. Belt. $100

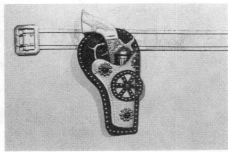

158. White & russet. Cut-out, red jewels, studs & belt. $85

159. White & dark blue. Badge cut out, bullets & studs. $45

160. L-White-red loop straps. R White. With jewels - studs. $45

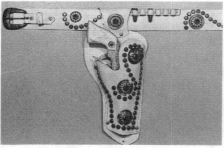

161.White- red diamonds, with multi-color jewels - studs. $150

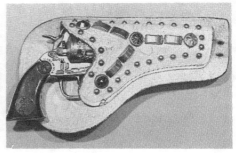

162. White, silver conchos and studs. Multi-color jewels. $50

163. White & red. Red jewels, silver studs & conchos. $125

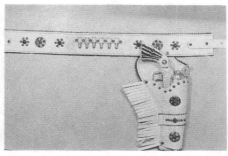

164. White. Gold studs, conchos & buckles. Large. $125

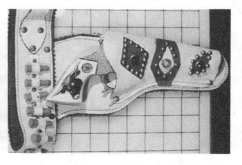

165. White-tan cut-outs. Multi-color jewels. Silver studs. $125

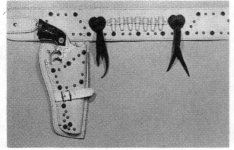

166. White- red hearts & straps Red jewels & silver studs. $125

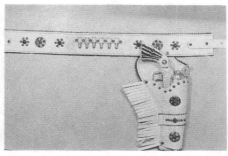

167. White- red trim, fringe & red jewels, gold conchos. $125

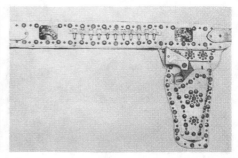

168. White. Many gold studs & conchos, red jewels. Large $145

169. Sally Starr set. Red, white & blue. Artwork. Double. $130

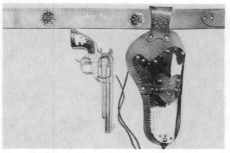

170. Hoppy- cowhide front, red jewels. Heart strap. $250

171. Tooled plastic garter set. Red lace, black holster. $15

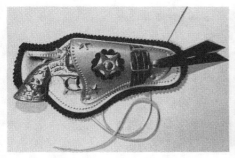

172. Metallic silver & blue. The stars & conchos are silver. $50

173. White & dark blue cutouts has colored jewels, studs. $145

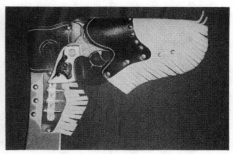

174. Annie Oakley set. Blue & tan. Fringe & silver studs. $175

175. Wild Bill Hickok set- B&W with turquoise & silver. $150

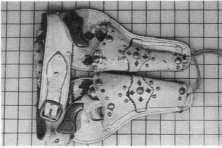

176. Early double. White-red trim, cut-outs & studs. $150

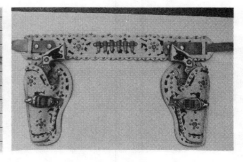

177. Superb double! White-red, silver trim, studs, jewels. $225

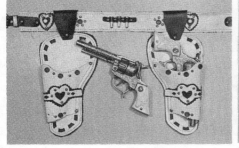

178. Early double- white & red, hearts, red jewels, studs. $150

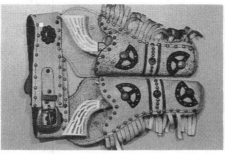

179. White- blue cut-outs. Red trim, jewels, fringe, studs. $150

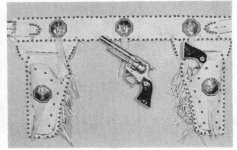

180. White. Gold conchos and studs. Fringe. Large. $150

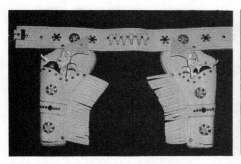

181.White double. Fringe, red jewels, gold studs. $145

182. Superb double. White, red jewels, gold studs. Cuffs. $225

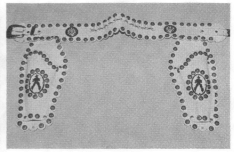

183. Double in white. Cowboy conchos. Gold studs. $145

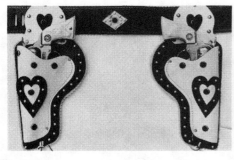

184. White & red double. Red jewels, silver studs, hearts.$175

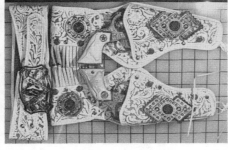

185. Printed floral art. White & silver trim, red jewels. $125

186. Texas Ranger. B&W Red jewels, cut-outs, studs. $100

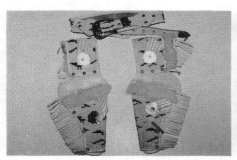

187. Unusual Indian set. Fringe red fur, beads, studs. Rare $200

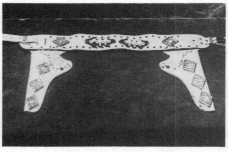

188. White slim set. Red jewels & silver studs, conchos. $125

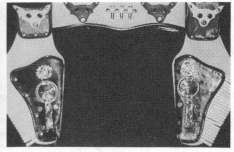

189. White with fur. Fringe & fox cut-outs, studs. $145

190. White & red. Multi-color jewels, cut-outs, conchos. $145

191. King of the Wild West set. Metallic front & studs. $165

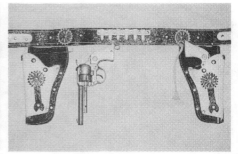

192. Tooled B&W, gold conchos & studs. Cut-outs. $135

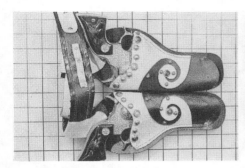

193. Burgundy & white. Silver studs, jewels, cut-outs. $125

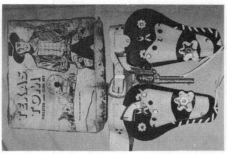

194. Texas Tom- B&W, multi-color jewels, badges, lace. $125

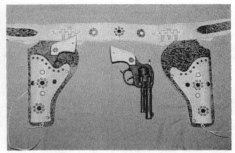

195. Tan & alligator-type, with-multi-color jewels, studs. $135

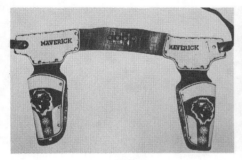

196. Maverick. B&W. Silver conchos & studs. Bullets. $150

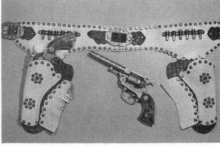

197. Red & white. Fringe,studs, jewels, bullets. Large. $150

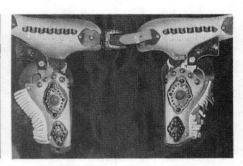

198. White & tone gray. Fringe conchos and turquoise. $145

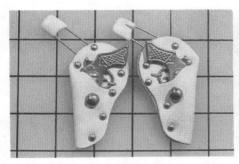

199. White leather diaper pins with silver studs. Small. $5

200. The Texan box for the set in alligator-type leather-right.

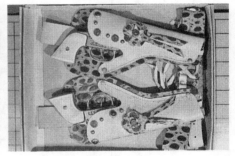

201.The Texan set. White, tan & russet. Cut-outs-jewels. $185

202. Carnel Roundup set. Art-work is printed. Small holsters.

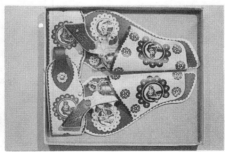

203. Roundup set. White & red -all decorations printed. $45

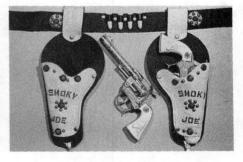

204. Rare Smokey Joe. White & red. Metal type, jewels. $165

205. Anco Star Ranger. Box lid with cowboy art in blue.

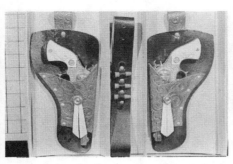

206. Anco set. Tooled in black & tan, conchos. Small. $65

207. Early, large russet set with silver studs & straps. $85

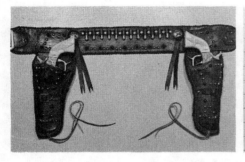

208. Early, large tan set, jewels, studs, conchos, bullets. $185

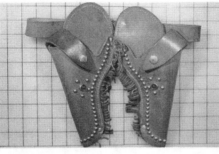

209. Keyston B. Tan, snap strap studs & jewels. Fringe. $150

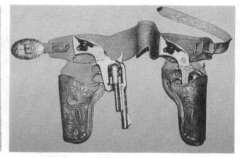

210. Tan completely floral and border tooled. Large. $145

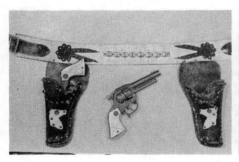

211. B&W, early, horse cut-outs jewels, studs, large. $135

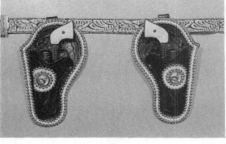

212. Early, tooled B&W, many silver studs & conchos. $185

213. Tan with many studs and medallions. Cross straps. $165

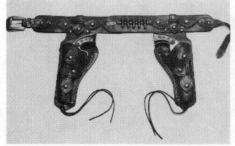

214. Gunfighter. Rare loops-tan Silver studs-bullets-early. $225

215. Early, tan with silver studs and conchos. Loop top. $145

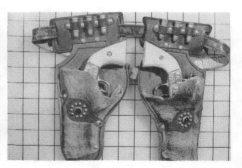

216. Small cowhide front with studs, jewels and bullets. $75

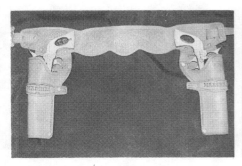

217. Tan tooled belt, Marshal strap holsters. Large. $150

218. Tan, cowhead embossed, stud, jewels & conchos. $135

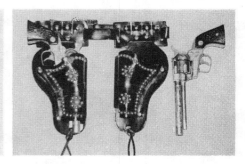

219. Black, silver studs and red jewels. Bullet loop top. $100

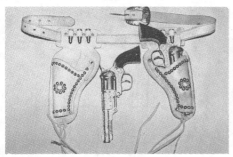

220.Tan, silver studs and green jewels. Bullet loop top. $100

221. Narrow pouch, black with conchos & studs. $125

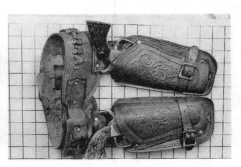

222.Large, tooled gunfighter set- straps & bullet loops. $165

223. Em-Jay Mustang set. Box lid for set on right.

224. Large, early, B&W, studs & cut-outs. Bullets. $145

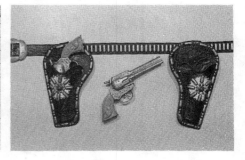

225. Early, tooled set. Unusual silver conchos & studs. $185

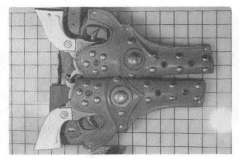

226. Large, tan slim set. Silver studs & big cross straps. $165

227. Tooled black, loop top has cut-outs, jewels & studs. $135

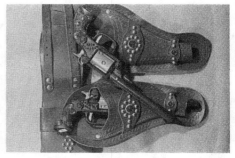

228. Early Keyston B.-tan, studs and jewels. Tooled-straps. $185

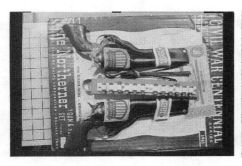

229. C.W. Northerner set. Black narrow with artwork. $145

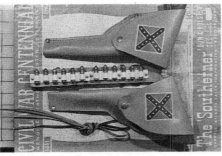

230. C.W. Southerner set. Gray narrow with artwork. $145

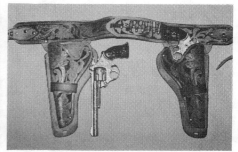

231. B & tan tooled narrow set in gunfighter-style. $175

232. Boyville box lid for tan set at right. Sears Roebuck & Co.

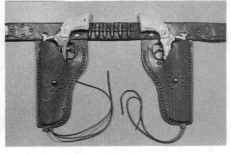

233. Boyville tan gunfighter set with small studs, bullets. $150

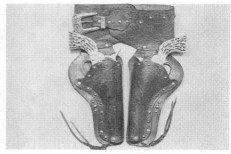

234. Tooled tan gunfighter set with steerheads & studs. $145

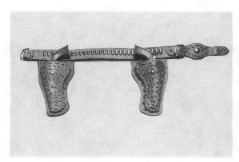

235. Gunfighter-Rare buckels & stud treatment-tan-laced. $200

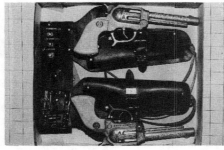

236. Russet gunfighter set with cross straps. Plain, large. $125

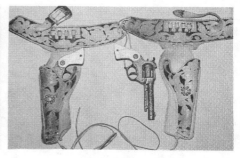

237. Tan, tooled gunfighter set with red jewels & studs. $175

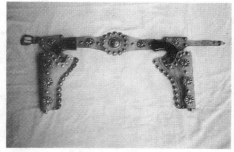

238. Large tan set with large silver conchos & studs. $165

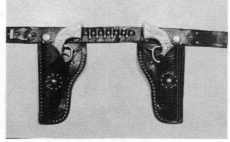

239. Boyville similar to 233 but in black leather. Sears. $150

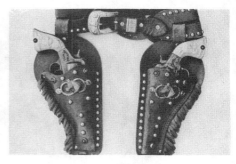

240. Tan, fringe, silver horseheads, studs & red jewels. $175

241. Small cowhide front set. Straps & bullets. $75

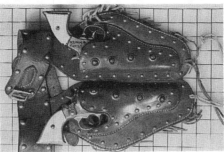

242. Large tan gunfighter set . Fringe, jewels & studs. $200

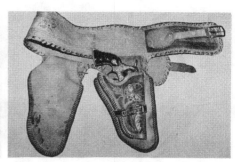

243. Tan gunfighter, tooled has laced edges. Large. $165

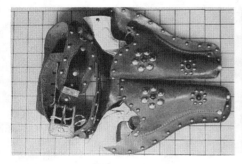

244. Tan gunfighter with studs and red jewels. Large. $165

245. Early black set with silver hearts & studs. Large-rare. $200

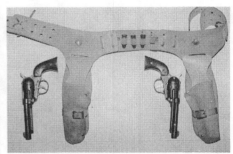

246. Daisy low-slung buckskin gunfighter set. Bullets. $100

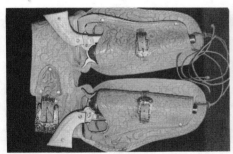

247. Superb large, tooled set. It is top quality & rare set. $245.

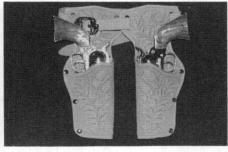

248. Small, tan tooled set with loop top & small belt. $35

249.McKinnon, NY tan set has studs & cross straps. $50

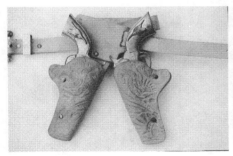

250. Very small, tan tooled set with small belt. $25

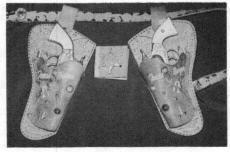

251. M.A. Henry- Texas Ranger set-jewels-studs & artwork. $95

252. Western Ranger Bike set in B&W with studs & jewels. $85

253. Marx dura-hide gunfighter set. Tooled. Black. $25

254. Daisy mini gunfighter set. Buckskin for 4" guns. $25

255. Vinyl, Little sharpshooter set with jewels & studs. $25

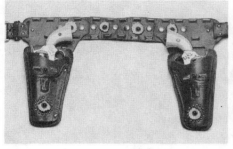

256. Early gunfighter-tan-cows-studs-blue jewels-cutouts. $200

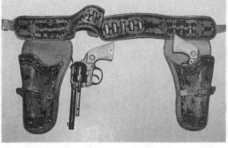

257. B & tan gunfighter. Tooled with jewels & bullets. $135

258. High quality gunfighter in tan, lined leather. Tooled. $150

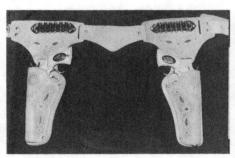

259. Tan, tooled Wagon Train. Turquoise & red jewels. $150

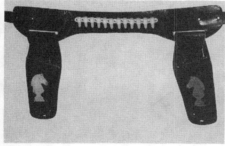

260. Plain black. Metal chess pieces & bullets. Paladin? $145

261. Ric-O-Shay. Black. Loop top with R-L holsters. $85

262. Russet gunfighter. Silver horses-studs-jewels-edged. $165

263. Tooled, tan Marshal gunfighter. Large. $175

264. Small black, loop top. Cut outs, horses & studs. $125

265. Tan & cowhide fur front. Jewels & studs, gunfighter-$135

266. Gunfighter. Silver studs & star conchos. Straps. $150

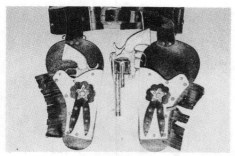

267. B&W loop top. Cutouts & fringe-studs-jewels. $135

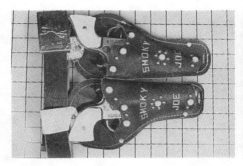

268. Black Smoky Joe. Metal brass type-jewels-studs. $165

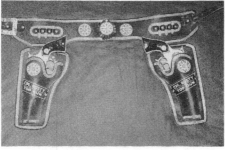

269. Rin-Tin-Tin Rusty. Black & silver art-jewels-conchos. $150

270.Sheriff-small. Loop top in B&W studs-bullets. $50

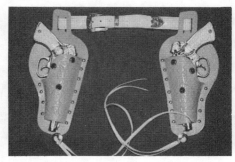

271. Early plastic. Tan, jewels & studs. White belt. $35

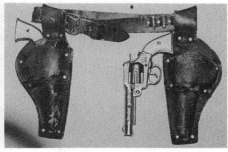

272.Early Star Ranger. Russet-loop top-studs-braid. $135

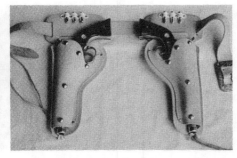

273. Nichols large leather silver studs, bullets. $135

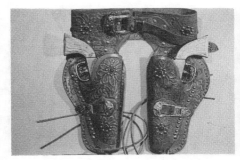

274. Superb-tooled gunfighter, fancy b'kles-jewels-studs. $200

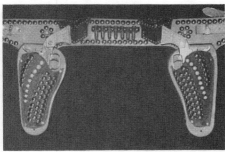

275. Fantastic studs! Cream & tan with 2 pouches. Large $250

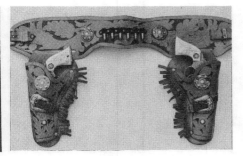

276. B&T tooled-fringe-yellow jewels & conchos. Large. $185

277. Esquire- tan-has embossed horses & silver studs. $150

278. Similar to 277. Scalloped edge-painted horses. $165

279. Unusual shape. Black with conchos,studs & cut-outs. $165

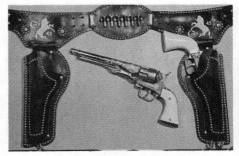

280. Very large Colt .45. Black. Silver studs & bullets. $250

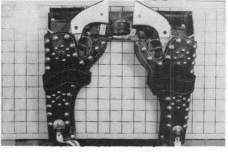

281. Early large Hoppy. Black-Multi-color jewels, studs. $450

282. Large-russet-scalloped & many studs-badges. $225

283. Unusual shape-black-early cow cut-outs-jewels-studs. $200

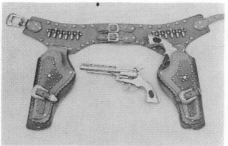

284.Super-gunfighter-tan-studs scalloped edge-buckles. $225

285. Small-early-tan-has silver studs & conchos. $150

286. Slim-tan-laced edge. Studs & multi-color jewels. $150

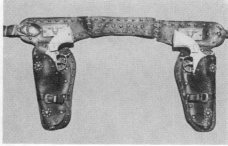

287. Large black gunfighter with silver conchos-studs. $185

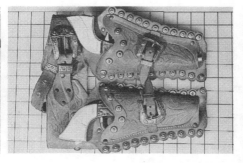

288. Early tooled tan set. Gold buckles- studs-scalloped $200

289. Tan gunfighter-Jewels with silver studs & buckles. $145

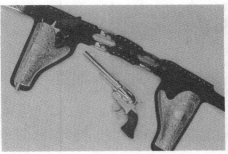

290. Beautiful black & metallic silver-floral pattern. Med. $300

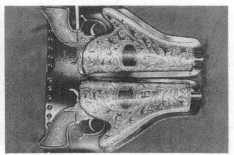

291. Detail of holster fronts & belt from 290. Made in 3 sizes.

292. Large Blk.-basketweave & silver conchos & studs. $165

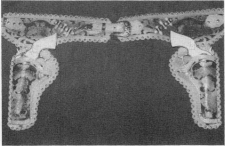

293. Large gunfighter-Tooled & scalloped. Studs-bullets. $165

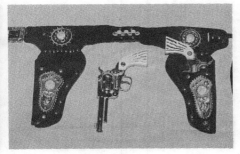

294. Black-large conchos-studs and red jewels-bullets. $135

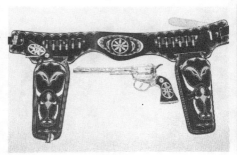

295. Very Lrg. Multi-color cut-outs. Fancy cow heads. $250

296. Early-unusual shape. B&W jewels-studs-cut-outs. $175

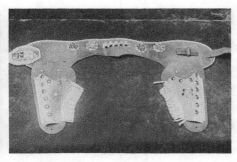

297. Small-tan-buckskin. Fringe & silver studs-conchos. $135

298. Lrg. gunfighter. Russet & white. Studs-big conchos. $200

299. Tan gunfighter. With large conchos & studs. Fringe. $165

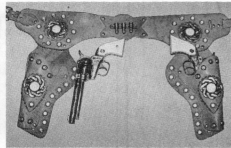

300. Tan gunfighter. Orange jewels-silver conchos. $165

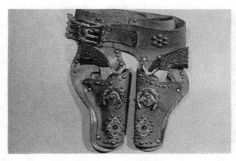

301. Early gunfighter. Large conchos & silver studs. $165

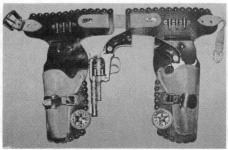

302. Lrg. fancy set-scalloped & tooled with studs. $185

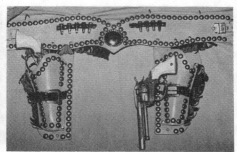

303. Lrg. cross-draw set. Fringe & large studs-medallion. $225

304. Small tan-tooled set. Loop top. Large conchos. $85

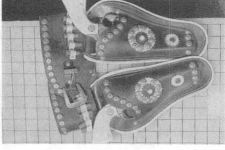

305. Large gunfighter. B&W edged & silver studs. $165

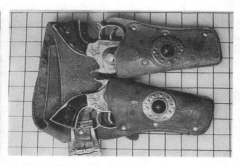

306. Early Texas Ranger. Tan-tooled-conchos & jewels. $150

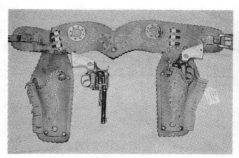

307. Cross-draw-fringe-cutouts-jewels-studs. Keyston B. $225

308. Very lrg. Blk. Fringe-studs-cut-outs-bullets. Wow! $275

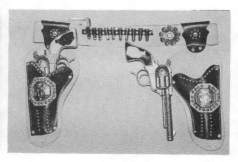

309. Loop top. T&B. Medallion & silver studs-bullets. $150

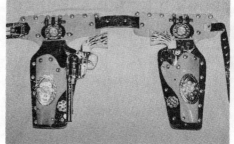

310. B&T. Large conchos, jewels-studs. Scalloped. $200

311. Russet- studs- silver horse conchos-scalloped. $175

312. Lrg. Blk.-many studs-buckles & bullets. $185

313. Super lrg. set. Tooled-studs conchos & bullets. $200

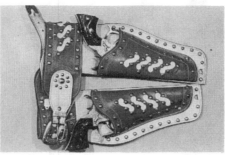

314. Unusual set. W&T Cutout design seldom seen. Studs $200

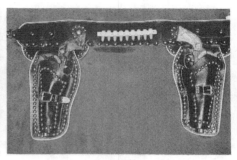

315. Lrg. black-many studs. Has edging & bullets. $200

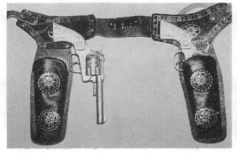

316. Black R-L set. Multi-color conchos-printed border. $145

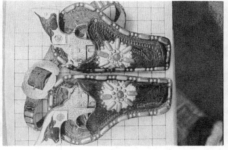

317. Early Keyston B. Tooled & numerous silver conchos. $185

318. Superb Lrg set. Black with-cut-outs-jewels-buckle. $225

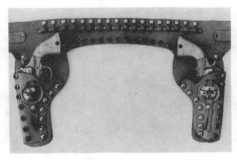

319. Early tan- silver conchos & studs.18 bullet loops. $165

320. Superb-very lrg. B&W cut-outs-jewels-studs-borders. $245

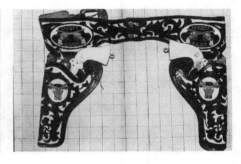

321. Wyatt Earp B&W tooled & colored. Studs. $175

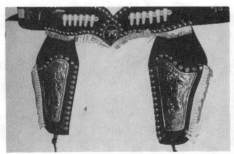

322. Keyston B. cross-draw has metal fronts-fringe-studs. $225

323. Box lid for a Texan holster set 324 at right.

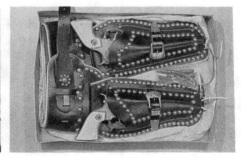

324. Box set 323. Black-many silver studs-buckles-large. $200

325. Box lid for a Pony Boy set. Esquire Novelty. See 326

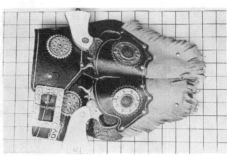

326. Pony Boy. Buckskin & blue. Fringe-conchos. $150

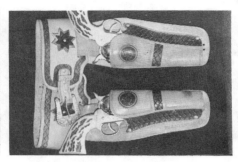

327. Esquire. Wells Fargo set. Braided edge-conchos. $175

328. Box lid for Halco Smoky set. See 329

329. Fancy Smoky Joe. B&T & jewels-studs-bullets. $200

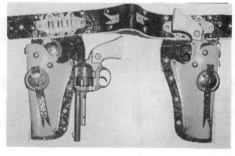

330. B&T. Conchos-studs with black area tooled. $150

331. Classy Roy R. set- conchos & RR studs-buckle. Large $350

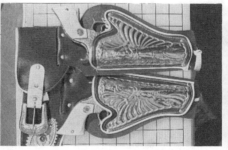

332. Large black set has metal fronts. Conchos-studs. $165

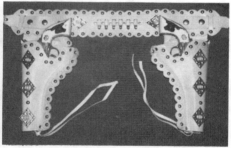

333. Hubley set. Tan-scalloped edge, concho-studs. $175

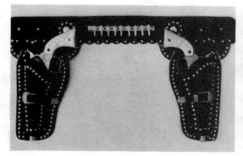

334. Large russet has numerous studs, scalloped-buckles. $200

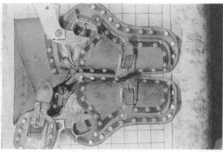

335. Early Roy R. set. B&T has RR studs & silver buckle. $300

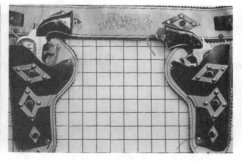

336. Red Ranger. B&T-jewels, studs-cut-outs & art. $145

337. Superb lrg. set. Black with numerous studs & jewels. $275

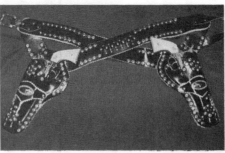

338. Rare gunslinger. Black has studs, conchos & jewels. $350

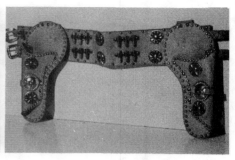

339. Large loop gunfighter. Tan -studs-conchos & bullets. $225

340. Large white set with gold studs-conchos & 3-D art. $175

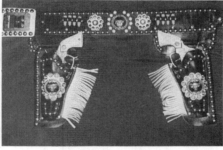

341. Lrg. B&W- Fringe-cut-outs studs-conchos-buckle. $325

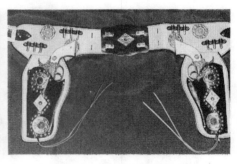

342. Lrg. B&W-Conchos-studs-jewels-bullets-buckle. $200

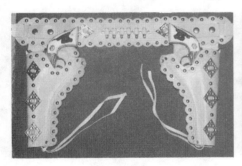

343. Lrg. Tan-Scalloped edge & conchos-studs-bullets. $175

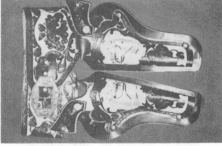

344. Esquire- B&W tooled. Art work in color-studs. $165

345. Lrg. Black-Fringe-conchos-studs-bullets-buckles. $300

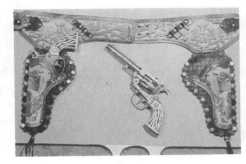

346. Superb B& gray. Tooled-cut-outs-studs-bullets-Lrg. $225

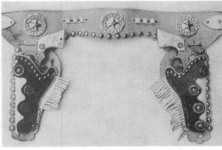

347. Lrg. Russet-tan. Fringe has cut-outs-studs-conchos. $250

348. Lrg. B&W. Studs-3-D conchos-bullets-artwork. $250

349. Superb cross-draw. Blk. & metal fronts-studs-fringe. $275

350. Red & Tan- Tooled-studs-conchos-red jewels. $165

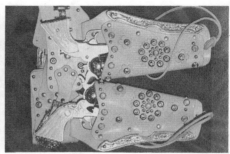

351. Lrg.-Tan- metal edge-studs red jewels-bullets. $165

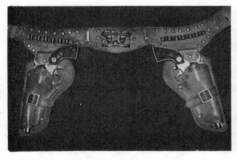

352. Russet-Lrg.- Has turquoise jewels-conchos-studs. $250

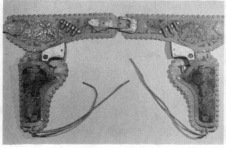

353. B&T tooled-scalloped edge studs-bullets-buckles. $165

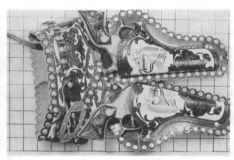

354. B&W& red. Studs-jewels-color art- scalloped edge. $175

355. Hubley-small Range Rider. Tan-concho,fringe-studs. $65

356. Box lid for Halco Texan set. See 357.

357. Tex set. Tan-fringe-studs-large conchos-jewels.Small $85

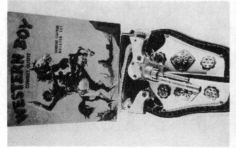

358. Western Boy set. B&W-has conchos-studs-jewels. $145

359. Lrg.- B&T with gold metal fronts-studs & conchos. $350

360. Wild Bill set. Tan & gray. Fringe & silver cochos. $75

361. B&T-silver studs & star conchos-straps. Large. $175

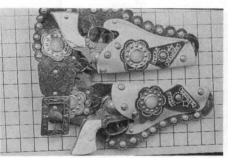

362. Texas Ranger-Tooled red & white. Conchos-studs. $145

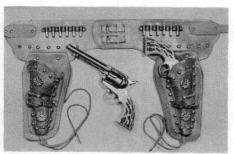

363. Large-tan-studs- jewels-conchos-bullets-buckles. $200

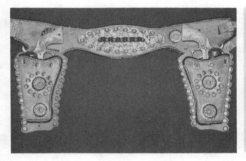

364. Cowhide-Tan&B. Red jewels-studs-conchos-bullets. $250

365. Lrg. Russet-silver conchos-studs-jewels-buckles. $225

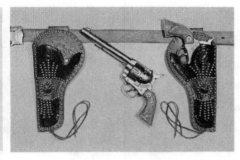

366. Early-russet-tan-jewels & many silver studs-tooled. $275

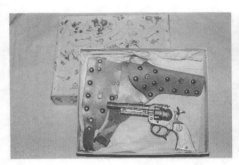

367. Early Texan-Russet-studs & red jewels. Simple. $145

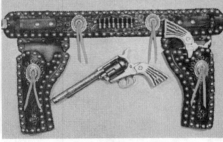

368. Lrg. Hubley-Black-silver studs-blue jewels-tooled. $250

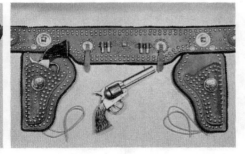

369. Lrg.-Tan-many silver studs conchos-red jewels. $250

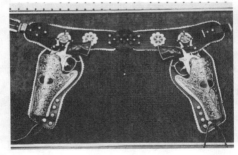

370. Lrg. B&W-with gold floral fronts-conchos-studs. $350

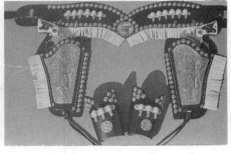

371. Lrg. Cross-draw-B&W set-fringe-metal-studs-cuffs. $300

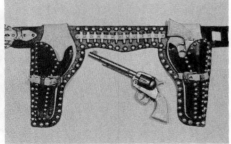

372. Lrg loop B&T numerous studs-buckles-bullets. $250

373. Small Black-gold metal on front. Gold studs-bullets. $275

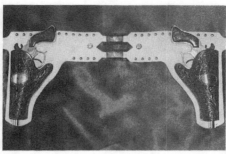

374. Unusual tan- with antique bronze metal fronts-studs.$275

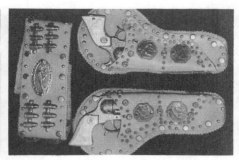

375. Lrg. Tan-red jewels-studs-conchos-bullets. Loop. $200

376. Lrg. B&T-horse conchos-studs-straps-bullets. $225

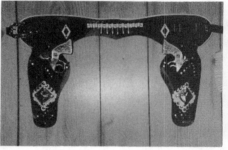

377. Black-edged-silver studs & conchos-knife sheath. $250

378. Lrg. Russet-silver conchos-studs-red jewels. $225

379. Lrg. B& plain gold belt & holster-conchos-jewels. $165

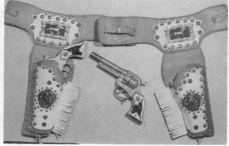

380. Tan & white-fringe-studs-3-D conchos-jewels. $200

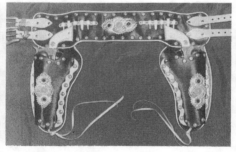

381. B&W Lrg.-Conchos-studs-jewels-2 straps-buckles. $200

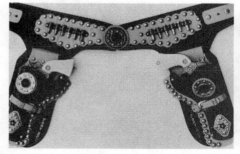

382. Lrg. B&T -Unusual shape. Conchos-studs-jewels. $250

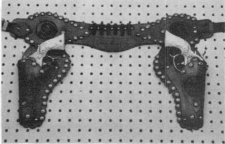

383.Early G. Autry. Tan-studs-tooled-scalloped edges. $300

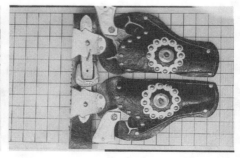

384. Lrg. loop top. B&W-studs-conchos-jewels. $150

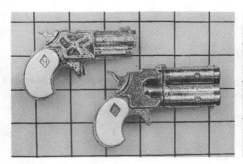

1. Halco-L-H-'60. *Top:* Hide-A-Way. *L.* Swivel Double. *$30-55*

2.Maverick-L-H '60. Chrome with display card . Rare-$50-85

3. Halco-L-H-'60. Dull finish & bullet. Ivory grips. $30-45

4. Hamilton-'55. Secret Agent-engraved-red grips-O/U. $35-50

5.Hamilton Hide-A-Way. Same as #4, but dull finish. $30-45

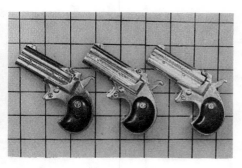

6. L- R.'61 Nichols cap. Nichols bullet. Kusan cap '62. $35-65

7. Avenger. Nichols cap '62 on a Kilgore card. $30-50

8. Western Heritage-Nichols '61 cap shooter on card. $35-55

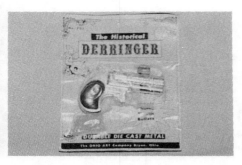

9. Derringer-Ohio Art - Kusan '65 cap & shootin' shell $35-65

10. Potshot-Mattel '62. Shootin shell-engraved-small. $20-35

11. Potshot-Mattel '62. Shootin shell-engrv.-dull finish. $15-30

12. Classy '60. Roy Rogers Hide Away. Tiny. Engraved. $35-65

13. Carnell '62- Hide-A-Mite in holster-L-H or Nichols. $35-50

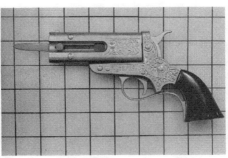

14. Hubley Dagger-Derringer '60 O/U-push-dagger. $75-130

15. Lone Star-Eng. '62 Pepper Box-4 shot-4 barrels. $65-100

16. Hubley-'60. Panther Pistol O/U derringer-boxed. $65-125

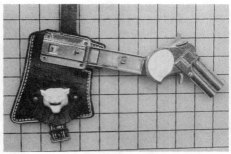

17. Reverse of wrist strap on a Panther. Note 3-D head.

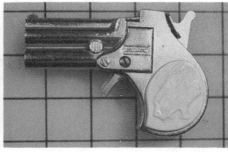

18. Close-up of Panther. Gun snaps into shooting position.

19. Esquire '55. Hideaway. Ant bronze. O/U bullets. $35-65

20. Esquire '55. Hideaway pair. Ant. Brnz. & Gold. Enr. $35-65

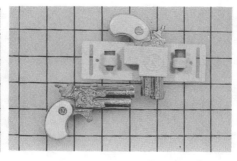

21. Nichols Dyna-mite '57. Pair Nik./white & Gold/blue.$30-60

22. Nichols Dyna-Mite '57 Nik. on card/ mini holster. $35-50

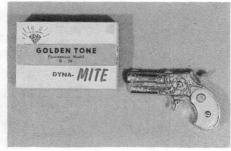

23. Nichols Dyna-Mite '60 Gold/blue grips-box. $50-75

24. Sheriff's Derringer-Ohio Art Bullet-Nik-Hong Kong. $15-25

25. Lone Star-Eng. '65 Black caps-red grips-engraved. $15-25

26. Outlaw miniatures. British Cast Metals-Eng '60. $45-100

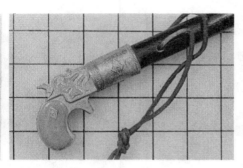

27. Halco '60 Cane handle derringer-Engr-red grips. $45-75

28. Remington-1876 Bucklegun Mattel on card/bul. '62. $50-85

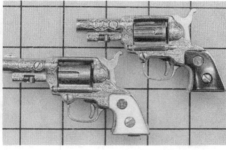

29. Pinto-Nichols '59. Bullets. Nik/black. Gold/blue. $30-55

30. Pinto on original card $.98. Nickel finish-white grp. $35-60

31. Paint- N ichols '60. Bul-caps Nickel/blk. on card. $35-60

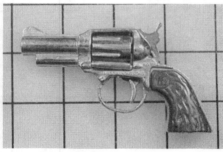

32. Ranger-Zee Toys-'65 Hong Kong. Nik/Turquoise. $10-20

33. Derringer. CK- Japan. '75 Black/walnut. $10-20

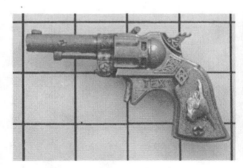

34. Tex- Revue Prod./L-H. '59 in Wagon Train sets. $35-65

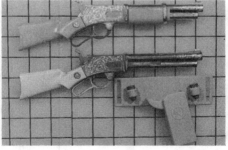

35. Spitfire-Nichols '58. Early have no forend. Nik. $25-45

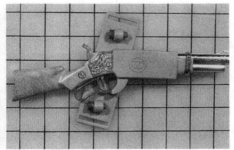

36. Spitfire-Nichols '59. Model with forend & holster. $30-50

1. Dime Pistol Bank-Elliott- Era 1920. Polished. Rare $65-100

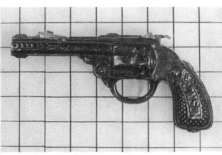

2. Ronson-1920-30. Sparks and cap shooter. Black. $35-70

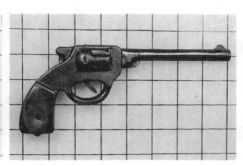

3. Early long barrel clicker. Era-1925. Black. $15-25

4. Daisy Model 80 Water pistol. Buzz Barton -1930 Blk. $65-100

5. Daisy #14 clicker-1935.Note embossed star. Black, $35-75

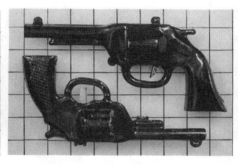

6. Wyandotte clicker on top. A Marx dart gun lower. $25-50 Ea

7. Marx-1930. Silver. G-Man is embossed. Lanyard Rg. $35-70

8. Marx 1940. 5 Star. R-W&B. Silver clicker. $25-50

9. Marx 1940. Scroll art in red-blue-gold. Dart gun. $30-55

10. Marx-1940. 2 Red Rangers. Blue & Silver with art. $25-50

11. Marx-1935. Clicker. "Me & My Buddy" animated. $75-150

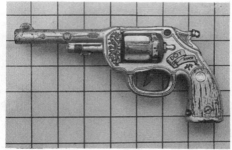

12. Wyandotte clicker 1940. In silver. "Y&• Ranch." $45-100

13. Marx- 1948. Sgt. Preston. Clicker-jewels-lanyard. $65-100

14. Wyandotte-1950. Small Red Ranger. clicker-black. $25-45

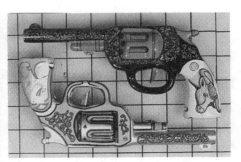

15. 1950 Full color clickers. *T*-Ohio Art. *L*- Marx. $35-65 ea.

16. 1935 Unknown. Engraved clicker-Indian. "#554". $45-85

17. Right side 16. "Ben" with a cowboy on the grips. Rare toy.

18. Marx-1945. Deluxe Target .45 Cal dart gun. Rare. $50-100

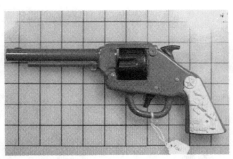

19. Wyandotte-1940. Rare Red Ranger cap. Rev. Cyl. $45-85

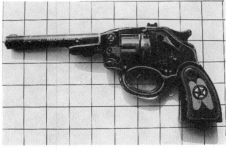

20. Marx. 1945 Officers Model Rev. Cyl.-.45 Cap.Rare $50-100

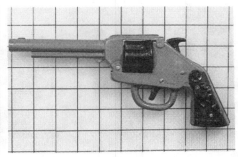

21. Wyandotte-1940. Ranger similar to 19. Blk. Grp. $45-85

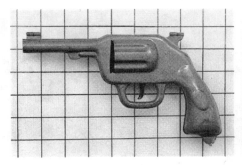

22. Wyandotte-1935. Rare cap shooter. Hinges. Red. $50-100

23. No. 22 opened to show the cap mechanism. Unusual toy.

24. Hubley-1960. Jailer's Key & Pad Lock cap shooter. $75-135

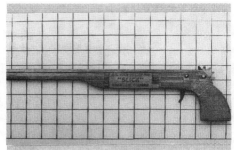

1. "Slick Cleaner"-1930 rubber band 6-shooter. Wood. $10-25

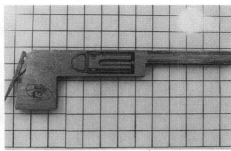

2."Bando"-1950 rubber band 6 shooter. Wood. $5-10

3. WW-II composition. Star in circle six gun. Black. $35-65

4. WW-II Scout composition. A horse & scroll. B&W. $45-85

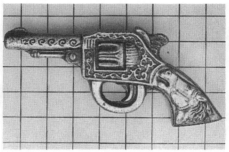

5. WW-II composition. Silver-horsehead-engraving. $45-85

6. WW-II similar # 4. No-name. B&W-lanyard ring. $45-85

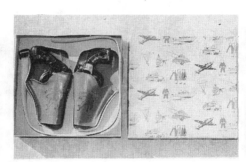

7. Let'er Buck WW-II composition set. Victory guns. $50-100

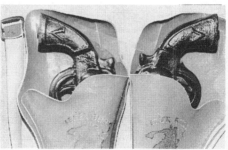

8.Close-up of #7. Note the "V" for victory on each grip. Black.

9. WW-II Compo'n in silver US Army/Gen MacArthur. $75-125

10. WW-II Hubley composition Texas Jr. with Colt. $75-125

11. WW-II Hubley composition Texas Jr. with star. $65-115

12. WW-II pair composition. A Ranger & MacArthur. $65-115

13. WW-II 3-composition guns. Unknown- Blk.& silver.$35-100

14. WW-II Comp. L-R Hubley, Molex, and Hamilton. $45-100

15. Detail of Molex in #14. The engraving is superb! Blk. paint.

16. WW-II rubber 6-guns. Black is Auburn.-Red is Arcor. $35-75

17. Arcor Ranch set-1945. Box lid in orange & blue. $45-100

18. Set from #17. Gun, knives, tomahawk & sheath. $45-100

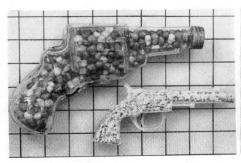

19. WW-II candy containers. A glass & plastic variety. $5-85

20. Tom Mix wooden gun. 1st model-1933. Opens. $145-250

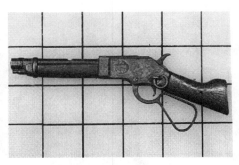

21. Marx-Wanted Dead or Alive miniature-caps. 1960. $25-65

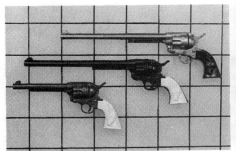

22. Marx miniature Colts-1960. Reg. $10-25 Buntlines $65-125

23.Amer. Min. Gun Co., CA '55 Colt Nik/Pearl. Works.$125-200

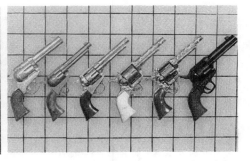

24.Colt Min. Armodelli-Esquire (2) Hubley-BCM & Zee. $20-35

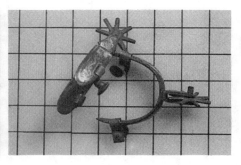

1. Real Child's spurs & leather straps. 1900. $150-250

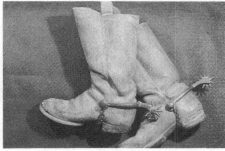

2. Child's boots with original spurs attached. 1900. $150-250

3. Original child's spurs with silver inlays. Rare. $200-350

4. Ruff N Ready. Gold-black straps/conchos. Boxed $65-100

5. Texas Ranger. L-H. Silver/tan cloth straps. Boxed $55-100

6. Lasso Em Bill- Keyston Bros. Silver/tan straps-Boxed $65-120

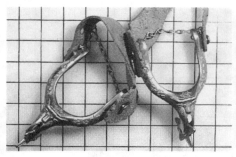

7. Hubley- Engraved-silver/tan scalloped straps. Rare-$65-125

8. Detail of #7 showing Hubley Toy casting on inside of spur.

9. Very Rare Keyston B. C.I. set of G. Autry spurs.Tan $200-350

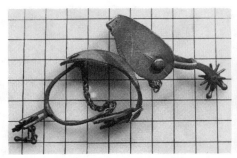

10. Tumbleweed Hoppy box set silver/white/jewels/studs. $275

11. Detail of #10 showing the lettering-jewels-studs-casting.

12. Tex-Spurs. Grimland Bros.- Waco, TX. Aluminum. $35-75

13. Box for a set of Hubley spurs. 1955-65 era. Box $15

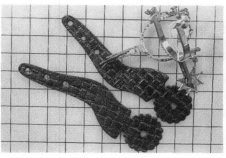

14. Hubley spurs found in #13. Silver/ basketweave. $45-85

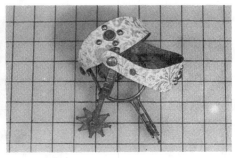

15. L-H set 1950. Tooled white-studs -jewels-silver. $35-65

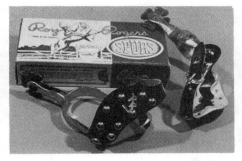

16. Classy/Schmidt Roy Rogers clover rowel. Boxed. Rare $300

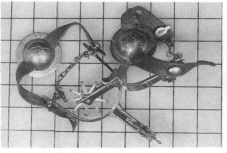

17. Superb Dodge-Melton set-1945-50. Silver/tan. $100-165

18. Detail of concho back from #17 showing maker-top quality

19. Hubley-1960."Trail Boss" on tan strap/silver spurs.$35-70

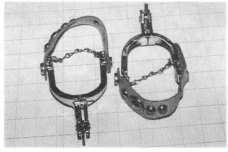

20. Esquire-1960. Heavy alloy-silver-tan/studs. $30-55

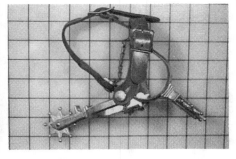

21. L-H-1955. Silver & gold. Tan buckle strap. $35-75

22.G-Schmidt. Buck'n Bronc'55 Lrg. conch-engr.-box.$75-165

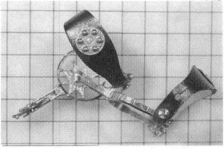

23.Esquire-1955-60. Chrome-black strap/concho. $35-65

24. Texas Ranger- L-H '55. Box-dull gray/tan straps. $45-85 Bx.

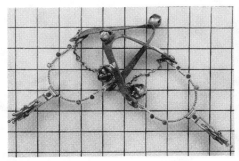

25. L-H Girl set. Color jewels & bells/tan straps. Rare. $65-100

26. Detail Leslie-Henry Texas Ranger box. R-W&B art. $25

27. Spurs from #26. Superb set has steerhead conchos-$75-145

28.G. Schmidt-Hoppy set with black straps. Boxed. $135-285

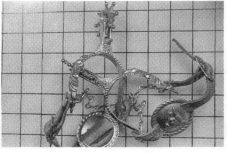

29. G. Schmidt superb set with engr. & steerhead con. $85-150

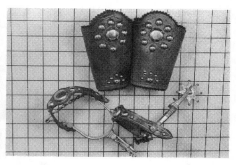

30. L-H cuffs & spurs. Dull gray tan-silver studs. $100-165 Set

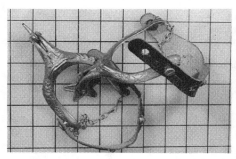

31. Hubley steerhead-style with engr./blk. straps-studs. $65-135

32. Esquire-Restless Gun set. Lrg. conchos/tan. $125-185 Set

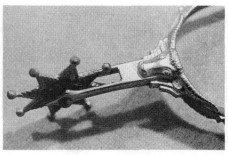

33. Detail of steerhead on spurs shown in #32. Superb quality!

34. Western Star boxed set. Tan & silver-steer conchos. $85-150

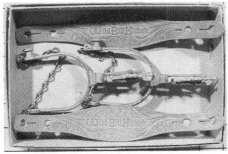

35.L-H Wild Bill Hickok boxed set/ tan tooled strap. $75-135

36. Detail of tooled strap in #35. Wild Bill Hickok.

37. L-H-1950. Dull gray/plain tan straps. $30-50

38. C Bar K-Corkale Mfg Co.CA Superb Gold-Sil. Box--rare $200

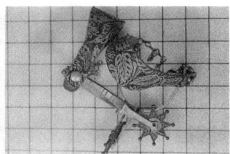

39.Esquire-1960. Dull gray/tan & black tooled strap. $35-65

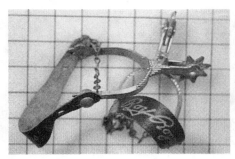

40. G. Schmidt. Multi-colored & silver/tan/conchos. $65-100

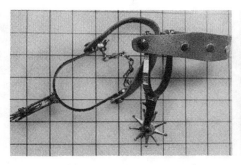

41.L-H-1955. Nickel-tooled tan strap & silver concho. $35-65

42.G. Schmidt-Hoppy. Gold & silver-blk/gold studs. $150-285

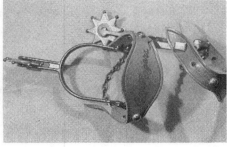

43. Classy-Roy Rogers-silver & black strap/sil. name. $100-175

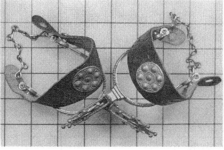

44.L-H Roy Rogers. Silver & tan gold name/details. $100-175

45. Kilgore Roy Rogers. Silver & gold-buckles-RR-studs $150-250

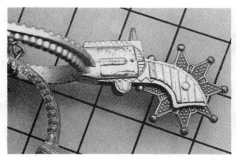

46. Detail of the superb & rare 6 gun spur & rowel of #47-48.

47. Classy- Dale Evans. Rare DE butterfly-gun/rowel. $150-250

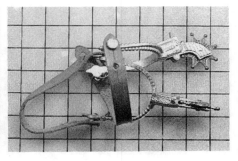

48. Classy- Polished 6 gun set-gold/silver/plain strap. $85-150

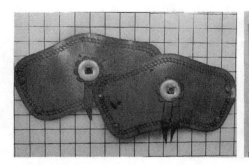

1. Pre 1940- Early-Tan-Border & silver concho/jewels. $50

2. Pre 1940 boxed cuffs & lariat Mordt Co. N. Plymouth, MA

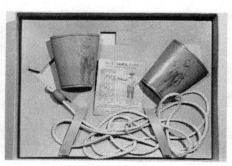

3. Contents of #2. Cowboy art on tan cuffs-lariat. Boxed $85

4.Leslie-Henry 1940 boxed set holster- cuffs with art. Set $150

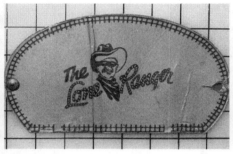

5. Tan fabric-composition cuff with L.R. artwork. Pair $35

6.Pre-1940 Keyston Bros. boxed set-white-tan-studs-jewels $135

7.Pre-1940 Keyston Bros. Boxed set. Orange box different #6.

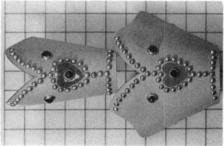

8. Contents of #7. Tan-silver studs/heart/jewels. Boxed $150

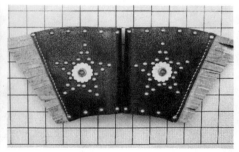

9. Super '40 set. Black-tan-studs fringe-jewels-concho-star. $100

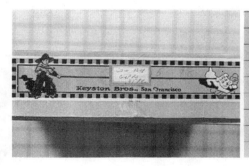

10. Label '40 era box -Keyston Bros. "Cowboy Cuffs" @ $.98.

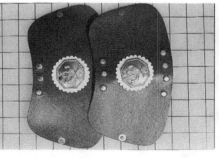

11. Contents #10- B&W-studs-crossed pistols concho. $50

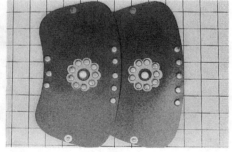

12. Contents #10-Red & tan-silver studs-cut-out. $50

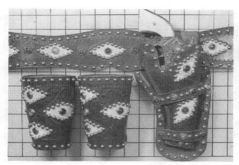

13. Super! K. Bros.-Tan-tooled-painted-studs-jewels. $150

14. *L.*-Tan-studs-jewels-border. *R.* White-red-studs-jewel.$60 ea

15. Esquire-B&W-cut-outs-jewel-silver concho-studs. $75

16. Black-tooled-cut-outs-studs-jewels. Large. $85

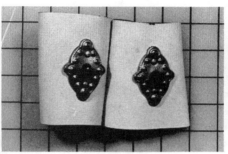

17. Simple cowgirl set. White-silver conchos-red jewel. $35

18. Restless Gun set. Black with silver artwork-border. $50

19. Hubley box for cuff set. Very rare. 1955-60 era. $35 box

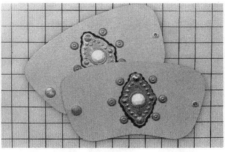

20. Cuff from #19. Tan & black white jewels-silver studs. $45

21. Super set. B&Tan-cut-outs-jewels-studs-tooled. $85

22. Pony Boy box. Esquire-Rare box. Red /white. 1950-60. $35

23. Cuff in #22. Black-gold-cut-outs-jewels-edged-star. $75

24. Super-Tan-steerhead concho studs-white jewels. Y&•. $125

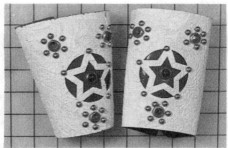

25. L-H Cowgirl set-white-red jewels-stars-studs. $65

26.Tan-large decorative concho yellow & red jewels-studs. $65

27. Red with white star cutouts and silver studs. L-H. $40

28. Texas Ranger-tan-tooled art embossed-jewels-studs. $75

29. Texas Ranger-russet-white art-jewels-silver studs. $50

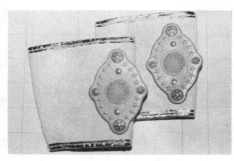

30. Hubley-Cowgirl-white-red & black edge-concho-jewel $45

31. L-H G. Autry-tan-tooled-red jewels-studs. 1950 era. $150

32. Detail of cuff #31. Note the Gene Autry & tooling. Rare set.

33. L-H G. Autry-red/silver stud & star jewels-gold name. $150

34. Cowgirl-white-gold steerhd. concho-studs-jewels. Y&• $125

35. Cowgirl-white & red- gold studs-blue jewels. $65

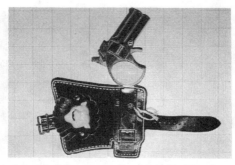

36. Hubley Panther cuff. Black-white panther head. Gun. $85

37. Fancy-black-silver steerhead & studs. edged-thong. $120

38. Hoppy-black-silver studs & white jewels. $165

39. Hoppy-black-gold conchos-studs-tooled-name. Rare $225

40. Hoppy-black-silver concho-studs-gold bust. Rare $200

41.Hoppy similar #40-gold stud & Hoppy busts. Rare. $225

42. Super set-black tooled-silver studs-red jewels. Key. Bro. $150

43. *L.* Red-cutouts-studs-jewels. *R.* Tan-gold studs-jewels. $85 pr

44. Tan-silver studs-tooled border-edged. $65

45. B&W cowhide-white cutout silver concho-jewels. Rare $145

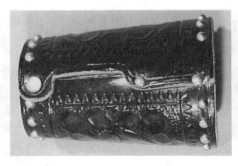

46. Keystone Bros. Back side of cuff. Note 3 rivets-do not open.

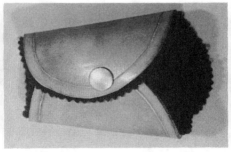

47. Back side of #44. Note felt lining and large snap closure.

48. Keyston Bros. Back side of cuff. Note rivets & snap closure

1. Roy Rogers-Trigger-white art brown cloth-vinyl- fringe. $125

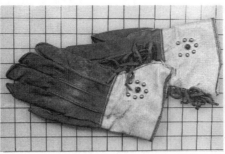

2. Roy R.-Trigger-Tan leather & vinyl-studs-jewels-fringe. $150

3. D. Crockett-Brown cloth & vinyl-fringe-color art. $75

4. Lasso 'em Bill-Black leather-white cutouts-studs. Rare $200

5. Buffalo B.-Red Ryder-Young Buffalo B.- Fabric-vinyl. $65 ea.

6. Roy Rogers similar #1 except in black with gold art. $125

7.Super! Roy R.-total deerskin & red jewels-studs-fringe. $225

8. Hoppy- Black leather white art-fringe. Rare. $150 (Hake's Am)

9. Tom Mix. Suede tan leather-artwork-1930s. $150 (Hake's Am)

10. Roy R. Brown fabric-vinyl gauntlets-frng. $125 (Hake's Am)

11. Roy R. 3 pairs in leather & vinyl gauntlets-fringe. $165 ea.

12. Leather with jewels-studs & conchos-fringe-Cowboy $85 ea.

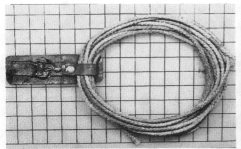

1. Sash cord- Belt hanger with silver saddle & snap loop. $55

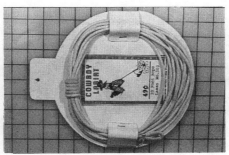

2. Keyston Bros. 20' sash cord on display card #303. $65

3. Autry Ranch Set lariat. Red, white & blue braided 12 ft. $10

4. Tom Mix cowboy rope. 15 ft. Ralston cereal premium. $45

5. Little Brahman-R&W braided Cleveland Mills, NC-12 ft. $25

6. Nichols Spinning lariat. 12 ft has end tassel & belt strap. $35

7. Lasso 'em Bill-10 ft. has loop honda. Keyston Bros. Box. $85

8. Lasso 'em Bill-12 ft. has loop honda. Keyston Bros. card. $65

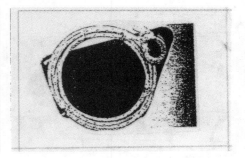

9. Western rope-14 ft. Leather honda for spinning. K.B. $75

10. Hoppy Trick rope-12 ft. has safety honda. Boxed. $125

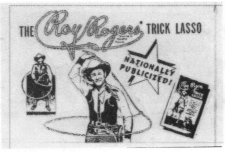

11. Roy R. Trick Lasso- Safe for spinning. 10'-Swivel. Box $125

12. G. Autry Steer-Roping Lasso 14 Ft. with safety honda. $125

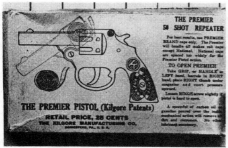

1. Federal-Kilgore-1920s- Note: Fed-Buster Corp. Pa. Rare $50

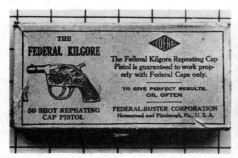

2. Buffalo Bill-Stevens-1940s. Early-style. $35

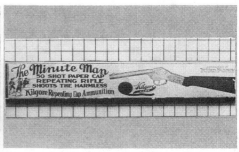

3. Minute Man Rifle-Kilgore-Mid 1930s. Very rare. $150

4.Premier Safety-Kilgore-1915. Kilgore-Homestead, Pa.? $35

5. 6 Shot-Stevens-1930s. Rarely found box. $65

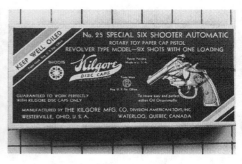

6. Special 6 shooter-Kilgore. 1935 era. Price $.35. $35

7. Bango- Stevens. Pre 1940. $25

8. Bango-Stevens-1940 era. Top gun is engraved-grips? $30 ea.

9. Texas-Kenton-1930- $65 & Kilgore-Invincible-1935- $45

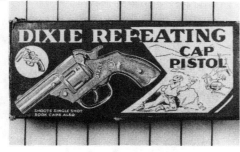

10. Dixie-Kenton- Mid 1930s. $55

11. Rodeo-Hubley-1940s. Rather common box. $25

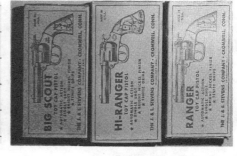

12.Big Scout-Hi-Ranger-Ranger. All Stevens-1940 era. $35 each.

13. Six Shooter & Buc-a-roo by Kilgore-1940 era. $55 each.

14. Two Ranger models-Kilgore 1940s. Special on one. $85 ea.

15. Lone Ranger-Kilgore-1940s. Very desirable box. $100-150.

16. Ranger Engraved-Kilgore 1940 era. Very rare box. $100

17. Ranger-Kilgore-1940s. Box end marked SPECIAL Pol. $85

18. Texan & Cowboy C.I. 1940-Hubley. Fairly common. $65 ea

19. Lawmaker-Kenton-1950-51. Rare box. Last of the C.I. $125

20.Bulls Eye-Kenton-1950-51. Rare box. Last of the C.I. $100

21. Sheriff-Stevens. Texan, Jr by Hubley. K.Carson-Kilgore.$35ea

22. American-Kilgore-1940 era. $1.49. Very desirable. $150

23. Long Tom-Kilgore-1940 era. Extremely desirable box. $200

24. Roy Rogers-C.I.-Kilgore. Pre 1940. Extremely rare. $300-500

25.G Autry-CI Kenton-1940 (2)
& L-H Buzz Henry. $100-150

26. 3 Cowboy King-Stevens-'40
L-R Nickel-Gold-A. Brnz. $125

27. Roy Rogers-49er. Gold L-H-
1950 era. Rare.$175

28. Hopalong Cassidy-1950 era
Wyandotte. Desirable $100-175

29. G. Autry-1950-55. Leslie-
Henry. Gold box. Rare $150

30. Early '50- Roy Rogers. Leslie
-Henry. Desirable. $135

31. G. Autry .44 L-H-1955 era.
T-Nickel. L-Gold. Rare. $175 ea

32. Roy Rogers-G. Schmidt-'50.
Schmidt boxes are rare. $175

33. Ruf Rider-LATCO & Buck'n
Bronc-G. Schmidt. Rare. $65 ea

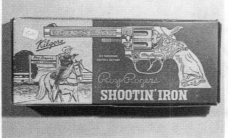

34. Alan Ladd- G. Schmidt '50.
Extremely rare! Shane. $225

35. Roy Rogers-Kilgore '55. A
rare DC box. $1.39. $125-185

36. Grizzly-Kilgore-'55. Top is
gold- lower nickel-2 piece $100

37. Red Ranger Jr.- Wyandotte-
1950s. Unusual DC box. $35

38. Lone Rider-M.A Henry- '50s
Buzz Henry SS. Rare box. $50

39. Silver Colt - Silver Mustang
by Nichols. Pre-1950. $50 each

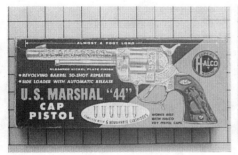

40. U.S. Marshal-L-H 1950s. A
Halco box-bullets. Rare. $65-85

41. Cowboy Classic-Hubley '50
Presentation box-gold gun. $75

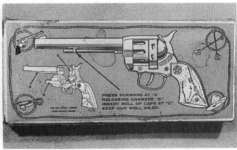

42. Cowboy-Hubley-'50s. Back
of box showing action. $45

43. Stallion/twin set by Nichols
$35 & Cowboy Jr- Hubley- $25

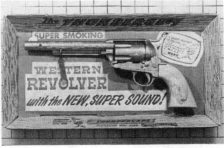

44. Thundergun-Marx-1955 era
display box. Rare. $65

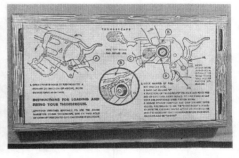

45.Thundergun-Back of display
shows loading of Thundercaps!

46. Marshal 6-7 Shot-L-H-Halco
Very rare 1955 era. $85

47. Marshal 6-7. Back of box
shows assembly & firing notes.

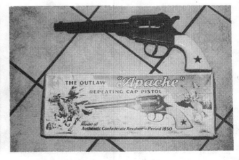

48. Apache-Lone Star-Eng. box.
Rarely seen die cast box. $25

49. Bronc-Schmidt-$75. Bronco Kilgore-$30. Buc-a-roo-Kilg.$55

50. Coyote-Hubley-1950s. $25

51. Hubley Pioneer-$25 & the Hubley Dagger Derringer. $35

52. Mustang 500-Nichols-1960. Front & back side of box . $65

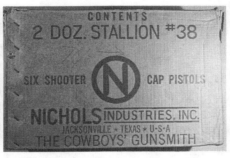

53. Nichols shipping carton '50 for Stallion .38s. Unusual $50

54. Stallion .38 & .32 Stallions-Nichols-1950 era. $25

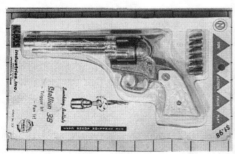

55. Stallion .38-Nichols-1950s. Display card. $1.98. $10 Card

56. Stallion .38-Nichols-1950s. Different box design. $25

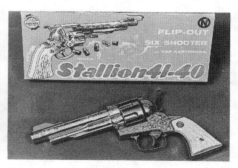

57. Stallion 41-40-Nichols-1958 Rare gun & box. $65

58. Stallion .45 MK II-Nichols-1950s Metallic silver lid. $100

59. Stallion .45 MK II-Nichols. Gold Tone G-45 gold gun.$300

60. Stallion .45 1950 era. 1st model Nichols. Rare box. $125

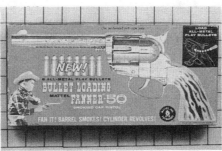

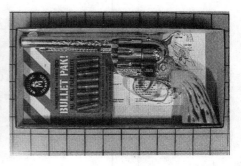

61. Fanner .45-Mattel-1960 era. Rare display frame-bullets. $85

62. Fanner 50-Mattel-1960 era. Revolving cylinder lid. $75

63. Fanner 50-Mattel. Interior of box in #62. Note bullet pack

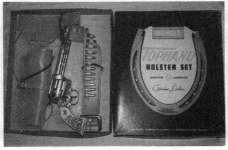

64. Fanner Shootin' Shell- 1960 Mattel. Cartridges & noses. $65

65. Tophand Set-Nichols-1960s Mustang 500 fast-draw $30 box

66.Stallion .45 MK II-Nichols-Steel-Blu. Kusan display. $35

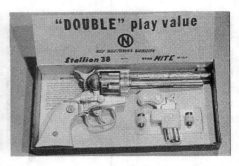

67.Ric-O-Shay-Hubley-1960s-Frame display with ammo. $25

68. Model 61-Nichols-Display. Kusan-Nashville, TN label. $35

69. Nichols Twin set display. A Stallion 38 & Dyna-Mite. $35

70. Texan Jr.-Hubley-Golden Jubileers. Twin set-rare. $45

71. L. Ranger- Fienburg-Henry Holster & gun box. Rare. $125

72. Lone Ranger - M.A. Henry Holster & gun set. Rare. $150

73. Cavalry Set-L-H Halco. Gun & holster set- 1961-65. $45

74. Champion-Kilgore. Timer-fast draw DC gun box. $25

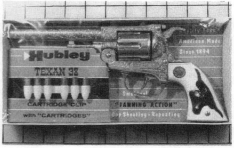

75. Texan .38-Hubley '50s box with acetate display cover. $25

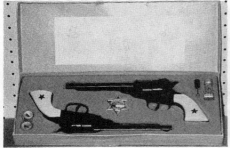

76. Apache .44 -BCM-Eng. A presentation set-red lined. $25

77. Rustler .45-Crescent- Eng. Large-full color. $65

78. Rustler .45-Crescent-Eng-Large-full color. $65

79. Range Rider MK II-Lone Star- Eng. Large-full color. $75

80. Range Rider Mk II-Lone Star- Eng. Large-full color. $75

81. Rustler .38-Crescent Toys-Eng. Full color box. $45

82. Rustler .38-Crescent Toys-Eng. Full color box. $45

83. Buntline Special-British Cast Metals-Eng. Rare box. $85

84. Byk-Olster-Western Ranger. Box for bicycle holsters. $20

85. Lasso 'em Bill set-Keyston B box for single holster. $75

86. Lasso 'em Bill set-Keyston B box for double set. Rare. $100

87. Early Keyston boxes. Note store labels-Lazarus - F. Schwarz

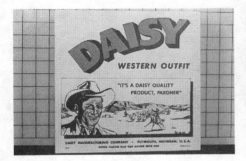

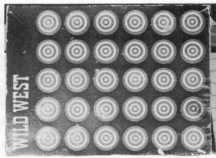

88. Western Holster set-Daisy-Plymouth, Mich. Rare. $65

89. Wild West- Large box for a holster set. No name. $25

90. Western-Style Holster set. Western Novelty-Chic. IL. $30

91. Lasso 'em Bill set-Keyston B Buffalo Bill sets. Boxes-$75 ea.

92. State Ranger holster set box 1950 era. R & S Toys-NYC $45

93. Texan Holster Box-Halco-1940s. $2.98 Early. Rare. $75

94. Dale Evans box. Full color. Rare 1955 set. Yankiboy. $300

95. Sharpshooters-Peg shooter box-Milton Bradley C0. $85

96. Red Indian Shooting game. Chad Valley-Eng. Full col. $125

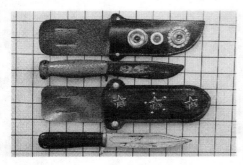

1. Keyston Bros. Superb leather sheath with rubber knives. $75

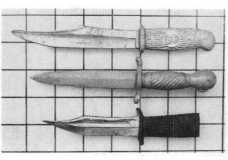

2. 3 Rubber Knives-1955-60 An Indian Scout on top. $15-35ea.

3. Rare Davy Crockett. Sheath fits on holster set. Rubber. $85

4. Hubley Bowie Knife. Vinyl with stag handle. 1960. $35

5. Detail: Hubley logo & name on the blade. Note stag handle.

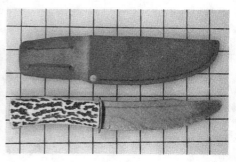

6. Mattel Buffalo Skinner-Buckskin sheath-stag handle. $75

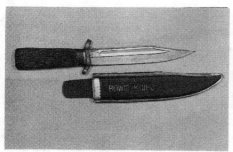

7. Esquire-Bowie knife - sheath-brown handle-rubber. $35

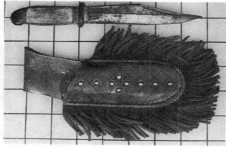

8. Arcor hunting knife-rubber-leather sheath-studs. $75

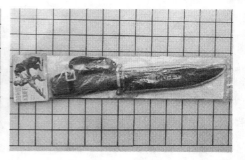

9. Bowie Knife-Elvin Co. Note bear & fighter. Packaged. $45

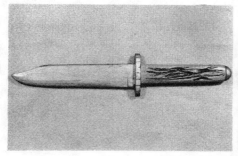

10. Bowie knife-stag handle of wood construction. $35

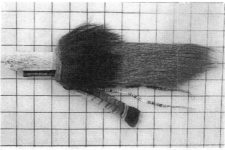

11. Indian-like sheath-fur-bead & feathers. Rubber knife. $75

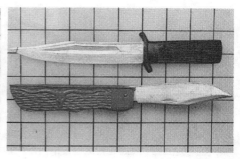

12. Arcor Bowie & folding pocket knives of rubber. $30 each

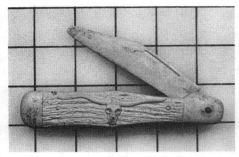

13. Folding Jack Knife-Auburn Rubber, IN. Yellow & silver. $50

14. Folding Jack Knife-Auburn Rubber, IN. Red & gold. $50

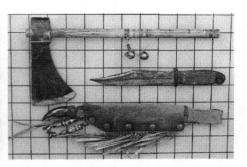

15. Wood tomahawk with bells rubber knife-fringe-beads $45ea

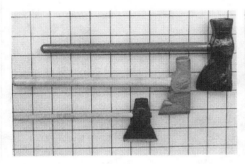

16. 3 rubber tomahawks. Black-red- Sun Rubber Co.OH. $45ea

17. Keys-Skillman Hardware,NJ & Jimilu Prod. Wash. DC. $65

18. Hickock Keys- L-H 1960 on original card. Large ring. $75

19. Maverick Canteen. Plastic-J. Gardner photo. $50 (Hakes Am.)

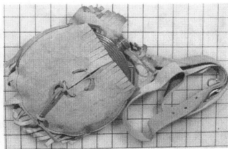

20. Plastic canteen in the suede leather pouch. Daisy 1960. $75

21. Marx plastic canteen with a strap and compass! Rare. $45

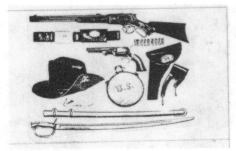

22. Marx 1961 C.W. Set. Sword $75. Plastic U.S. canteen-$65

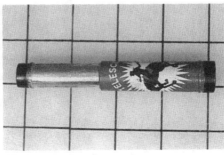

23. Pocket telescope. Works-has cowboy on bronc. Rare. $25

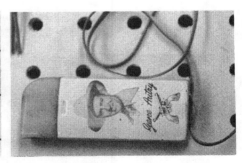

24.G.Autry flashlight & leather thong. Bantam Lite. Rare. $45

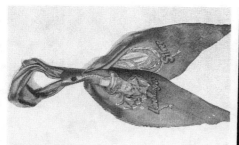

1. L. Ranger & Silver '55- Red-
Keyston B. jeweled slide. $85

2.H-Bar-O-Bobby Benson-1935-
Yellow-Rangers Club-$75 (Hakes)

3.Tom Mix-Purple-Brown-white
1930. Rare kerchief-$100 (Hakes)

4. Buck Jones & Silver-Very rare
Brwn-purple-W. '35 $175(Hakes)

5. Hopalong Cassidy-B&W has
metal steerhead slide. '50. $135

6. Hopalong Cassidy-Blue -'55
has metal steerhead slide. $135

7. Roy Rogers & Trigger-'55-Red
& black on yellow. $100

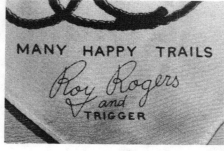

8. Detail of #7 Roy showing his
signature on the bottom.

9. Roy Rogers & Trigger-'55-Red
kerchief & white artwork. $100

10. Roy Rogers & Trigger-'60 in
Red-yellow-black. Slide. $125

11. Detail of rare slide on #10.
Note gun & signature. $45 ea.

12. Davy Crockett-'54-yellow &
brown. Keyston B. slide. $75

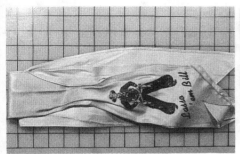

13. Lasso 'em Bill-1935. Yellow & black. Rare kerchief. $75

14. Blue & White check with a red & gold star. Kerchief. $35

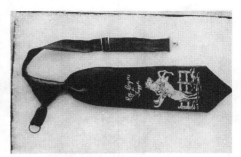

15. Roy Rogers & Trigger tie. '55 Red. Unusual. Rare. $75

16. Scalloped edge blue kerchief with metal slide. $35

17. Straight Arrow-1949-red-white-blue. Rare. $85 (Hakes Am.)

18. Ken Maynard 1930 era-Rare bandanna. $85 (Hakes Am.)

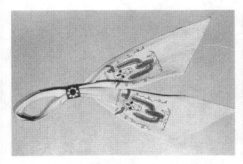

19. Steerhead-red jewel eyes. A Keyston B. studed slide. $75

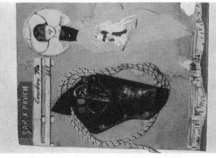

20. Bar X Ranch red kerchief-cowboy-leather slide. '45. $55

21. Riegel, NY-Pony Exp. Glove & Ker. Set. Invisible Note! $85

22. Keyston- Indian bandanna in red-yellow-black. Rare. $55

23. Keyston B.-Cowgirl bandanna. Unusual artwork. $55

24. Keyston B.-Square Dancers. Oval cowboy on holsters. $55

1.Hopalong Cassidy boots with original box. Acme $225 Boxed

2. G. Autry -Servus Rubber Co. Boots in original box. $175

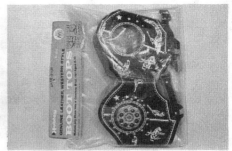

3. Hubley Booters-shoe top-'60. Black-jewels-studs-Pack. $100

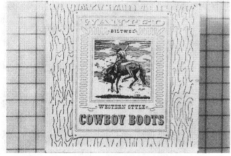

4. Bilt-Well box for kid's western boots. See #5. Note artwork

5. Bilt-Well black & white pair of cowboy boots. $150 Boxed

6. L-H booters for shoe tops. A cowgirl set in red-white. $85

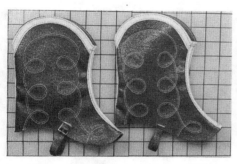

7. Hubley Booters-tan & brown with orange-green stitches. $75

8. Box for a pair of Roy Rogers socks. Roy art work. Rare. $65

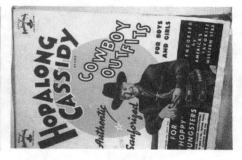

9. H. Iskin Co-Hoppy box for a cowboy outfit. $125 Box only.

10. Roy Rogers 8" leather boots with art. Early 1950s. $200

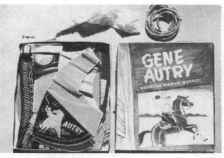

11. G. Autry Ranch outfit. Box-vest-chaps-kerch.-rope-$450 set

12. Pla-Master Annie Oakley boxed cowgirl outfit. $350 set.

1. 1920 era cast iron handcuffs. Unmarked. Seldom seen. $50

2.Early cuffs: JP Co., NY- Marks B. Ma.- Gardner, Ma.- Unm.$50

3.Early CI & steel cuffs Gardner Screw Co. Gardner, MA-Pol $50

4. 1950 Hale-Nass Co, NY cuffs on card- cowboy art. Steel. $45

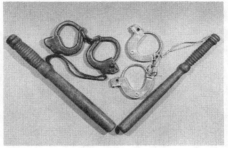

5. Lawman Billy clubs & cuffs. Wood-CI & tin. Clubs $25 each

6. Keyston B. bicycle saddlebag with tooling & conchos. $150

7. Kit Carson color set. Like a tooled leather saddle bag. $75

8. Davy Crockett bike dispatch bag. 7" X 8". $75   (Hakes Amer.)

9. Wagon Train bike saddle in blk. & red leather.-conchos.$85

10. Bob Steele western branding iron set. Uses letters. $175

11. Knox-Reese-Roy-R. Ranch-branding iron set. Rare. $200

12. Cavalry Flag for 101st Cav.-Rin-Tin-Tin item. Yel-Blu. $75

1. Roy Rogers-Plus Brand.-Black with B&W band. Laced. $125

2. Red with silver lacing & star. White neck cord. $35

3. Matt Dillon-Arlington Hat Co. Black/fabric label. $85

4. Roy Rogers-Plus Brand-Tan with beaded band. $150

5. Pla-Master- Red with white decoration & edging. $50

6. Roy R. Quick-Shooter- Black-B&W band & gun. Ideal. $200

7. Superb Hoppy! Black- B&W band-B-W & red pin. $350

8. Detail of #7 band & Hoppy pin on band. Outstanding hat!

9. Detail #7 interior label for Bailey of Hollywood. Sheriff.

10. Bat Masterson-black derby & cane. Carnell-Brooklyn. $125

11. Straw- Black trim. Printed B & W Desperado. $35

12. Roy R. Black. Red & gold trim. B&W band. Plus B. $130

13. Roy R. Red- B/W& red bead band. White lace. Plus B. $135

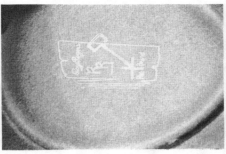

14. Detail of #13 showing Plus Brand logo. Made many hats.

15. Cream straw-white trim-red & green western art. $65

16. Black-red & gold trim--with silver studs. Arlington Hat. $65

17. Yellow-tan has brown band & silver stars-red keeper. $100

18. Rare Hubley autograph hat. White vinyl-plaid string. $150

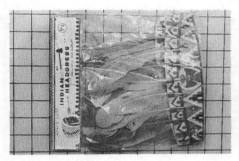

19. Packaged Indian Chief set-beads & feathers. Coronet. $45

20. Dale Evans blk. hat. Queen of the West. $125   (Hakes Amer.)

21. Gene Autry braces. Carded with Sheriff's badge. $185

22. Roy R. belt & gold-red 3-D buckle-pearl grips.Tooled. $200

23. A. Oakley & Davy Crockett belts on cards. Rare. $75 - $65

24. Gene Autry belt. Carded & Sheriff's badge. $200

1.Lasso 'em Bill- Key. B. Red & white leather vest. Studs $85

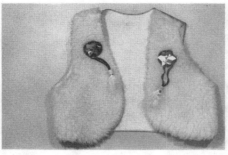

2. Natural Sheepskin vest with silver stars. Cowgirl vest. $85

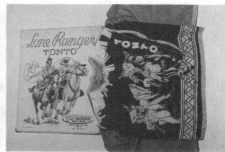

3.Tonto outfit. Full-color top & tan pants. Pla-master Rare $165

4.Cowgirl set-Keyston B-Yellow with brown trim-fringe. $135

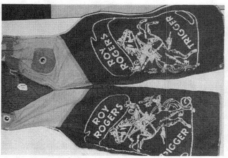

5. A. Oakley dress-skirt-vest. In yellow-red- full color-rare $200

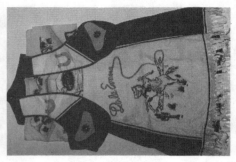

6. Dale Evans-top-skirt & vest by Yankee B Yelw-blk-red. $300

7. G. Autry-Keyston B.--Red & black leather. Studs. Rare $425

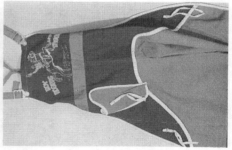

8. Roy Rogers fabric chaps. Tan-brown-white-red. $125

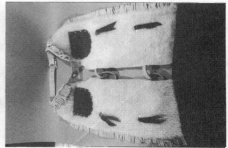

9. Roy Rogers fabric overalls set in black & red. Holster. $100

10. G. Autry. Chaps & vest-red-blue-yellow. Great art! $550

11. Superb Keyston B. Leather vest-chaps-Red & W. Stars.$225

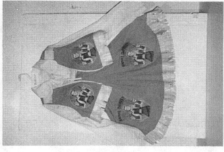

12. Wooly chaps! Tan & brown leather trim. Super! $100

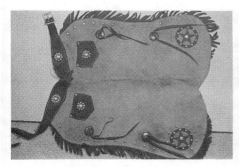

13. Super chaps in russet with black fringe-trim by Texian $85

14. Buckskin chaps with brown trim & silver conchos. $65

15. Wooly chaps with tan trim. Silver star conchos. $125

16. G. Autry shirt-Gray & black Gold. Calif. Ranchwear. $125

17. B&W western shirt. Walls-Texas. Silver gun buttons. $85

18. B & Tan shirt with embroidered western figures. $85

19. Sgt. Preston set. Pla-master-Iskin Co. Red-Blue. Rare. $325

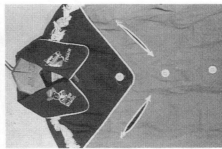

20. Roy Rogers shirt by Rob Roy in Black-white-red. $125

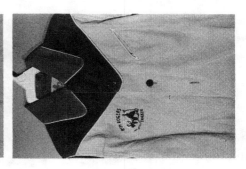

21. Roy Rogers shirt by Rob Roy in white & purple. $125

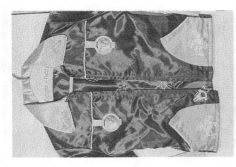

22. Pistol Pete jacket by Impreg-nole 1943. Red & Black. $135

23. Detail #22-note the two gun pistol Pete zipper & conchos.

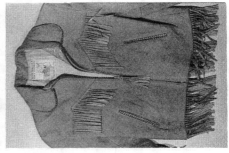

24. Superb, Roy Rogers suede leather jacket with fringe! $350

1. Early sheet caps: Boot-er-oo-Kilgore-National-Andes. $20 ea.

2. Early sheet, Super Mammoth caps. Kilgore Mfg. Co. $20

3. Sheets & roll. National-Acme & Kilgore. $10-15.

4. Repeating Cane & Pistol caps National Fireworks. $15

5. Blanks, sheet books & rolls. Pressman-Nichols-UnXld. $15

6. Rolls & round caps. Kilgore-Kent-Marx Stevens-Hubley $10

7. Yan-kee Boy-St Louis Super! Sheets. Rare. $20-30

8. Rolls & Caps. Nichols-Acme-Western-Clipper-Crescent. $20

9. Caps & Paper. Kilgore-Buddy L-Paper Buster-Jatina Mfg. $10

10. Young Buffalo Bill 1,500 shots! Cherry rolls. $5-10

11. Blank cartridges for Kenton & other blank shooters. $35

12. Kenton Blanks. Note that the gun is on the box. Rare $75

13. Counter display box. 8"X8" Cowboy Caps-60 packs. $25

14. Counter display box. 6"X7" Action Caps-Stevens 60 Bx. $20

15. Counter display box. 5"X7" Super Nu-Matic Paper rolls. $15

16. Counter display box. 6"X7" Bang-Kilgore. 60 boxes. $25

17. Counter display box-6"X13" Early Backes-Hot Spot caps $35

18. Counter display box-6"X10" Shur-Fire-Stevens. $20

19. Nichols counter display boxes for .45 & .38 clips. $15ea

20. Counter display box-6"X10" Cowboy roll caps. $30

21. Counter display box-5"X10" Nichols Ind. Round caps. $25

22. Counter display box-6"X10" Acme Brand caps. $20

23. Counter display box-7"X13" Nichols-Fury roll caps. $35

24. Counter display box- 6"X8" Acme-Mammoth disc caps. $25

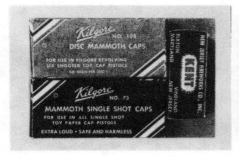

25. Kilgore -No. 108 & No. 75.
Kent, Vineland, NJ. caps-$10 ea

26.Counter display boxes for
Hubley & Nichols bul.clips.$25

27.Counter display box-5"X10"
Nichols Stallion rnd. caps. $20

28. Bullets & caps. Mattel-Fury-
Nichols Stallion-Hubley. $5-15

29.50 roll box-2500 shots-Bang
Kilgore & Jatina Ranger. $15 ea

30.Roll caps-Herbie-Halco-Stars
Campbell-Daisy-Kusan O. $5 ea

31. Exploding corks-Depyfag in
box. Foreign. Unusual. $25

32. Hubley display boxes-Bullet
clips-.38 & .45. $25 each. Box

33. Display box- Nichols .32 &
.38 bullet clips. $25 Box

34.Contents of #33 Nichols .32
& .38 clips of 6 bullets. $20/clp

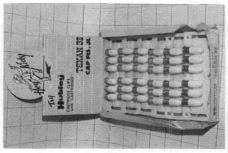

35. Contents #32 Hubley clips
for .38. Clip of 6 bullets.$35 ea

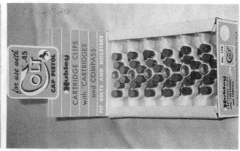

36. Contents #32 Hubley clips
for .45 & compass. 6 bul.$75 ea

37.Hubley bubble pack-Colt 45 clip of 6 bullets & compass $85

38. Stallion 45 Display box $25 Clip with 6 bullets. $65

39. Nichols bullet packs. Plastic 38-45 & Early 6-45 box. $30-65

40. Nichols belt bullet clips for 45 Stallion-$65 32 Stallion-$30

41. Detail of Hubley belt clip for Colt .45 with compass. $75

42.Hubley shells for the Dagger Derringer & Rem .36. $35 Card

43. Mattel counter display box for Shootin' Shells. $30

44. Mattel Bullets-8-Pak $15 & 3 SS cartridges & 30 noses $30

45. Nichols Stallion early box of 6-.45. $65 Target peas! $10

46.Nichols Firing shell kit- Rare Note different caps. $50 ea. pak

47. Unusual & rare bag of corks for a Daisy double barrel. $20

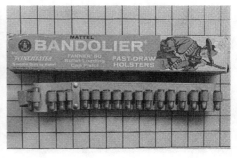

48.Mattel bandolier-tan leather has 32 metal bulls.$100 Boxed

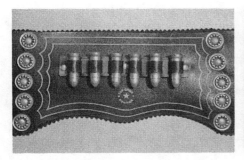

49. Typical gun belt bullet loops for plastic shells. Esquire Co.

50. Rare package of smoke for the P.E.C. Frontier Smoker. $25

51. Unusual patriotic card of 2 darts. Ohio Art Co. Rare. $10

52. Unusal head-stamp. Harvel-Kilgore metal bulls-H-K gunbelt

53. LECO-U.S.A. head-stamp on both silver & gold bullets.

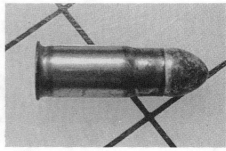

54. Mattel metal play bullets for Mattel guns. Super brass & lead

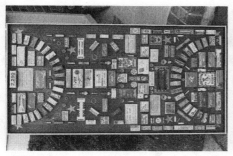

55. Large 24" X 48" display case for caps, bullets & ammunition

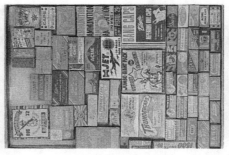

56. Smaller 12" X 18" display case for various boxes of caps.

57. Wow! 16 bullets on this Roy Rogers double set by Classy.

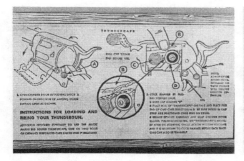

58. Loading instruction for the Marx Thundergun. 2 rolls caps.

59. Lone Ranger Ball pen set & belt. Similar silver bullets. $100

60. Instructions for metal shells in a G. Autry L-H 44 cylinder.

1. Nickel steerhead. L-H Gene Autry set 1950 era.

2. Nickel steerhead & fence on an early leather set. 1940 era.

3. Beautiful-nickel with pearl horns & background. Cowgirl.

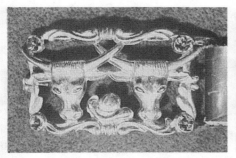

4. Double steerheads & hat. Nickel. Unknown maker,

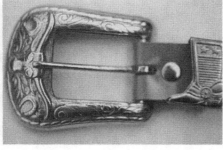

5.Steerhead & boot on Hubley Cowboy set. Nickel. 1950-60.

6.Three steerheads. Pearl horns on large one. Nickel. Unknown

7.Gold steerhead buckel. 1955-60. Engraved. Halco holster.

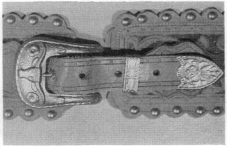

8. Steerhead & flowers. Nickel Hubley double holster set.

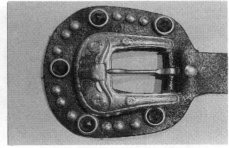

9. Steerhead-Nickel. Leather on back with jewels. Roy by Classy

10.Steerhead-horse-thunderbird -saddle. Nic. Maverick-Esquire.

11.Unusual steerhead & flowers. Nickel. Esquire-Pony Boy.

12. Gold steerhead & flowers on a Trackdown set by Classy.

13. Beautiful Keyston Bros-with dark metal & silver horse/rider

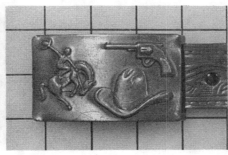

14. Nickel-Bronco-hat & gun. A Halco holster set. Late 1940s.

15. Bronco-horseshoes-fence & cowboys. Large nickel. Halco.

16. Large, very heavy. Silver & gold bronco. Jewels. S Bar M

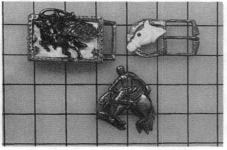

17. Small buckles. Zorro-gold & pearl. Plastic horsehead. Bronc.

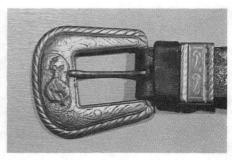

18 Early-Pre '40- Bucking bronc nickle with engraving.

19. Money buckle! Calf roper & cowboy. Early style. No name.

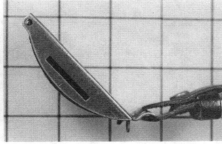

20. Detail of top of #19. Note the slot for coins! Unusual-rare.

21. Detail #19 shows buckle opened to reveal internal bank.

22. Large nickel buckle with a cowboy-horse & floral design.

23.Small buckle has exceptional detail of bull dogger! Rare.

24. Steerhead-guns-hats-flowers stars-horseshoes. Nickel Esquire

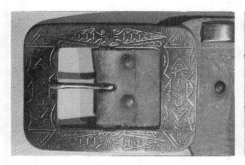

25. Large nickel buckle with geometric Indian art-Keyston B

26. Simple nickel buckle with a Daisy Bullseye Logo. 1958-62

27. Large buckle-nickel. Flower & scroll engraved. Early Halco.

28. Superb nickel buckle with engraved designs. Keyston Bros

29. Early nickle buckle has geometric art. Early Sears holster.

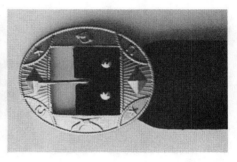

30. Guns-stars-rope-etc. Esquire Wells Fargo holster set. Nickel.

31. Indian-horse-gun-steer-stars Esquire-Nickle-Gunsmoke set.

32. Cowboy-Indian & Pony on Esquire holster set. Early style.

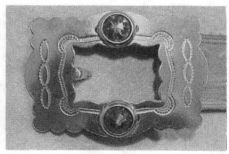

33. Large nickel with engraved art & two red jewels. Halco set

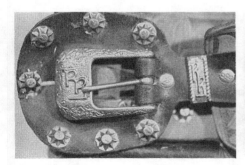

34. Roy R. nickel-engraved-RR keeper-silver flower stud-Classy

35. Mattel-Shootin' Shell Buckle has Remington Derringer. Card

36. Mattel Buckle similar to #36 but in presentation box. 1960.

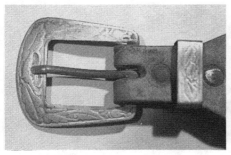

37. Simple floral scrolls on an early nickel buckle. Keyston Br.

38. Hubley Sheriff- Jailer's key shooting buckle. Unusual.

39. Rin-Tin-Tin & Rusty in Nik-yellow & blue. Esquire-Actoy.

40. Roy Rogers-large nickel has image & horse shoe. Classy set.

41. Nickel-red & black Lone Ranger buckle. Esquire set.

42. Nickel & black-Pony Boy with pony medallion. Esquire.

43. Roy R. Holster buckle-Scroll & RR on keeper & end. Classy.

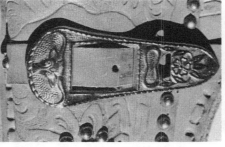

44. Holster buckle-nickel-steer-head & flower. Wagon Train set

45. Holster buckle. nickel horse shoe shape. Hubley-Halco set.

46. Holster belt decorative con-cho. Nickel running horse.

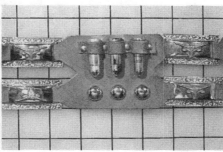

47. Adjustable belt buckles. In gold & silver. Metallic G. Autry

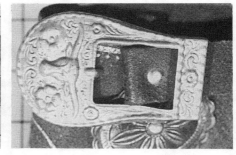

48. Steerhead-flowers & scrolls on a Wyatt Earp set. Esquire.

1. Folk art interpretation of a steer. Unusual holster top.

2. Hoppy gun belt with Bar-20 Ranch and silver steerhead.

3. Beautifully tooled Longhorn & floral carving. Hubley-Halco.

4. Embossed steerhead, jewels, studs and silver conchos. Halco

5. Cowgirl set- B&W tooled has jewels-studs-buckle-May be L-H

6. Tooled- Tan & Blk. has silver concho & fringe. Hubley-Halco

7. Tooled floral design-has silver concho-jewels-studs. Keyston B

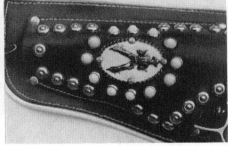

8. Large oval is pearl with 3-D blk. cowboy-silver studs. Key. B

9. Unusual metal front-cowboy & horse-silver studs. Keyston B

10. Buckin' Bronc silver medallions & star studs. Keyston B. ?

11. Detail of a silver Buckin' Bronc medallion.

12. Large silver horse medallion on a horse shoe. L-H. 1950

13. Embossed horse. Jewel eyes. Stud briddle-cut mane. Key. B.

14. 3-D silver horse head. Studs & Saddle King of Texas stamp.

15. Silver horsehead with two rope loops-jewels-studs-fringe.

16. Pony medallion. Scalloped edge cut-out. Tiny studs. Esq.

17. Printed Restless Gun art in silver with studs. Esquire Nov.

18. Lone Ranger-embossed art-Hi-Yo-Silver-jewels. M.A. Henry

19. Colt 45 & Colt logo printed in gold on black. Hubley 1960

20. Embossed Gene Autry and Flying "A" Ranch logo. L-H '55

21. WW II patriotic American-God Bless America-U.S. shield.

22.Embossed bust of Cheyenne on holster top. Daisy set. 1959

23. JC Higgins-Sears stamped back of 1950 era leather holster

24. Boyville Steerhide stamp on back of 1951 Sears holster.

25. John Wayne's likeness was embossed in holster front. Rare

26. Unusual 6-point star with a cowboy in the center. Silver.

27. Silver concho with crossed six guns & horse shoe.

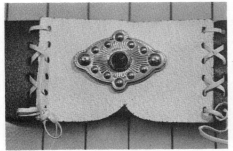

28. Adjustable section of a gun belt with silver concho & jewel

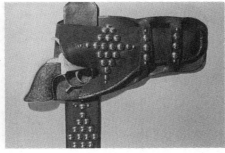

29. Rare pattern of silver studs on holster and gun belt.

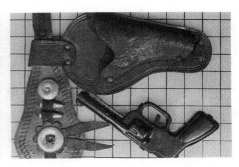

30. Unusual belt shape-border stamping-silver conchos. Early.

31. Gene Autry metallic-floral-plastic holster front. Rare set.

32. Large silver concho showing Connestoga wagon. Hubley set

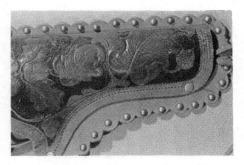

33. Scalloped edge-oak leaf-nut tooling. Superb! Hubley 1950s.

34. Detail of oak leaf-nut tooling on belt of #33. Hubley set.

35. Tinted horsehead-oak leaves tooling-basketweave. Hubley

36. Texas Ranger-multi color jewels & studs. Tooled- L-H ?

37. Beautiful tooled floral scroll design on double holster. R & S

38. Tooled flowers & embossed lettering- The Texan. Halco

39. Deeply tooled with 2 colors & gold lettering. Esquire Nov.

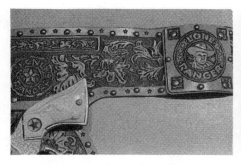

40. Embossed designs in Neolite for L. Ranger set-tan. BarashCo

41. Embossed pony in 2 colors with studs & jewels. Esquire N.

42. Floral tooled Roy R. with many jewels & studs. Classy P.

43. Embossed Roy R. in metallic silver-studs-jewels. Classy Prod.

44. Embossed Roy R.- leather with many RR studs. Classy P.

45. Superb cast Roy R. silver RR concho for holster. Classy P.

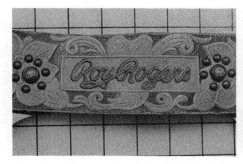

46. Embossed flowers & Roy R. name in 3 colors. Rodeo King

47. Embossed Roy Rogers & a silver steerhead. Halco-1950

48. Unbelievable RR conchos & studs. Note all RRs. Classy P

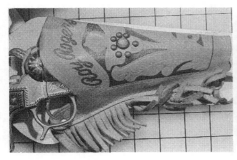

49.Floral tooling & Roy R.-with jewel-studs. See #46. Rodeo K.

50. Gun belt buckle for superb Roy Rogers-Trigger set. Classy P

51. Typical raised "RR" studs found on many Roy Rogers sets

52. Roy Rogers on holster strap & "RR" on snap. G. Schmidt

53. Embossed Roy Rogers on a metallic foil holster front.

54.Roy on an early narrow belt with steerhead & studs. L-H

55. Floral design & Roy's name on a metallic foil holster-Classy

56. Unusual shape buckle on a Roy set. Note the "RR" details.

57. Unusual star detail on this cowgirl set in blue & silver.

58. Horsehead-horse shoe cut-out-fringe-tooling. Betty Leach

59 Unusual trim-cut-outs-white fringe-gold conchos-studs. Esq.

60.Nichols-Crazy 8 money belt has secret $-pocket & derringer.

1.Deep floral engraving behind cylinder. Kilgore Sharpshooter.

2. Leaf engraving on the barrel & frame of a Stevens Bango.

3. Leaf & border engraving on a Stevens Big Scout

4. Scroll & flower engraving on a Stevens 49-er.

5. Scroll & buck engraving on a Kilgore American 2nd Model.

6. Simple scrolls on a Kenton Bulls Eye in dark finish.

7.Nearly identical to #6 is Gene Autry engraved gun by Kenton

8. Early Hubley Texan, Jr. has nice scrolls. Dummy -Colt logo

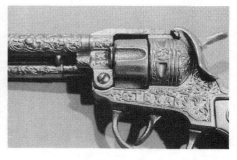

9.Heavy scrolls on barrel-frame of early Hubley Texan. Classic.

10. Kilgore 1st model Bronco DC - Bucking Horse on frame.

11.Simple scrolls - Wyandotte Hoppy. Note "Y&•" logo.

12. Deep scrolls-stippled background. 44 Lesie-Henry Texas R

13. Raised scrolls on frame of a L-H DC Roy Rogers.

14. Incised scrolls on the frame of a L-H DC Wyatt Earp.

15. Unusual scrolls & brands with stippled frame-Stevens DC

16.Nice scrolls-borders-stippled background. Lone Star-Eng-Roy

17. Beautiful scrolls on Hubley DC Texan Jr. in antique bronze

18. Scrolls & name on Hubley DC Pioneer-Note early compass

19.Late Hubley DC Texan Jr. in A. bronze. Superb engraving!

20. Simple scrolls on Halco-L-H Texas Ranger DC.

21. Unusual scrolls & longhorn on Crescent Toys, Eng.-Rustler.

22. Fine scroll & stippling on a Halco Marshal DC.

23. Detailed flowers & scrolls on Classy No name DC model.

24. Unusual tiny scrolls on a rare G.Schmidt Maverick DC.

25. Very fine scroll engraving on a Hubley DC Texan .38.

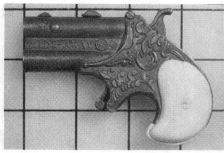

26. Beautiful floral scrolls on a Hide-Away derringer by Actoy.

27.Deep relief scrolls-horse and steerhead grips.-L-H Maverick.

28. Fine quality scrolls on a DC Nichols 41-40 Stallion.

29. Exceptional relief. Note the acorns on barrel-Hubley-Drngr.

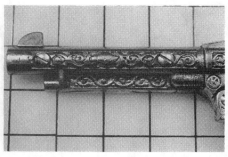

30. Scrolls & buffalo on barrel of a Kilgore CI American.

31. Floral scrolls on the barrel of a Stevens CI 49-er.

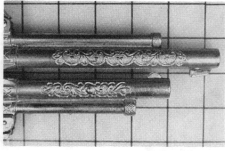

32. Scrolls on the barrels of L-H long & short barrel varieties.

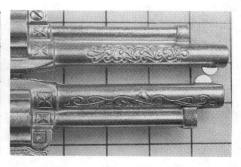

33. L-H barrel scrolls for early model (lower) & later (top).

34. Simple scrolls on Actoy DC L. Rangers. Note stag varieties.

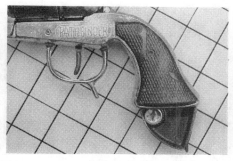

35. Engraved copper grips with checkering. Schmidt-Pathfinder

36. Very fine raised scrolls on a Plainsman by C. Lawyer Co.

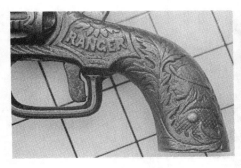

1. Folk art scroll & cowboy cast into grips. Stevens Ranger 1880

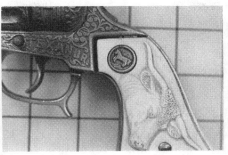

2. Very familiar Hubley ivory-style steerhead grips. Colt logo.

3. Superb imitation pearl insert grips on early Mordt. 1930 era.

4. Black HI-YO SILVER & Rider grips on Kilgore L. Ranger-1940

5. Imitation pearl with rearing horse-Kenton Autry - 6 Shooter

6. Rare Patriotic U.S.A. & Eagle on WW II Bango white grips.

7. All metal cast grips with logo & checkering-Kilgore-6 Shooter

8. Superb ivory-style, diving eagle on Kilgore American.

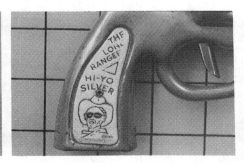

9. Rare inset celluloid has Lone Ranger art-Marx tin clicker- '38

10. Rearing Horse. Many colors on a Kilgore Six Shooter. 1940s

11. Early white horsehead grip on Stevens Bango. 1938 era.

12. Later white horsehead with jewel. Stevens Bango. 1940s.

13. Detail of early Hubley CI Cowboy with Colt oval logo.

14. Indian Chief on white grips of Stevens Big Chief DC. Super!

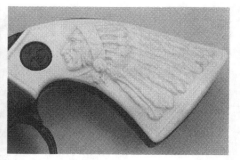

15. Fantastic Indian Chief on a BCM Buntline & Lone Star Roy.

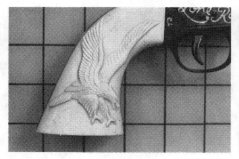

16. Beautiful screaming eagles from a Marx Lone Ranger gun.

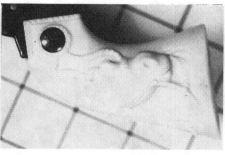

17. Horsehead & rope from a Marx plastic clicker pistol.

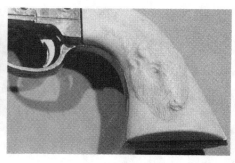

18. Fantastic ivory-like Buffalo head on a Marx Thundergun!

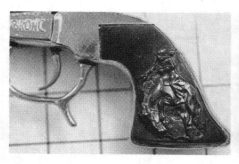

19. Rare Schmidt Buck'n Bronc black on black from gold guns.

20. Horsehead grip with square hole screws. L-H Can. Hickok.

21. Black horsehead on L-H 44 gold Gene Autry. L-H oval.

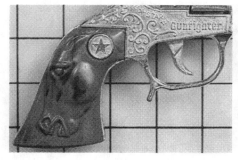

22. Super red-black swirl horsehead on Lone Star Gunfighter.

23. Rare L-H Steerhead oval has square hole screw. W. Earp gun

24. Fantastic metallic scroll grip from Classy. Gold-pewter-brass

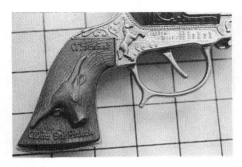

25. Copper grips W.B. Hickok & steerhead. L-H Pop-up cap box.

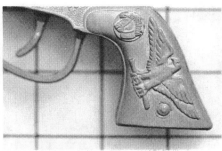

26. All metal Actoy eagle grips from Korean war era-Pony logo

27. Detail of transparent Kusan grips of Nichols circle "N" logo

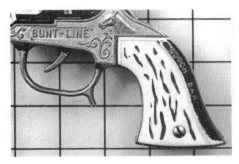

28. Unusual Notch Bar stag grip on a Lone Star Bunt-Line gun.

29. Timer mechanism on the Kilgore Champion Fast Draw.

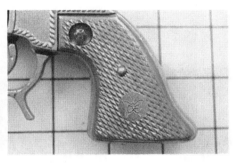

30. Schmidt copper. Dale Evans DE butterfly logo & jewel. Rare.

31. Schmidt copper. Roy Rogers "RR" logo & jewel. Rare grip.

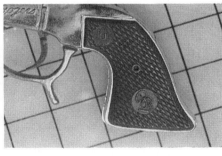

32. Schmidt copper. Roy Rogers & Trigger logo at top.. RR also.

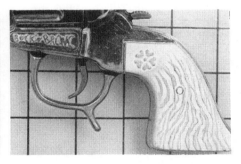

33. Schmidt painted white-tan stag on Buck'n Bronc. Rare.

34. Frame detail of standard Colt .45. & Colt logo. Hubley.

35. Extremely rare Texan .45 & Hubley Logo. Anniversary gun.

36. Frame detail of standard Model 1860 Cal. 44. Hubley.

1. Display card has Gene's signature. Kenton-1938-Rare $750

2. Appollo Theater promotion-Maine '39- G. Autry. Rare $850

3. Counter display-1929 -Fox double barrel shotgun. $200

4. Leslie-Henry Gene Autry .44 counter display-1955 Rare $400

5. Roy Rogers display for Geo. Schmidt guns. 1955 Rare $500

6. Roy Rogers display - Kilgore DC guns. 1950-55. Rare $500

7. Hubley store display board. 1960 era. 5 guns in gold. $125

8. Hubley store display rack '55 is wall hung for sales. $135

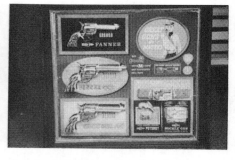

9. Mattel store display-1960 era has guns & Buckles. Rare $350

10. Nichols store display for a counter. 3 gun model. $100

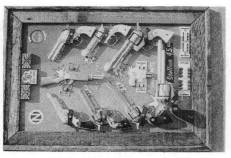

11. Nichols display board for 9 guns, caps & bullets-1960 $200

12. Nichols display board for 7 guns & bullets-1958 $175

13. Nichols-Halco presentation boards for sales. Rare-'61- $350

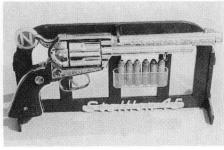

14. Nichols plastic counter display for Stallion 45 MK II $200

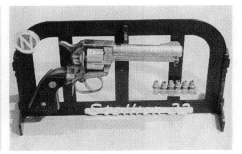

15. Nichols plastic counter display for Stallion 32. $165

16.Mattel counter display for 4 rifle models. Cardboard. $200

17. Window poster for Kenton CI Gene Autry 1940 era. $150

18. Large poster for Gene Autry Kenton guns '40. Signed. $400

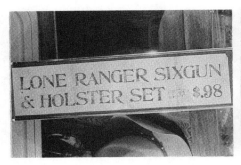

19. Poster for Lone Ranger set. '40. Same source as #18. $200

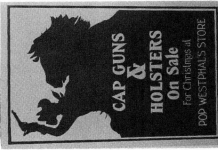

20.Recreation-Christmas poster for cap guns & holsters. $75

21. 1954 calendar-18 X 24 has two buckeroos & TV. $85

22. Owner ID paper under grip of Gene Autry Kenton CI. 1949

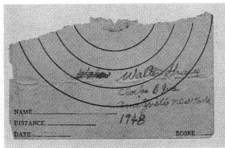

23. Owner ID paper under grip of CI Hubley Texan. 1948

24.Owner ID library card under grip of Nichols Stallion 45- '50

1.Stallion 45-1st model with a library card found under grip.

2. Hubley DC Cowboy with the owner's name engraved on top.

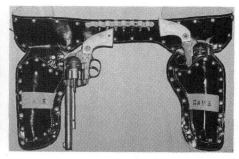

3. Pair of Hubley holsters with owner's name in metal letters.

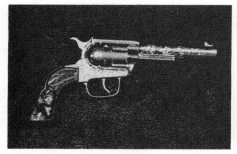

4.Texan Jr.-50th Anniv.'91 gold Com. Classic & Parris Mfg. $50

5. Hopalong Cassidy-Topper. A rocking horse-Rich Toys. $450

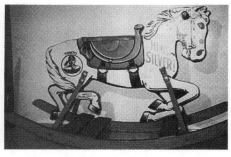

6. Lone Ranger-Silver rocking horse. 1940. $350

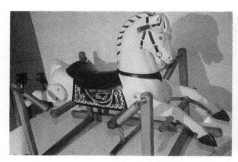

7. Davy Crockett rocking horse 1954-55 Rich Toys. $250

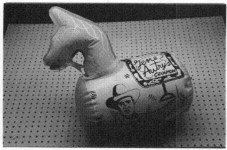

8. G. Autry-Champion air-filled horse-Plastikaire Prod, NY $185

9. Detail of Schmidt Cowhand with rare dummy hammer.

10. Detail of Kenton - G. Autry rare short barrel dummy gun.

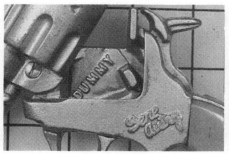

11.Kenton G. Autry long barrel dummy has scalloped hammer.

12. Rare Hubley DC Cowboy with a dummy hammer.

1.Various lawman badges. Vary $15-35-Cattleman-W. Earp $50

2. RCMP Mountie badges. Rare $35-50. Center badge $85

3.Various lawman badges. Vary $30-50. Annie Oakley pin $45

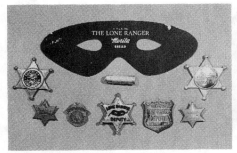

4. Lone Ranger badges & mask. $25-75 -Chief Scout badge$200

5.Various lawman badges. Vary $30-50. Ponderosa badge $65

6.Various lawman badges. Vary $20-50. Wild Bill & Jingles $85

7.Various lawman badges. Vary $25-65. Police shld- G-Man$75

8. Rare G. Autry Deputy Sheriff 12 points (Smilo & Sons) $100

9. Gene Autry ring. Very rare Buckaroo accessory. $150

10.Gene Autry tie clasp. This is a seldom seen accessory. $85

11.Gene Autry Deputy-Champ Crackshot Cowboy- Rare $175

12. Hoppy buckle-$85. Badges- $35-75. Lone Star rare (Rt. top)

13.L. Ranger-Deputy has secret comp.'49-$100. C. Scout $200

14.Roy R-Deputy-whistle-secret comp.'50-$100. Small Dep-$50

15.Badges & pins. Various Lawman. $20-$85. (Repros exist.)

16.Tom Mix-Decoder '41-$125. Dobie County- siren '46 -$100

17. T. Mix Rings- Magnet-Strat. Shooter-Initial-Look Arnd. $85

18. Roy R. Rings-Branding Iron & Microscope-1948-49-$85-100

19. L. Ranger Safety C. Merita & Harris-Boyer Bread. $50 each

20.L. Ranger silver bullet Pencil sharpener & Secret comp. $75

21. T. Mix Wrangler & Straight Shooter badges-1938. $125-$75

22.Gabby Hayes Cannon-$145 & Roy R.saddle ring-$185-1950

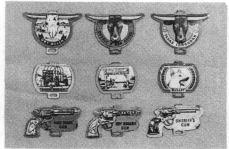

23. Roy R. tin medals-27 varieties. Full color 1954. $15 ea.

24. Hoppy badge display-Lone Star 10" X 15" 1955 Card $125

KENTON'S
NEW ENGRAVED
Gene Autry
REPEATER CAP PISTOLS

GENE AUTRY Sr.

NO. 60

The cap pistol with the outstanding reputation. Just ask any youngster—they all know this model. It is an engraved scale model of Gene Autry's own six shooter. Nickel plated finish with brilliant red plastic grips. Gene Autry's script signature engraved on each grip. 9" long. Each pistol packed in an attractive three-color display box, showing a large photograph of Gene Autry. Packed ¼ gross per shipping carton. Carton weight 37 lbs.

No. 60-C Gene Autry Sr. Same as No. 60, except in imitation gun metal finish with ivory plastic grips. Gene Autry's script signature engraved on each grip.

NO. 55
GENE AUTRY Jr.

The Junior model of the regular Gene Autry pistol in a lower price range. Nickel plated finish with brilliant red plastic grips. Gene Autry's script signature engraved on each grip. This pistol has break action and appeal for every youngster. 7¼" long. Each packed in an attractive three color display box. Packed ½ gross per shipping carton. Carton weight 53 lbs.

No. 55-C Gene Autry Jr. Same as No. 55 except in imitation gun metal finish with ivory plastic grips. Gene Autry's script signature engraved on each grip.

REPEATER CAP PISTOLS
WESTERN TYPE REPEATING CAP PISTOLS

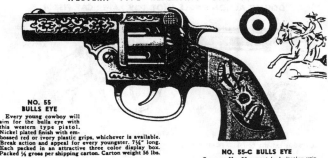

NO. 55
BULLS EYE
Every young cowboy will aim for the bulls eye with this western type pistol. Nickel plated finish with embossed red or ivory plastic grips, whichever is available. Break action and appeal for every youngster. 7¼" long. Each packed ½ gross per shipping carton. Carton weight 56 lbs.

NO. 55-C BULLS EYE
Same as No. 55 except in imitation gun metal finish with embossed ivory plastic grips.

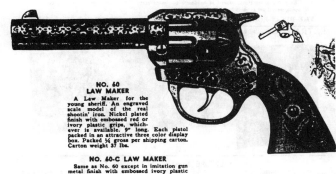

NO. 60
LAW MAKER
A Law Maker for the young sheriff. An engraved scale model of the real shootin' iron. Nickel plated finish with embossed red or ivory plastic grips, whichever is available. 9" long. Each pistol packed in an attractive three color display box. Packed ¼ gross per shipping carton. Carton weight 37 lbs.

NO. 60-C LAW MAKER
Same as No. 60 except in imitation gun metal finish with embossed ivory plastic grips.

Kilgore TOY CAP PISTOLS
ROY ROGERS SHOOTIN' IRONS

NO. 77 ROY ROGERS SIX-SHOOTER

A realistic western six-shooter type toy cap pistol. Entire cylinder revolves as each cap is fired . . . six shots to a loading. The only genuine six-shooter type cap pistol endorsed by a "Western Star". "Swing-out" cylinder for easy loading. Barrel is engraved with authentic ranch brands, additional decorative engraving on sides of gun. Sturdy, pearl plastic grip is embossed with head of "Trigger." An official Roy Rogers Shootin' Iron . . . look for his signature above the trigger guard.

ACTUAL SIZE

NO. 108 DISC MAMMOTH CAPS
Realistic six shots per disc. Contain special lubricant to make pistol work easier, last longer. Larger and louder than repeating caps.

SPECIFICATIONS

No.	Length Overall	Quantity Per Case	Weight Per Case	Price Per Doz.
77	10½	1/6 gr.	36 lbs.	$
108		5 or 10 gr. boxes per case	3 lbs. per gr.	

SIX SHOOTER — 50-SHOT REPEATING — SINGLE SHOT TOY CAP PISTOLS
WORLD'S LARGEST MANUFACTURER OF TOY CAP PISTOLS AND TOY CAPS

ⓚ *Kilgore* INC. WESTERVILLE, OHIO U.S.A.

No. 8 HI-HO

LUSTROUS
INLAID
SHEL-GLO
PLASTIC
GRIP

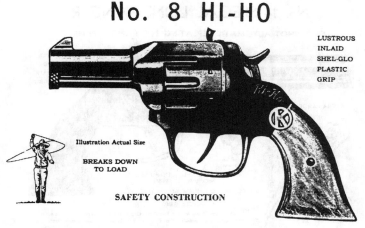

Illustration Actual Size

BREAKS DOWN
TO LOAD

SAFETY CONSTRUCTION

The Hi Ho Repeater combines beauty of appearance and complete automatic action.

Easy to load and shoot. A real Scout's gun. Made of durable cast iron. Finish optional — rich gun metal or nickel plate.

Shoots Kilgore Perforated Repeating Caps—No jamming—No slipping.

Each Hi Ho Repeater packed in an attractive two-color carton—one-half gross to shipping case. Shipping weight per gross, 122 lbs.

THE HI-HO SHOOTS KILGORE PATENTED PERFORATED REPEATING CAPS ONLY

50 SHOTS TO
THE ROLL
5 ROLLS TO
THE CARTON

LOUDEST
50-SHOT
REPEATING CAP
MADE

THE KILGORE MANUFACTURING CO.
WESTERVILLE, OHIO, U.S.A.   Waterloo, Quebec, Canada
AMERICA'S LARGEST MAKERS OF TOY PAPER CAP PISTOLS AND TOY PISTOL PAPER CAPS
Printed in U.S.A.

No. 24 BUC-A-ROO

(Cast Iron)

DOUBLE ACTION SINGLE SHOT TOY PAPER CAP PISTOL

REPEATING
HAMMER
ACTION

LENGTH 8½ INCHES

EXTRA LARGE SIZE

LUSTROUS INLAID COLORED PLASTIC GRIP

A genuine reproduction of the pistol used by the daring cowboys in the early days of the West.

Safety hammer cannot release until trigger is pulled. Recoil completely absorbed. Made of durable cast iron. Optional finish—bright nickel plate or rich gun metal.

Each Buc-a-roo Pistol packed in handsome two color carton. One-half gross to shipping carton. Shipping weight per gross 98 lbs.

THE BUC-A-ROO SHOOTS KILGORE PENNY MAMMOTH SINGLE SHOT CAPS

EXTRA LOUD— 72 Mammoth Caps to the Box — (1 Gross to Carton) — 5 Gross to Shipping Case

ACTUAL SIZE

THE KILGORE MANUFACTURING CO.

WESTERVILLE, OHIO, U. S. A.   Waterloo, Quebec, Canada

AMERICA'S LARGEST MAKERS OF TOY PAPER CAP PISTOLS AND TOY PISTOL PAPER CAPS

Printed in U. S. A

No. 100 ROY ROGERS

TOY PAPER CAP PISTOL

BREAKS DOWN TO LOAD
LIKE A REVOLVER

Illustration Actual Size
Length 11 Inches

SAFETY CONSTRUCTION
CAP CHAMBER ENCLOSED

An extra large Western type toy paper cap pistol. Finished in bright buffed and polished nickel plate with beautiful inlaid plastic grip simulating a real bone handle. Entire cylinder revolver—six loud, rapid reports with one loading.

Packed one each in beautiful two-color display set-up box. One-fourth gross to shipping carton. Shipping weight per gross 196 lbs.

SHOOTS KILGORE DISC MAMMOTH CAPS

18 DISCS
TO THE BOX
108 SHOTS

Kilgore
DISC CAPS
PAT. PEND. IN U.S. AND CANADA

THE KILGORE MANUFACTURING CO.

WESTERVILLE, OHIO, U. S. A.   Waterloo, Quebec, Canada

AMERICA'S LARGEST MAKERS OF TOY PAPER CAP PISTOLS AND TOY PISTOL PAPER CAPS

Printed in U. S. A

No. 14 SPECIAL LONE RANGER

FIFTY SHOT AUTOMATIC REPEATING TOY PAPER CAP PISTOL

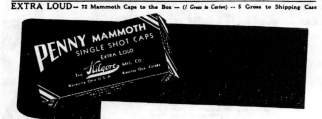

LUSTROUS
INLAID
BELL SHAPE
PLASTIC GRIP

EXTRA LARGE SIZE   Length 9¼ Inches

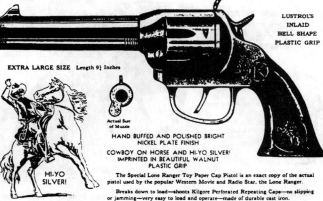

Actual Size
of Muzzle

HAND BUFFED AND POLISHED BRIGHT
NICKEL PLATE FINISH

COWBOY ON HORSE AND HI-YO SILVER!
IMPRINTED IN BEAUTIFUL WALNUT
PLASTIC GRIP

HI-YO
SILVER!

The Special Lone Ranger Toy Paper Cap Pistol is an exact copy of the actual pistol used by the popular Western Movie and Radio Star, the Lone Ranger.

Breaks down to load—shoots Kilgore Perforated Repeating Caps—no slipping or jamming—very easy to load and operate—made of durable cast iron.

Each Special Lone Ranger Cap Pistol packed in beautiful two-color box. One-half gross to shipping carton. Shipping weight per gross, 156 lbs.

THE LONE RANGER SHOOTS KILGORE PERFORATED REPEATING CAPS ONLY

50 SHOTS TO
THE ROLL
5 ROLLS TO
THE CARTON

Kilgore
PERFORATED CAPS

LOUDEST
50-SHOT
REPEATING CAP
MADE

THE KILGORE MANUFACTURING CO.

WESTERVILLE, OHIO, U. S. A.   Waterloo, Quebec, Canada

AMERICA'S LARGEST MAKERS OF TOY PAPER CAP PISTOLS AND TOY PISTOL PAPER CAPS

Printed - U. S. A.

No. 12 LONE RANGER

FIFTY SHOT AUTOMATIC REPEATING TOY PAPER CAP PISTOL

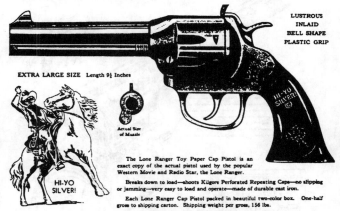

LUSTROUS
INLAID
BELL SHAPE
PLASTIC GRIP

EXTRA LARGE SIZE   Length 9¼ Inches

HI-YO
SILVER!
(C)

Actual Size
of Muzzle

HI-YO
SILVER!

The Lone Ranger Toy Paper Cap Pistol is an exact copy of the actual pistol used by the popular Western Movie and Radio Star, the Lone Ranger.

Breaks down to load—shoots Kilgore Perforated Repeating Caps—no slipping or jamming—very easy to load and operate—made of durable cast iron.

Each Lone Ranger Cap Pistol packed in beautiful two-color box. One-half gross to shipping carton. Shipping weight per gross, 156 lbs.

COWBOY ON HORSE AND HI-YO SILVER! IMPRINTED ON GRIPS

OPTIONAL FINISHES
No. 12 N. B.—Finished in Bright Nickel Plate with Lustrous Black Plastic Grip.
No. 12 G. M.—Finished in Rich Gun Metal with Pearl Plastic Grip.

THE LONE RANGER SHOOTS KILGORE PERFORATED REPEATING CAPS ONLY

50 SHOTS TO
THE ROLL
5 ROLLS TO
THE CARTON

LOUDEST
50-SHOT
REPEATING CAP
MADE

THE KILGORE MANUFACTURING CO.

WESTERVILLE, OHIO, U. S. A.   Waterloo, Quebec, Canada

AMERICA'S LARGEST MAKERS OF TOY PAPER CAP PISTOLS AND TOY PISTOL PAPER CAPS

Printed - U. S. A.

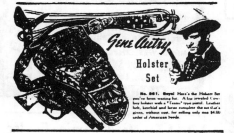

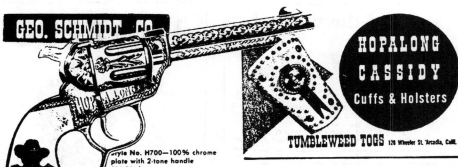

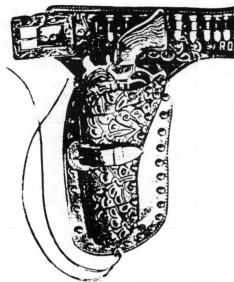

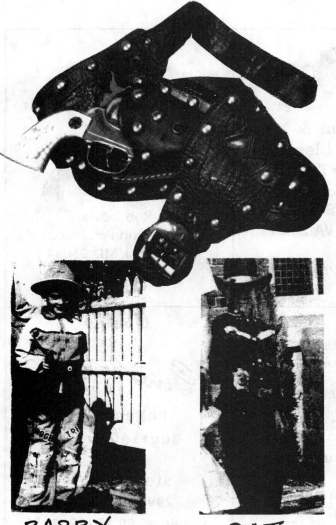

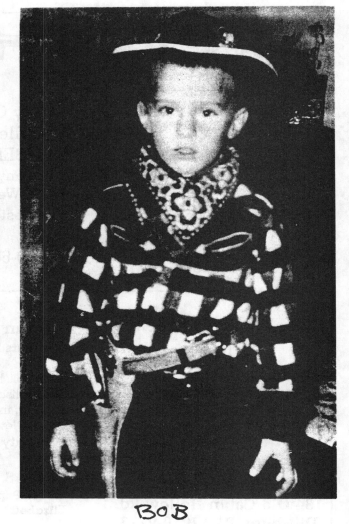

BARRY   PAT   BOB
                           ANNA MARIE

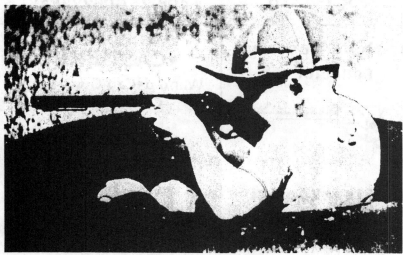

DAVE

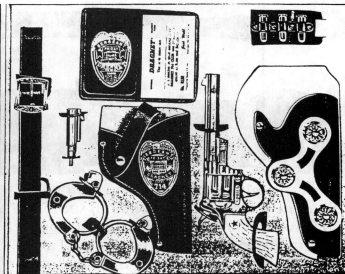

OFFICIAL "**DRAGNET**" DETECTIVE AND WESTERN HOLSTER COMBINATION SET.
"2 in 1" Hubley 50 shot repeater-convertible pistol.
A change of barrels makes the gun a detective or a western pistol.
• One Western holster and one **DRAGNET** police holster.
• Handcuffs, **BADGE 714**, identity card in carrying case, and bullet clip.

PACKING: Individually packed in combination box, all on platform, one dozen per carton.
WEIGHT: 21 pounds per dozen.

Hoot Gibson
holster set.
1930 era.
(Hakes Americana)

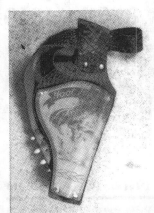

Buck Jones, Rangers
Club of America
holster. 1930 era.
(Hakes Americana)

BE THE FASTEST DRAW IN YOUR NEIGHBORHOOD!
IF YOU CAN BEAT YOUR FRIENDS---**THIS CERTIFICATE IS YOURS!**

This is to Certify that

_____

has qualified as a

Fast-Draw & Faming Expert

by outdrawing and fanning the first shot in
individual contests with the following persons:

(1)_____ (2)_____ (3)_____

(Note: Three (3) signatures must be obtained above
for proper qualification.)

Mattel Fast-Draw Certificate • 1959

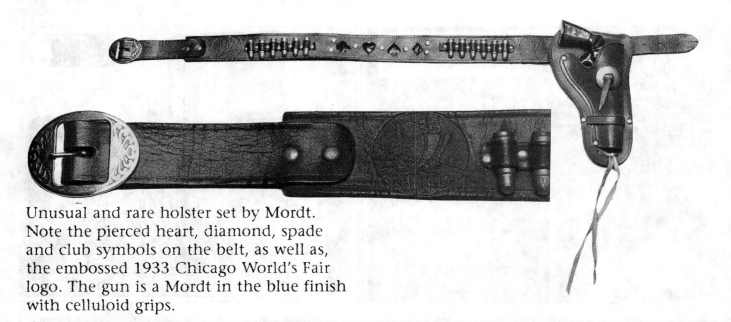

Unusual and rare holster set by Mordt.
Note the pierced heart, diamond, spade
and club symbols on the belt, as well as,
the embossed 1933 Chicago World's Fair
logo. The gun is a Mordt in the blue finish
with celluloid grips.

Original box for Mordt set with the address
of North Plymouth, Mass., USA.

Daisy Buzz-Barton
6-Shot Water Pistol

*Cyclist's
Safeguard*   25c

Repeating Water Pistol. Price Postpaid

Thanks for the memories Aunt Blanche!

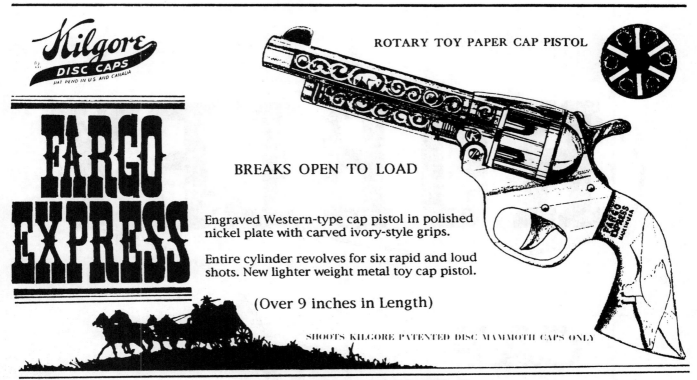

Kilgore DISC CAPS
PAT PEND IN US AND CANADA

FARGO EXPRESS

ROTARY TOY PAPER CAP PISTOL

BREAKS OPEN TO LOAD

Engraved Western-type cap pistol in polished nickel plate with carved ivory-style grips.

Entire cylinder revolves for six rapid and loud shots. New lighter weight metal toy cap pistol.

(Over 9 inches in Length)

SHOOTS KILGORE PATENTED DISC MAMMOTH CAPS ONLY

THE KILGORE MANUFACTURING CO.
WESTERVILLE, OHIO, U. S. A.   Waterloo, Quebec, Canada
AMERICA'S LARGEST MAKERS OF TOY PAPER CAP PISTOLS AND TOY PISTOL PAPER CAPS
Printed in U. S. A.

BUZZ BARTON HOLSTER SET
6-Shot Daisy Water Pistol
Complete with Holster

Buzz Barton says: "A six-shooter without a holster and belt is just like a cowboy without a horse." Hence this Daisy Buzz Barton Holster Set. It is the Daisy Buzz Barton six-shot Water Pistol described above (our No. 2915) complete with a Holster and Belt. The Holster and Belt are made of genuine top-grain leather, beautifully embossed, and with Buzz Barton's signature burned into the face of the Holster. The Holster proper is 8½ inches long and 5 inches wide. The Belt is 31 inches long, with nickel-plated tongue buckle. A quality outfit in all respects.

No. 7491. DAISY BUZZ BARTON HOLSTER SET. Price Postpaid....... 50¢

CAP
PISTOLS
1950

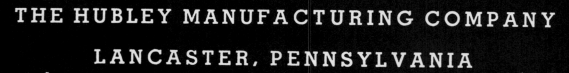

THE HUBLEY MANUFACTURING COMPANY
LANCASTER, PENNSYLVANIA

★ ★ ★ HUBLEY CAP PISTOLS ★ ★ ★

TEXAN

No. 285 TEXAN

Length 10¼ inches. Photograph actual size.
Packed 1 in a beautiful display box; 1 doz. to a carton.
Weight per gross 144 lbs.
Nickel finish with plastic handles and engraved stock
and barrel. Has revolving cylinder with automatic
opening device. Shoots standard roll caps.

Pat. No. 1993916
2088891

No. 286 TEXAN

Size and description same as above.
Packed 1 in a beautiful display box; 1 dozen to a carton.
Weight per gross 156 lbs.
Gold plated finish with beautiful plastic handles.

THE HUBLEY MANUFACTURING COMPANY, LANCASTER, PA.

No. 24 BUC-A-ROO

(Cast Iron)

DOUBLE ACTION SINGLE SHOT TOY PAPER CAP PISTOL

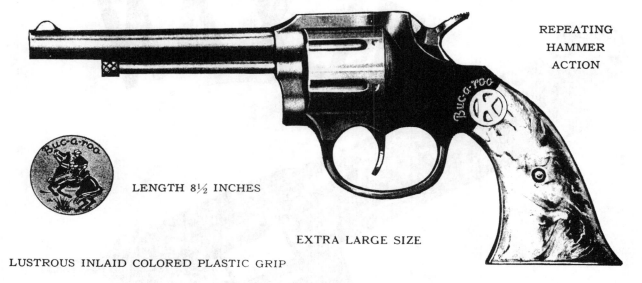

REPEATING
HAMMER
ACTION

LENGTH 8½ INCHES

EXTRA LARGE SIZE

LUSTROUS INLAID COLORED PLASTIC GRIP

A genuine reproduction of the pistol used by the daring cowboys in the early days of the West.

Safety hammer cannot release until trigger is pulled.   Recoil completely absorbed.   Made of durable cast iron.   Optional finish—bright nickel plate or rich gun metal.

Each Buc-a-roo Pistol packed in handsome two color carton.   One-half gross to shipping carton. Shipping weight per gross 98 lbs.

THE BUC-A-ROO SHOOTS KILGORE PENNY MAMMOTH SINGLE SHOT CAPS

EXTRA LOUD-- 72 Mammoth Caps to the Box -- *(1 Gross to Carton)* -- **5 Gross to Shipping Case**

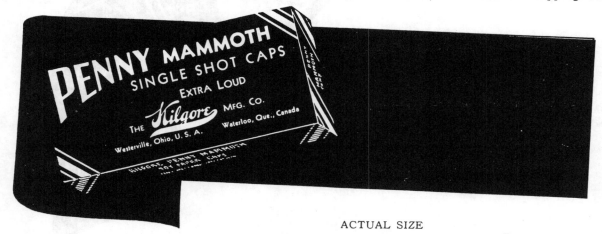

ACTUAL SIZE

THE KILGORE MANUFACTURING CO.

WESTERVILLE, OHIO, U. S. A.   Waterloo, Quebec, Canada

AMERICA'S LARGEST MAKERS OF TOY PAPER CAP PISTOLS AND TOY PISTOL PAPER CAPS

Printed in U.S.A.

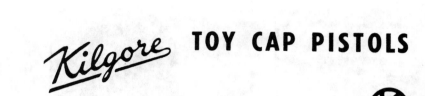

TOY CAP PISTOLS

No. 9 PAL

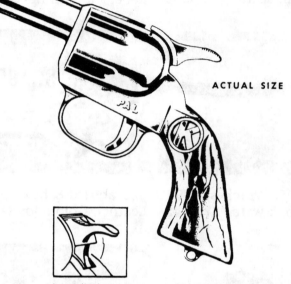

ACTUAL SIZE

Single shot model — especially designed for the little fellow's first cap pistol. An exclusive special feature is that it will receive but one cap at a time . . . no overloading. Die cast of zinc alloy . . . plated with Kilgore's sparkling Dura-Gleam finish. Western design. Permanently assembled and built to take rough handling. Hammer locks in cocked position for easy loading. Grip handsomely designed with embossing, built to fit small hand. The biggest "little" cap pistol on the market. Looks like — and is big value.

Large, hood-type hammer provides full protection.

NO. 75 SINGLE SHOT CAPS

Used in the *Pal* and all other single-shot cap pistols, 72 caps per box, 144 boxes per carton. Mammoth size, very loud. Contains special lubricant to increase life of pistol.

Rivets, cast on left side of gun, are spun over for tight, permanent assembly. Can't be taken apart — eliminates unsightly nuts and bolts.

Accepts only one cap at a time . . . preventing overloading.

SPECIFICATIONS

No.	Length Over-All	Quan. Per Case	Weight Per Case	Price Per Doz.
9	6"	½ Gross	12 lbs.	$
75	2 Gr. per case — 3 lbs. per Gr.			

This "K" Means O.K.

Kilgore INC. WESTERVILLE, OHIO U.S.A.

New York Office
Room 751
Fifth Ave.
Bldg.

Chicago Office
Room 14-102
Mdse. Mart

1.Marx 1960 prototype J.Yuma-Rebel. 12" Bar. Scattergun.$350

2. Detail of cap box in butt of Rebel shotgun never produced.

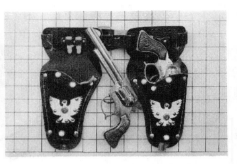

3. Small Roy R. set with eagles & small Schmidts. $275-600.

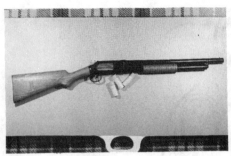

4. Mattel-1965. Winchester '97 shotgun. Cap & water. $75-145

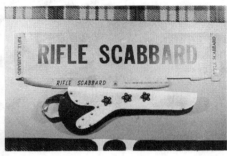

5. Scabbard & box. Colchester Leather, Colorado. Rare $150

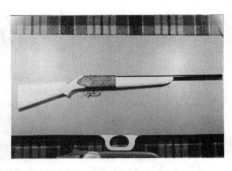

6. Hubley Girl's Frontier Rifle-white stock. Caps. $85-150 rare

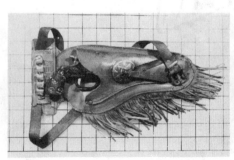

7. Early Key. Bros. Concho and fringe. Gun-Lasso em Bill. $125

8. L. Ranger Volunteers theater poster. Free clickers. 1942. $300

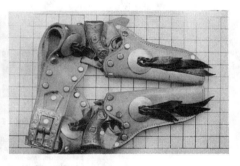

9. Early double with conchos. Herman Friedrick - NYC. $225

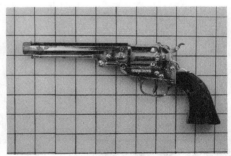

10. Mustang by British Cast M. 1965 era. Cap rep.-Nic $75-125

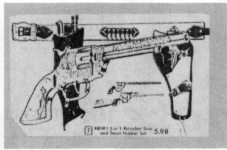

11.L-H Can.'61. Ricochet 5 in 1 holster set. .44 RC. $300-500

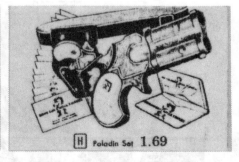

12. Paladin '61 Derringer, holster & cards. Rare set. $50-100